THE COMPLETE
COOKERY COURSE

A STEP-BY-STEP GUIDE
FOR ALL OCCASIONS

THE COMPLETE
COOKERY COURSE

A STEP-BY-STEP GUIDE
FOR ALL OCCASIONS

TREASURE PRESS

Contents

Introduction 7

Quick and Easy Cooking

8

Friendly Family Meals

72

Cooking for Special Occasions

136

Oven Magic

200

First published in 1982 by Octopus Books Limited

This edition published in 1989 by
Treasure Press
Michelin House
81 Fulham Road
London SW3 6RB

© 1981 Octopus Books Limited

ISBN 1 85051 348 8

Printed in Czechoslovakia
50430/2

Notes

In some parts of the world cooks are already at ease with metric measures. In other countries the changeover to metrics is recent or still going on. I have included both metric and imperial measures to make the recipes as easy as possible. It is advisable to buy the equipment approved by the Standards Association of Australia.

All spoon measurements are level.
All cup measurements are level.
Use a measuring cup or jug for liquids.
Plain flour and granulated sugar are used, unless otherwise specified.
Standard eggs of 55 g weight are used, unless otherwise specified.
All ovens should be preheated to the specified temperature, particularly for cakes, biscuits and pastry recipes.

Introduction

Here is a careful guide to all the basics of good cooking – a true cookery course for everyone from beginners to experienced cooks wanting to brush up on special recipes and techniques.

More than that, it shows you how to use the basic skills of good cooking to create beautiful, varied food for every occasion. It is a book to encourage your own creative flair, backing up your ideas and imagination with the sort of practical help you've been looking for.

In all the recipes, the method is fully spelt out, so even with a dish that's brand new to you there should be no problems. Many recipes are illustrated with close-up pictures of each step and special hints to give you 'picture-perfect' results. It's a bit like having me in the kitchen beside you, showing you the way as we go along!

I have also divided the book into four chapters to fit in with the way we live today, when most of us have to be many cooks in one.

When you want good food in a hurry, you can go straight to the 'Quick and Easy' chapter. If you have to stretch the budget to provide nourishing food for a group of people, look at 'Friendly Family Meals'. If there's a party or celebration coming up, you will find marvellous ideas for entertaining in the big section on 'Special Occasions'. And when you feel in the mood for some heart-warming, old-fashioned baking, it's all there for you in 'Oven Magic'.

To sum it up, my *Creative Cookery Course* is for all the cooks you are now, or want to be . . . imaginative, practical, versatile and expert!

I wish you joy of it.

Margaret Fulton

Quick and Easy Cooking

Quick and Easy Cooking

Quick and easy cooking can still be the sort of cooking we all look forward to – that is, nourishing, interesting and, of course, appetizing.

The idea is to take advantage of quick techniques and foods that do not need long or elaborate preparation.

It is quick and easy to sauté, deep fry and grill. Eggs and fish are quick and easy, and so are cheese dishes, salads and vegetables, pasta and pancakes.

The Chinese have perfected the 'stir fry' method which produces wonderful main courses literally in minutes, and the Danes have contributed those luscious open sandwiches with piled-up fillings – a meal on a slice of bread!

We should not neglect canned and frozen foods, nor today's convenience meats like chicken pieces, ham and sausages, and the benefits of food that can be largely prepared ahead and easily assembled at the last moment.

Quick and easy cooking shouldn't call for a large range of equipment or utensils, but on top of your basics I do recommend you try for a blender and food processor to help you, a good big frying pan with a heavy base, and a wok for Chinese dishes.

I have chosen recipes that range from snacks to main meals and ideas for easy entertaining. I think you will find them helpful for all those occasions when you want something good to eat without fuss – and with the pace of life now, that's about a daily requirement.

Here's to quick and easy cooking for the cook and happy eating to everyone she cooks for!

Eggs . . . Meals in a Moment

What a lot of good cooking begins with the egg!

For breakfast they are indispensable; and there is nothing more welcome for a light meal than an omelette, baked eggs or some other savoury egg dish.

Eggs are one of the quickest foods to cook and one of the easiest. Be careful, though, to avoid high heat and overcooking as both toughen the white and darken the yolk.

Fresh eggs keep up to 2 weeks in the refrigerator but it is useful to leave at room temperature those that will be needed during the day. They are less likely to crack in hot water and the yolks and whites mix better.

Whole eggs in the shell cannot be frozen, but yolks and whites freeze well if separated. Stir yolks lightly with a pinch of salt for each yolk. Freeze whites just as they are; they will whip up like fresh ones when thawed.

Eggs come in 3 sizes. The 55 g middle-size egg is the standard size used in all recipes, unless otherwise stated.

Scrambled Eggs; Poached Eggs; Fried Egg

Boiled Eggs

Eggs should be at room temperature. If they are very cold, bring them to room temperature in warm water. Place them in boiling water to cover. When the water reboils, turn down to a simmer and count cooking time from then.

SIZE	SOFT	MEDIUM	HARD
45 g (small)	2 min. 40 sec.	3 min. 20 sec.	7 min.
55 g (standard)	3 min.	3 min. 50 sec.	9 min.
65 g (large)	3 min. 20 sec.	4 min. 15 sec.	11 min.

Lift the eggs out of the water and tap the shell at one end to prevent further cooking. Tap hard-boiled eggs all over and store in cold water to prevent darkening round the yolk.

Poached Eggs

Use very fresh cold eggs (they are firmer and hold their shape better). Half-fill a shallow pan with water, add a drop of vinegar and bring to the boil. Break each egg into a saucer and slide it gently into the water. Put the lid on, remove from the heat and leave $3\frac{1}{2}$ minutes for very soft eggs, 4 minutes for medium. Lift the eggs out in the order in which they went in, using a slotted spoon or slice. Drain over absorbent paper towels and trim off any untidy edges. Serve on toast spread with butter or anchovy paste or on a bed of smoked haddock or spinach.

Fried Eggs

Heat a little butter, bacon fat or oil in a frying pan. Break each egg into a cup and slide into the pan just before the fat starts to sizzle. The fat should splutter very gently round the eggs; if too hot it will toughen the whites; if not hot enough the whites will not set before the yolks. Spoon hot fat over the eggs until the whites are set but the yolks are still wobbly, about 3 minutes. Lift out carefully with an egg slice and serve with fried or grilled bacon, sausages, hamburgers or corned beef hash.

Scrambled Eggs

Allow 2 eggs per person. Season with salt and freshly ground pepper and add 1 tablespoon of milk or cream per egg. Beat with a fork until well mixed. Heat a nut of butter in a small saucepan, preferably non-stick. Add the eggs and stir with a wooden spoon over a very gentle heat until thick and creamy but a little softer than you want them. Remove from the heat and serve immediately; their own heat will make them a little firmer as you do so. Serve with buttered toast for breakfast or with asparagus tips or sautéed mushrooms for a first course.

Variations

Stir about 1 tablespoon of flavouring for every 2 eggs into the uncooked mixture. Grated cheese, chopped cooked ham or bacon, flaked cooked or smoked fish, crabmeat or prawns are good. Serve hot, or serve cold on open-face sandwiches or in pastry cases.

Stuffed Eggs

6 large eggs	1 teaspoon French mustard
3 tablespoons mayonnaise, cream or sour cream or 2 tablespoons soft butter	salt cayenne or seasoned pepper

Boil the eggs in simmering water for 11 minutes, stirring for the first 6 minutes so that the yolks are centred. Plunge into cold water, lightly cracking the shells. Shell and cut in halves lengthwise with a stainless steel knife (so as not to discolour the eggs). Cut a tiny slice from the bottom of each half to make it sit on the plate.

Remove the yolks and put the whites into cold water to prevent drying out. Mix the yolks with mayonnaise, cream or butter and mustard. Season to taste with salt and pepper. Stir in flavourings using what you have on hand (see ideas below).

Remove the egg whites from the water and dry. Pile or pipe the yolks back into the whites. *Garnish and serve as an appetizer, or with salad vegetables as a light meal for 3 or 4.*

Variations

Herb 1 tablespoon finely chopped fresh herbs or 1½ tablespoons parsley sprigs chopped with ¼ teaspoon dried herbs. Sprinkle with chopped parsley or snipped chives.
Ham and Cheese 1 tablespoon finely chopped ham and 2 tablespoons grated Cheddar or blue cheese. Garnish with slivers of ham.
Curry 1–2 teaspoons of curry powder or curry paste and a spring onion, finely chopped (including some of the green top). Garnish with shreds of spring onion.
Tuna, Salmon or Crab 2 tablespoons of any of these or other cooked, canned or fresh fish, finely flaked, and 1 teaspoon lemon juice. Garnish with capers or paprika.

Baked Eggs in Ramekin (en Cocotte)

Stuffed Eggs au Gratin

Don't stop at stuffed eggs served cold: they make an excellent hot savoury dish with an easy sauce based on canned soup.

12 stuffed egg halves, any flavour (see recipe)	2 teaspoons snipped chives or chopped parsley
1 × 440 g can cream of chicken or mushroom soup	salt freshly ground pepper
¼ cup milk	½ cup fresh breadcrumbs, tossed in a little melted butter
60 g (2 oz) butter, melted	

Arrange the stuffed eggs in a shallow ovenproof dish. Empty the canned soup into a bowl and stir in the milk, melted butter and chives or parsley. Season with salt and pepper and pour over the eggs. Sprinkle with crumbs and bake in a moderate oven (180°C/350°F) for 20 minutes until golden brown and hot. *Serves 4 to 6*

Baked Eggs in Ramekins (en Cocotte)

Preheat the oven to 180°C (350°F). Butter individual ovenproof ramekins. Put 1 tablespoon cream into each one and drop in 1 or 2 eggs. Season with salt and freshly ground pepper and finally put another spoonful of cream or butter on top. Place in a shallow pan with hot water and bake for 8 to 10 minutes until the whites are just set and the yolks soft. Serve in the ramekins.

Spanish Baked Eggs

60 g (2 oz) butter	6 eggs
1 clove garlic, crushed	salt
125 g (4 oz) sliced Chorizo (Spanish sausage) or salami	freshly ground pepper
1 green pepper, seeded and finely chopped	6 tablespoons cream

Heat the butter in a flat flameproof dish and gently fry the garlic, sausage and green pepper until the pepper is softened. Break the eggs over the top, season well with salt and pepper, then spoon the cream over. Bake in a preheated moderate oven (180°C/350°F) for 8 to 10 minutes, or until the whites are set and yolks soft. *Serves 3 as a main course, 6 as a first course.*

French Savoury Omelettes

An omelette is the exception to the rule that eggs are cooked on gentle heat. It is cooked fast, but very briefly.

Allow 2 eggs per person and choose an omelette pan the right size, 18 cm (7 inch) for 2 eggs. An omelette pan has special rounded sides to help the omelette roll out, but a thick frying pan can be used.

Omelette Fines Herbes

2 eggs	salt
1 tablespoon chopped fresh herbs (parsley, chervil, tarragon, chives or others)	freshly ground pepper
	15 g (½ oz) butter
2 teaspoons water	parsley sprigs, to garnish

To cook the omelette, see step-by-step pictures at right. *Serves 1*

Variations

Cheese Omelette Mix 2 tablespoons grated cheese, instead of the chopped herbs, into the beaten eggs.
Stuffed Savoury Omelette Make a plain omelette (see recipe for Omelette Fines Herbes) omitting the herbs, and spoon a savoury filling onto the centre of the omelette just before folding it over. Allow 2–3 tablespoons of cooked filling for each person. Sliced mushrooms, chopped ham or bacon, crisp bread croûtons, potato cubes and chopped onion, asparagus tips, spinach purée, flaked cooked, canned or smoked fish are all good. Fry the filling in butter and keep warm while you make the omelette.

Omelette Fines Herbes

Omelette Fines Herbes
1 Beat the eggs with a fork. Mix in the herbs, water and salt and pepper to taste. Heat butter until it sizzles but do not allow it to brown. Pour in the egg mixture, keeping heat high.

2 With a palette knife, draw the mixture from sides to middle of pan and tilt pan so the uncooked egg runs underneath.

3 When the underneath is set but the top still slightly runny, fold the omelette in half (if using 4 eggs, fold the omelette in three). Roll the omelette out onto a hot plate. Run a dab of butter on the point of a knife over the top; garnish and serve at once.

Crowns on Toast (page 16)

Warsaw Concerto

This was one of Noel Coward's favourites for an after-theatre supper. The touch of vinegar with fried onions is reminiscent of Polish cookery, hence the title.

90 g (3 oz) butter	freshly ground pepper
2 large onions, thinly sliced	½ cup fresh breadcrumbs,
2 teaspoons vinegar	tossed in a little melted
6 eggs	butter
salt	¼ cup grated Swiss cheese

Melt the butter and fry the onions gently until golden. Stir in the vinegar, turn the heat up and fry, stirring, until lightly browned.

Turn the contents of the pan into a shallow ovenproof dish and spread out to line it. Shell the eggs and slide them into the dish. Season with salt and pepper. Mix the buttered crumbs with the grated cheese and sprinkle over to cover the eggs. Bake in a hot oven (220°C/425°F) for 6 minutes and serve immediately. *Serves 3 to 6*

Puffy Baked Eggs, Arnold Bennett

Omelette Arnold Bennett, flavoured with smoked haddock, was created at the Savoy Hotel for the famous writer. This dish uses the same ingredients but in a different way.

375 g (12 oz) cooked smoked	a little butter
haddock	1 tablespoon each grated
7 eggs	Cheddar and Parmesan
½ cup cream	cheese
freshly ground white pepper	salt

Flake the haddock, removing skin and bones. Separate one egg, reserving the white. Mix the yolk with one-third of the cream, then blend into the fish. Season with pepper and spoon into 6 buttered ramekins. Lightly whip the remaining cream, add the cheese and a little salt and pepper. Whisk the reserved egg white stiffly and fold in.

Break an egg into each dish and cover with the cheese mixture. Bake in a hot oven (200°C/400°F) for 5 to 6 minutes. Serve hot. *Serves 6*

Soufflé Egg and Bacon Toasts

4 eggs	4 slices buttered toast
4 slices bacon, cooked and	TO GARNISH:
chopped	chopped parsley or snipped
4 tablespoons grated cheese	chives

Separate the eggs. Beat the yolks and stir in the bacon and cheese.

Whisk the whites until soft peaks form, then fold through the yolk mixture. Divide among the slices of toast, covering the toast completely. Grill under a low heat for 5 minutes and serve immediately, garnished with parsley or snipped chives. *Serves 4*

Eggs with Watercress Mayonnaise

1 bunch watercress	½ cup homemade mayonnaise
2 tablespoons cream	6 hard-boiled eggs, quartered

Pick the sprigs of watercress from the stalks, and purée half in a blender or food processor, gradually adding the cream. Combine with the mayonnaise and spoon over the eggs. Garnish with the remaining watercress. *Serves 4 to 6*

Fried Eggs in Sweet and Sour Sauce

4 eggs	1 tablespoon soy sauce
oil for frying	1 tablespoon tomato paste
SAUCE:	1 tablespoon sugar
1 tablespoon cornflour, mixed	1 tablespoon vinegar
to a paste with	2 tablespoons orange juice
4 tablespoons cold water	

Fry the eggs in oil, arrange on a heated serving dish and keep warm. Mix all the ingredients for the sauce in a small saucepan, bring to the boil and simmer, stirring, until thick and translucent. Pour over the eggs and serve at once. They are good with rice, noodles or on toasted muffins. *Serves 4*

Scrambled Egg Mayonnaise

6 eggs	¼ cup mayonnaise, preferably
salt	homemade
freshly ground pepper	TO GARNISH:
60 g (2 oz) butter	2 teaspoons chopped parsley
1 small fillet smoked fish (any	or snipped chives, or a
kind), cooked and flaked	mixture of both
3 tablespoons cream	

Beat the eggs, season them and cook gently in the butter, stirring, until set. Add the flaked fish and cream, and allow to cool. Serve piled on a dish with mayonnaise spooned over and sprinkled with herbs. *Serves 4*

Luncheon Omelette Cake

A splendid idea for a summer luncheon. This omelette looks like a beautiful cake, delicately browned, and is served cut in wedges. Young green beans may be substituted for the zucchini and any canned or cooked dried beans (for example, soy or butter beans) are delicious instead of the limas.

3 zucchini	4 tablespoons oil
1 × 300 g can baby lima beans	pinch of nutmeg
2 ripe medium tomatoes	salt
1 onion	freshly ground pepper
2 cloves garlic	2 tablespoons chopped parsley
2 medium potatoes, cooked and peeled	7 eggs, lightly beaten

Wash the zucchini, cut them into slices and sprinkle lightly with salt. Leave to stand for 20 minutes, then drain and pat dry with absorbent paper towels. Drain the beans and rinse under cold running water. Peel and seed the tomatoes and chop them roughly. Slice the onion thinly and crush the garlic. Cut the potatoes into thick slices.

Heat 2 tablespoons oil in a heavy saucepan. Add the vegetables, nutmeg, salt and pepper to taste. Cook gently for 4 to 5 minutes, stirring often, until the onion and zucchini are tender but firm. Stir in the parsley.

Heat the remaining 2 tablespoons of oil in a heavy frying pan which can go into the oven. Pour the eggs into the pan, add the vegetables and stir gently. Cook over a medium heat, without stirring, until the bottom of the omelette is set, about 3 to 4 minutes (the top will still be runny).

Put the pan into a hot oven (220°C/425°F) for 6 to 8 minutes, or until the top is brown and puffy. Alternatively, place under a preheated grill to cook and brown the top. Slide the omelette onto a plate and allow to cool. Serve cut in wedges with salad. *Serves 4 to 6 as a hearty main course.*

Spicy Egg Curry

Curried eggs used to be a 'Sunday evening' special in many homes. Why not revive the custom?

8 hard-boiled eggs	½ teaspoon chilli powder (or to taste)
2 cloves garlic, crushed	
1 large onion, finely chopped	2 tablespoons sesame seeds
1 tablespoon oil	½ teaspoon salt
1 teaspoon each ground coriander and cumin	1 cup natural yogurt
	2 tablespoons lemon juice

Shell the eggs. Cook the garlic and onion in oil until soft. Add the remaining ingredients, except the yogurt and lemon juice, and cook for 1 minute, stirring. Blend in the yogurt and juice and cook for 5 minutes. Cut the eggs in half lengthwise, add to the sauce, and heat through. Serve with boiled rice. *Serves 4*

Egg Salad Sandwiches

4 hard-boiled eggs, chopped	4 tablespoons mayonnaise
2 spring onions, chopped	salt
1 tender stick celery, chopped	freshly ground pepper
1 gherkin, finely chopped	

Mix all the ingredients together and use as a sandwich filling on wholegrain bread. *Makes 4 sandwiches*

Pickled Eggs

These are an English specialty, sometimes found on the counter in nice old pubs. They are good to serve in your own home when friends drop in for a drink; and they keep for a month or more in the refrigerator.

2 cups white vinegar	½ teaspoon celery seed
1 cup water	3 tablespoons sugar
1 teaspoon salt	12 hard-boiled eggs
1 teaspoon mixed pickling spice	2 cloves garlic, crushed

Place the vinegar, water, salt, pickling spice, celery seed and sugar in a large saucepan. Bring to the boil and simmer for 5 minutes. Cool. Shell the eggs and place in a wide-mouthed jar. Strain the pickling liquid over them, and add the garlic. Cover tightly and leave in the refrigerator for 3 days before serving. Serve whole or cut in halves. *Makes 12*

Crowns on Toast

2 large eggs	2 slices wholemeal toast, buttered
salt	
freshly ground pepper	2 parsley sprigs, to garnish

Separate the eggs. Whisk the whites with salt and pepper until soft peaks form. Pile half onto each piece of toast, make a hollow in the centre using a half shell and slip the yolk into the hollow. Bake in a moderate oven (180°C/350°F) until browned and the yolk is set. Garnish with a parsley sprig. *Serves 2*

Cold Hungarian Eggs

This is a lovely egg salad, and a pleasant alternative to stuffed eggs. Serve with lettuce and crisp radishes.

1 small onion, grated	freshly ground pepper
2 teaspoons paprika	½ cup mayonnaise, preferably homemade
½ teaspoon Worcestershire sauce	¼ cup thick sour cream
salt	8 hard-boiled eggs

Blend together all the ingredients, except the eggs, tasting for seasoning. Peel the eggs, cut them in half lengthwise and coat with the paprika sauce. Serve cold. *Serves 4 as a luncheon dish, 8 as an appetizer.*

Curried Egg and Potato

4 eggs	2 teaspoons snipped chives
1 medium potato, boiled and peeled	salt
	freshly ground pepper
60 g (2 oz) butter	4 slices hot buttered toast
1 tablespoon curry powder	

Boil the eggs for 5 minutes and shell them. Chop the potato roughly. Melt the butter and lightly fry the curry powder. Add the chopped potato and fry until the edges go crispy. Add the eggs and chop all together. Season with half the chives and salt and pepper to taste. Pile onto the toast and heat under the grill for a few minutes. Sprinkle with the remaining chives. *Serves 4*

Egg and Vegetable Squares

Use any leftover vegetables that you have on hand, or make up the quantity with canned vegetables.

1 medium onion, chopped	*½ teaspoon salt*
30 g (1 oz) butter	*freshly ground pepper*
4 cups cooked vegetables	*a little oil*
6 eggs	

Sauté the onion in the butter until golden. Chop the vegetables and stir in. Remove the pan from the heat and cool a little. Break the eggs into a bowl, season with salt and pepper and beat lightly. Add the vegetables and mix lightly together. Oil a shallow baking dish and pour in the egg mixture. Bake in a moderate oven (180°C/350°F) for 20 to 30 minutes, until set. Remove from the oven, cut into squares and serve hot. *Serves 6*

Sweet Soufflé Omelette

3 eggs, separated	*pinch of salt*
1 tablespoon sugar	*15 g (½ oz) butter*
2 teaspoons flour	*2 tablespoons jam, warmed*
1 tablespoon cream	*caster sugar for dusting*
grated rind of ½ lemon	

To cook the omelette, see step-by-step pictures at right. *Serves 2*

Variations

Use fresh or canned fruit instead of jam, well sugared or flavoured with a little liqueur or brandy.

When the omelette is placed on the serving dish, flame it with rum. Warm 1 tablespoon rum, set light to it with a match and pour flaming over the omelette.

For a gala occasion, give the omelette the spectacular look you see in top restaurants. After filling and folding, sift icing sugar over to cover the top. Have two metal skewers heated over a flame to red hot. Use them to mark a lattice design on the icing sugar; it will caramelize as you press it lightly. Serve immediately.

Sweet Soufflé Omelette

Sweet Soufflé Omelette

1 Preheat the oven to 190°C/375°F. Lightly beat the egg yolks with the sugar, flour, cream and lemon rind. Whisk the egg whites with the salt until firm peaks form. Pour in the yolk mixture and fold in gently.

2 Heat the butter in a large omelette pan or other heavy pan that can go into the oven. When the butter is sizzling, but not brown, pour in the omelette mixture. Gently level and smooth the top.

3 Place the pan in the oven for 12 to 15 minutes or until golden and risen. Spoon warm jam down the centre, fold the omelette over, dust with caster sugar and slide onto a heated dish. Serve immediately.

Everybody Likes Hot Snacks

There could be nothing simpler than a slice of hot buttered toast, but it's something we never seem to tire of. When fillings and toppings are added, the result is hot snacks in endless variety, always welcome for impromptu family eating and quick and easy entertaining.

Add extra interest by using different kinds of bread or muffins and crumpets as the base for ingredients, and try different toasting methods. Some fillings (especially those with cheese on top) can go directly under the grill for a bubbly, golden surface. Others are made into sandwiches and then toasted on both sides under the grill or in a jaffle iron or snackmaker.

For parties, toast cups provide an interesting change from pastry cases, and they are simple to make. Cut rounds about 6 cm (2½ inches) in diameter from white sandwich bread, and press into well-buttered muffin or patty tins. Bake in a moderately hot oven (190°C/375°F) for 10 minutes, or until golden brown, then remove from the tins and add fillings.

A toasted snack can make a complete meal when you add a bowl of soup or a crisp salad, and don't forget old favourites like cinnamon toast and marmalade toast for those with a sweet tooth. There's a toasted snack for every occasion – and best of all, everyone enjoys them.

Chef's Club Sandwich

This is one of the most popular snacks in the world, served by good clubs and hotels everywhere. Arrange the filling so that it 'overflows' the edges a little, for a tempting generous look.

3 thick slices of sandwich bread	freshly ground pepper
butter for spreading	1 tablespoon mayonnaise
4 small, crisp lettuce leaves	3–4 thin slices cooked chicken
2 thin slices Swiss cheese	salt
2–3 slices tomato	TO GARNISH:
1 large rasher crisp, grilled bacon, rind removed	1 large green or stuffed olive on a toothpick

Toast the bread on both sides and spread one side of each slice with butter. On the first slice put two lettuce leaves, then the cheese, tomato and bacon. Grind a little pepper over. Spread the second slice of toast with mayonnaise, place on top, and arrange the remaining lettuce and the chicken on it. Season with salt and pepper and add the third slice of toast. Cut in two diagonally and garnish with an olive on a toothpick. *Serves 1*

Curried Chicken Pies

These little 'pies' are really toasted sandwiches made in a snackmaker, but they're so filling and nutritious they're just right for lunch with a crisp salad.

1 cup chopped, cooked chicken	2 teaspoons curry powder
1 stick celery, finely chopped	1 tablespoon lemon juice
2 spring onions, finely chopped	½ green pepper, finely chopped (optional)
1 tablespoon desiccated coconut	salt
¼ cup mayonnaise	freshly ground pepper
	8 slices bread
	butter for spreading

Mix all the ingredients together, except the bread and butter. Taste the mixture and adjust the seasoning if necessary. Butter the bread slices on one side only. Place 4 slices in a snackmaker, buttered side down, and divide the filling among them. Top with the remaining bread slices, buttered side up, and toast until crisp and brown. *Serves 4*

Cream Cheese and Date Dreams

If you haven't tried a combination like this, I can assure you it's quite delicious, and with cheese, bacon, egg and milk, you have a good high-protein snack that is a meal in itself.

4 rashers bacon	2 eggs
125 g (4 oz) cream cheese, softened	⅔ cup milk
¾ cup chopped, stoned dates	pinch of salt
8 slices white bread	butter for frying, if needed

Remove the rind from the bacon, cut each rasher into halves and fry slowly until crisp. Remove with a slotted egg slice, drain on absorbent paper towels and keep warm.

Mix the cream cheese and dates together. Spread on 4 slices of bread and cover with the remaining 4 slices. Beat the eggs with the milk and salt. Dip the sandwiches into the mixture and fry on both sides in the bacon fat until golden brown, adding a little butter if needed. Top each sandwich with 2 slices of bacon and serve hot. *Serves 4*

Spiced Apricot Crunchies

Here's an easy snack that's sweet but not too rich.

2 tablespoons sugar	6 slices of French bread, cut on the diagonal, about 2.5 cm (1 inch) thick
2 tablespoons lemon juice	½ teaspoon ground ginger
2 tablespoons water	2 teaspoons cinnamon
60 g (2 oz) butter	3 tablespoons apricot jam

Place the sugar, lemon juice, water and butter in a saucepan and heat until the sugar is melted. Pour into a flat dish and dip both sides of the bread into the mixture. Arrange the bread slices on a greased baking tray. Mix the ginger and cinnamon together and sprinkle over the top, then spread each slice with apricot jam. Bake in a preheated hot oven (200°C/400°F) for 5 to 6 minutes, until the edges are crisp and golden and the jam is bubbly. *Serves 6*

From the back clockwise: Cream Cheese and Date Dreams; Egg and Cheese Scramble (page 20); Spiced Apricot Crunchies; Danish Surprise (page 20)

Danish Surprise

This dish is a surprise because it's so easy to make, yet so sumptuous – a truly super snack that could also be served as the first course at a dinner party or very special luncheon.

6 slices rye bread	2 Bismark (pickled) herring
60 g (2 oz) butter, softened	fillets, cut into thin strips
1 tablespoon prepared	50 g (1¾ oz) caviar
horseradish	TO GARNISH:
50 g (1¾ oz) smoked salmon,	sour cream
cut into thin strips	fresh dill sprigs or parsley

Lightly toast the bread and spread with butter blended with horseradish. Cover with alternate strips of smoked salmon, herring and caviar. Serve at once, garnished with a spoonful of sour cream and a sprig of fresh dill or parsley. *Serves 6*
NOTE: Real caviar and the best smoked salmon make this a luxury snack for very special occasions, but you can cut costs by using lumpfish roe and smoked salmon schnitzel (the shredded pieces that come in a jar). Still delicious!

Hamburger Muffins

Meat patties are cooked directly on top of toasted muffins for a hearty snack the whole family will enjoy.

3 muffins	500 g (1 lb) minced steak
butter for spreading	salt
about 3 tablespoons of your	freshly ground pepper
favourite chutney or pickle	1 tablespoon Worcestershire
HAMBURGER MIXTURE:	sauce
2 slices bread, crusts removed	1 small onion, grated
¼ cup evaporated milk or	1 egg, beaten
cream	

Make the hamburger mixture first. Soak the bread in milk or cream until soft, then beat with a fork. Mix with the steak, salt, pepper, sauce, onion and egg. Using wet hands, shape the mixture into 6 patties the same diameter as a muffin.

Split the muffins in two and lightly toast both sides under a grill. Spread the tops with butter, and then a good spoonful of chutney or pickle.

Put a hamburger on each muffin, patting it out to cover the top completely. Also pinch down around the edges of the muffin to prevent it shrinking away during cooking. Place under a medium grill and cook for 10 to 12 minutes, or until the patties are cooked through. Serve with a crisp green salad and pass the tomato sauce for those who can't enjoy a hamburger without it. *Serves 6*

Cinnamon Nut Toast

4 slices white bread	2 teaspoons cinnamon
60 g (2 oz) butter	2 tablespoons crushed nuts
1½ tablespoons honey	

Toast the bread on one side only. Mix the remaining ingredients well together and spread on the untoasted side. Place under a medium grill until the topping is golden and bubbly. Cut in fingers to serve. *Serves 2 to 4*

Corned Beef and Cabbage

6 thick slices from a large loaf	12 thin slices cooked corned
of rye bread	beef
Thousand Island Dressing (see	6 slices Swiss, Gruyère or
below)	Jarlsberg cheese
6 tablespoons sauerkraut,	
rinsed in cold water and	
well drained	

Toast the bread on one side only and spread with dressing. Add a layer of sauerkraut, top with two slices of corned beef, then a slice of cheese. Place under a medium grill until the filling is heated through and the cheese melted (about 5 minutes). *Serves 3 to 6, depending on appetites.*

Thousand Island Dressing

⅓ cup mayonnaise	6 green or black olives, finely
2 teaspoons tomato sauce	chopped
dash of Tabasco	salt
1 hard-boiled egg, chopped	freshly ground pepper
2 spring onions, chopped	

Combine all the ingredients in a small bowl and adjust the seasoning as required.

Egg and Cheese Scramble

scrambled eggs (using 4 eggs)	2 tablespoons grated Cheddar
2 slices bread	cheese
butter for spreading	mint sprigs, to garnish
1 tablespoon chutney	

Make scrambled eggs, as described on page 13. Toast the bread and spread one side with butter and chutney. Pile the eggs onto the toast, sprinkle cheese over and grill until melted. Garnish with mint sprigs. *Serves 2*

A man's favourite: Corned Beef and Cabbage

Speedy Pizza Submarine

Instead of making a dough or pastry base, the topping for this 'pizza' goes on crusty bread and then under the grill. You get all the robust flavour of real Italian pizza with the minimum of effort.

1 × 825 g can peeled tomatoes, drained and chopped	1 long French loaf or 2 small Italian loaves
1 clove garlic, crushed	12 thin slices Mozzarella cheese
1 tablespoon chopped fresh oregano or 1 teaspoon dried	12 slices of your favourite salami
¼ cup olive oil	1 can flat anchovies
salt	¾ cup grated Parmesan cheese
freshly ground pepper	

Put the tomatoes, garlic, oregano, oil and salt and pepper to taste in a saucepan and simmer for 10 minutes until the flavours are well blended.

Split the bread lengthwise (the French loaf will be easier to handle if you cut it in half first). Put the bread on a baking tray, and spoon the hot tomato mixture evenly over it. Arrange the cheese and salami slices alternately on top, slightly overlapping. Cut the anchovies into small pieces and scatter on top, then drizzle with the oil from the can. Sprinkle with grated Parmesan and place under a medium grill until the topping is golden and bubbly, 4 to 6 minutes. Cut into diagonal slices to serve.
Serves 6 to 8

Variation
Instead of anchovies, you can add sliced, ripe black olives, chopped green pepper or spring onions.

Ham and Pineapple Sandwiches

Ham and pineapple go so well together, especially in a creamy sandwich filling with the crunch of toasted almonds. Cut into fingers, these sandwiches make interesting appetizers to serve with drinks – or cut them in halves diagonally for a quick, light lunch.

12 slices white sandwich bread	4 spring onions, finely chopped (including green tops)
butter for spreading	
FILLING:	
1 small can crushed pineapple	2 tablespoons finely chopped toasted almonds
2 cups finely chopped ham	
1 × 125 g packet Philadelphia cream cheese, softened	3 teaspoons soy sauce
	salt
	freshly ground pepper

Make the filling first. Drain the pineapple, reserving the syrup. Combine the pineapple with the remaining filling ingredients, seasoning to taste with salt and pepper and adding just enough pineapple syrup to give a spreading consistency. Butter the bread on one side, and divide the filling evenly among 6 of the slices on the unbuttered side. Top with the remaining slices, buttered side up. Toast the sandwiches on both sides under a medium grill, turning them carefully with an egg slice or spatula. *Serves 6 as a light meal, 10 to 12 as an appetizer.*
NOTE: The sandwiches may also be made in an electric snackmaker. Place 6 slices of bread in the snackmaker, buttered side down, and spoon in the filling. Top with the remaining slices, buttered side up, and toast until golden.

Extra Touches for Convenience Foods

Convenience foods – that is, prepared or partly prepared foods – are part of our busy way of life. Frozen and canned fruits and vegetables, canned soups, stock cubes, cooked meats, cake and pastry mixes are all useful standbys when there's no time to prepare fresh ingredients, or when they are scarce or out of season. At the same time, you can still add personal touches to make them more inviting and interesting – and here are some ideas to start you off.

Asparagus Parmesan

Mixed Beans with Garlic Butter

1 × 310 g can butter beans	2 cloves garlic, crushed
1 × 310 g can red kidney beans	salt
1 × 220 g can green beans	freshly ground pepper
90 g (3 oz) butter	chopped parsley, to garnish

Drain the beans and rinse under cold water. Melt the butter in a frying pan and gently fry the garlic until soft. Add the beans and stir until piping hot. Season to taste with salt and pepper, and sprinkle with parsley to serve. *Serves 6 to 8*

Variation

Add a teaspoon of Mexican-style chilli powder along with the garlic for a spicy flavour.

Asparagus Parmesan

Canned asparagus makes a delicious hot vegetable baked with butter and cheese.

2 × 425 g cans asparagus spears or cuts	½ cup grated Cheddar cheese
60 g (2 oz) butter, melted	salt
½ cup grated Parmesan cheese	freshly ground pepper
	1 cup fresh breadcrumbs

Drain the asparagus. Pour half the melted butter into a small casserole dish. Arrange half the asparagus in the dish and top

with half the grated cheese, adding salt and pepper to taste. Repeat the asparagus and cheese layers, then top with breadcrumbs and spoon over the remaining butter. Bake in a preheated moderate oven (180°C/350°F) for 20 minutes, until the asparagus is heated through, the cheese is melted, and the crumbs are golden. *Serves 4 to 6*

Mexican Bean Dip

Canned baked beans make a spicy dip for a crowd. Serve with corn chips, toasted Lebanese bread or potato crisps.

1 × 425 g can baked beans in tomato sauce	2 teaspoons Worcestershire sauce
½ cup grated tasty cheese	2 cloves garlic, crushed
1 teaspoon salt	dash of cayenne
1 teaspoon Mexican-style chilli powder (or more to taste)	2 rashers bacon, grilled until crisp, and crumbled
2 teaspoons vinegar	

Place all the ingredients, except the bacon, in a blender and whirr until smooth. Taste, and add extra chilli powder as desired. Turn into a bowl, sprinkle with crisp bacon and serve as a dip. *Makes about 3 cups*

Liverwurst Cheese Ball

Liverwurst from the delicatessen is seasoned, shaped into a ball and 'iced' with cream cheese – an interesting idea for a party.

250 g (8 oz) liverwurst (chicken, Latvian, calf's liver, etc.)	salt
	freshly ground pepper
1 clove garlic, crushed	1 × 125 g packet Philadelphia cream cheese
2 tablespoons finely chopped green olives	2 teaspoons milk
1 tablespoon Dijon-style mustard	1 tablespoon snipped chives

Place the liverwurst in a bowl and mash with a fork to soften. Blend in the garlic, olives, mustard and salt and pepper to taste. Shape into a ball and chill. Meanwhile, allow the cream cheese to soften at room temperature. Beat with a fork until smooth and stir in the milk and chives. Spread over the ball of liverwurst (like icing a cake) and chill until serving time. Surround with buttered French bread or crisp crackers. *Makes enough for 10 to 12 appetizer servings.*

Quick Tuna Medley

30 g (1 oz) butter	1 × 340 g can tuna in oil, drained
1 medium onion, finely chopped	½ cup milk
1 × 305 g can asparagus or celery soup	freshly ground pepper
	chopped parsley, to garnish
1 × 220 g can mixed vegetables, drained	

Heat the butter in a large frying pan and fry the onion until soft. Stir in the remaining ingredients, except the parsley, separating the tuna into chunks with a fork. Heat gently until piping hot; turn into a serving dish and sprinkle with chopped parsley. *Serves 4*

Cheese Chowder with Hot Crackers

Variation

Use oyster soup instead of asparagus and a 440 g can of red salmon instead of tuna. Serve over crisp fried noodles.

Cheese Chowder

1 onion, finely chopped	*2 cups milk*
60 g (2 oz) butter	*1 carrot, finely chopped*
1 tablespoon flour	*2 sticks celery, chopped*
1 × 440 g can chicken soup (cream type)	*dash of salt and paprika*
	½ cup grated tasty cheese

Fry the onion in butter until soft. Blend in the flour off the heat, then return to the heat and stir in the remaining ingredients, except the cheese. Simmer for 15 minutes, stirring occasionally. Add the cheese, cook for a minute until the cheese melts, then pour into soup bowls. Serve with hot crackers, if wished. *Serves 4*

Hot Crackers

Use round crackers, rye wafers or other small savoury biscuits. Brush the tops with melted butter and arrange on a greased baking tray. Sprinkle with a little onion or celery salt and top with poppy seeds, caraway seeds, or sesame seeds (or a mixture). Bake in a moderate oven (180°C/350°F) for 5 minutes, or until crisp and hot. Serve with soup or as a snack.

Sweet and Spicy Frankfurts

The sauce for this is so simple, but the flavour's special.

¼ cup Dijon-style mustard	*500 g (1 lb) cocktail*
¾ cup redcurrant jelly	*frankfurts*

Heat the mustard and jelly in a saucepan, stirring until combined. Add the frankfurts to the sauce and heat through. *Serves 8 to 10 as an appetizer.*

Celery with Caviar and Sour Cream

An impressive snack for gourmet friends!

6 tender sticks celery	*1 small jar caviar or lumpfish*
1 carton thick sour cream	*roe*
	fresh lemon juice

Remove any strings from the celery, wash, and pat dry with absorbent paper towels. Spoon the sour cream into the hollows and top with caviar. Sprinkle a little lemon juice over and cut into bite-size pieces on the diagonal. Serve immediately. *Serves 8 to 10 as part of an appetizer tray.*

Sandwiches for a Crowd are Easy

How to produce stylish snacks or a casual meal for a crowd without being marooned in the kitchen and missing all the fun? Prepare ahead with one or more of these super-sandwiches.

Submarine Sandwiches

These take their name from their shape, and they're beautifully practical for a crowd because they're made the day before and can be eaten hot or cold. They carry well too, if that's a consideration. Vary the filling to suit yourself, using ham, corned beef or chicken with such additions as chopped celery, sliced mushrooms, mustard, chopped dill pickles or sauerkraut.

1 long French loaf or 2 small Italian loaves	1 small can flat anchovy fillets
¼ cup olive oil	2 or 3 canned pimientos, drained
12 thin slices Swiss cheese	freshly ground pepper
4 medium tomatoes, thinly sliced	black or green olives, stoned
12 thin slices of your favourite salami	parsley sprigs, to garnish

If using a French loaf, cut it in two to make it easier to handle. Slice the bread lengthwise and remove some of the crumbs. Brush the insides of the bread with oil.

Place the cheese slices in an overlapping pattern on the bottom halves of the bread; top with overlapping tomato slices, then the salami slices.

Drain the anchovies and split the fillets lengthwise. Cut the pimientos into halves or quarters. Arrange the anchovies, pimientos and olives alternately on top of the salami and grind a little black pepper over. Put the top halves of the bread on and wrap tightly in foil. Place in the refrigerator with a weight on top (such as a couple of tins standing on a bread board) for several hours or overnight.

To serve cold, remove from the refrigerator about 1 hour before needed. At serving time, unwrap and cut across in thick slices. Garnish with parsley.

To serve hot, place the wrapped bread in a moderate oven (180°C/350°F) for 20 minutes, when the cheese will be melted and the crust crispy. Cut across into thick slices. For a complete meal, add a simple salad. *Serves 6 to 8*

Variation

The submarine may be served open-faced. Divide the filling evenly among the halves of bread, finishing with a topping of cheese. Place under a heated grill until the cheese is bubbly and melted.

Submarine Sandwich

Sausage-Stuffed Rolls

12 long, soft bread rolls	12 grilled sausages
125 g (4 oz) butter, melted	French mustard
6 spring onions, finely chopped	salt
4 tablespoons mixed, chopped fresh herbs, or 4 tablespoons parsley sprigs chopped with 2 teaspoons mixed dried herbs	freshly ground pepper

Cut the rolls in halves lengthwise and pull out part of the crumb from each piece (use another time for breadcrumbs). Brush the insides with melted butter and sprinkle with chopped spring onions and herbs. Split the sausages lengthwise, spread the insides generously with French mustard and put back together.

Place a sausage in each hollowed roll, season with salt and pepper and replace the top half of the roll. Wrap tightly in aluminium foil in packages of 3 or 4 rolls and leave overnight in the refrigerator. When the rolls are required, heat the packages straight from the refrigerator in a moderate oven (180°C/350°F) for 20 minutes. *Makes 12 rolls*
NOTE: You can use ordinary sausages, or, for a more sophisticated version, Continental-style sausages such as bratwurst.

Appetizer Pies

Each 'pie' is really a big round open-face sandwich with the toppings arranged decoratively in circles. Fun to offer with drinks, cut into wedges, or as a casual meal with a salad.

1 day-old loaf of round bread, preferably wholegrain	1 × 125 g can devilled ham
butter for spreading	2 teaspoons prepared horseradish
EGG TOPPING:	CHEESE TOPPING:
4 hard-boiled eggs, chopped	1 × 250 g packet Philadelphia cream cheese, softened
¼ cup mayonnaise	2 tablespoons crumbled blue cheese
2 tablespoons finely chopped spring onion	pinch of cayenne or ¼ teaspoon seasoned pepper
1 teaspoon French mustard	
salt	TO FINISH:
freshly ground pepper	2 medium green cucumbers
HAM TOPPING:	
125 g (4 oz) ham, finely chopped	

Make the toppings by combining the ingredients for each in a separate bowl.

Cut the top off the loaf and cut the bread across into 4 thick horizontal slices, discarding the bottom crust. Spread each slice with butter.

Spread the egg topping in a circle in the middle of each slice, and add the ham topping in a ring round it. Finally spread the cheese topping round the outside. Wash and dry the cucumbers and score the rind from end to end with a fork. Cut into very thin slices and arrange, overlapping, in a circle over the join of the ham and cheese toppings. Serve cut into wedges. *Makes about 24 wedges*
NOTE: If you want to make Appetizer Pies ahead of time, place each finished pie on its serving platter, cover with plastic wrap and lay a damp disposable cloth lightly over the top. Refrigerate, but remove about 45 minutes before serving to allow the pies to come to room temperature.

Lebanese Bread Pockets

3 rounds Lebanese bread	¼ cup finely chopped parsley
10–12 thin slices roast lamb	¼ cup finely chopped fresh mint
spray of parsley or mint, to garnish	¼ cup grated Parmesan cheese
SALAD:	2 tablespoons olive oil
½ cup burghul (cracked wheat)	2 tablespoons lemon juice
1 large ripe tomato, peeled and chopped	salt
3 spring onions, finely chopped (including some green tops)	freshly ground pepper
	½ small lettuce, shredded

To make the salad, cover the burghul with boiling water, leave for 10 minutes, then drain through a sieve and rinse with cold water. Squeeze out as much water as possible with your hands, then put the burghul into a tea-towel and wring out to dry further.

Place the burghul in a bowl, add the tomato and spring onions and toss. Add the herbs, cheese, oil, lemon juice and salt and pepper to taste and toss again. Just before serving, mix the lettuce lightly through the salad.

Cut each round of bread into 4 wedge-shaped pieces, like a pie. Pull the top and bottom crusts gently apart. Fill the 'pocket' thus formed with thinly sliced roast lamb (cut large slices into pieces as needed) and salad.

Pile the pockets onto a large platter and garnish with a big spray of parsley or mint. *Makes 12 pockets*

Toasted Crab and Olive Wedges

1 flat round loaf of bread (often called a cottage loaf)	2 × 170 g cans crabmeat, drained
butter for spreading	⅓ cup mayonnaise
185 g (6 oz) Swiss cheese, grated	⅓ cup stuffed olives, sliced
	1 tablespoon drained capers, chopped

Slice the bread in half horizontally and cut each half into 6 pie-shaped wedges, cutting down to the bottom crust but not all the way through. Spread with butter and lightly toast the cut sides. Mix the other ingredients together and spread on top. When required, place in a hot oven (200°C/400°F) for 10 to 15 minutes until hot and bubbly. Finish cutting apart. *Makes 12 wedges*

Toasted Cheese and Mushroom Wedges

bread and butter as in recipe above	⅓ cup thick sour cream
250 g (8 oz) mushrooms, finely chopped	⅓ cup chopped parsley
185 g (6 oz) Swiss cheese, grated	salt
	freshly ground pepper

Cut, butter and toast the bread as for Crab and Olive Wedges. To remove excess moisture from the chopped mushrooms, put them on a clean cloth, fold the cloth over them and wring out with both hands.

Mix the mushrooms with the remaining ingredients and finish as for Crab and Olive Wedges. *Makes 12 wedges*

Fish fillet frying in batter

From the Frypan . . . Fast Fish Dishes

Everybody enjoys succulent fish fillets in a crisp, golden coating of breadcrumbs or batter.

Here are a few points to keep in mind:

Go over the fillets carefully and remove any scales and bones. Small kitchen pliers or strong tweezers do an instant job of bone removal!

Allow the egg and breadcrumb coating to harden for at least 10 minutes, preferably in the refrigerator, before frying the fish.

For fish in batter, dust the fillets lightly with flour, then dip each fillet in batter and place it straight into the hot oil in the pan.

Packaged crumbs are convenient for coating fish. Alternatively, you can make your own breadcrumbs by baking crusts in a slow oven until crisp, then crushing them with a rolling pin.

When the fish is cooked, drain it on crumpled kitchen paper towels. If you need to keep the first batch warm while more are cooking, arrange the fillets in one layer on a baking tray and place in a warm oven. Don't pile them on top of one another or they will lose their crispness.

Fish cooked this way freezes well, so you might like to make two or three batches at one time and freeze them for later use. Wrap each portion individually in freezer wrap, then store in freezer bags or covered containers. To reheat frozen fish, do not thaw but place the frozen portions on a greased baking tray and leave in a preheated moderate oven (180°C/350°F) for 20 minutes, or until the outside is crisp and the fish heated through.

Crisp Batter for Fish

The secret of a really light, crisp batter is to use beer or soda water as the liquid and to add a stiffly beaten egg white just before using.

1 cup flour	*60 g (2 oz) butter or*
pinch of salt	*margarine, melted*
2 eggs	*1 cup beer or soda water*

Sift the flour with the salt into a bowl and make a well in the centre. Lightly beat one whole egg and one egg yolk (keep the second white for later) and pour into the well with the melted butter or margarine. Stir round and round, incorporating the flour gradually and adding beer or soda water little by little. Stir until the mixture is smooth, then cover and stand in a warm place for 1 hour. Just before using, whip the remaining egg white to a firm snow and fold into the batter. *Makes sufficient batter for 4 thick fillets.*

Fillets of Fish Fried in Batter

Remove any scales and bones from the fillets, then trim them and dry with paper towels.

Heat 1 cm (½ inch) of oil in a frying pan until a slight haze rises from it. Coat the fillets with flour, shaking off the surplus. Dip them in batter, holding them by the tail for a moment over the bowl to allow the surplus batter to drip off. Place in the oil, skinless side down, and fry for 3 to 4 minutes or until golden underneath. Turn and fry on the other side. Do not crowd the pan; fry in batches if necessary, adding a little more oil as required. Drain on crumpled paper towels.

Crumbed Fillets of Fish

Suitable fish include bream, flathead, sole, snapper and whiting. Allow about 185 g (6 oz) filleted fish per person, either 2 small fillets or 1 large fillet. Large ones are easier to handle if cut in half.

To crumb and cook, see step-by-step pictures at right.

Tartare Sauce

This is the classic accompaniment to fried and grilled fish.

1 teaspoon finely chopped capers
2 teaspoons finely chopped gherkins
1 teaspoon finely chopped spring onion
2 teaspoons finely chopped parsley
½ cup mayonnaise
mustard and lemon juice to taste

Scatter all the finely chopped ingredients over the mayonnaise in a small bowl. Fold in lightly and season with mustard and lemon juice. *Makes ½ cup*

Fish Fillets with Ginger

This pretty dish, with its scattering of green and white spring onion, has an intriguing spicy flavour. It is a good choice for a special little dinner.

500 g (1 lb) bream or snapper fillets, skinned
juice and grated rind of 1 lemon
60 g (2 oz) butter
1 medium onion, finely chopped
2 teaspoons grated fresh ginger
2 cloves
1 teaspoon brown sugar
1 tablespoon dry white wine
salt
freshly ground pepper
2 spring onions (including some green tops), to garnish

Cut the fillets into serving-size pieces; spoon the lemon juice over and set aside.

Melt the butter in a large frying pan, add the onion and ginger and cook gently until golden. Stir in the lemon rind, cloves, brown sugar and wine. Push to one side and arrange the fish in the pan. Season with salt and pepper and spoon the onion mixture over. Cover tightly and cook on a very low heat for 8 to 10 minutes, or until the flesh is white and tender when tested with a toothpick.

Arrange the fish on a hot serving platter and spoon the sauce over. Scatter with spring onions cut on the long diagonal into shreds, and serve immediately with plain boiled rice. *Serves 2 to 3*

Crumbed Fillets of Fish
1 Spread seasoned flour in a flat dish, and dry crumbs on a sheet of greaseproof paper. Beat an egg and pour into a shallow dish. Coat a fillet with flour; shake off surplus, and dip into egg.

2 Draw the fillet out over the side of the dish to remove surplus egg, allowing the egg to drip back into the dish, not into the crumbs.

3 Lay the fillet skinless side down in the crumbs. Use the edges of the paper to toss more crumbs over the fish. Sprinkle on more crumbs if necessary.

4 Press the fillet down firmly into the crumbs. Lift by the tail, shake off loose crumbs and lay skinless side up on a tray. Repeat coating with remaining fillets; place on tray and refrigerate for at least 10 minutes to harden egg.

5 Heat enough oil or vegetable shortening to come halfway up the fillets. When a slight haze forms, put in fillets, skinless side down, and fry until golden underneath. Turn with a fish slice and fry other side. Don't crowd the pan; fry in batches if necessary.

6 Drain the fish well on paper towels and keep warm until all are done. Arrange skinless side up on a heated serving plate. Garnish with lemon and parsley. Serve with Tartare Sauce if liked (see recipe at left).

Fish Fillets Italian Style

750 g (1½ lb) white fish fillets	1 teaspoon salt
3 tablespoons olive oil	¼ teaspoon freshly ground
2 tablespoons chopped parsley	pepper
1 clove garlic, crushed	2 teaspoons chopped fresh
2 ripe tomatoes, peeled and	mint or oregano or ½
chopped	teaspoon dried

Wipe the fillets with damp paper towels and cut into serving pieces. Heat the olive oil in a frying pan, add the parsley and garlic and cook gently for 3 minutes without browning. Add the chopped tomatoes and bring to simmering point. Add the fish and remaining ingredients. Cover and simmer very gently for about 8 minutes, or just until the fish is white and tender when tested with a toothpick. *Serves 4 to 6*

Crispy Herrings in Oatmeal

This is the traditional Scots way of cooking herrings to give a beautiful crunchy outside – and it makes a marvellous breakfast. You can buy frozen herrings in some fine food stores and delicatessens, otherwise use fillets of mackerel or mullet.

4 herrings weighing about	185 g (6 oz) butter
280–350 g (9–11 oz) each, or	TO GARNISH:
about 750 g (1½ lb) mackerel	lemon wedges
or mullet fillets	parsley sprigs
milk	
medium oatmeal (from health	
food shops) for coating	

To prepare and cook, see step-by-step pictures below. *Serves 4*

Fish with Vegetables

A whole nourishing, well-balanced meal that's made quickly in one pan. It's particularly good for children or older people because it's easy to eat and to digest – but anyone would relish this good combination of fresh vegetables, herbs and fish.

30 g (1 oz) butter or margarine	1 small bay leaf
2 or 3 carrots, peeled and	2 teaspoons chopped fresh
thinly sliced	herbs (thyme, parsley,
1 small onion, peeled and	chives, tarragon, chervil), or
thinly sliced	2 teaspoons fresh parsley
2 small or 1 large stick celery,	chopped with ¼ teaspoon
thinly sliced	mixed dried herbs
500 g (1 lb) fillets of white fish	salt
(gemfish, flathead, bream)	freshly ground pepper
2 tomatoes, peeled and	2 tablespoons cream
chopped	chopped parsley, to garnish
1 tablespoon water or white	
wine	

Melt the butter or margarine in a frying pan, add the carrots, onion and celery and cook gently until soft, without browning.

Wipe the fish with damp kitchen paper and cut into serving pieces. Push the vegetables to one side, place the fish in the pan and cook for 1 minute on each side. Spoon the vegetables over the fish.

Add the tomatoes, water or wine, bay leaf and herbs. Season with salt and pepper, then cover and cook gently for 7 to 10 minutes or until the fish is white and tender when tested with a toothpick.

Remove the fish to a hot serving dish. Stir the cream into the contents of the pan and spoon over the fish. Sprinkle with chopped parsley and serve at once. *Serves 3 to 4*

Crispy Herrings in Oatmeal
1 Check that the fish is well scaled and cleaned. Slit the belly right down to the tail. Cut off the head, fins and tail. Open out flat and place, skin side up, on a board. Dip thumb and forefinger in salt and hold tail end firmly. Press down with knuckles all along the backbone to loosen it.

2 Turn the herring over and with the point of a knife ease out the backbone in one piece, starting at the tail end. Pull out as many of the small bones as possible. Wipe the fish with damp kitchen paper.

3 Dip the fish in milk and coat with oatmeal, following the method for egg and breadcrumbs (page 27). Fry in hot butter, skinless side first, until crisp, then turn and fry other side. Drain on crumpled kitchen paper. If the herring has roe, coat and fry it separately and place down the centre of each fish. Garnish with lemon wedges and parsley and serve very hot.

Crispy Herrings in Oatmeal

Smoked Fish Hash

250 g (8 oz) smoked fish, cooked and flaked	1 teaspoon grated lemon rind
2 medium potatoes, cooked, peeled and diced	freshly ground pepper
1 tablespoon grated onion	2 tablespoons sour cream
1 tablespoon chopped parsley	60 g (2 oz) butter
	1 teaspoon extra chopped parsley, to garnish

Mix together all the ingredients, except the butter and extra parsley. Heat the butter in a frying pan, add the hash mixture and cook, stirring occasionally, until very hot and lightly browned. Sprinkle with chopped parsley and serve immediately. *Serves 2 to 3*

Whitebait Fritters

Fresh whitebait are such a delicacy that you will want to do something lovely with them when they are in season. They are superb presented in crisp, light fritters. Canned whitebait are also good treated this way.

2 eggs	TO GARNISH:
1 cup fresh whitebait or 1 × 185 g can	lemon wedges
salt	parsley sprigs
freshly ground pepper	
oil for frying (preferably peanut)	

Beat the eggs in a bowl and stir in the whitebait. Season with salt and pepper. Heat enough oil to film the bottom of a heavy frying pan. When the oil begins to haze, spoon in the whitebait mixture to form large fritters. Keep the fritters apart; cook in batches if necessary. Fry for 2 minutes or until golden on one side, turn with a fish slice and fry the other side. Drain briefly on crumpled paper towels and serve very hot, garnished with lemon wedges and parsley sprigs. *Makes 4 to 6 large fritters*

Devilled Fish

When you want something fast, hot and really savoury, this could be the one – any time from breakfast to a late supper. It's especially useful because you can have the ingredients always on hand – frozen fillets do very well.

2 medium onions, finely chopped	2 tomatoes
2 teaspoons curry powder (or to taste)	1 tablespoon lemon juice
30 g (1 oz) butter	salt
500 g (1 lb) skinless fillets of gemfish or other white fish	pinch of cayenne
	chopped parsley, to garnish

Fry the onions and curry powder gently in butter until golden. Cut the fish into pieces. Peel, seed and chop the tomatoes. Add the tomatoes to the pan, top with the fish and cook, covered, over a low heat without stirring, until the fish juices begin to run. If using frozen fish, continue cooking until the fish is completely thawed. Raise the heat to medium, and cook, stirring lightly and flaking the fish with a fork, until the sauce thickens slightly. Stir in the lemon juice and season with salt and cayenne to taste. Sprinkle with chopped parsley and serve immediately with hot buttered toast or fried bread. *Serves 4*
NOTE: The fishmonger will usually skin fillets if you ask him, but you should check for any little bones before cooking.

Fish Steaks Casalinga

Italian cooks have devised a variety of splendid sauces for fish. This is a simple but impressive way with fish steaks.

125 g (4 oz) butter	1½ tablespoons beurre manié (see note)
1 onion, chopped	salt
½ cup dry white wine	freshly ground pepper
1 tablespoon chopped parsley	1½ tablespoons lemon juice
4 thick fish steaks	
5 canned anchovy fillets	

Melt half the butter in a large heavy frying pan, add the onion and cook gently until golden. Add the wine and parsley, then place the fish in the pan. Simmer, tightly covered, for about 8 minutes or until the flesh is white and can be pushed away from the bone slightly with a toothpick.

While the fish is cooking, rinse the anchovies under cold water and pound to a paste with a pestle and mortar, or with the end of a rolling pin in a small bowl.

When the fish is cooked, lift it from the pan onto a hot platter and keep warm.

Blend the pounded anchovies into the liquid in the pan and beat in the beurre manié. Stir over a medium heat for 5 minutes. Season with salt and pepper to taste; remove from the heat and stir in the remaining butter and the lemon juice. Spoon some sauce over the fish and serve the rest separately. *Serves 4*
NOTE: Beurre manié is butter blended with flour, used as a thickener. For this quantity, put 15 g (½ oz) softened butter into a small bowl and mix in thoroughly 1 tablespoon flour. Beat into the simmering liquid, bit by bit.

From the Frypan... Fast Meat Dishes

When a French girl marries and leaves home, she takes at least one *sauteuse* or frying pan with her. She knows that no other single piece of equipment is more vital to the cook who wishes to produce beautifully cooked food with a minimum of fuss.

When meat is perfectly sautéed, the outside is sealed to a golden brown crustiness, the inside moist and tender with all the succulent flavour sealed in.

Many sautéed foods are enjoyed plain, but if a little sauce is required it too is quick and easy: the savoury brown bits left in the pan are quickly scraped up and swirled with a few spoonfuls of stock, cream, wine or water and seasoning.

Meats for Sautéing

Because the method is so quick, tender meat should be chosen. Chicken pieces, lamb chops and steaks, escalopes of veal, thinly sliced pork chops, hamburger patties, liver and kidneys, tender beef steaks (not too thick) and ham steaks are all suitable.

Choosing the Pan

The type of metal is not the vital factor. The pan might be cast iron, stainless steel with a copper base, or aluminium or iron coated with enamel. The important thing is that it has a very heavy base and is large enough to take food without crowding. Because sautéing takes place over brisk heat, a heavy base is essential to distribute the heat properly and allow the food to brown evenly and cook through without scorching.

The sides should be no deeper than 5 cm (2 inches) and should be straight. This allows the food to move back and forward in the pan quickly as it is tossed over high heat.

Escalopes of Veal Viennoise

3 thin slices veal steak (escalopes), each weighing about 125 g (4 oz)	TO GARNISH:
	1 hard-boiled egg
seasoned flour	2 teaspoons drained capers
1 egg, beaten	3 flat anchovy fillets
dry breadcrumbs for coating	lemon wedges
2 tablespoons vegetable oil	parsley sprigs
60 g (2 oz) butter	TO ACCOMPANY:
	Tartare Sauce (page 27)
	Sauté Potatoes (see below)

Put the escalopes between sheets of greaseproof paper and beat with a rolling pin until they are very thin. If large, cut in two. Coat with seasoned flour, dip in beaten egg and then in crumbs, firming them on with the flat of the hand (for details of egg-and-breadcrumbing, see step-by-step pictures for Crumbed Fillets of Fish, page 27). Leave for at least 10 minutes, preferably in the refrigerator.

Heat a sauté pan, pour in the oil and heat; then add the butter and heat until the foam subsides. Place the escalopes in the pan and fry briskly for 3 or 4 minutes until the undersides are golden; turn and cook the other sides. Remove from the pan and drain on crumpled paper towels. Arrange on a hot serving dish.

While the escalopes are cooking, shell the hard-boiled egg and separate the yolk and white. Chop the white finely and sieve the yolk. Garnish each escalope with capers and an anchovy fillet, with a row of egg white and yolk on either side. Add the lemon wedges and parsley. *Serves 3*

Sauté Potatoes

A favourite accompaniment to almost any meat or fish dish.

3 medium-size old potatoes, boiled and skinned	30 g (1 oz) butter
	salt
1 tablespoon oil	2 tablespoons chopped parsley

Pork Fillet with Mushrooms and Sour Cream

Cut the potatoes into thick slices. Heat a sauté pan, add the oil and heat it; then add the butter and heat until the foam subsides. Place the potatoes in the pan and cook briskly, shaking the pan and turning the potatoes continually until they are brown and crusty on the outside. Sprinkle with salt and chopped parsley and serve immediately without draining the potatoes. *Serves 3*

Lamb Roll Dijon

The method is the 'quick and easy' benefit here! The lamb cooks in a superb marinade and needs no gravy – the pan juices are simply poured over.

1 boned and rolled shoulder of lamb, about 1.75 kg (3½ lb), with excess fat removed before rolling	1 tablespoon soy sauce ¼ teaspoon ground ginger 1 clove garlic, crushed 1 teaspoon dried rosemary
¼ cup Dijon-style mustard	1 tablespoon oil

Place the meat on a rack in a baking dish. Mix the remaining ingredients together and spread all over the roast. Allow to stand for 1 hour at room temperature.

Roast in a moderately slow oven (160°C/325°F) for 1½ hours, or until done to your liking. Allow to rest for 20 minutes, then serve cut in thick slices with the heated pan juices poured over. (Add a little water if necessary). *Serves 6*

Pork Fillet with Mushrooms and Sour Cream

An elegant luxury dish, perfect for a dinner party, but quite quick and simple to make. It's a good idea for a busy working woman or man who wants to entertain within an hour or two of coming home. Finish the dish with a piped border of creamy mashed potato and serve with a simple green salad.

500 g (1 lb) pork fillet	2 teaspoons chopped mixed fresh herbs or ½ teaspoon dried
90 g (3 oz) button mushrooms	
2–3 tablespoons flour	
60 g (2 oz) clarified butter (ghee)	salt
2 tablespoons sherry or vermouth	freshly ground pepper
	1 cup stock (or water and stock cube)
½ cup sour cream	TO GARNISH: fried mushroom caps paprika

To prepare and cook, see step-by-step pictures below. *Serves 4*

Pork Fillet with Mushrooms and Sour Cream

1 Trim any fat or skin from the fillet and cut across into slices 2.5 cm (1 inch) thick. Place between sheets of greaseproof paper and flatten slightly with a rolling pin. Trim mushroom stalks and wipe caps with a damp cloth. This can all be done ahead of time.

2 Flour the pork, shaking off any surplus. Heat butter in a sauté pan; when foam subsides add pork in a single layer. Fry briskly until crisp underneath; turn and fry other side. Add the mushrooms and cook for 5 minutes, shaking pan frequently.

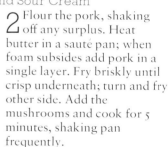

3 Pour in the sherry or vermouth and boil, scraping up brown bits from bottom of pan. Cook gently for a minute or two.

4 Lower the heat and stir in sour cream. Add the herbs, salt and pepper to taste and

mix well. Stir in sufficient stock just to cover the pork. Cook gently for 7 to 10 minutes or until the pork is tender. Taste, and adjust seasoning as necessary. Make a border of mashed potatoes and spoon in the pork and sauce. Garnish with fried mushroom caps and paprika.

Lamb with Rosemary

4 lamb steaks or chump chops	salt
30 g (1 oz) butter	freshly ground pepper
1 clove garlic, crushed	1 tablespoon flour
1 teaspoon chopped fresh	1 teaspoon wine vinegar
rosemary or ¼ teaspoon	½ cup dry white wine
dried	½ cup water

Trim any excess fat from the meat. Heat the butter and, when foam subsides, brown lamb well on both sides. Add the garlic, rosemary, salt and pepper and cook gently without a lid for 10 minutes, turning meat once.

Remove the meat and set aside. Add flour to the pan and cook, stirring, for 2 minutes. Mix the vinegar, wine and water together and stir in gradually. Continue stirring until the mixture boils, then check seasoning. Return the meat to the pan, cover, and simmer until tender, 15 to 20 minutes. *Serves 2 to 4*

Pork Chops with Peppercorns

If 'butterflied' chops are unavailable, use loin chops or shoulder steaks.

4 butterfly pork chops	1 tablespoon Dijon-style
salt	mustard
freshly ground pepper	1⅓ cups cream
1 tablespoon oil	TO GARNISH:
SAUCE:	a tomato rose (see note)
2 teaspoons green or pink	
peppercorns, drained	

Season the chops with salt and pepper. Heat the oil in a large sauté or frying pan and fry the pork for 4 to 5 minutes on each side, until golden brown and cooked through. Remove to a heated platter and keep warm.

Pour off any excess fat. Add the peppercorns to the pan and fry for a few seconds, then add the mustard and cream. Stir well to pick up the brown gravy bits on the bottom of the pan, and continue cooking gently until the sauce thickens. Add salt to taste, spoon the sauce over the pork, and serve garnished with cress or parsley and a tomato rose. *Serves 4*
NOTE: To make a tomato rose, peel a small, round tomato as you would an orange. Roll the tomato skin to make one large or two small roses. This is surprisingly easy, as the rose seems to fall naturally into shape. Finish with a rose leaf from the garden, or blanch a few spring onion stalks in boiling water for 20 seconds and arrange as leaves.

Beef and Cheese Cake

60 g (2 oz) butter	3 eggs
250 g (8 oz) lean minced beef	3 tablespoons water
1 onion, finely chopped	375 g (12 oz) grated semi-firm
1½ teaspoons salt	cheese such as Jarlsberg
freshly ground pepper	

Heat the butter and fry the beef briskly until it changes colour, stirring and breaking up lumps with a fork. Add the onion and fry for 3 minutes, adding salt and pepper to taste.

Beat the eggs and water together and stir in all but ½ cup of cheese. Stir this mixture into the contents of the pan, spread out evenly and press down. Sprinkle the remaining cheese over the top. Put a lid on the pan and cook over a moderate heat for 10 minutes. Remove the lid, put a plate over the pan and turn the meat cake out onto the plate, then reverse onto another plate. Serve cut in wedges, with crusty French or Italian bread and a mixed salad. *Serves 4*

Liver au Poivre

Liver is a top source of vitamins and minerals (especially iron) and this is an interesting new way of serving such a nutritious and economical food.

500 g (1 lb) calf's liver or 1	2 tablespoons oil
lamb's fry	salt
1 tablespoon black	finely chopped parsley, to
peppercorns	garnish

Remove the outer membrane from the liver and cut into strips about 1 cm (½ inch) thick, discarding any veins.

Crush the peppercorns with a pestle and mortar, or by placing between two sheets of plastic wrap and pounding with the end of a rolling pin.

Sprinkle the strips of liver with the crushed peppercorns and press in with the flat of your hand. Heat the oil in a frying pan until a faint blue haze rises. Quickly sauté the liver slices, turning with a spatula until lightly browned on all sides.

The secret of tender liver is not to overcook it. As soon as the strips have lightly browned and stiffened, without being hard, they are done – about 3 minutes.

Transfer at once to a heated serving plate, sprinkle with a little salt and finely chopped parsley, and serve.

Sautéed onion rings and a green vegetable or salad are good accompaniments. *Serves 3 to 4*
Variation
Liver au Poivre Vert Instead of black peppercorns, sprinkle the strips with crushed green peppercorns (sold in small cans as Poivre Vert). Drain the peppercorns and dry by patting with absorbent paper towels before crushing them. If you wish, a little cream may be added to the pan after the liver is cooked, and heated with the pan juices to make a gravy.

Ham with Vermouth and Cream

Rich, luxurious and ready in minutes. This dish is a specialty of the Savoie district of France.

60 g (2 oz) butter	½ cup dry vermouth
8 thin slices cooked ham	salt
125 g (4 oz) button	freshly ground pepper
mushrooms	(preferably white)
1 cup pouring cream	

Melt the butter, add the ham slices and heat very gently. Lift out the ham with a slotted egg slice and arrange the slices, folded in half, down the centre of a hot serving dish. Cover and keep warm.

Add the mushrooms to the pan, cover, and cook gently for 4 minutes. Remove the lid and stir in the cream and vermouth. Season to taste with salt and pepper and simmer for 3 to 4 minutes until thickened a little.

Spoon the sauce over the ham and serve with mashed potatoes or buttered noodles. *Serves 4*

Pork Chops with Peppercorns

34

Veal Steaks Normandy

6 thick veal steaks	salt
60 g (2 oz) butter	freshly ground pepper
½ cup dry white wine	60 g (2 oz) mushrooms, sliced
2 teaspoons Dijon-style mustard	3 tablespoons cream
	1 egg yolk

Put the steaks between 2 sheets of greaseproof paper and beat them with a rolling pin to flatten them a little.

Heat the butter in a large frying pan and, when the foam subsides, brown the steaks well on both sides. Remove and keep warm.

Add the wine to the pan and stir and scrape up all the brown bits on the bottom. Blend in the mustard, salt and pepper and simmer, uncovered, for 10 minutes. Add the mushrooms and simmer for a minute. Whisk the cream and egg yolk together and stir in. Heat very gently, stirring, until the sauce thickens a little and becomes glossy, but do not let it boil.

Pour the sauce over the veal and serve very hot. *Serves 6*

Coppiette

Coppiette are little rissoles, Roman style – excellent for lunch with a fresh tomato sauce, or marble size with drinks.

750 g (1½ lb) lean minced beef	freshly ground pepper
60 g (2 oz) fatty ham or pork, finely chopped	¼ teaspoon nutmeg
1 clove garlic, crushed	¼ cup milk
1 tablespoon finely chopped parsley	2 eggs, lightly beaten
2 teaspoons finely chopped fresh marjoram or ½ teaspoon dried	4 tablespoons grated Parmesan cheese
	1 tablespoon sultanas
2½ tablespoons soft breadcrumbs	1 tablespoon pine nuts
salt	fine dry breadcrumbs
	oil for frying

Mix together all the ingredients except the dry breadcrumbs and oil and knead well. Break off small pieces and shape into flattened balls. Roll in the dry breadcrumbs, place on a tray in one layer and leave in the refrigerator for at least 30 minutes.

Heat enough oil in a frying pan to come halfway up the rissoles. When a faint blue haze rises from the oil, place the rissoles in the pan in one layer. Fry until golden underneath, then turn and fry the other side. Do not crowd the pan, but fry in batches if necessary. Drain each batch on crumpled paper towels and keep warm.

If liked, serve with Quick Tomato Sauce. *Serves 6*

Quick Tomato Sauce

1 tablespoon olive oil	1 teaspoon chopped fresh basil or oregano, or ¼ teaspoon dried
1 small onion, finely chopped	
1 × 875 g can peeled tomatoes	1 bay leaf
salt	2 teaspoons tomato paste
pinch of sugar	
freshly ground pepper	

Heat the oil, add the onion and cook over a high heat for 4 to 5 minutes, stirring until lightly browned. Chop the tomatoes, add to the pan with the juice and the remaining ingredients. Simmer, covered, for 15 minutes. *Enough for 6 servings*

Fried Liver and Bacon

4 rashers bacon	flour for dusting
60 g (2 oz) butter	1 small onion, chopped
4 tomatoes, halved	½ cup red or white wine or stock
salt	
freshly ground pepper	parsley sprigs, to garnish
500 g (1 lb) calf's liver or 1 lamb's fry	

To prepare and cook, see step-by-step pictures below. *Serves 4*

Arrange the liver on a hot serving dish, surrounded by bacon and tomatoes; pour gravy over and garnish with parsley.

Accompaniments for Fast Meat Dishes
When a meat dish is quick and easy, it's often ready to serve before conventionally cooked vegetables are ready! Cooked potatoes are easy to slice and brown in a little butter, and quick-cooking noodles can be tossed with chopped spring onions, herbs or poppy seeds.

Fried Liver and Bacon
1 Remove rind from bacon and cut each rasher in half. Place in a cold frying pan and cook slowly until crisp, pouring off fat as it runs. Remove and keep warm. Return bacon fat to pan, add butter and heat. Fry the tomatoes on both sides, until turning golden. Season with salt and pepper.

2 Meanwhile, skin the liver, slice 5 mm (¼ inch) thick and remove any gristle. Dust with flour on both sides.
When the tomatoes are done, remove from pan and keep warm. Arrange the liver slices in pan, being careful to avoid splashing.

3 Fry the liver briskly until brown, about 2 minutes on each side. Do not overcook or it will be hard. Season with salt and pepper; remove and keep warm. Add onion to pan and fry, stirring, until golden. Stir in the wine or stock, scraping up all the brown bits from the pan. Bring to the boil, simmer for a minute or two and correct seasoning.

Veal Chops Rosé

Rosé wine and sour cream go into a simple but interesting sauce for veal chops. Serve on a bed of freshly cooked noodles, and add a green salad or fresh green vegetable.

8 veal chops	freshly ground pepper
flour for dusting	¾ cup rosé wine
60 g (2 oz) butter	¾ cup light sour cream
salt	

Lightly dust the veal chops on both sides with flour. Heat the butter in a heavy sauté or frying pan and brown the chops well on both sides. Season with salt and pepper. Add the wine to the pan, cover, and simmer gently for 20 minutes or until the chops are tender.

Remove the chops and keep warm. Scrape up the brown bits from the bottom of the pan and add the sour cream. Heat without boiling, taste for seasoning, and pour over the chops. Serve on a bed of noodles. *Serves 4*

Buttered Noodles

1 × 500 g packet egg noodles	salt
60 g (2 oz) butter	freshly ground pepper
4 spring onions, chopped	2 tablespoons poppy seeds

Cook the noodles in plenty of boiling salted water until tender. Drain well and toss with the remaining ingredients. Serve at once. *Serves 4*

Quick Oyster Chicken

1 onion, sliced	1 teaspoon sugar
3 tender sticks celery, sliced on the diagonal	1 tablespoon soy sauce
1 green pepper, seeded and cut into strips	2 teaspoons oyster sauce
375 g (12 oz) boneless chicken fillet	¾ cup water
3 tablespoons peanut oil	salt
3 teaspoons cornflour	freshly ground pepper
	coriander sprigs or chopped spring onions, to garnish

Have the vegetables prepared. Cut the chicken into strips about 1 cm (½ inch) wide. Heat the oil in a wok or heavy frying pan and toss the vegetables in the hot oil until tender-crisp, about 3 minutes. Remove with a slotted spoon. Blend the cornflour with sugar, soy sauce and oyster sauce and mix to a smooth paste with the water. Have ready.

Reheat the oil remaining in the pan and add the chicken. Fry briskly over a high heat, turning frequently, until golden brown and cooked through, 3 to 4 minutes. Return the vegetables to the pan and add the cornflour mixture. Stir over a medium heat until the sauce is clear and thickened. Add salt and pepper to taste. Simmer for 1 minute and serve garnished with coriander sprigs or chopped spring onions. *Serves 3 to 4*

Fried Liver and Bacon

Meat and Chicken from the Grill

Hamburgers with Herb and Lemon Stuffing

Ask any man to name his favourite food and at least one out of two is sure to answer, 'grilled steak!'. Few things can match the sight and aroma of meat acquiring that lovely savoury brown crust on a grill or barbecue.

Grilling is also a marvellously quick way to cook, but because it is so quick it requires careful timing to keep the food tender and succulent. One way of testing grilled meat is to press it with your forefinger. If it feels soft and spongy, it is not cooked through; if soft but springy it is medium-done; when well-done, it is firm with little springiness. If you are uncertain, insert a fine skewer into the thickest part and check the juice that comes out. If it is red, the meat is rare; if pink, medium; if clear, well-done. Chicken has pink juice when underdone, clear juice when cooked through.

Always preheat the grill and grill rack before cooking. Just before you put the meat on the rack, brush the rack with a little oil to prevent sticking. Also brush lean cuts like chicken or lean pork with oil or melted butter.

Thick cuts of red meat should be grilled at high heat, but not so close to the heat that the surface is charred before the inside is cooked to your liking.

Meat that requires longer cooking, chicken for example, should be grilled at moderate heat, far enough away from the grill for it to be cooked through by the time it is golden brown.

Grind a little pepper over the meat before cooking, if you wish, but add salt only after cooking as salt draws out the juices. Be sure to trim off excess fat before cooking – you not only cut down on calories, but on smoke, too!

Grilled Rump Steak

Have the steak cut 4 cm (1½ inches) thick. If you have between 2 and 4 people to serve, buy one large piece and cut it into portions after cooking. Trim the border of fat and nick at 2.5 cm (1 inch) intervals to prevent the meat from curling when cooked. If the steak is large, curl it around into a neat shape and secure with a skewer.

Grind some black pepper over the steak when you take it from the refrigerator and leave for about 30 minutes for the meat to come to room temperature. Preheat the grill until very hot. Just before beginning to cook, brush the grill rack and meat with oil.

Grill at high heat until brown and crusty on both sides, then if further cooking time is required, lower a little away from the heat or turn heat down a little to complete cooking. Allow about 4 to 5 minutes each side for rare steaks, 6 to 7 minutes for medium and 8 minutes for well done. These times are an indication only, the effectiveness of your grill must be taken into account. To check for degrees of 'doneness', see instructions at left.

Grilled steak needs no sauce, but a pat of plain or flavoured butter placed on just before serving gives a beautiful glaze. A green salad, grilled tomatoes, fried onions, mashed or French-fried potatoes or fresh green vegetables are lovely accompaniments. Don't forget to offer a choice of good mustards and horseradish, too.

Hamburgers with Herb and Lemon Stuffing

750 g (1½ lb) hamburger steak	½ teaspoon chopped fresh thyme
1 teaspoon Worcestershire sauce	1 teaspoon finely snipped chives
1 teaspoon salt	30 g (1 oz) butter, melted
freshly ground pepper	salt
30 g (1 oz) butter, melted	freshly ground pepper
FILLING:	½ teaspoon grated lemon rind
1 cup fresh breadcrumbs	
1 egg, beaten	
2 teaspoons chopped parsley	

Mix the hamburger steak, Worcestershire sauce, salt and a good grinding of pepper lightly with a fork. Place on a board and pat out to a flat cake. Cut into 12 even-sized pieces and, with wet hands, shape each into a thin flat patty.

Mix all the filling ingredients lightly together with a fork. Spoon onto 6 of the patties, top with the remaining patties and press edges together to seal. Brush the hamburgers with melted butter and grill on a preheated oiled grill rack at high heat for about 5 minutes on each side. *Makes 6 hamburgers*

Sweet and Spicy Ham

4 ham steaks	¼ teaspoon ground ginger
15 g (½ oz) butter, melted	pinch of salt
¼ cup apricot jam	1 tablespoon water
½ teaspoon dry mustard	

Preheat the grill and oil the grill bars. Brush one side of the ham steaks with butter and grill on this side for 4 minutes. Mix the remaining ingredients together. Turn the steaks, spread with the mixture and grill for a further 5 minutes, or until the glaze is lightly browned. *Serves 4*

Devil-Crumbed Chicken

A crisp and piquant coating adds zest to the flavour of chicken and keeps the meat tender and juicy.

This is also a lovely dish to take on a picnic, as it packs well wrapped loosely in foil and tastes just as good warm as hot. In this case, add a container of crisp salad and perhaps some buttered rolls.

4 half breasts of chicken	dash of cayenne
60 g (2 oz) butter, melted	2 teaspoons Worcestershire
DEVIL MIXTURE:	sauce
60 g (2 oz) butter	1 cup fine, fresh breadcrumbs
1 teaspoon dry mustard	
½ teaspoon salt	

Preheat the grill to medium and cover the grill rack with oiled foil. Brush the chicken breasts with melted butter and grill for 10 minutes with the skin side down, brushing once or twice with butter.

Meanwhile, make the devil mixture. Soften the butter with a wooden spoon and work in the mustard, salt, cayenne, Worcestershire sauce and crumbs.

Remove the chicken from the grill and, when it is cool enough to handle, press the crumb mixture firmly over the skin side of each breast.

Place the chicken on the grill again, crumb side up, and grill at medium heat for a further 10 to 12 minutes, until the topping is golden brown and the juices run clear when the flesh is pierced with a fine skewer. (If the crumbs seem to be colouring too much, turn the heat down or move the chicken further away from the heat. You can take it off the rack and put it in the grill pan itself.) Serve hot with a green vegetable: a purée of peas or creamed spinach would make a good texture contrast. *Serves 4*
NOTE: The breadcrumbs required are the ones made from fresh bread – very easy if you have a blender, or you can rub the bread through a sieve. For the sieve method, bread a day or two old gives quicker results.

Marinated Grilled Lamb Chops

6 baby lamb loin chops	1 bay leaf, finely crumbled
6 tablespoons dry white wine	salt
6 tablespoons olive oil	freshly ground pepper
2 cloves garlic, finely chopped	

Trim the skin and excess fat from the chops and nick the fat. Combine the remaining ingredients and pour over. Leave for at least 2 hours to absorb the flavours, turning the chops occasionally.

Preheat the grill until it is very hot. Curl the tails of the chops round neatly and secure with toothpicks or small skewers. Brush the grill bars with oil and grill the chops at high heat, brushing several times with the marinade. Cook for 4 minutes on each side or until the meat feels soft but springy when pressed with the forefinger. The chops will be slightly pink and juicy inside at this stage. Grill 2 minutes longer on each side if you like them well done. *Serves 4*

Mixed Grill

2 lamb cutlets or loin chops	4 large mushrooms
oil for brushing	2 rashers bacon
2 sausages	watercress, to garnish
2 lamb's kidneys	MINT BUTTER:
2 tomatoes	2 tablespoons chopped fresh
salt	mint
freshly ground pepper	60 g (2 oz) butter
sugar	lemon juice
butter	

Make the mint butter before cooking the grill. Beat the mint into the butter and add the lemon juice to taste. Shape into a roll and chill. Slice when hard.

To prepare and cook, see step-by-step pictures below. *Serves 2*

Mixed Grill
1 Trim the skin and excess fat from the cutlets or chops. Brush with oil. Preheat grill, oil grill bars and place cutlets and sausages on. Grill about 5 minutes, turning the sausages but not the cutlets, until brown.

2 Meanwhile, cut the kidneys in half; skin and remove cores with scissors. Thread on a skewer to prevent curling while cooking. Brush with oil. Halve the tomatoes across, not downwards. Season with salt, pepper and a little sugar and dot with butter. Remove the mushroom stems, season undersides with salt and pepper and dot with butter.

3 Stretch the bacon rashers with the back of a knife and remove rind and gristle. Roll up and skewer. When the cutlets are brown on first side, turn with tongs and add the kidneys, bacon rolls, tomatoes and mushrooms. Turn kidneys, sausages and bacon as needed but not cutlets or vegetables.

4 When the cutlets are brown on the second side, place them on a heated serving dish or two individual plates and arrange the rest of the mixed grill around them. Top the cutlets with mint butter and garnish with watercress.

Kebabs and Brochettes from the Grill

Skewered foods are some of the nicest things that can come from a grill. Don't save them only for outdoor barbecues! They're quick, interesting and economical for everyday meals; they dress up beautifully for entertaining and they take just as easily to grilling in the kitchen as outside.

Two points to note: if filling skewers with a variety of foods that need different cooking times, precook the slower ones (such as chunks of corn on the cob or small whole onions) a little before adding them to the skewers. Secondly, use metal skewers that are flat or square, not round; then, as the food softens in cooking, it will not slip round when the skewers are turned. Round wooden skewers (such as those little satay sticks that are available in most hardware stores) have enough grip to hold the food firmly, but must be soaked in hot water for at least 30 minutes before using to prevent scorching.

Kofta

Kofta, richly spiced sausages moulded directly onto skewers, come in many versions throughout the Middle East.

500 g (1 lb) boneless lean lamb or beef, or a mixture of both, finely minced	freshly ground pepper
	2 tablespoons finely chopped parsley
1 onion, peeled and grated	1 teaspoon ground cumin
1 egg, lightly beaten	¼ teaspoon ground coriander
1 teaspoon salt	

Place all the ingredients in a bowl and pound or knead until very smooth. If you have a food processor, you can prepare the mixture in a flash: put the meat and onion, which need not be minced or grated, just cut into pieces, into the processor bowl with all the other ingredients and process until smooth.

Divide the mixture into 4 and mould each portion into a sausage shape round a skewer. Grill at high heat on a preheated oiled grill, for 7 to 8 minutes, turning several times until browned all over.

Serve on a bed of plain boiled rice or push the meat off the skewers into pockets of warm Lebanese bread – even nicer if you put the bread, opened out, under the grill while cooking the meat so that it catches the spicy juices. *Serves 4*

Smoked Eel Brochettes

A sophisticated first course.

750 g (1½ lb) smoked eel	2 green cucumbers
3 lemons	18 small bay leaves
freshly ground pepper	60 g (2 oz) butter, melted

Remove the skin from the eel, cut into 18 pieces and remove the bone. Sprinkle with the juice of 1 lemon and freshly ground black pepper and leave for 1 hour. Cut the cucumbers and remaining 2 lemons into 21 slices (lemons will be thin).

Thread 6 skewers, beginning and ending with cucumber and lemon and threading a bay leaf next to each piece of eel. Brush all over with melted butter and grill for 5 to 6 minutes, turning and basting several times. *Serves 6*

Skewered Lamb with Plum Sauce

750 g (1½ lb) boneless lamb, cut from leg or shoulder	3 tablespoons lemon juice
	1½ tablespoons soy sauce
salt	1 clove garlic, crushed
freshly ground pepper	2 teaspoons sugar
MARINADE:	¼ teaspoon dried basil
1 × 500 g can plums	

Remove any fat and skin from the lamb and cut into bite-size cubes. Drain the plums (reserving syrup), remove the stones, and rub them through a sieve or whirr in a blender. Combine the plums and syrup with the remaining marinade ingredients. Pour over the lamb, cover and leave in the refrigerator for several hours or overnight.

Thread the meat on skewers and season lightly with salt and freshly ground pepper. Grill on an oiled rack under a preheated grill at high heat for about 10 minutes, or until well browned but still springy when pressed. Turn during the cooking time and baste several times with the marinade.

When the meat is almost cooked, boil the remaining marinade in a small saucepan, without a lid, until it is reduced to the consistency of thin gravy. Serve in a separate bowl. *Serves 6*
Variation
Cubes of pork are also excellent marinated in this fruity sauce and grilled. Grill at high heat for 2 minutes each side, then turn the heat down to medium and grill 10 to 15 minutes more.

Ham and Fruit Kebabs

Ham is perhaps the best of all meats to combine with fruit. Serve these savoury-sweet kebabs on a bed of rice.

3–4 thick ham steaks	BASTING SAUCE:
oranges	60 g (2 oz) butter
prunes	⅓ cup orange marmalade
hot tea, if needed (see recipe)	2 teaspoons lemon juice
slices of fresh or canned pineapple	1½ teaspoons dry mustard

Cut the steaks into pieces about 3 cm (1¼ inches) square. You will need about half as many orange segments, prunes and pineapple pieces as squares of ham, so judge quantities accordingly. Cut the oranges into small wedges. Soak the prunes (unless they are the large, soft kind) in hot tea for 10 minutes to plump them; drain and stone. Remove the core of the pineapple (if fresh) and cut each slice into 6 segments. Thread skewers with ham, orange, prune, ham, pineapple, ham and so on, ending with a piece of ham. Melt the butter in a small saucepan, stir in the other sauce ingredients and heat gently until blended.

Brush the basting sauce over the ham and fruits and grill at a moderately low heat on an oiled rack for 10 to 15 minutes, turning and brushing with sauce several times. *Serves 6 to 8*

Ham and Fruit Kebabs

Fish, Fruit and Vegetables from the Grill

For many, there is no better way than grilling to cook fish steaks, thick fillets and small whole fish. Fruit and vegetables also grill to perfection. It is a cooking method favoured by weight-watchers, but it produces succulent results that everyone enjoys.

Grilled Fish
This is the step-by-step method for golden fish with moist, tender flesh. Note that the fish, unless very thick, is grilled on one side only, not turned during cooking.

Choose thick steaks, thick fillets or small whole fish. For whole fish, slash both sides diagonally two or three times to allow the heat to penetrate.

Cover the grill pan or a shallow metal tray with foil and heat it under the grill at high heat for a few minutes. Add enough butter to coat the fish when melted – about 60 g (2 oz) should be enough for 4 pieces of fish. Put the pan under the grill again and heat the butter until the foam subsides.

Meanwhile, lightly dust the prepared fish all over with a little flour and season with salt and pepper.

Lay the fish in the hot butter and turn about so that all sides are coated. Place the pan under a high heat and grill without turning until browned on top and cooked through. This will take about 8 minutes for fish 2.5 cm (1 inch) thick, 4 to 5 minutes for thinner pieces. If the top is getting too brown before the fish is cooked through, lower the pan away from the heat or turn the heat down. During grilling, spoon the buttery pan juices over the fish once or twice, and, if liked, add a squeeze of lemon juice and a sprinkle of spring onion or parsley to the juices. Pour any remaining liquid in the pan over the fish.
NOTE: Fish is cooked as soon as the flesh turns white, offers little resistance to a toothpick inserted in the thickest part and can be flaked. Don't overcook; just a minute or two can make the difference between succulence and dryness.

Grilled Fruit and Vegetables
Many fruits and vegetables grill beautifully. To keep them moist and juicy, they are basted with a little butter or liquid during cooking, or topped with buttery crumbs. Grill them on medium heat, far enough away from the source of heat for them to cook through without browning too much on the outside. If you don't have a grill with an adjustable rack, they could be placed in the grill pan itself. Line the pan with foil, and you will have the buttery juices to pour over when serving.

Grilled Mushroom Caps
Cut off the stem ends level with the caps. Wipe with damp kitchen paper dipped in a little lemon juice. Season with salt and pepper and arrange on a heated and oiled foil-lined grill rack, skin side down. Put a dab of butter in the middle of each cap and grill at medium heat for about 5 minutes. You may add a sprinkle of herbs, grated cheese or chopped bacon before grilling.

Grilled Tomatoes Provençale
Combine 1 crushed clove garlic, 3 tablespoons chopped parsley, ¼ cup oil and 1 cup soft white breadcrumbs with salt and pepper to taste. Cut 4 large tomatoes in half crosswise, season with salt and pepper and top each with a spoonful of the crumb mixture. Grill for about 10 minutes under medium heat. If the crumbs are browning too quickly, cover the tops with aluminium foil, then remove it for the last few minutes.

Grilled Eggplant Slices
Wash a firm eggplant and cut across into slices about 2 cm (¾ inch) thick. Sprinkle with salt, leave for 20 minutes, then rinse and pat dry with paper towels. Arrange on a greased baking tray. Combine 1 crushed clove garlic, 1 grated small onion and ¼ cup olive oil or melted butter.
Brush the eggplant with the oil mixture and grill under a medium heat for 5 minutes, basting twice with the oil. Turn and brush with more oil. Cook another 2 or 3 minutes until tender.

Glazed Pineapple Slices
Peel a ripe pineapple, cut across into thick slices and remove the core. Cream 60 g (2 oz) butter with 2 tablespoons brown sugar and 1 teaspoon cinnamon. Dot half this mixture on the pineapple and arrange on a greased baking tray. Grill under medium heat for 3 minutes, turn and dot with the remaining butter mixture. Grill 3 minutes more. Pour any syrup in the tray over the slices and serve hot with ice-cream.
For variety, sprinkle with dark rum during grilling or with desiccated coconut just before they are done.

Bananas in their Jackets
Bananas are the simplest of all fruit to grill. Simply place medium-ripe bananas on the grill rack and grill for about 3 minutes each side or until soft when tested with a fine skewer. Peel, sprinkle with brown sugar and lemon juice and serve hot with ice-cream or whipped cream.
Bananas may also be served as an accompaniment to grilled meats – in this case, don't add sugar.

Opposite: Grilled Mushroom Caps and Tomatoes Provençale;
Above: Grilled Oriental Fish

Grapes Brûlée

500 g (1 lb) seedless grapes
300 ml (1¼ cups) thick sour
  cream

¾ cup brown sugar

Wash the grapes well. Chill the grapes and the sour cream until
icy cold. Place the grapes in a deep layer in a flameproof serving
dish. Cover with sour cream, then cover the cream completely
with brown sugar. Place under a preheated grill and grill at high
heat until the sugar is melted and bubbly – watch very carefully
that it doesn't burn.

    This is a simple but superb dessert, as the grapes remain cold
and contrast with the smoothness of the cream and the crunchy
hot topping. *Serves 4*

Grilled Stuffed Peaches

6 ripe fresh peaches or 12
  halves canned peaches
1 cup stale cake crumbs or
  crumbled macaroons
30 g (1 oz) butter, softened

1 tablespoon finely chopped
  mixed peel or glacé ginger
1 tablespoon brandy, sweet
  sherry or light rum
ice-cream

Peel and halve the fresh peaches, if using. Arrange the peaches in
one layer on a buttered baking tray. Mix together the remaining
ingredients, except the ice-cream, and place in the hollows of the
peaches, dividing evenly. Grill under a medium heat for 6 to 8
minutes. Serve hot or cold with ice-cream. *Serves 6*

Grilled Oriental Fish

This Chinese-style marinade gives a sensational flavour and rich
colour to fish. Serve with plain boiled rice and a cucumber and
bean sprout salad, or just a bowl of crisp radishes, lettuce and
celery.

6 thick serving-size pieces of
  white fish fillets
2 tablespoons soy sauce
2 slices of fresh ginger, peeled
  and chopped
¼ teaspoon 5-spice powder

2 tablespoons oil
pinch of sugar
pinch of pepper
2 tablespoons dry white wine
coriander sprigs and spring
  onion brushes, to garnish

Wipe over the fish and remove any visible scales or bones.
Combine the remaining ingredients, except for the garnish, in a
flat dish. Place the fish in the dish and turn about to coat. Leave
for 1 hour, turning the fish once.

    Line the grill pan with foil, heat under the grill and place the
fish in, skin side up. Pour over half the marinade and grill at high
heat for 4 to 5 minutes. Pour over the remaining marinade and
grill for a further 4 to 5 minutes. Transfer to a heated platter and
pour over any marinade remaining in the pan. Garnish with
coriander sprigs and spring onion brushes and serve
immediately. *Serves 6*

Variation
Grilled Curried Fish Omit the soy sauce and substitute
½ teaspoon curry powder for the 5-spice powder. Continue as
above.

The Magic Baked Potato

For most of us, potatoes help to 'make the meal' and nothing is more inviting than a potato baked in its jacket, with its flavourful skin, soft mealy inside and a golden pat of butter melting on top.

How to Cook

Start with old potatoes of uniform size and scrub them well so the delicious skins can be enjoyed (there are valuable vitamins and minerals under the skin).

Place directly on the oven rack and bake in a moderate oven (180°C/350°F) for 20 minutes. Take out and pierce with a fork. This stops the steam from gathering inside the skin, which makes the potato soggy instead of fluffy. Return to the oven and cook until tender – an average-size potato will take an extra 40 to 45 minutes. Immediately you take them from the oven, cut a cross in the top with a sharp knife, and squeeze the bottom of the potato so the cross opens up. Serve at once, seasoned with salt and pepper and a pat of butter. Or add a spoonful of sour cream and a sprinkling of snipped chives or chopped parsley.

Seasoning

If the potatoes are to be mashed and seasoned, do not cut a cross in the top. Instead, cut an oval-shaped slice from the top, or cut the potato in half if large. Scoop out the pulp with a spoon and press it through a sieve or mash well with a fork. For each potato, add 2 tablespoons of cream, plus 1 egg yolk for 4 potatoes, and season with salt and pepper. Other flavourings may be mixed in if you wish, e.g., grated cheese, chopped herbs, or crumbled bacon.

Replace the potato pulp in the shells and sprinkle the top with cheese or dab with butter. Place in a moderate oven (180°C/350°F) for 5 to 6 minutes, or until heated through and nicely browned.

Baked Potato with Chicken Livers

Serve this as a complete meal, with a crisp green salad.

3 large old potatoes	$\frac{1}{4}$ cup cream
250 g (8 oz) chicken livers	salt
90 g (3 oz) butter	freshly ground pepper
125 g (4 oz) mushrooms, sliced	chopped parsley, to garnish
$\frac{1}{4}$ cup dry white wine	

Scrub and dry the potatoes and place them on the middle shelf of a preheated moderate oven (180°C/350°F). Bake for 20 minutes, pierce with a fork to release the steam and continue baking until tender, about 40 minutes more.

While the potatoes are cooking, make the filling. Trim any membrane and discoloured parts from the livers; cut in halves,

Baked Stuffed Potatoes

and pat dry with absorbent paper towels. Melt the butter and fry the livers over a medium-high heat until lightly browned and firm – this takes only a few minutes. Remove the livers with a slotted spoon and place in a bowl.

Add the mushrooms to the pan and fry gently for a few minutes until softened. Remove with a slotted spoon and add to the livers. Pour the wine into the pan and cook for a minute, scraping up any brown bits from the bottom. Add the cream, turn the heat to low, and simmer the sauce for a few minutes until it thickens a little. Season to taste with salt and pepper.

When the potatoes are cooked, cut in halves lengthwise and scoop out the flesh leaving a shell about 1 cm ($\frac{1}{2}$ inch) thick. Dice the flesh and mix with the reserved livers and mushrooms. Pile back into the shells and return the potatoes to the oven for 5 minutes, until heated through. Spoon the hot sauce over, sprinkle with parsley, and serve. *Serves 6 as a light luncheon dish or entrée.*

Baked Potato with Peas and Chives

4 medium-size old potatoes	freshly ground pepper
$\frac{1}{2}$ cup cream or 60 g (2 oz) butter	1 cup cooked, seasoned green peas mixed with 2
1 egg yolk	tablespoons snipped chives
salt	2 tablespoons grated cheese

Bake the potatoes in a moderate oven (180°C/350°F) until soft when pierced with a fork, about 1 hour. Cut a slice from the top of each potato, scoop out the pulp and mash. Stir in the cream or butter, egg yolk, and salt and pepper to taste. Fill each potato shell half full with the mixture, then divide the peas and chives equally between them. Pile the rest of the potato on top, sprinkle with cheese, and return to the oven for 12 minutes until heated through and browned on top. *Serves 4*

Potatoes Garbo

Baked potatoes this way are said to be a favourite of Greta Garbo. One serving has approximately the same joules (calories) as a small apple.

2 large old potatoes	$\frac{1}{2}$ cup chopped parsley or
15 g ($\frac{1}{2}$ oz) butter, melted	watercress, or 1 cup cooked
salt	spinach
freshly ground pepper	

Scrub and dry the potatoes and place them on the middle shelf of a preheated moderate oven (180°C/350°F). Bake for 20 minutes, then pierce with a fork to release the steam. Continue baking until tender, about 40 minutes.

Cut each potato in half and scoop out the flesh, leaving a shell about 1 cm ($\frac{1}{2}$ inch) thick. Brush the insides with melted butter and season with salt and pepper. Return to the oven and bake for 10 minutes. Serve the shells sprinkled liberally with chopped parsley or watercress, or fill with cooked spinach. *Serves 4*
NOTE: Use the scooped-out flesh to make a lovely Swiss-style potato cake next day. Chop finely and combine with a small chopped onion and salt and pepper to taste. Heat a thin film of oil in a small frying pan and add the potato, pressing it down into a firm cake. Cook over a medium heat until brown and crusty on the bottom, then turn and brown the other side. Serve topped with grilled tomatoes and bacon. *Serves 4*

And who can resist French Fries?

French-fried potatoes, the beloved *pommes frites* of France, are favourites everywhere. Others call them 'chips', part of the equally loved 'fish and chips' of England.

These golden fingers of potato that are crispy outside and soft and mealy inside are natural accompaniments for fried fish, excellent with grilled meats, hamburgers and sausages, and a special treat as a snack.

Other vegetables take kindly to this deliciously crisp finish, too. French-fried onions, sweet potatoes and parsnips make an interesting change, and deep-fried parsley gives a stylish finish to fried and grilled dishes.

Vegetable oil or solid vegetable shortening may be used for deep frying. If you have an electric deep-fryer, follow the manufacturer's instructions. Otherwise, use a heavy-based saucepan large enough to allow the vegetables to float in the oil, but never fill it more than two-thirds full. A frying basket helps you to add and remove a whole batch of food at once. Failing a basket, put the food in loose, being sure not to crowd the pan, and remove it as it cooks with a skimmer or slotted spoon. Drain food quickly on crumpled kitchen paper and serve it very hot. If you have to keep it hot for a short time while frying another batch, spread it out on trays in a very slow oven (120°C/250°F).

French-Fried Onion Rings

1 large onion
½ cup milk
seasoned flour

oil for deep frying
salt

Peel the onion and cut into 5 mm (¼ inch) thick slices. Separate into rings. Dip the rings in milk, then into seasoned flour, shaking off any surplus.

Heat deep oil to 190°C/375°F (when a bread cube browns in 25 to 30 seconds). Put the onion rings in a heated frying basket (see Step 2 in instructions for chipped potatoes) and fry for 2 to 3 minutes until crisp and golden. Drain on crumpled kitchen paper, salt lightly and serve very hot. *Serves 4*

Fried Parsley

Divide parsley into sprigs, wash and dry very well. Heat deep oil to 190°C/375°F (when a bread cube browns in 25 to 30 seconds). Drop in the sprigs and fry for just a few seconds; remove while still green and crisp. Drain on crumpled kitchen paper and use at once.

French-Fried Potatoes (Potato Chips)

Perfect, crisp French fries are produced by frying twice. The first frying can be done hours ahead of the meal, the second takes only 1 to 2 minutes and should be done just before serving. Allow 250 g (8 oz) of old potatoes for each serving.

To prepare and cook, see step-by-step pictures below.

French-Fried Potatoes
1 Choose even-sized old potatoes. Peel and wash. Cut into slices, then into sticks of the same thickness. Standard size is 1 cm (½ inch) thick, cut with a knife or wavy cutter; 'matchsticks' are thinner and shorter. The ends can be squared off and trimmings used for soup. Dry on a clean cloth and keep covered or they will discolour. If kept in cold water they tend to lose vitamin C.

2 Fill a deep-fryer or deep saucepan two-thirds full with oil. Put in the frying basket and heat it in the oil or food will stick to it. Heat oil to 170°C/340°F, when a bread cube browns in about 1 minute. Lift out the basket, put in a thick layer of chips, lower into the oil and cook 3 to 4 minutes until the chips are soft but not coloured. Lift out, drain, and place on crumpled kitchen paper. Reheat oil between batches.

3 Just before the chips are required, reheat the oil to 190°C/375°F when a bread cube browns in 25 to 30 seconds. Fry the chips, a batch at a time, for 1 to 2 minutes or until crisp and golden. Drain on crumpled kitchen paper, salt lightly and serve very hot.

Deep-Fried Parsnips

4 medium parsnips
1 egg
salt
freshly ground pepper

seasoned flour
dry breadcrumbs
oil for deep frying

Peel the parsnips and cut into short sticks about 1 cm (½ inch) thick. Parboil in salted water to cover for 8 minutes, then drain and dry on absorbent paper towels. Cool.

Beat the egg lightly with a little salt and freshly ground pepper. Dip the parsnip sticks into the seasoned flour and shake off surplus. Then dip into the egg, roll in breadcrumbs and refrigerate for 10 minutes to set the coating.

Heat oil to 190°C/375°F (when a bread cube browns in 25 to 30 seconds) and fry the parsnip sticks until golden brown. Drain on crumpled paper towels and serve at once. *Serves 6*

Variations

Other vegetables such as cauliflower or broccoli pieces, or artichoke hearts, may be prepared in the same way as parsnips, cooking lightly before coating with flour, egg and breadcrumbs. Eggplant, green pepper, zucchini and mushrooms may be coated and deep fried in the same way, but do not need to be cooked first.

French-Fried Onion Rings; French-Fried Potatoes; Matchstick Potato Chips; Crinkle-Cut Potato Chips; Fried Parsley

Sweet Potato Fries

2 large sweet potatoes
oil for deep frying
2 teaspoons brown sugar

1 teaspoon salt
freshly grated nutmeg

Wash the potatoes and parboil for 10 minutes. When cool enough to handle, peel and cut into 5 mm (¼ inch) thick slices. Heat oil to 190°C/375°F (when a cube of bread browns in 25 to 30 seconds) and fry the potato slices until golden brown. Drain on crumpled paper towels; then sprinkle with brown sugar and salt, grate a little nutmeg over and serve immediately. *Serves 6*

Oven 'French Fries'

When you can't give the cooking your full attention, it may be easier to bake chips to 'French-fried' crispness. The texture is a little different, but very good.

4 medium-size old potatoes
1 teaspoon paprika

60 g (2 oz) butter, melted, or 3 tablespoons oil
salt

Peel the potatoes and cut into sticks about 1 cm (½ inch) thick. Dry well with absorbent paper towels. Spread in a single layer in a shallow baking tin and sprinkle with paprika. Pour butter or oil over and turn the potatoes about until they are coated.

Place in a preheated very hot oven (230°C/450°F) and bake for 30 to 40 minutes, turning several times, until golden brown and tender. Drain on crumpled paper towels. Serve sprinkled with salt (be careful not to over salt). *Serves 4*

Vegetable Variety the Easy Way

There is a quiet 'Vegetable Revolution' taking place among thoughtful cooks these days! Vegetables are no longer being treated as an afterthought to the main dish, but as a vital part of the meal – sometimes as the meal itself.

Greengrocers are adding their support to the new approach by stocking a wide variety of vegetables, and growers are sending them to the markets young, firm and dewy.

Freshly cooked vegetables are tempting in their own right if they are lightly cooked (never stewed) and simply seasoned with salt, freshly ground pepper and butter. At the same time, they blend beautifully with other foods like bacon, cheese, garlic, eggs, sour cream, nuts and herbs, and can be combined in interesting but easy ways.

There is as much satisfaction in turning out a lovely vegetable dish as there is in making a glamorous cake; and, since we should eat vegetables every day, there is even more of a challenge to provide variety!

I think you will enjoy the ideas on these pages.

Above: Cauliflower with Cream Sauce; Broccoli with Lemon Butter and Cheese

Broccoli with Lemon Butter and Cheese

500 g (1 lb) young broccoli spears	salt
90 g (3 oz) butter	freshly ground pepper
2 tablespoons lemon juice	2 tablespoons grated Parmesan cheese

Trim any tough ends from the broccoli stalks and discard coarse leaves. Arrange the spears in a wide pan and cover with boiling salted water. Cook until just tender, about 10 to 12 minutes. Drain, and place in a heated serving dish. Heat the butter in a small saucepan, stir in the lemon juice and salt and pepper to taste, and pour over the broccoli. Sprinkle with cheese and place under a preheated grill for 30 seconds. *Serves 4*

Cauliflower with Cream Sauce

1 small whole cauliflower	2 tablespoons lemon juice
½ carton thick sour cream	salt
60 g (2 oz) Philadelphia cream cheese, softened	freshly ground pepper
	2 spring onions, finely chopped

Trim the outside green leaves of the cauliflower and wash well. Place stalk side down in boiling salted water and simmer for 15 minutes, or until just tender when tested with a skewer (be sure not to overcook). Drain the cauliflower, place in a heated serving bowl and cover with sauce.

To make the sauce, place the sour cream and softened cream cheese in a saucepan. Stir over a gentle heat until the cheese is melted. Add the flavourings and heat just to boiling point. Spoon over the cauliflower at once. *Serves 6 to 8*

Zucchini and Cheese Scallop

500 g (1 lb) zucchini	*freshly ground pepper*
salt	*45 g (1½ oz) butter*
185 g (6 oz) Gruyère cheese, grated	

Cut the zucchini in halves lengthwise if large, then cut into 5 cm (2 inch) lengths. Cook for 1 minute in boiling salted water and drain well.

Butter a shallow ovenproof dish and arrange a layer of zucchini in it. Sprinkle with one-third of the grated Gruyère and season with salt and pepper. Repeat twice more, ending with a layer of cheese. Cut the butter into small pieces, dot over the top and bake in a hot oven (200°C/400°F) until golden brown, about 30 minutes. *Serves 6*

Creamy Paprika Cabbage

1 small white cabbage, about 500 g (1 lb)	*salt*
60 g (2 oz) butter	*freshly ground pepper*
1 small onion, chopped	*½ cup light sour cream*
1½ teaspoons paprika	*a little extra paprika*

To prepare and cook, see step-by-step pictures below. *Serves 4*

Celery with Parmesan

1 bunch celery	*½ cup grated Parmesan cheese*
2 cups chicken stock	*60 g (2 oz) butter, melted*
salt	*¼ cup pouring cream*
freshly ground pepper	

Wash the celery and trim away roots and tough strings. Cut into 10 cm (4 inch) lengths. Bring the chicken stock to the boil in a large saucepan; add the celery and simmer until almost tender, about 15 minutes. Drain, place in a buttered square baking dish and season with salt and pepper to taste. Sprinkle with cheese, then pour over the butter and cream mixed together. Bake in a moderately slow oven (160°C/325°F) for 15 minutes, or until the celery is tender and topping golden. *Serves 4 to 6*

Broad Beans with Bacon

250 g (8 oz) shelled broad beans, fresh or frozen	*½ cup cooking liquid from beans*
4 bacon rashers, rind removed	*salt*
15 g (½ oz) butter	*freshly ground pepper*
1 small onion, chopped	*1 tablespoon chopped parsley*
2 teaspoons flour	

Cook the beans until tender in boiling salted water (20 minutes if fresh). Meanwhile, cut the bacon into dice. Heat the butter and fry the bacon and onion for 3 to 4 minutes, or until the onion is soft, stirring often to prevent sticking. Blend in the flour off the heat. Drain the beans and reserve half a cup of the cooking liquid. Return the pan to the heat and add the bean liquid. Bring to the boil, stirring, and simmer for 1 minute. Add the beans and reheat gently. Taste, add salt and pepper as required, and stir in the chopped parsley. *Serves 4*

Hot Orange Beetroot

The underlying flavour of orange is a classic complement to the sharp-sweet flavour of beetroot. It may be a surprise to find it as a hot dish, but it is very good – especially with rich meats such as pork or duck.

½ cup sugar	*2 tablespoons grated orange rind*
1 tablespoon cornflour	*¼ cup orange juice*
½ teaspoon salt	*1 × 425 g can small whole beetroot, drained*
½ cup white vinegar (cider, if possible)	*30 g (1 oz) butter*
2 tablespoons water	

Put the sugar, cornflour, salt, vinegar and water into a saucepan and blend together. Stir over a medium heat until the mixture boils and becomes clear.

Add the orange rind and juice and the beetroot and simmer gently until heated through. Stir in the butter and serve immediately. *Serves 6 to 8*

Creamy Paprika Cabbage

1 Remove any coarse outer leaves from the cabbage. Cut into quarters, discard the tough stalk, and shred finely (as for coleslaw). Place in a colander, wash under running water, and drain.

2 Heat butter in a flameproof casserole or saucepan and gently fry the onion until soft. Stir in the cabbage and continue cooking and stirring over a low heat until the cabbage is beginning to soften, about 2 minutes.

3 Stir in paprika, salt and pepper to taste, and sour cream. Mix well together, cover with a lid, and cook over a low heat on top of the stove for 10 minutes, or until the cabbage is cooked.

4 Remove the lid and sprinkle the cabbage with paprika to serve. It could also be garnished with sautéed apple slices, strips of green pepper or crumbled, cooked bacon. An interesting accompaniment for meat loaves, grilled sausages and pan-fried ham slices.

Tomatoes with Yogurt

This refreshing salad is a good one for weight-watchers to remember, and goes beautifully with cold roast veal or lamb as well as hot, grilled meats.

½ cup natural yogurt	good pinch of dry mustard
1 tablespoon mayonnaise	salt
2 teaspoons chopped fresh dill	freshly ground pepper
or pinch of dried	3 large ripe tomatoes
2 teaspoons lemon juice	

Place the yogurt in a bowl and stir in the mayonnaise, dill, lemon juice, mustard, and salt and pepper to taste. Allow to stand for 30 minutes to blend the flavours. Peel the tomatoes and cut into slices. Arrange in overlapping rows on a serving platter, and spoon the yogurt dressing over just before serving. *Serves 6*

German-Style Vegetable Platter

500 g (1 lb) green beans	salt
500 g (1 lb) tender green peas	freshly ground pepper
1 small cauliflower, broken	2 tablespoons chopped fresh
into florets	herbs or 2 teaspoons dried
6 small young carrots	½ cup cream
SAUCE:	2 tablespoons lemon juice
60 g (2 oz) butter	finely chopped parsley, to
250 g (8 oz) mushrooms,	garnish
sliced	
1½ tablespoons flour	

Prepare the vegetables and cook separately in boiling salted water until just tender; be careful not to overcook. Drain, reserving 1½ cups of cooking liquid, and arrange separately on a serving platter. Keep warm.

To make the sauce, heat the butter in a heavy frying pan and sauté the mushrooms until just tender, about 3 minutes. Stir in the flour off the heat, then return the pan to the stove and add the reserved vegetable liquid. Bring to the boil, stirring all the time, and add salt and pepper to taste. Stir in the herbs and cream and simmer for 2 minutes, then add the lemon juice. Spoon the mushroom sauce over the vegetables and sprinkle with parsley. *Serves 6*

Oriental Spinach

This dish takes less than five minutes to cook, yet tastes exotic!

1 medium bunch spinach	2 cloves garlic, crushed
3 tablespoons peanut oil	1½ teaspoons salt
4 spring onions, chopped	2 tablespoons soy sauce
(including green tops)	1½ teaspoons sugar
1 slice fresh ginger, finely	1 tablespoon dry sherry
chopped	1 tablespoon light sesame oil

Discard any tough white stalks from the spinach, wash thoroughly, and cut into thin slices. Place in a tea-towel and wring out any excess moisture. Heat the oil in a wok or heavy frying pan and fry the spring onions, ginger and garlic for 2 minutes, stirring constantly. Add the spinach and cook for 2 minutes, stirring. Add the remaining ingredients and stir until everything is well blended. Turn into a heated serving bowl and serve at once. *Serves 4 to 6*

Broccoli with Wine

White wine and garlic lend robust Italian flavour to this popular vegetable. If fresh broccoli is out of season, the frozen kind does very well.

500 g (1 lb) broccoli	salt
2 tablespoons olive oil	freshly ground pepper
2 cloves garlic, crushed	1 cup dry white wine

Remove any tough or wilted leaves from the broccoli, and woody ends if necessary. Cut the tender stems into thin slices and separate the heads into florets. Wash and drain.

Heat the oil in a heavy frying pan and sauté the garlic until soft but not brown. Add the broccoli stems and florets, and toss in the hot oil until well coated. Season with salt and pepper, add the wine, and cover the pan. Cook over a low heat for 15 minutes, or until the broccoli is tender, stirring now and again. Serve with the pan juices poured over. *Serves 4*

Sauerkraut with Apples and Caraway

Sauerkraut is good served cold as a salad, and also makes an interesting hot vegetable. For a mellow flavour, always rinse with cold water and drain thoroughly first.

3 cooking apples	salt
60 g (2 oz) butter	freshly ground pepper
2 medium onions, chopped	1–2 tablespoons sugar
1 × 500 g can sauerkraut,	1 cup beef stock (or stock cube
rinsed and drained	and water)
½ teaspoon caraway seeds	½ cup grated raw potato

Peel and core the apples, and cut into thin slices. Heat the butter in a heavy saucepan and gently fry the onions and apples until soft but not brown, about 5 minutes. Add the sauerkraut, caraway seeds, and salt, pepper and sugar to taste. Stir in the beef stock, bring to the boil, and simmer for 5 minutes. Add the raw potato and simmer for another 5 minutes, or until the potato is cooked. Adjust seasoning before serving. *Serves 6*

Purée of Brussels Sprouts

500 g (1 lb) Brussels sprouts	2 cups chicken stock
90 g (3 oz) butter	½ cup hot milk
2 medium-size old potatoes,	salt
peeled and diced	freshly ground pepper

Remove any discoloured leaves from the sprouts, trim the stem ends, and parboil for 5 minutes in salted water. Drain well. Heat 60 g (2 oz) of the butter in a heavy frying pan, and toss the sprouts until well coated. Add the potatoes and chicken stock, bring to the boil, then cover the pan tightly and simmer for 15 to 20 minutes, or until the vegetables are very tender. Cool slightly, then whirr in a blender until smooth. Return the purée to the pan and add the hot milk and remaining butter. Season with salt and pepper to taste, turn into a heated serving bowl, and serve at once. *Serves 6*

NOTE: Serve the purée topped with crisp little squares of fried bread (croûtons) or chopped toasted almonds.

German-Style Vegetable Platter

Hurry-Up Salads

Though simple to make, salads give scope for the original touches all cooks enjoy. The lovely bright colours and interesting shapes of the basic ingredients delight the eye as well as the palate.

There is an ever-increasing demand for salads of all kinds. Big, beautifully arranged salads look well on a buffet table; or a salad can be served as a first course on individual plates, or as an accompaniment to the main dish, when it can help to balance the meal; and don't neglect the possibility of serving a salad as the meal itself.

Rice, cold pasta, cracked wheat and barley form the basis of wholesome salads with an international flavour – nutritious and interesting as well as filling. Cold meats, seafood, cheese and eggs may be combined with cooked or raw vegetables, or a combination of both. Fruits, nuts, and crunchy sprouts add excitement.

Making a Green Salad

The greens must be fresh and crisp. Try for a variety of them – the more you toss together, the more interesting the salad. Many greengrocers are now stocking more than one kind of lettuce, so look for cos with its long, soft leaves, and the tiny mignonette lettuce, as well as the familiar round iceberg variety. The pale green witloof with its pointed ends (also called chicory or Belgian endive in some shops) is an interesting addition, and so are young, baby leaves of spinach.

Greens must be fresh, so buy only what you need for a day or two. If necessary, discard any dry or tough outer leaves. Don't wash or break up the heads before storing in the refrigerator crisper, but separate the leaves and wash them as you need them. When washing, use plenty of cold running water to float away any sand or grit hiding in the crevices of leaves. Dry the leaves thoroughly by patting with absorbent paper towels or a tea-towel, or whirling in a salad basket. When the leaves are quite dry, wrap them in a clean tea-towel or place in a plastic bag and return to the crisper until it's time to make the salad.

Salad Niçoise; Witloof and Apple Salad; Mixed French Salad

The Dressing

The oil generally used for salads is olive oil. I prefer a light olive oil, but any good, fresh oil will do. Buy only as much as you can use in a reasonably short time and keep in a cool place – the refrigerator if necessary.

Other oils may be used alone or in combination with olive oil to suit your own taste and add interest to salads. Walnut oil is light and delicate with just a hint of walnut flavour – when you add some walnut pieces as you toss the salad the result is superb. You can also consider peanut oil, light sesame oil, the polyunsaturated oils, and apricot oil for salads containing fruit.

For the acid content of dressings, use vinegar or lemon juice or a combination of the two. Any vinegar – wine, malt or cider – may also be flavoured with herbs. To make herb vinegar, simply place a handful of the fresh herb of your choice (eg. tarragon, rosemary, thyme, marjoram) in the bottle, cork tightly, and allow to stand in a warm place for about two months. (Don't chop the herbs, leave them in long sprigs on the stalk.)

Other Dressings

Tossed green salads require the piquancy and simplicity of a good French dressing (or vinaigrette) but there are many salads which call for the velvety smoothness of a mayonnaise, salad cream, or sour cream dressing. Other dressings may contain yogurt, buttermilk, fruit juices or cottage cheese – good for weight-watchers.

The important thing is to match the dressing to the salad, so in all my salad suggestions the appropriate dressing is recommended.

A Final Word on Simplicity

While it is interesting to experiment with different combinations of ingredients and different dressings, don't go overboard! Some of the simplest salads are the most delicious. A ripe avocado half with a little vinaigrette is perfection itself. Learning when not to 'gild the lily' is a great part of the art of good cooking – and, incidentally, makes the good cook's job easier and quicker into the bargain!

Salad Niçoise

This is a hearty, full-flavoured salad that is often served as a complete meal in itself.

3 ripe tomatoes, peeled and seeded	*1 can flat anchovies*
1 green pepper, seeded	*French Dressing (see right)*
1 large onion, thinly sliced	*1 cup cooked green beans*
1 small head lettuce	*8 black olives, stoned*
1 × 100 g can tuna in oil	*2 hard-boiled eggs, cut in 4*

Cut the tomatoes into quarters and slice the green pepper. Separate the onion into rings. Wash and dry the lettuce and separate the leaves. Drain and flake the tuna. Cut the anchovy fillets in half lengthwise.

Place half the French dressing in a large salad bowl and toss the lettuce and beans until well coated. Arrange the tuna on top with the tomatoes, onion rings, green pepper slices and olives. Top with hard-boiled eggs and anchovy fillets, and sprinkle the remaining dressing over. *Serves 6*

Mixed French Salad

The classic French salad is made of greens, but other vegetables are often added for colour and flavour contrast.

1 head lettuce, Cos or Iceberg	*½ small cucumber, peeled,*
few leaves of curly endive	*seeded, and cut into chunks*
watercress sprigs (optional)	*French Dressing (see right)*
2 ripe tomatoes, peeled, seeded	*finely chopped spring onion,*
and cut into quarters	*to garnish*
4 radishes, thinly sliced	

Wash and dry the greens. Separate the lettuce into leaves; if the leaves are large, tear them into pieces with the fingers, do not slice. Combine all the ingredients in a salad bowl and toss with the dressing. Serve at once, sprinkled with spring onion. *Serves 4 to 6*

French Dressing Mix together ½ teaspoon salt, ½ teaspoon Dijon-style mustard and ¼ teaspoon pepper and stir in 2 tablespoons wine or cider vinegar. Add 6 tablespoons olive oil, little by little, whisking until slightly thickened.

Witloof and Apple Salad

2–3 heads witloof	*lemon juice*
(sometimes called Belgian	*Sour Cream Dressing (see*
endive)	*below)*
3 red-skinned apples	*4 tiny whole beetroot (freshly*
4 tender sticks celery, finely	*cooked or canned)*
chopped	*walnut halves, to garnish*

Trim the witloof stems and remove any discoloured leaves. Set aside some outer leaves to line the salad bowl and chop the remainder. Core two of the apples, cut into dice and add to the witloof with the chopped celery. Cut the remaining apple into slices and sprinkle with lemon juice.

Line a pretty salad bowl with witloof leaves. Toss the celery, chopped witloof and apple with the dressing and spoon into the bowl. Top with tiny whole beetroot and apple slices and garnish with walnuts. *Serves 6*

Sour Cream Dressing Mix together ½ cup thick sour cream, 1 teaspoon Dijon-style mustard, 2 teaspoons caster sugar and 1 tablespoon lemon juice until well blended. Add salt and freshly ground pepper to taste.

Spinach and Yogurt Salad

This makes a refreshing companion to spicy Eastern dishes or curries.

1 bunch spinach (about	*2 small cloves garlic, crushed*
1 kg/2 lb)	*with salt*
salt	*freshly ground pepper*
1 cup natural yogurt	

Cut the spinach leaves off the thick stems and wash thoroughly. Salt lightly and place in a heavy saucepan. Cover tightly and cook until wilted, shaking occasionally to prevent sticking, about 2 minutes. Drain and cool, then chop coarsely. Beat together the yogurt, garlic and salt and pepper to taste and fold through the spinach. Serve chilled. *Serves 4 to 6*

Turkish Barley Salad

Apple and Walnut Salad

This light, healthy, fruit and nut salad is a delightful, easily made change from the usual green salad. Serve with chicken, grills, or cold meats.

1 head lettuce, Cos or Iceberg	DRESSING:
2 large red-skinned apples	*½ teaspoon salt*
1 tablespoon lemon juice	*freshly ground pepper*
1 red or white onion, or 6	*1 teaspoon Dijon-style*
spring onions	*mustard*
small bunch watercress	*1 tablespoon wine vinegar*
(optional)	*2 tablespoons olive oil*
½ cup chopped walnuts	*1 tablespoon walnut oil*

Separate the lettuce into leaves and wash and dry well. If the leaves are large, tear them into smaller pieces. Place in a salad bowl. Core the apples (do not peel), slice thinly and toss with the lemon juice. Peel and slice the onion and separate into rings.

If you are able to find red onions, these are lovely and mild in salads. Spring onions with their green tops are also good. If using these, slice into long, thin shreds.

Arrange the apple slices and onion over the lettuce leaves. Add sprigs of watercress, if using, and sprinkle with walnuts. Combine all the ingredients for the dressing in a jar. Shake well to thicken, or beat well in a small bowl.

Just before serving, toss the salad with the freshly mixed dressing. *Serves 6*

Melon Salad

This elegant melon salad is just right with ham or pork.

1 rock melon	*½ teaspoon ground ginger*
1 honeydew melon	*juice of 1 lime or lemon*
freshly ground pepper	

Halve the melons, scoop out the seeds and peel. Cut the flesh into thin crescents or small cubes. Grind some pepper over and sprinkle with ground ginger and lime or lemon juice. Arrange the crescents on a platter, or place cubes in a bowl, and cover and chill until serving time. *Serves 6 to 8*

Cauliflower and Seafood Salad

Serve this luscious green, white and red salad as a first course, or as a light lunch with hot rolls or herb bread.

1 small cauliflower, divided	*salt*
into florets	*freshly ground pepper*
1 × 170 g can crabmeat,	*½ cup mayonnaise*
salmon or tuna	*½ cup sour cream*
2 cups cooked prawns,	*1 small lettuce or 1 bunch*
scallops or firm white fish	*endive*
cut into chunks (or a	TO GARNISH:
combination)	*chopped parsley*
4 spring onions, finely	*cherry tomatoes or tomato*
chopped (including some	*wedges*
green tops)	
1 teaspoon chopped fresh	
tarragon or ¼ teaspoon dried	

Drop the cauliflower into boiling salted water to cover and cook for 2 minutes. Drain, cool under running water, and drain again. Place in a large bowl. Drain the crabmeat, pick over to remove any cartilage, and break into lumps (or drain salmon or tuna and break into lumps). Add to the cauliflower with the other seafood, onions and herbs, salt and pepper to taste, mayonnaise and sour cream. Fold lightly together. Serve on a bed of lettuce or endive leaves, sprinkled with parsley and garnished with cherry tomatoes or tomato wedges. *Serves 6*

Turkish Barley Salad

1 cup barley	*4 spring onions, shredded into*
1 small cucumber, peeled,	*matchstick lengths*
seeded and chopped	*salt*
2 large ripe tomatoes, peeled,	*freshly ground pepper*
seeded and chopped	*endive leaves, to serve*
½ bunch radishes, thinly sliced	DRESSING:
¼ cup chopped parsley	*3 tablespoons lemon juice*
2 tablespoons chopped fresh	*1 teaspoon salt*
mint	*½ cup olive oil*

Cover the barley with cold water and bring to the boil. Remove from the heat, cover, and stand for 1 hour. Drain, cover again with salted cold water, bring to the boil and simmer until tender, 1 to 1½ hours.

Meanwhile, make the dressing: put the lemon juice and salt into a bowl and gradually whisk in the oil. Drain the barley, and toss gently with the dressing. (This can be done hours ahead of time.)

Toss the barley with the chilled vegetables and herbs and season with salt and pepper to taste. Serve on lettuce leaves. *Serves 6*

Mexican Orange Vegetable Salad

1 large crisp lettuce, broken	*1 green pepper, seeded and*
into chunks	*sliced*
1 medium orange, peeled and	DRESSING:
sliced	*½ cup olive oil*
½ cucumber, thinly sliced	*2½ tablespoons wine vinegar*
1 onion, thinly sliced	*½ teaspoon salt*

Place the lettuce in a bowl and arrange the orange slices and vegetables over it. Blend the oil with the vinegar and salt, pour over the salad and mix lightly. *Serves 6*

Luncheon Tomatoes

6 large ripe tomatoes
salt
freshly ground pepper
2 cups natural yogurt
1 small cucumber, chopped
2 spring onions, finely chopped (including some green tops)
1 stick celery, finely chopped
½ green pepper, seeded and finely chopped
1 cup finely chopped corned beef
6 lettuce leaves, to serve

Cut a slice from the top of each tomato and scoop out most of the flesh, leaving a shell about 1 cm (½ inch) thick. Salt the shells lightly inside and turn upside down to drain.

Discard the seeds from the scooped-out flesh; chop the flesh and the slices from the top, and place in a bowl. Add the yogurt, other chopped vegetables, beef and salt and pepper to taste and fold lightly together. Spoon into the tomato cases, chill, and serve each tomato on a lettuce leaf. *Serves 6*

Herb Bread

French bread served this way is good with any salad.

1 loaf French bread
90 g (3 oz) butter
3 tablespoons chopped fresh herbs or 2 teaspoons dried, chopped with fresh parsley
salt
freshly ground pepper

Slice the loaf almost through to the bottom crust at 2 cm (¾ inch) intervals. Soften the butter and blend with the herbs and salt and pepper to taste. Butter the bread in between the slices and over the top. Wrap tightly in aluminium foil and bake in a preheated moderate oven (180°C/350°F) for 20 minutes. *Serves 6*

Smoked Fish and Potato Salad

This substantial salad combines smoked fish and new potatoes in a beautifully flavoured creamy dressing. It is served warm, not chilled, and needs just a crisp green salad to go with it. It makes a delightful meal to serve out-of-doors on a summery day.

1 kg (2 lb) new potatoes
500 g (1 lb) smoked cod or haddock
1 large onion, chopped
¾ cup light sour cream
2 tablespoons capers, drained
2 tablespoons prepared horseradish
freshly ground pepper
¼ cup chopped parsley

Place the potatoes in cold salted water and bring to the boil. Cover and simmer until tender. Drain, peel, and cut in thick slices. Set aside in a salad bowl.

Poach the fish with the chopped onion in just enough water to cover for about 10 minutes, or until it flakes easily with a fork. Drain the fish and onion, remove any skin and bones from the fish and flake into large pieces. Combine the fish and onion with the potatoes. Blend the sour cream with the capers and horseradish, and toss lightly with the potatoes and fish. Season well with freshly ground pepper and sprinkle with parsley. Serve warm. *Serves 4 to 6*

Smoked Fish and Potato Salad

Rice is Nice ... Sweet or Savoury

Rice is the staple food of more than half the world's population, and it is hard to think of another food which is more economical or versatile. The cooking method varies according to the type of dish.

What Rice to Use

Short plump grains of white rice, when cooked, are tender and moist, and are inclined to cling together – this makes it ideal for risottos, puddings, rice rings and moulds.

Long-grain white rice cooks to a different texture: it is light and fluffy, with the grains separate. It is usually preferred as a side dish with curries, for combination dishes and salads.

Brown rice is the most nutritious kind because the outer covering containing the germ and bran is left on. This also gives the cooked rice an interesting chewy texture and slightly nutty flavour. Brown rice is chosen for many 'meal-in-one' vegetarian casseroles, and makes an interesting change for side dishes and salads.

Golden rice is polished like white rice but is then enriched with some of the nutrients of brown rice. It is a good, all-purpose kind to keep on the pantry shelf.

With Indian curries and other highly spiced foods, the perfumed Basmati rice is a perfect accompaniment.

Remember that rice approximately triples in bulk when cooked, so one cup of uncooked rice gives you 3 cups of cooked. As a side dish, plan on approximately half a cup of cooked rice per person for average appetites, with a little over.

Boiled Rice

8 cups water	*2 slices lemon*
2 teaspoons salt	*1 cup rice, long or short grain*

Bring the water, salt and lemon slices to the boil in a large saucepan. Add the unwashed rice slowly, so the water continues to boil. Boil for 12 to 15 minutes, uncovered, until the grains are tender and have no hard centre when pressed between the fingers.

Drain at once through a colander, and make a few small holes in the rice with the handle of a wooden spoon to allow the steam to escape. Remove lemon slices before serving. *Makes 3 cups of rice*

NOTE: To keep hot, put the colander of drained rice over a pan of simmering water and place a lid on top. To serve plain, fork a good knob of butter through the rice and season with salt and freshly ground pepper to taste.

Variations

Add one or more of these to the hot, cooked rice: finely chopped onion, fried until soft in a little butter or oil; toasted pine nuts or toasted, slivered almonds; cooked, sliced mushrooms; snipped chives or finely chopped spring onions (with their green tops); finely chopped ham; sliced olives.

Steamed Rice

This method of cooking rice results in well-defined grains with excellent flavour. The rice will have absorbed all the liquid by the time it is cooked, so the liquid itself may be flavoured with stock cubes, herbs, lemon peel or a knob of butter to give added flavour to the finished dish.

The simple formula is to use 2 cups of water – plain or with flavourings – to 1 cup of rice.

Bring the water to the boil and add salt to taste. Sprinkle the rice in slowly, so that the water doesn't stop boiling. Stir the rice when it is all added, then cover the pot with a tight-fitting lid and turn the heat as low as possible. Cook very gently for 17 to 20 minutes, or until all the liquid is absorbed and the rice is fluffy and tender. Remove the pan from the heat, take the lid off and allow the steam to escape for a minute or two, then fluff up the rice with a fork.

Kedgeree

375 g (12 oz) smoked cod or haddock	3 tablespoons lemon juice
4 hard-boiled eggs	salt
90 g (3 oz) butter	freshly ground pepper
4 cups cooked, long-grain rice (1½ cups raw rice)	TO GARNISH: lemon slices cut in butterfly shapes (see picture)
3 tablespoons chopped parsley	

Put the fish in a wide saucepan or frying pan, cover with cold water and bring to the boil. Turn the heat down and simmer for 10 minutes, or until the flesh is white and opaque all through at the thickest part. Drain the fish, remove any skin and bones, and separate into large flakes.

Shell the hard-boiled eggs. Chop two whole eggs into pieces (not too small). Separate the yolks and whites of the other two eggs, and finely chop the yolks and whites separately.

Melt the butter in a frying pan over a medium heat and add the fish, rice, the two whole chopped eggs, half the parsley and the lemon juice. Gently stir until heated through, about 4 minutes, and season well with salt and freshly ground pepper. Turn onto a heated platter and decorate with strips of hard-boiled egg yolk and white and the remaining parsley.

Garnish with lemon butterflies and serve at once. *Serves 4 to 6*

Risotto Espagñol

The rice is browned in olive oil, then cooked with garlic, onion, stock and seasonings. It is a way of treating rice that is found in many countries, Spain among them. Risotto makes a perfect accompaniment to spicy chicken dishes, meat balls and stews – and adds interest to plain grills and sausages. For a main course dish, cooked meats, seafood or poultry can be stirred through and heated when the rice is cooked.

½ cup olive oil	1 cup grated, well-flavoured cheese
1 large onion, finely sliced	
2 cloves garlic, crushed	salt
1½ cups long-grain rice	freshly ground pepper
2 cups chicken or beef stock (or water and stock cubes), combined with 1 cup tomato juice	1 tablespoon lemon juice or more to taste
	green pepper slices or chopped parsley, to garnish
½ teaspoon dried thyme or oregano	

Risotto Espagñol

1 Heat the olive oil in a heavy frying pan, and gently fry the onion and garlic until soft but not brown, stirring constantly. (Don't allow it to colour or it will burn when you are frying the rice.) Add the unwashed rice and continue cooking and stirring over a moderate heat until it turns a very pale gold colour.

2 Pour the stock and tomato juice into the pan. Continue cooking over a low heat, stirring frequently so the rice doesn't stick to the bottom. By the time the rice is tender (about 20 minutes) almost all the liquid should be absorbed. If there is too much liquid, raise the heat a little and continue cooking until it has evaporated.

3 Remove the pan from the heat and add the thyme and grated cheese to the rice. Stir lightly to blend, taste for seasoning, and add salt and freshly ground pepper as needed, with enough lemon juice to give a little 'bite' to the flavour. At this stage, the risotto is ready to serve as an accompaniment, garnished with pepper slices or parsley. If required for a main course, follow Step 4.

4 Choose one or more of the following and add to the risotto:
250 g (8 oz) shelled prawns
250 g (8 oz) chopped, cooked chicken
250 g (8 oz) ham, cut into cubes
250 g (8 oz) salami-type sausage, peeled and cut into cubes
250 g (8 oz) whole small mushrooms, lightly sautéed
sliced, blanched green pepper cut into slices and added with a can of drained tuna or salmon.

Opposite: Kedgeree; Risotto Espagñol

Brown Rice

1½ cups brown rice
3 cups water, stock or stock cubes and water
1½ teaspoons salt
1 bay leaf

Place the rice in a colander and rinse in cold running water. Turn into a bowl, cover with cold water, and allow to soak for 30 minutes. Drain, and place in a saucepan with the water or stock, salt and bay leaf. Bring to the boil, then cover the pan and simmer over a gentle heat for 40 to 45 minutes, or until the rice is tender and liquid absorbed. Toss lightly with a fork to fluff up, and use in the following recipe.

Brown Rice with Cheese and Vegetables

4 tablespoons oil
1 clove garlic, crushed
2 onions, finely chopped
4 tender sticks celery, thinly sliced
1 green pepper, seeded and thinly sliced
1 tablespoon chopped fresh basil or 1 teaspoon dried
cooked brown rice (see above)
½ cup beef or chicken stock (use stock cubes if necessary)
salt
freshly ground pepper
2 large tomatoes, peeled, seeded and thinly sliced
1 cup grated tasty cheese
finely chopped parsley, to garnish

Heat the oil in a large frying pan. Gently fry the garlic, onions, celery and green pepper until they are soft. Stir in the basil, rice and stock, and season well with salt and pepper. Toss lightly with a fork until heated through. Spoon the mixture into a flameproof casserole dish and arrange the tomato slices on top. Sprinkle with grated cheese and place under a hot grill for 2 to 3 minutes until the cheese is golden and bubbly. Sprinkle with chopped parsley and serve. *Serves 4 to 6*

Nidos de Arroz con Huevo

This Mexican dish is good for brunch, lunch or supper. Use cooked rice – either white or brown – and any firm well-flavoured cheese.

2 cups cooked rice
60 g (2 oz) butter, melted
2 tablespoons snipped chives or finely chopped parsley
salt
freshly ground pepper
1 cup grated well-flavoured cheese
6 eggs
3 rashers of bacon, rind removed

In a bowl, blend the rice with the melted butter, chives or parsley, salt and pepper to taste, and half the grated cheese. Place the rice mixture in a greased baking dish, then make 6 hollows in the rice with the back of a spoon to form nests. Drop one egg into each nest, season with salt and pepper, and sprinkle the rest of the grated cheese on top.

Bake in a moderately hot oven (190°C/375°F) for about 12 minutes, until the eggs are set and the cheese is melted. Lift the squares carefully from the dish with an egg slice and place on individual plates. Serve with halved grilled rashers of bacon. *Serves 6*

Curry Soup with Rice

60 g (2 oz) ghee or 2 tablespoons oil
2 onions, thinly sliced
1 clove garlic, crushed
1 teaspoon turmeric
2 teaspoons curry powder
¼ teaspoon ground ginger
4 cups chicken or beef stock
1 cup cooked rice
salt
freshly ground pepper
1 tablespoon lemon juice

Heat the ghee or oil in a heavy saucepan and gently fry the onions and garlic until soft and golden, stirring to prevent sticking. Add the turmeric, curry powder and ginger to the pan and continue frying for a minute. Pour in the stock, bring to the boil and simmer for 10 minutes. Add the rice and cook for another minute or two until the rice is heated through. Add salt and pepper to taste, and the lemon juice. Pour into individual bowls and serve. *Serves 4 to 6*

Arroz Con Coco

2 cups cooked, short-grain rice
½ teaspoon salt
¾ cup sugar
½ cup desiccated coconut
2 teaspoons cinnamon
1 cup milk (or half milk and half cream)
1 teaspoon grated lemon rind

Place all the ingredients, except the lemon rind, in a saucepan. Bring just to boiling point over a medium heat, then simmer for about 15 minutes, stirring now and again. When the mixture is thick and creamy, remove from the stove, stir in the grated lemon rind and serve either hot or cold. *Serves 4*

Chicken and Rice Salad

3 whole chicken breasts, lightly poached (see below)
3 cups cooked, long-grain rice (white, brown or gold)
6 spring onions, finely chopped (including some green tops)
6 radishes, cut into fine slices
1 red or green pepper, seeded and finely sliced
4 tender sticks celery, finely sliced
DRESSING:
2 tablespoons toasted sesame seeds
2 tablespoons Dijon-style mustard
2 tablespoons lemon juice
1 teaspoon salt
1 teaspoon sugar
1 teaspoon ground coriander
freshly ground white pepper, to taste
¼ cup chicken stock (from poaching chicken)
½ cup walnut oil
TO SERVE:
lettuce or other salad greens, or bean sprouts

Skin and bone the chicken breasts and cut into bite-size cubes. Lightly toss with the rice, spring onions, radishes, pepper and celery. Chill. Mix all the ingredients for the dressing together and, just before serving, stir through the chicken mixture. Serve on a bed of crisp greens or bean sprouts. *Serves 6 to 8*

TO POACH CHICKEN: Place the chicken breasts in a saucepan with 1 teaspoon salt, 2 slices of fresh ginger, and a chopped spring onion. Cover with cold water, bring to the boil, then reduce the heat and simmer with the lid on for 8 minutes. Allow to cool in the stock before using.

Chicken and Rice Salad

Pasta and Easy Pasta Sauces

What a huge variety of pasta we can choose from today. Spaghetti (which means 'little strings'), macaroni and noodles are the names of the basic groups, but these can take hundreds of shapes. The many shapes and sizes are not only interesting to look at, but which one you choose will influence the flavour of the finished dish. The texture will vary, and different amounts of sauce will be included with each mouthful.

Italian-style pasta is made from a coarsely ground, hard wheat flour that is creamy yellow in colour. The Chinese and Japanese use a wide assortment of noodles often containing buckwheat flour, rice, even seaweed, and enriched with extra protein. In health food shops we can also find pasta made from wholemeal flour and sometimes vegetable purées.

Pasta is not only the basis of thousands of different dishes, it is good for you. Even without a sauce it contains useful amounts of protein, vitamins and minerals, and is well within a weight-watcher's regime if accompanied by a simple salad with fresh fruit to follow.

Pasta sauces come in as many varieties as pasta itself. The slow-simmered kind is only one of them and, for me, many of the most delicious sauces are simple ones quickly made from fresh ingredients.

To Cook Pasta

The basic rule is to cook pasta in an abundant amount of rapidly boiling, salted water – about 12 cups for each 250 g (8 oz) of pasta. Add a spoonful of oil to stop the pasta sticking together, and stir now and again as an added precaution.

The exact cooking time will vary between different kinds of pasta and even the different brands. If you are following instructions on the packet, it is a sensible idea to lift out a piece a minute or so before the cooking time suggested, and test it by biting. Many people like pasta cooked until just *al dente* – that is, still firm to the bite. Others prefer it a little softer. Cook it until it tastes just right to you, then drain at once in a colander or large sieve.

If the pasta is to be served hot, return it to the saucepan and add salt and freshly ground pepper to taste and a little butter, turning it gently through the pasta so the strands are coated. If you intend having pasta cold (and cold pasta is delicious) add a little oil to the hot pasta instead of butter.

Cooking Long Spaghetti

There is no need to break long spaghetti to fit it into the pot. Hold a handful at one end and dip the other end in the rapidly boiling water. It will soften almost at once, and you can keep dipping it further into the pan, coiling it around to fit until the whole length is covered with water.

Quick-Cooking Noodles

There are some Japanese and Chinese noodles that are cooked in only a small amount of liquid. In this case, they are usually not drained, but the liquid is seasoned and used as a soup or sauce. Simply follow the directions on the packet.

Cooking Times

These times are approximate. The only true test of 'is it cooked?' is to try for yourself.

Ordinary spaghetti	10 to 12 minutes
Very thin spaghetti (spaghettini or vermicelli)	8 to 10 minutes
Tagliatelle and long macaroni	10 to 12 minutes
Macaroni shells	15 to 18 minutes
Broad noodles such as lasagne	10 to 12 minutes
Alphabet macaroni, pastini, small stars	5 to 7 minutes
Cannelloni	10 to 12 minutes

Adding Sauce to Pasta

Place the drained, buttered pasta in a heated serving bowl and add part of the sauce. Using 2 forks, lift the pasta so the sauce coats the strands, just as you toss a salad. Top with the remaining sauce and sprinkle with grated cheese at the table. Alternatively, the pasta and sauce may be served separately.

To Keep Pasta Hot

Hot pasta is best served freshly cooked, so you should try to have the sauce ready at the same time.

If this isn't possible, drain the pasta and toss with a little butter – about 90 g (3 oz) for 6 servings. Place in a colander, cover with a lid, and put the colander over a pan containing a small amount of simmering water.

An alternative method is not to drain the pasta. Just leave it in the water, cover the pan, and turn off the heat. When required, reheat the water to boiling, then drain and toss with butter.

Eating Spaghetti (The Easy Way)

With practice, it is possible to eat spaghetti neatly using just a fork. But, even in Italy, a spoon and fork are often used together to make the job quicker and easier.

First, using a fork and spoon together, turn the spaghetti in the sauce so a few strands are coated. Then spear a few strands with the fork, hold the fork against the inside bowl of the spoon, and twirl the strands around the fork. When a neat package is formed, lift it from the plate and enjoy yourself!

Quantities

Appetites vary, but, as a guide, you could allow 500 g (1 lb) of pasta to serve 4 people as a main course or 6 as a first course.

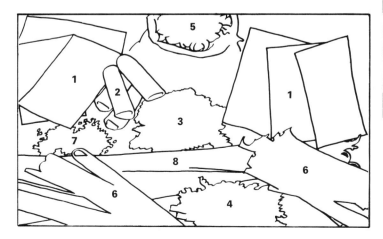

Lasagne (1), cannelloni pipes (2), corkscrew rotini and spirals (3, 4), shells (5), ribbon noodles (6), tiny pastini (7) and spaghetti (8).

Tagliatelle alla Bolognese

This traditional sauce from Bologna includes chicken livers as well as minced beef.

2 tablespoons olive oil
2 rashers bacon, rind removed, and coarsely chopped
1 onion, chopped
1 tender stick celery, sliced
125 g (4 oz) mushrooms, chopped
125 g (4 oz) minced beef
60 g (2 oz) chicken livers, cleaned and chopped
2 tablespoons tomato paste
½ cup red wine
1 cup beef stock (or stock cube and water)
1 tablespoon chopped fresh basil or ½ teaspoon dried
1 teaspoon sugar
pinch of nutmeg
salt
freshly ground pepper
250 g (8 oz) tagliatelle
1 cup grated Parmesan cheese

To prepare and cook, see step-by-step pictures below. *Serves 4 as a first course.*

Tagliatelle alla Bolognese
1 Heat the oil in a large saucepan and gently fry the bacon, onion, celery and mushrooms until soft. Add the minced beef and chicken livers and continue cooking, stirring frequently, until the meat is brown.

2 Stir in the tomato paste, then the wine and stock. Add the basil, sugar, nutmeg and salt and pepper to taste. Bring to the boil, stirring, then cover the pan and simmer the sauce for 45 minutes.

3 Fifteen minutes before the sauce is ready, start to cook the tagliatelle in plenty of boiling salted water. (It will take about 12 minutes – test by biting a strand.) Drain well, season with salt and pepper and fork through a knob of butter. Arrange in a heated serving dish.

4 Taste the sauce and adjust the seasoning if necessary, then spoon over the tagliatelle. Serve with a bowl of grated Parmesan cheese handed separately and a tossed green salad.

Spaghetti with Gorgonzola

Here is a lovely creamy sauce that really is made in minutes. If Gorgonzola isn't available, substitute Roquefort or any creamy blue cheese – but try to get fresh Parmesan; it adds so much to the flavour.

500 g (1 lb) spaghetti	SAUCE:
60 g (2 oz) butter	*1 cup pouring cream, or ½ cup*
½ teaspoon nutmeg	*cream and ½ cup milk*
4 spring onions, finely chopped	*250 g (8 oz) Gorgonzola*
(including green tops)	*cheese, cut into small dice*
½ cup freshly grated Parmesan	*salt*
cheese	*freshly ground pepper*

Cook the spaghetti in plenty of boiling salted water until done to your taste, 10 to 12 minutes. Drain at once, return to the saucepan, and toss with the butter, nutmeg, spring onions and Parmesan cheese.

Meanwhile, make the sauce. Heat the cream in a saucepan. When hot, add the Gorgonzola and stir gently until melted. Season with salt and freshly ground pepper.

Turn the spaghetti into a heated serving bowl and top with the sauce. Serve immediately on hot plates, accompanied by extra grated Parmesan and a peppermill of black peppercorns, so diners can grind a little extra pepper to suit their taste. *Serves 4 to 6*

Spaghettini with Tomatoes and Basil

Here is just about the simplest sauce of all, made in your blender in a moment. However, if you use ripe tomatoes, fresh basil and good quality olive oil, it has a freshness and flavour unsurpassed by the most complicated sauces.

500 g (1 lb) spaghettini or	*3 tablespoons chopped parsley*
vermicelli	*¼ cup chopped fresh basil*
SAUCE:	*¼ cup olive oil*
4 large ripe tomatoes	*salt*
2 cloves garlic, crushed	*freshly ground pepper*

Peel, seed, and coarsely chop the tomatoes. Place with the garlic, parsley, basil and oil in a blender and blend to a purée. Heat gently in a saucepan to boiling point, then taste and season well.

Meanwhile, cook the pasta in plenty of boiling salted water until tender but still firm to the bite – about 8 to 10 minutes. Drain well and toss at once with the fresh tomato sauce. Serve with crusty French bread. *Serves 4 to 6*

NOTE: When fresh basil is not in season, substitute 1 tablespoon chopped fresh oregano or marjoram.

Vermicelli with Garlic and Broccoli

There are only a few ingredients in this dish, but they combine to produce a robust flavour – and it has such a fresh and appetizing look, with its green and white colours. As you will note, the garlic is chopped, not crushed; in Naples, where the dish originated, they like to bite into the garlic!

1 bunch fresh broccoli	*approximately 2 cups water*
½ cup olive oil	*250 g (8 oz) vermicelli or*
6 cloves garlic, peeled and	*spaghetti, broken into*
coarsely chopped	*5 cm (2 inch) lengths*
freshly ground pepper	*salt*

Cut the florets from the broccoli and trim any woody ends from the stems. Peel the stems and cut into slices. If the florets are large, separate into halves or quarters, then cut in 5 cm (2 inch) slices.

Put the olive oil and garlic in a heavy-based frying pan over medium heat. Season liberally with freshly ground black pepper. When the oil is hot, but not smoking, add the broccoli stems and florets, 1 cup of water and the uncooked vermicelli. Mix well to combine all the ingredients, and place a lid on the pan. Cook over moderate heat, lifting the lid occasionally to give the mixture a stir – the pasta must not stick to the bottom. If necessary, add a little water from time to time. By the time the vermicelli is cooked (about 8 minutes) the broccoli will be tender, and there should be just enough pan liquid to make a sauce. Take the pan from the heat, add salt to taste, mix well and serve piping hot. *Serves 4*
NOTE: Cheese is not usually served with this dish, but you may pass a bowl of grated cheese if you wish.

Macaroni, Bean and Tuna Salad

This is a lovely, fresh-tasting salad, worthy of your best virgin olive oil and special enough for entertaining.

250 g (8 oz) green beans	*freshly ground pepper*
250 g (8 oz) elbow macaroni,	*4 ripe tomatoes, peeled, seeded*
or use little shells or	*and coarsely chopped*
corkscrew shapes	*6 spring onions, chopped,*
6 tablespoons olive oil	*(including green tops)*
1 tablespoon chopped fresh	*1 × 425 g can tuna in oil*
basil or ½ teaspoon dried	*3 tablespoons chopped parsley*
salt	

Top and tail the beans, string if necessary and cut into julienne (matchstick) strips. Bring a large pot of salted water to the boil and add the macaroni and green beans together. When the macaroni is cooked to the *al dente* stage (about 10 minutes), drain at once, and rinse the macaroni and beans with cold water. Drain well.

Place in a large salad bowl and add 4 tablespoons of the olive oil with the basil, salt and freshly ground pepper to taste. Toss gently with 2 forks to coat the beans and macaroni with oil. Add the tomatoes and spring onions, the drained tuna separated into chunks and the parsley. Toss lightly to combine, and taste for seasoning, adding more oil, salt and pepper if necessary. Do not refrigerate, but serve the salad at room temperature, with Italian bread and a glass of chilled rosé or light red wine. *Serves 4*

Creamy Noodles with Fresh Herbs

If you have fresh herbs growing in your garden or on the windowsill, you have almost all that's needed for this simple sauce.

500 g (1 lb) flat noodles	*1 tablespoon chopped fresh*
2 cloves garlic, crushed	*oregano or marjoram*
60 g (2 oz) butter	*salt*
½ cup pouring cream	*freshly ground pepper*
2 tablespoons chopped parsley	TO SERVE:
2 tablespoons snipped chives	*freshly grated Parmesan or*
1 tablespoon chopped fresh	*Romano cheese*
basil	

Cook the noodles in plenty of boiling salted water until tender but still firm to the bite, about 10 minutes. Drain thoroughly and toss with the crushed garlic and butter.

Heat the cream just to boiling point, and add the chopped parsley, chives, basil and oregano. Season to taste with salt and plenty of freshly ground pepper. Pour over the buttered noodles and toss gently but thoroughly until mixed. Serve at once in heated bowls, and pass freshly grated cheese at the table. *Serves 4*

Spinach Pesto

This is a different version of the classic Pesto Sauce, which is made with fresh basil. Here, spinach gives the bright green colour and good flavour.

⅓ cup shelled walnuts	*½ cup olive oil*
2 cloves garlic, crushed	*¼ cup grated Parmesan cheese*
⅓ cup water	*1 teaspoon salt*
2 cups chopped fresh spinach	*freshly ground pepper*
(green parts only)	

Place the walnuts, garlic and water in a blender or food processor fitted with the steel blade and process until the nuts are chopped. Add the spinach in small amounts alternately with the oil, and process until smooth. Add the Parmesan cheese, salt, and pepper to taste, and blend. Toss with 500 g (1 lb) of hot, freshly cooked pasta. Alternatively, the sauce may be made ahead and reheated when required. *Serves 4*

Salami Carbonara

Make sure the pasta and sauce are ready at the same time – the eggs mustn't be allowed to overcook before they are tossed with the hot pasta.

250 g (8 oz) salami in one piece	*freshly ground pepper*
4 eggs, lightly beaten	*90 g (3 oz) butter*
2 tablespoons pouring cream	*500 g (1 lb) hot, freshly cooked*
¼ cup grated Parmesan or	*spaghetti*
Romano cheese	*2 tablespoons snipped chives*
½ teaspoon salt	*or finely chopped parsley*

Skin the salami and chop into small dice. Combine the eggs with the cream, cheese, salt and freshly ground pepper to taste. Heat the butter in a heavy-based frying pan and lightly brown the salami. Add the egg mixture and cook, stirring, over a medium heat, until the eggs are just beginning to thicken. Toss at once with the hot spaghetti and snipped chives or parsley. *Serves 4*

You can do such a lot with Pancakes

There is nothing tricky about making beautiful pancakes if you keep the following simple tips in mind.

The Pancake Pan

If possible, keep a separate pan just for pancakes and omelettes. A sensible size for pancakes to be rolled is one with a diameter of 15 cm (6 inches). If the sides slope out, the pancakes will be easier to turn.

Don't wash the pan. After using, simply wipe over with a drop of oil on a paper towel. If it gets burned or sticky, rub with a damp cloth dipped in coarse salt, then wipe over with a little oil. To season a new pan, pour in enough oil to cover the bottom, leave for 24 hours, then pour off the oil and wipe with a paper towel.

Cooking Pancakes

Greasing the pan is important. You don't want the pancakes to stick or to be 'fried' in the ordinary sense.

First heat the pan, then wipe the base with oil or clarified butter. A pastry brush is good for this, or dip a piece of clean cloth in a little oil (don't burn your fingers!).

When the pan is greased and thoroughly hot, test the batter to see if it's the right consistency. You should be able to make about 2 tablespoons of batter spread evenly over the base of a 15 cm (6 inch) pan. Add a little liquid if the batter is too thick, and use a jug or large spoon for measuring. Pour the batter into the centre of the pan, then twist it quickly in a clockwise action to spread a film of batter evenly over it. When the underside is golden brown and little bubbles appear on top (about 1 minute), loosen the edges with a spatula, slide the spatula underneath and turn the pancake over. Cook the other side for 1 minute, or until set and brown, then turn out onto a clean tea-towel spread on a wire cake rack. Fold the edges of the tea-towel over the pancake and leave until the next one is cooked. Open the towel, drop the next pancake on top of the first one, and fold the towel over again. Repeat this process as each pancake is cooked. The trapped steam will stop the pancakes from sticking together, and there is no need to place paper in between.

Above: Pancakes can be rolled around a sweet or savoury filling.
Left: Savoury Stuffed Pancakes

Basic Pancake Batter

1 cup flour	*1 egg*
1 teaspoon baking powder	*1½ cups milk*
½ teaspoon salt	*15 g (½ oz) butter, melted*

Sift the flour with the baking powder and salt into a mixing bowl. Make a well in the centre and add the egg, milk and melted butter. With a wooden spoon, gradually draw in the flour. Beat the batter well, cover with a tea-towel and leave to stand for 1 hour.

Heat a little butter in a pancake or crêpe pan. Pour off any excess, reserving it for when the pan needs further greasing. Use a small jug to pour in enough batter to coat the surface of the pan (or you may measure it from a large spoon – about 2 tablespoons are right for a 15 cm/6 inch pan). Run the batter smoothly and evenly over the surface. Cook until small bubbles appear, about 1 minute, then use a metal spatula to turn the pancake over. Cook for 1 minute on the other side, or until set and golden brown. Lift out of the pan and fold in a clean tea-towel. Repeat the process for each pancake. *Makes about 14 pancakes*

To turn pancakes easily, loosen all round the edges first with a knife or spatula.

For sweet pancakes, turn onto paper dusted with icing sugar, then use paper to help roll up.

Savoury Stuffed Pancakes

8 thin pancakes (see Basic Pancake recipe, above)	*salt*
	freshly ground pepper
45 g (1½ oz) butter	*2 tablespoons lemon juice*
1 medium onion, finely chopped	*1 cup chopped cooked prawns, ham or chicken*
125 g (4 oz) mushrooms, sliced	*Cheese Sauce (see right)*
2 tender sticks celery, chopped	*2 tablespoons grated Parmesan cheese*
3 ripe tomatoes, peeled, seeded and chopped	*parsley sprigs, to garnish*
1 tablespoon chopped fresh basil or ½ teaspoon dried	

Make the pancakes first, then the filling.

Heat the butter in a heavy frying pan and gently fry the onion, mushrooms and celery until soft. Add the tomatoes and basil with salt and pepper to taste, and the lemon juice. Stir in the prawns or meat and allow to cool.

Spread the pancakes out flat and divide the filling among them. Fold over the sides of each pancake, then roll up and arrange seam-side down in a shallow greased baking dish. Pour the hot cheese sauce over the pancakes, sprinkle with grated cheese, and bake in a preheated hot oven (200°C/400°F) for 20 minutes, or until heated through and golden and bubbly on top.

Garnish with parsley sprigs and serve. *Serves 8 as a first course, 4 as a main course.*

Cheese Sauce Place 2 cups of grated, processed cheese (or the contents of 1 jar cheese spread), 1 teaspoon dry mustard, a pinch of cayenne and ½ cup milk in a bowl over simmering water and stir constantly until blended together. Add a little extra milk, if necessary, to give a pouring consistency.

Variation

Pancakes in a Pie Instead of filling and rolling the pancakes, you can bake them in layers like lasagne. Choose a round ovenproof dish or cake tin about 23 cm (9 inches) in diameter, and make your pancakes the same size. Butter the pancakes well, then add a little cheese sauce. Stack the pancakes in layers with the filling between. Also add a spoonful of sauce between the layers and spread the remaining sauce over the top. Bake in a moderate oven (180°C/350°F) until piping hot. Serve cut in wedges.

All-in-One Pancakes

For extra quick and easy sweet or savoury pancakes, stir the 'filling' into the batter and cook them together. This recipe with self-raising flour gives a slight 'rise' when the pancakes are cooked, making them light and tender.

1 cup self-raising flour	*1 cup of chosen flavouring ingredients (see suggestions)*
pinch of salt	
1 egg, lightly beaten	*oil for greasing pan*
1 cup milk	

Sift the flour and salt together. Mix the beaten egg and milk together and pour over the flour mixture, folding through gently with a rubber spatula or large metal spoon (the mixture will still be lumpy). Scatter the flavouring ingredients over and fold in lightly.

Heat a large heavy frying pan or griddle iron and grease the surface lightly. Place the mixture on in spoonfuls, dropping it from the tip of the spoon. When browned underneath and bubbles appear through the mixture, turn with a metal spatula and cook the other side. Lift onto a cloth-covered cake cooler. Re-grease the pan before cooking each batch. *Makes 24 to 30 small pancakes*

Flavouring Suggestions

Apple and Sultana ¾ cup chopped apple mixed with ¼ cup sultanas, 1 tablespoon sugar and ¼ teaspoon cinnamon. Sprinkle the pancakes with a little more sugar.

Apricot-Mint Soak 1 cup dried apricots overnight in water to cover. Drain well, and cut into small squares. Add to the pancake batter with 1 tablespoon finely chopped fresh mint. They can be served sprinkled with sugar and lemon for dessert, or as an accompaniment to roast pork.

Frankfurt 1 cup frankfurt slices, 1 teaspoon French mustard and 1 tablespoon fruit chutney.

Cheese ½ cup grated Cheddar cheese, ¼ teaspoon paprika and ¼ teaspoon seasoned pepper or a pinch of cayenne. Sprinkle each pancake with a little extra grated cheese while still hot.

Bacon 1 cup chopped, cooked bacon, 1 tablespoon finely chopped spring onion, ½ teaspoon Worcestershire sauce and a good grinding of pepper. Serve with grilled tomato halves for a light meal.

Corn 1 cup freshly cooked or canned corn (cream-style or whole kernel), 1 tablespoon finely chopped spring onion and a good grinding of pepper.

Ham and Herb ¼ cup chopped, fresh herbs (parsley, thyme, chives, oregano) and ¼ cup chopped ham.

Fillings for Rolled Pancakes

Quantities given here are enough to fill 8 pancakes about 15 cm (6 inches) in diameter.

Savoury Fillings

Spinach and Cheese Fold 1 cup chopped, cooked and drained spinach with ½ cup thick sour cream and ¼ cup grated Cheddar or Swiss cheese. Season with freshly ground black pepper and freshly grated nutmeg. Fill the pancakes and arrange in an ovenproof serving dish. Pour hot cheese sauce over, sprinkle with a little grated cheese and bake at 200°C/400°F for 20 minutes. (See Cheese Sauce recipe, page 63.)

Crab or Chicken Bengal Sauté 2 finely chopped spring onions in 30 g (1 oz) butter. Stir in 2 teaspoons curry powder, fry for 1 minute, then add ½ teaspoon Worcestershire sauce, a dash of Tabasco, ¼ cup each sour cream and natural yogurt and salt to taste. Fold in 1 cup of crabmeat or chopped, cooked chicken and heat gently. Fill the pancakes with the hot mixture and arrange in a flameproof serving dish. Spread with a little cream and place under a hot grill to glaze.

Sweet Fillings

Jamaican Pineapple Sauté 1 cup chopped fresh pineapple or chopped, well-drained canned pineapple in 60 g (2 oz) butter and 2 tablespoons brown sugar until lightly browned. Sprinkle over 1 tablespoon rum and cook for 1 minute more. Spread the pancakes with apricot jam, fill with the pineapple mixture, and arrange in a flameproof serving dish. At the table, set alight 3 tablespoons warm rum and pour over the pancakes while flaming. Serve with a bowl of chilled sour cream with a little brown sugar stirred through.

Cherry Sprinkle 1 tablespoon Kirsch over ¾ cup of stoned, canned or stewed black cherries. Mix with ¼ cup slivered almonds and fill the pancakes as usual. Arrange in an ovenproof serving dish, sprinkle well with caster sugar and place in a hot oven (200°C/400°F) for 3 or 4 minutes, until the sugar forms a glaze. Serve with chilled whipped cream.

Jam and Nut A super-quickie! Mix together 3 tablespoons strawberry or raspberry jam, 3 tablespoons crushed hazelnuts or walnuts and 1 tablespoon lemon juice. Fill and roll the hot pancakes, and top with a spoonful of whipped cream.

Soufflé Surprises

This lovely hot dessert is like a tender pancake folded around thick meringue.

4 eggs, separated	2 tablespoons flour
2 tablespoons sugar	¼ cup milk
½ teaspoon vanilla	butter
good pinch of salt	honey or preserves, to serve

Beat the egg whites until frothy. Add the sugar, vanilla and salt and continue beating until the mixture forms stiff peaks. Blend the egg yolks and flour together with a fork, then stir in the milk.

Grease a 20 cm (8 inch) omelette pan with a little butter and heat. Pour in one-quarter of the yolk mixture, about 3 tablespoons. Spread evenly by rotating the pan and immediately spoon one-quarter of the whites on one side of the yolk layer. Cook for 1 minute, then use a spatula to lift up the side with the egg white filling and fold it over the other side. Cook another minute so the whites will heat through, and remove from pan.

Repeat the process with the remaining mixtures, adding a little butter to the pan each time. (Place the cooked soufflés in a very slow oven until all are ready.) Serve hot with honey or preserves. *Serves 4*

Lemon Pancake Gâteau

4–5 large pancakes, about 20 cm (8 inches) in diameter (see Basic Pancake recipe, page 63)	¼ teaspoon salt
	½ cup orange juice
	3 tablespoons lemon juice
	1 teaspoon grated lemon rind
candied lemon or orange peel, or grated lemon rind	30 g (1 oz) butter
LEMON FILLING:	3 egg yolks, beaten
2½ tablespoons cornflour	TO SERVE:
¾ cup sugar	a bowl of whipped or sour cream (optional)

Mix the cornflour, sugar and salt together and blend to a paste with a little of the orange juice. Add the remaining juices, lemon rind and butter, and cook over boiling water until the mixture thickens, stirring constantly. Remove from the heat and stir in the beaten egg yolks. Return to the stove and cook for 3 minutes longer, stirring. Allow to cool before assembling the gâteau.

To assemble, spread the filling between the pancakes and over the top, stacking each layer to make a cake. Sprinkle with candied lemon or orange peel, or grated rind. Leave to stand at room temperature for half an hour to allow the flavours to mellow, and serve cut in wedges like a cake. Pass a bowl of whipped cream or sour cream, if desired. *Serves 6 to 8*

Cottage Cheese Blintzes

8 small cooked pancakes, about 10 cm (4 inches) in diameter (see Basic Pancake recipe, page 63)	1 egg yolk
	1 teaspoon vanilla
	TO SERVE:
	sugar and cinnamon, mixed together
15 g (½ oz) butter	a bowl of sour cream (optional)
½ tablespoon oil	
FILLING:	
1½ cups cottage cheese	

Cook the pancakes, then make the filling by blending the cheese, egg yolk and vanilla together. Fill the pancakes with the cheese mixture, tuck in the ends and roll up. At this stage they can be refrigerated until required.

Heat the butter and oil together in a heavy frying pan and place the blintzes in, seam-side down. Fry to a golden brown, then turn carefully with a spatula and fry the other side. Serve at once, and pass a bowl of sugar and cinnamon and another of sour cream, if desired. *Serves 4*

Jiffy Blintzes

For these super-quick blintzes the cheese is added to the pancake mixture and cooked all-in-one. Serve with maple syrup, honey, lemon and sugar or your favourite jam.

1 cup flour	1 cup light sour cream
1 tablespoon sugar	1 cup cottage cheese
½ teaspoon salt	4 eggs, well beaten

Sift the flour, sugar and salt into a large bowl. Stir in the remaining ingredients and blend until just combined (do not over mix). Cook by tablespoonfuls in a hot greased frying pan turning to brown both sides. *Makes about 24*

Cottage Cheese Blintzes

Ideas for the Griddle

There are many close relatives of the pancake that are often cooked on a greased griddle or hotplate, making them quick and easy to prepare in quantities.

Pikelets

1 cup self-raising flour	*½ cup milk with 1 teaspoon*
pinch of salt	*lemon juice added*
¼ teaspoon bicarbonate of soda	*15 g (½ oz) butter, melted*
2 tablespoons sugar	*a little extra butter for cooking*
1 egg	

Sift the flour, salt and bicarbonate into a medium-size bowl. Make a well in the centre and add the sugar, egg, milk and melted butter. Stir the mixture from the centre, gradually drawing in the flour from the sides, until you have a smooth batter. Grease a hotplate or heavy frying pan with a little butter and heat. Drop the mixture by tablespoonfuls into the pan and cook over medium heat until the bottoms are brown. Turn carefully and brown the other sides. (If the batter thickens too much, thin with a little milk.) Serve them warm with butter and honey or a good berry jam and a spoonful of whipped cream. *Makes 10 to 12 pikelets*

Variations

Add 60 g (2 oz) seedless raisins or sultanas to the batter, or stir in 1 tablespoon golden syrup instead of sugar.

Wholegrain Griddle Cakes

Try these for breakfast with butter, maple syrup and grilled sausages – a favourite idea from the U.S.A.

¾ cup self-raising flour	*2 eggs*
¾ cup wholemeal self-raising	*1 cup milk*
flour	*30 g (1 oz) butter, melted*
1 teaspoon salt	*a little extra butter for cooking*
2 tablespoons sugar	

Sift the flours with the salt and sugar. Separate the eggs. Beat the yolks with the milk and melted butter, and whip the whites separately until they stand in peaks. Stir the milk mixture into the flour, then fold in the egg whites. Cook by placing tablespoonfuls on a hot greased griddle or in a heavy frying pan, making sure the undersides are browned before turning over. Serve at once. *Makes about 14 griddle cakes*
NOTE: In America, these griddle cakes are served in stacks, with butter melting in between. About 4 to a stack should be enough for the average appetite.

Drop pikelet batter from the top of a metal spoon, allowing room for spreading.

Cook for 2 to 3 minutes until bubbles show on top, then turn and cook other side.

Irish Potato Cakes

500 g (1 lb) floury old potatoes	*freshly ground pepper*
60 g (2 oz) butter	*1 cup flour (approximately)*
salt	*butter for spreading*

To prepare and cook, see step-by-step pictures at right. *Makes 12 to 16 potato cakes*

Crisp Corn Flapjacks

These are good served with bacon and grilled tomatoes – and very nutritious.

$\frac{1}{2}$ *cup plain flour*	*1 teaspoon baking powder*
$\frac{2}{3}$ *cup yellow cornmeal*	$\frac{1}{4}$ *cup self-raising flour*
(polenta)	*60 g (2 oz) butter, melted*
1 teaspoon salt	*2 cups buttermilk*
$\frac{1}{2}$ *teaspoon bicarbonate of soda*	*1 egg, beaten*

Sift together the plain flour, cornmeal, salt, bicarbonate, baking powder and self-raising flour. Blend together the butter, buttermilk and egg. Make a well in the centre of the cornmeal mixture and pour in the liquid. Stir from the centre with a wooden spoon until the dry ingredients have been moistened and you have a smooth batter. Do not over mix. Drop the batter onto a hot greased griddle or frying pan, making flapjacks about 10 cm (4 inches) in diameter. When the undersides are brown, turn over and cook the other sides. If the batter thickens while the flapjacks are cooking, stir in a little extra buttermilk. *Makes about 10 flapjacks*

Irish Potato Cakes

1 Peel the potatoes and cook until tender. Drain, and shake the pan over the heat for a moment so potatoes dry off completely. Mash well and while still hot beat in the butter. Season with salt and pepper and work in enough flour to bind into a dough.

2 Divide the dough in half. Pat or roll each half out into a circle shape on a floured board, then cut each circle into 6 or 8 triangles. The dough should be about 1 cm ($\frac{1}{2}$ inch) thick.

3 Make sure the griddle or frying pan is well greased and heated through. Lift the potato cakes carefully with a spatula or egg slice, and cook for about 5 minutes each side until nicely brown.

4 Split each cake in two, and fill with a slice of butter. Serve very hot with grilled sausages, bacon and tomatoes, or fried eggs – or golden syrup for those with a sweet tooth.

Irish Potato Cakes; Pikelets

Desserts in 10 Minutes or Less

Most people like to finish a meal with 'something sweet'. It can be as simple as a piece of fresh fruit – and there's nothing more refreshing. But when we entertain, or when the main course has been a salad – or just for the fun of it – it's nice to serve a dessert.

Luckily for the quick and easy cook, there are many delectable desserts that can be made in minutes. Even spectacular Bombe Alaska takes only a few minutes of actual cooking time if it is prepared ahead; and if you have a supply of pancakes on hand in the refrigerator or freezer, you have the basis of superb desserts to make at the table in a chafing dish or in your frypan.

Brazil Sundaes

2 teaspoons butter	½ cup brown sugar, firmly
¾ cup coarsely chopped Brazil	packed
nuts or cashews	½ litre coffee ice-cream
½ cup pouring cream	extra chopped nuts, to
	decorate

Melt the butter in a small saucepan. Add the chopped nuts and stir until lightly toasted. Add the cream and brown sugar, bring to the boil, then simmer until well blended, stirring constantly. Spoon the hot sauce over individual servings of ice-cream, and sprinkle with a few extra chopped nuts. *Serves 6*

Cherry Nut Ice-Cream

½ cup drained maraschino	3 tablespoons finely chopped
cherries	walnuts or toasted almonds
2 tablespoons maraschino	1 litre vanilla ice-cream
syrup	extra syrup for topping

Remove the pits from the cherries and roughly chop with the 2 tablespoons of syrup. Add the chopped nuts. Let the ice-cream soften slightly and stir in the cherries and nuts (don't over mix, a rippled effect is attractive). Return to the freezer until serving time, then serve in individual scoops with a little syrup poured over. *Serves 6*

Ice-Cream Balls with Mincemeat Flambé

Freeze the ice-cream balls a day ahead so they're very firm.

1 litre vanilla ice-cream	¼ cup brandy
1 × 275 g jar fruit mince	

Scoop the ice-cream into balls with an ice-cream scoop. Freeze until ready to serve. At serving time, pile the ice-cream balls into a serving bowl, heat the mincemeat and spoon over the frozen ice-cream. Warm the brandy in the same pan, ignite, and pour flaming over the mincemeat. Serve at once. *Serves 6*

Gingered Melon Balls

3 cups melon balls or cubes	2 tablespoons gin (optional)
3 tablespoons honey	mint sprigs, to decorate
½ cup finely chopped	
crystallized ginger	

Combine the melon balls, honey, ginger and gin, if using. Place in the freezer compartment for 5 to 10 minutes, then spoon into individual bowls and garnish each bowl with a sprig of mint. *Serves 6*

Mixed Fruit Ambrosia

3 oranges, peeled and sliced	2 tablespoons lemon juice
1 cup shredded coconut	2 cups chopped fresh
2 ripe bananas, peeled and	pineapple (or drained,
sliced	canned pineapple)

Arrange the orange slices in the bottom of a large serving bowl (glass is attractive because you can see the fruits). Sprinkle with one-third of the coconut. Top with the bananas, sprinkle with lemon juice and another third of the coconut. Arrange the pineapple on top and sprinkle with the remaining coconut. Chill for 5 minutes, then serve at the table in individual bowls. *Serves 6*

Rum Babas

The traditional rum baba is made from a yeast mixture but this short-cut recipe has the same rich flavour.

1 single-layer sponge cake	1 tablespoon lemon juice
(from the cake shop)	3 tablespoons dark rum
½ cup sugar	1 cup cream
1 cup water	

Cut the cake into 4 circles, using a small glass as a guide. Place in individual dishes. Bring the sugar and water to a boil and simmer until the sugar is dissolved. Stir in the lemon juice and rum. Pour the hot syrup over the cake and, when cooled a little, place in the refrigerator until ready to serve. Whip the cream until stiff and spoon or pipe on top of the babas. *Serves 4*

Orange-Coconut Cream Cake

Homemade or bought Madeira cake, orange cake or sponge cake is suitable for this fresh-tasting dessert. Make ahead of the main course and chill for an hour or more so the flavours have a chance to mellow.

1 piece Madeira or orange	2 large oranges, peeled and
cake (enough for 4	finely sliced
servings), or 1 single-layer	½ cup desiccated coconut, or
sponge cake	toasted, flaked almonds
4 tablespoons sweet sherry or	1 cup cream, whipped with 1
orange-flavoured liqueur	teaspoon vanilla and 1
	tablespoon sugar

Split the cake in half and sprinkle both halves with sherry or liqueur. Arrange half the orange slices on one half of the cake. Gently fold the coconut or almonds into the sweetened whipped cream. Spread half the cream on the orange slices and cover with

the other half of the cake, spreading the remaining cream on top. Chill in the refrigerator until serving time. Just before serving, top with the remaining orange slices. *Serves 4 to 6*

Mixed Fruit Ambrosia

Bombe Alaska

This most spectacular of desserts may be prepared the night before and frozen until ready to cook.

1 single-layer sponge (bought or homemade)	*pinch of cream of tartar*
	pinch of salt
½ cup raspberry or strawberry conserve	*¾ cup caster sugar*
	TO FLAME:
1 litre ice-cream (vanilla, cassata, Neapolitan or strawberry)	*1 lump sugar*
	a little brandy or lemon essence
MERINGUE:	
6 egg whites	

Place the cake on a small wooden board and spread with raspberry or strawberry conserve. Arrange scoops of ice-cream on the cake, piling them up into a dome shape and leaving a margin of about 1 cm (½ inch) around the edge of the cake. Freeze while preparing the meringue.

To make the meringue, beat the egg whites with cream of tartar and salt until stiff (save half an egg shell for the top of the Alaska). Gradually beat in the sugar, 2 tablespoons at a time, and continue beating until the meringue is white, shiny, and very stiff.

Remove the cake from the freezer and spread with the meringue, completely covering both the cake and ice-cream, and forming a peak on top. Place half an egg shell in the centre with the hollow side up (you will be putting the sugar lump in here when the Alaska is cooked).

Return to the freezer until required.

At serving time, preheat the oven to very hot (220°C/425°F). Take the Alaska from the freezer and place at once in the hot oven. Leave for a few minutes, until the meringue has browned and puffed slightly. Meanwhile, soak the sugar lump in the brandy or lemon essence.

Take the Alaska from the oven, place the sugar lump in the egg shell, and light it. Carry the Alaska flaming to the table – if it's night time, turn the lights out to increase the dramatic effect – and serve at once. *Serves 8 to 10*

SOME POINTS TO REMEMBER: The wooden board used as the base of the bombe helps to insulate it and stop the ice-cream melting. (A metal tray heats too quickly.)

Make sure the meringue completely covers all the sides of the cake and the ice-cream. Any little holes will let the heat in.

Have the egg whites at room temperature, as they whip to greater volume.

Variations

It is easy to add different touches to Bombe Alaska:
Use chocolate cake and chocolate ice-cream.
Add a sprinkling of rum or sweet sherry to the cake.
Top the cake with a layer of well-drained sliced peaches or apricots instead of conserve. (Not suitable for freezing.)
Sprinkle the meringue with flaked or slivered almonds.
Sprinkle some desiccated coconut over the top just before baking; the coconut will turn a light brown as the meringue cooks.

Chicken with Cucumber

Quick and Easy Chinese Dishes

Many Chinese dishes are quick and easy. Perhaps the most familiar quick method is the 'stir-fry' one, but the Chinese do not stop here. They have a special way with cold foods and salads, with crisp-fried morsels and noodles, with soups and steamed dishes – the quick and easy list is endless. Here is an interesting cross-section for you to try.

Deep-Fried Prawn Balls

Serve these as an appetizer with drinks, or as a first course with a Chinese meal. Offer a little bowl of hot mustard and another one of chilli sauce or plum sauce for dipping.

500 g (1 lb) green prawns	*1 teaspoon salt*
3 water chestnuts, drained and chopped	*1 teaspoon cornflour*
2 slices fresh ginger	*1 teaspoon Chinese rice wine or dry sherry*
1 egg white	*oil for deep frying*

Shell the prawns and remove the black veins. Chop roughly. Place all the ingredients in a blender, and whirr until a smooth paste is formed. (If you don't have a blender, the prawns and ginger can be minced very finely by hand, then the other ingredients mixed in.) Shape teaspoons of the mixture into small balls – it won't stick to your hands if you dampen them. Deep fry in one or two batches in hot oil, using enough oil for the prawn balls to float. Serve hot. *Makes enough for 6 to 8 appetizer servings.*

Sweet and Pungent Eggs

This is an unbelievably simple way of turning a fried egg into an authentic Chinese delicacy!

6 eggs	*½ tablespoon sugar*
oil for frying	*pinch of monosodium*
1 tablespoon soy sauce	*glutamate*
½ tablespoon vinegar	

Fry each egg individually and, just before it is set, fold over into a half moon shape, pressing the edges together to seal. Place each egg as it is cooked on a plate. When all are cooked, replace them in the pan and add the soy sauce, vinegar, sugar and monosodium glutamate. Bring to the boil, then remove the eggs to individual plates, pour a little sauce over each, and serve. *Serves 6 as part of a meal, 3 for lunch or supper.*

Stir-Fried Pork with Celery

This very simple dish from Peking is a good one for beginners to try.

315 g (about ⅔ lb) pork fillet	*2 tablespoons soy sauce*
1 clove garlic, crushed	*1 teaspoon sugar*
½ tablespoon sugar	*½ teaspoon monosodium*
½ tablespoon soy sauce	*glutamate*
1 tablespoon cornflour	
4 tender sticks celery	
TO COOK:	
2–3 tablespoons oil	

Remove any fat or membranes from the pork and cut into slices about 5 mm (¼ inch) thick. Using the blunt edge of a chopper, or a heavy saucer, pound the meat lightly to tenderize and flatten it. Mix together the garlic, sugar, soy sauce and cornflour and stir into the pork. Allow to stand for 30 minutes.

Meanwhile, peel any strings from the celery and cut across into diagonal slices about 1 cm (½ inch) wide. Blanch in boiling water for 2 minutes, drain and rinse in cold water.

Heat 2 tablespoons of the oil in a wok or large, heavy frying pan. Fry the pork slices on both sides until golden brown (adding a little more oil, if necessary, to prevent sticking).

This should take about 4 minutes altogether. When the pork is browned, quickly stir in the soy sauce, sugar, monosodium glutamate and celery. Wait a moment until it is heated through, then transfer to a heated serving plate and serve at once. *This will serve 4 to 6 as part of a Chinese meal, or 2 as a main course with boiled rice.*

Chicken with Cucumber

Chicken lightly cooked this way retains all its juices. Serve chilled, with crispy cucumber and the interesting nutty sauce.

8 chicken fillets (boned, skinless breasts)	*1 tablespoon light soy sauce*
2 spring onions	*½ teaspoon dry mustard*
2 slices fresh ginger	*3 tablespoons water*
3 cups water	*1 teaspoon salt*
2 small young cucumbers	*1 teaspoon chilli oil (or 1*
SESAME SAUCE:	*teaspoon peanut oil with a*
1 teaspoon finely chopped spring onion	*dash of Tabasco)*
2 tablespoons sesame paste or crunchy peanut butter	*1 tablespoon brown sugar*
	TO GARNISH:
	spring onion brushes

Place the chicken fillets in a saucepan with the spring onions, ginger and water. Bring to the boil, reduce the heat, cover the pan and simmer gently for 6 minutes. Allow to cool in the stock, then remove and cut into julienne strips (the size of matchsticks).

Peel the cucumbers, leaving a few strips of green skin for colour, then halve them and scoop out the seeds with a teaspoon. Cut the cucumber into julienne strips the same size as the chicken. Cover the chicken and cucumber with plastic wrap and refrigerate until needed.

Place all the ingredients for the sesame sauce in a small bowl and mix well to combine.

Arrange the chicken on one side of a dish, and the cucumber next to it. Garnish with spring onion brushes. Just before serving, spoon a little sauce over the chicken and cucumber and serve at once as a first course or as part of a cold buffet. *Serves 6 to 8*
NOTE: Save the chicken cooking liquid and use in any recipe that calls for a light stock.

Sliced Beef with Green Peppers

375 g (12 oz) Scotch fillet	*4 green peppers, seeded and cut*
1 teaspoon soy sauce	*into thin strips*
1 teaspoon cornflour	*1 teaspoon salt*
pinch of bicarbonate of soda	*1 tablespoon soy sauce*
2 teaspoons water	*pinch of monosodium*
dash of black pepper	*glutamate*
7 tablespoons oil	

Cut the beef into thin slices, then into strips a little longer than a match. Mix together the 1 teaspoon soy sauce, the cornflour, bicarbonate, water and pepper and stir into the beef strips, turning them so all are covered.

Heat 3 tablespoons of the oil in a wok or heavy frying pan and add the green peppers and salt. Stir-fry for about 2 minutes, until the peppers are tender-crisp. Remove the peppers with a slotted spoon. Add the remaining 4 tablespoons of oil to the pan and fry the beef for 2 to 3 minutes until golden brown. Return the peppers to the pan with the 1 tablespoon of soy sauce and the monosodium glutamate. Stir for another minute until piping hot, then serve at once. *Serves 4 to 5 as part of a Chinese meal, or 2 as a main course with boiled rice.*

Minced Beef with Noodles

4 tablespoons oil	*2 cloves garlic, crushed*
500 g (1 lb) topside mince (lean beef mince)	*2 slices fresh ginger, chopped*
2 tablespoons Chinese rice wine or dry sherry	*2 teaspoons hot chilli sauce, or pinch of chilli powder*
4 tablespoons soy sauce	*1 cup water*
1 tablespoon cornflour	*salt*
2 teaspoons sugar	*2 × 55 g packets Chinese noodles*

Heat the oil in a wok or heavy frying pan. Add the mince meat and stir and turn until the meat is brown, breaking up any lumps with a fork. Add the rice wine or sherry, soy sauce, cornflour, sugar, garlic, ginger and chilli sauce or powder. Stir for a minute so everything is well blended, then add the cup of water. Stir again, taste the gravy, and add salt to taste if necessary.

Meanwhile, cook the noodles according to the packet directions and arrange on a heated serving plate. Pour the meat mixture over the noodles and serve at once. *Serves 4*

Hot Chicken Salad

2 tablespoons toasted sesame seeds	*½ teaspoon each salt and sugar*
2 tablespoons Dijon-style mustard	*pinch of 5-spice powder*
2 tablespoons lemon juice	*6 spring onions, chopped*
¼ cup chicken stock	*4 cups diced, cooked chicken*
	2 cups crisp shredded lettuce

Blend together all the ingredients, except the chicken and lettuce, in a frying pan and bring to the boil. Add the chicken and heat through. Taste, adjust the seasoning, and spoon the hot mixture over the cold lettuce. Serve at once. *Serves 6*

Friendly Family Meals

Friendly Family Meals

It's one of the greatest cooking challenges of all time to provide interesting and nourishing meals day in, day out, and not lose your enthusiasm for the job.

I think it helps to stay enthusiastic when you consider what you are doing for the family by offering good food in a happy atmosphere. You are giving them refreshment for the spirit as well as the body. No other times are remembered with such warmth as those relaxed moments around the family dining table. News is exchanged, friends are welcomed, problems are aired. Indeed, the fanciest restaurant cannot give what you give, because good food is only a part of family eating. Love and security are the priceless extras to be found at a happy table.

These recipes include shortcuts and new ideas as well as old-time family favourites. Many are simple enough for the novice cook to make; and I believe boys as well as girls should grow up feeling at ease in the kitchen – do encourage them to help!

Naturally, I have kept nourishment and economy in mind, so there is only one special touch waiting to be added – your own joy in cooking for your family.

Start them off Right with Soup

A pot of soup is a welcoming sight. It makes a wonderful first course for a family, or it can be turned into a complete meal by adding a sandwich or bread and butter. There are hearty soups for cold days, light soups for summer lunches and special soups for entertaining. Canned and packaged soups are great standbys, but even in today's busy world it's rewarding to make your own soup and your family will certainly taste the difference.

Basic Stocks

There is no doubt that good stock plays an important role in good cooking. Stock is not only the foundation of many soups, but it is also used to make sauces, gravies and entrées.

Stock is simple to make and need not be made fresh every time it is required. It will keep almost indefinitely in the refrigerator if it is reboiled every few days, and it freezes well. I think it is worthwhile making a few litres at a time and storing it for use through the week.

Of course, stock cubes and canned consommé can be wonderful aids if you are discriminating in their use, especially if you make them up with vegetable water or just simmer a few vegetables with them before using.

Using Stock

White stocks are used for light-coloured soups and sauces, brown stock for dark soups. Use veal bones for a basic white stock, a boiling fowl or chicken pieces for chicken stock, and beef bones plus a piece of stewing beef for brown stock.

White or Chicken Stock

Use this for light-coloured soups and sauces.

500 g (1 lb) meaty veal bones or chicken pieces (wings or backs)	1 stick celery
7 cups cold water	bouquet garni (3 parsley sprigs, 1 bay leaf and 1 sprig of thyme, tied together)
1 onion, halved	6 peppercorns
2 carrots, sliced	

To prepare and cook, follow step-by-step pictures at right.

White or Chicken Stock

1 Ask the butcher to crack the large bones. This will release the gelatine and give body to the stock. Remove any fat from the bones, wash them and place in a large saucepan. Cover with the water and bring to simmering point.

2 As the stock simmers, scum will rise to the surface. Remove it carefully, then add the vegetables, bouquet garni and peppercorns. Salt is not added to the basic stock, but goes into the recipe itself. Cover and simmer gently for 4 to 6 hours.

3 Strain the stock through a sieve into a bowl, discarding the solids. Allow the stock to cool, then refrigerate. The fat will settle into a solid layer on top and can be easily lifted off.

4 The fat of chicken stock will rise to the surface as it chills, but will remain soft. Spoon off as much as possible, then remove the remaining fat by carefully drawing an absorbent paper towel across the surface.

Brown Stock

Use the same ingredients as for White Stock but substitute
500 g (1 lb) beef bones and 125 g (4 oz) chopped gravy beef
for the veal or chicken.

Brown the bones, meat and vegetables in a hot oven
(220°C/425°F) for 20 minutes to give the stock a good brown
colour. If the bones are very lean, grease the baking dish with oil
or butter. Transfer the bones, meat and vegetables to a saucepan
and proceed as for White Stock.

Scots Broth

This is a hearty, nourishing soup full of meat and vegetables.
Serve the soup with buttered oatcakes (Scottish for preference)
or fresh crusty bread. Follow with a crisp salad and fresh fruit
for dessert and you have a complete meal for family or guests.

750 g (1½ lb) lamb neck chops	1 turnip, peeled and diced
8 cups cold water or white	1 parsnip, peeled and diced
stock (see opposite) or stock	1 large onion, chopped
cubes and water	2 leeks, washed and thinly
salt	sliced, or 1 extra onion
freshly ground pepper	3 tablespoons pearl barley
2 carrots, scraped and diced	chopped parsley, to garnish

Trim fat from the chops, then place in a large saucepan and add
the water or stock with salt and pepper to taste. (If using stock
cubes, add the seasoning later.) Bring to the boil and skim, then
cover tightly and simmer for 1 hour. Add the prepared vegetables
and barley and cook for another hour, or until the meat and
vegetables are tender. Remove the chops from the soup with a
slotted spoon and cut the meat into small pieces. Blot up any fat
on top of the soup with absorbent paper towels, return the
meat to the pot and reheat. Adjust the seasoning. Serve
sprinkled with chopped parsley. *Serves 6*
NOTE: If leeks aren't available, use an extra onion in the soup.
Be sure to taste before adding seasoning if you have used stock
cubes, as they will already be seasoned.

Potato Cheese Soup

So simple – yet absolutely delicious.

4 large potatoes, peeled and diced	white pepper
3 cups white stock (see opposite)	8 tablespoons grated Gruyère cheese
1½ cups milk, scalded	4 tablespoons grated
pinch of nutmeg	Parmesan cheese
salt	

Cook the potatoes in the stock until tender. Push through a sieve
or purée in a blender and return the potatoes and stock to the
pan. Add the milk, nutmeg, salt and pepper to taste and bring to
the boil. Pour into 4 flameproof bowls and sprinkle with the
Gruyère cheese, then the Parmesan cheese. Put under a preheated
grill for 2 minutes, or until the cheese melts. *Serves 4*
NOTE: When there is no time to make stock, canned chicken or
beef consommé is useful to have on hand; just make up to the
required amount of liquid with water. For a change, you can
also make the soup with pumpkin or carrots instead of the
potatoes. Use about 750 g (1½ lb) pumpkin, peeled and diced, or 4
to 5 large carrots. Warmed French bread is a perfect
accompaniment.

Scots Broth

Green Herb Soup

If you have a green thumb with herbs, here is a lovely fresh-flavoured soup that will show off your skills.

2 large onions, chopped	2 tablespoons chopped fresh
60 g (2 oz) butter	herbs (thyme, sage,
1 cup chopped parsley	marjoram, oregano)
2 tablespoons flour	3 cups milk
3 cups warm chicken stock	3 tablespoons cream
(page 76)	freshly ground pepper
1/3 cup rice	snipped chives, to garnish
salt	

Cook the onions gently in butter until soft but not brown. Stir in the parsley and cook for 1 minute, then add the flour and stir for another minute. Remove from the heat, cool a little, and add the chicken stock, blending well. Return to the heat and stir to boiling point. Sprinkle in the rice and salt to taste and simmer for 25 minutes. Cool slightly and push through a sieve or purée in batches in a blender. Return to the pan and add the chopped herbs, milk and cream. Taste and adjust the seasoning with salt and pepper. Sprinkle with chives to serve. *Serves 8*

Pea Soup with Frankfurts

Split peas and frankfurts are perfect partners for an economical, high-protein winter lunch or supper.

1 cup split peas	ham bone or bacon bones to
30 g (1 oz) butter	flavour
1 turnip, peeled and chopped	salt
1 large onion, chopped	freshly ground pepper
2 sticks celery, chopped	4 continental frankfurts
6 cups white stock (page 76)	1 tablespoon lemon juice

Soak the peas overnight in cold water to cover. Heat the butter in a large saucepan, add the turnip, onion and celery and cook very gently for 10 minutes, shaking the pan to avoid sticking. Drain the peas and add to the pan with the stock and ham or bacon bones. Cover and simmer gently for 3 hours, stirring occasionally. Remove the bones, cut any meat into small dice and return to the pan. Season the soup with salt and pepper to taste. Slice the frankfurts and heat gently in the soup for 3 minutes. Stir in the lemon juice and serve. *Serves 8*

Petite Marmite for a Crowd

This easy version of the famous French 'little pot' is full of succulent beef and vegetables, with the interesting addition of chicken livers.

1.5 kg (3 lb) gravy beef, cut in	4 sticks celery, sliced
slices 2.5 cm (1 inch) thick	250 g (8 oz) chicken livers,
4 litres (7 pints) water	trimmed of sinews and cut
1 tablespoon salt	in two
1/4 teaspoon pepper	3 beef stock cubes
1 bay leaf	CHEESE MIXTURE:
2 large onions, stuck with 6	60 g (2 oz) butter
whole cloves	1/2 teaspoon paprika
4 carrots, scraped and sliced	3 tablespoons chopped parsley
2 turnips, peeled and diced	1 cup grated Parmesan cheese

Place the beef, water, salt, pepper, bay leaf and onions in a large pot. Bring to the boil and skim the froth from the top. Cover the pot and simmer until the meat is tender, about 2 hours. Remove the meat and set aside. Remove and discard the bay leaf and onions.

Add the carrots, turnips, celery, chicken livers and stock cubes to the pot and simmer for a further 20 minutes. Dice the meat, add to the soup and heat through. Taste, and adjust the seasoning.

Meanwhile, cream the butter and mix in the paprika, parsley and cheese. Ladle the soup into bowls and top each one with a spoonful of the cheese mixture. *Serves 8 to 10*

Kidney Soup

This was a very popular soup in Edwardian times. It is dark, rich and smooth in appearance and flavour; and it's still an excellent way to begin a family meal.

4 lambs' kidneys or 1/2 an ox	1 medium onion, chopped
kidney	2 tablespoons flour
5 cups brown stock (page 77)	2 teaspoons tomato paste
bouquet garni (1 celery stick,	1/2 cup red wine or dry sherry
1 bay leaf, 1 sprig of thyme	salt
and 3 sprigs of parsley, tied	freshly ground pepper
together)	chopped parsley, to garnish
30 g (1 oz) butter	

Remove the skin and cores from the kidneys. Soak in warm salted water for 1 hour, then drain and cut into thin slices. Place in a large saucepan with the stock and bouquet garni. Cover the pan and simmer gently for 1 hour. Remove the bouquet garni, then put the kidneys and liquid into a bowl and rinse the pan.

Melt the butter in the same pan and gently fry the onion until brown. Stir in the flour and cook for 1 minute. Remove from the heat, cool a little, and stir in the tomato paste and 3 cups of kidney liquid. Blend well, return to the heat and stir until boiling. Add the remaining liquid with the kidneys and the wine or sherry. Season to taste with salt and pepper and simmer for 10 minutes. Rub the soup through a sieve or purée in batches in a blender or food processor fitted with the steel blade. Reheat and garnish with chopped parsley. *Serves 8*

Country Vegetable Soup

30 g (1 oz) butter	1 cup tomato juice, or 3
2 cups diced mixed vegetables	medium tomatoes, peeled,
such as onion, carrot,	seeded and chopped
turnip, parsnip, celery, leek	salt
2 tablespoons flour	freshly ground pepper
5 cups warm brown stock	2 tablespoons chopped
	parsley, to garnish

Melt the butter in a large saucepan and add the vegetables. Cover the pan and allow the vegetables to cook very gently for 20 minutes. Stir in the flour, cook for a few minutes, then remove from the heat. Allow to cool a little, add the stock, tomato juice or tomatoes and salt and pepper to taste. Stir until well blended, then cover and cook for 20 minutes or until the vegetables are tender. Sprinkle with chopped parsley to serve. *Serves 6*

Buttermilk Pepper Soup; Country Vegetable Soup

Italian Marriage Soup

6 cups rich beef or chicken
  stock (pages 77, 76), or
  canned consommé and water
60 g (2 oz) fine egg noodles
125 g (4 oz) unsalted butter

¾ cup freshly grated Parmesan
  cheese
4 egg yolks
1 cup cream
pinch of nutmeg

Bring the stock to boiling point in a saucepan or chafing dish. Add the noodles (broken into pieces if desired) and cook for 5 minutes, or until tender to the bite. Blend the butter with the cheese and egg yolks, and gradually add the cream. (This can be done in the kitchen beforehand and brought to the table.) Stir a little hot soup into the egg mixture, stir well, then pour back into the soup and stir until the mixture is thickened and creamy. Add the nutmeg and ladle at once into bowls. *Serves 6*

Pumpkin Soup

This is a golden soup with a good, rich flavour.

30 g (1 oz) butter
1 kg (2 lb) pumpkin, peeled
  and chopped
1 medium onion, stuck with 2
  cloves
2 teaspoons sugar
salt

2½ cups white stock or chicken
  stock (page 76)
1 cup milk
freshly ground pepper
freshly grated nutmeg, to
  garnish

Heat the butter in a large heavy saucepan. Add the pumpkin and stir until the pieces are well coated with the butter. Cover the pan and cook very gently for 10 minutes to develop the flavour. Add the onion, sugar, a pinch of salt and the stock. Replace the lid and cook over a low heat until the pumpkin is very tender.

Discard the onion, add the milk and adjust the seasoning.

Push the soup through a sieve, or purée in a blender or processor fitted with the steel blade. Reheat if serving hot, or cool and chill for a summer soup. Sprinkle with a little nutmeg to serve. *Serves 6*

Quick Crab Bisque

1 × 305 g can mushroom soup
1 × 305 g can oyster soup
1½ soup cans milk
1 cup pouring cream

1 × 170 g can crabmeat, flaked
¼ cup dry white wine
butter

Blend the soups in a saucepan and stir in the milk and cream. Bring just to boiling, add the crab and heat through. Stir in the wine, ladle into bowls and top with a spoonful of butter. *Serves 8*

Buttermilk Pepper Soup

A light soup for summer that is quickly made with the help of stock cubes and an electric blender.

1 medium onion, finely
  chopped
30 g (1 oz) butter
1 red or green pepper, seeded
  and finely chopped
2 chicken stock cubes
  dissolved in 1 cup hot water

1 × 600 ml carton buttermilk
1 teaspoon salt
¼ teaspoon white pepper
TO GARNISH:
snipped chives
whipped cream

Fry the onion gently in the butter until soft but not brown, about 5 minutes. Add the pepper, cover the pan and cook over a low heat for another 5 minutes. Add the stock, cover and simmer gently for 15 minutes. Add the buttermilk and salt and pepper and heat through. Purée the soup in batches in an electric blender. Serve hot or chilled, garnished with snipped chives and a swirl of cream. *Serves 4 to 6*

First Courses are Family Affairs

Soups are always welcome first courses, and you will find some delicious recipes on pages 76 to 79. I also like to serve cold vegetables with a piquant sauce, fruits, interesting spreads, hot little savouries (see the picture opposite) and appetizer salads.

Sardine Spread

Serve on hot wholegrain toast, crusty bread or crackers.

1 × 160 g can sardines	2 hard-boiled eggs, chopped
4 spring onions, chopped	1 tablespoon lemon juice
5 tablespoons mayonnaise	1 teaspoon curry powder

Drain the sardines, remove the backbones if large, and mash with the remaining ingredients. Taste and adjust the seasoning. *Makes about 1¼ cups*

Appetizer Salad

An interesting European way of serving leftover roast meat.

8–10 slices roast beef, lamb or pork	1 cup light sour cream
salt	lettuce leaves
freshly ground pepper	1 tablespoon capers, to garnish
1 tablespoon lemon juice	
1 onion, thinly sliced and separated into rings	

Slice the meat into thin strips. Season with salt, pepper and lemon juice. Fold the meat and onion rings into the sour cream. Serve in lettuce cups, sprinkled with capers. *Serves 6*

Pizza Muffins

An easy, hearty first course to serve before a main dish salad.

4 English muffins (plain or bran)	salt
1 clove garlic, crushed	freshly ground pepper
2 ripe tomatoes, peeled, seeded and chopped	1 cup grated mature Cheddar cheese
½ teaspoon dried oregano	125 g (4 oz) salami, diced
	¼ cup grated Parmesan cheese

Split the muffins and toast lightly on both sides under the grill. Mix together the garlic, tomatoes and oregano with salt and pepper to taste. Spread evenly over the muffins, top with the cheese and then the salami. Sprinkle with Parmesan cheese and place under a medium grill until the topping is golden and bubbly. *Serves 4 generously*

Crostini di Provatura

1 can flat anchovy fillets, drained	12 slices soft cheese (Mozzarella, Bel Paese, Provolone)
2 tablespoons milk	90 g (3 oz) butter, melted
½ loaf French bread	

Cover the anchovies with the milk and leave to soak. Cut the bread into 12 slices. Place a slice of cheese, trimmed to fit, on each slice. Arrange, slightly overlapping, in a long ovenproof dish. Bake in a moderately hot oven (190°C/375°F) for 7 minutes, or until bread is crisp and cheese melted. Drain the anchovies, chop coarsely and heat in the melted butter. Pour sauce over crostini and serve at once. *Serves 4 to 6*

Spiced Melon Cocktail

If you don't have a melon baller, simply cut the melons into cubes.

1 small ripe rock melon	2 teaspoons grated orange rind
1 small ripe honeydew melon	2 tablespoons lemon juice
½ teaspoon cinnamon	2 tablespoons brown sugar
½ teaspoon ground ginger	mint leaves, to garnish

Halve the melons and remove the seeds. Scoop out the flesh using a melon baller or cut into bite-size cubes. Place in a bowl. Scoop out any remaining flesh and push through a sieve to make a purée. Add the purée and the remaining ingredients to the bowl and stir. Cover the bowl and chill in the refrigerator for several hours. Serve in small deep dishes, garnished with mint leaves. *Serves 6 to 8*

Vegetables Vinaigrette

Beautiful as a course on its own or as an accompaniment to cold meats, grills or poultry. The appeal of this dish depends upon cooking the vegetables very lightly, so give the beans only about 4 to 5 minutes and the other vegetables no more than 2 to 3 minutes.

250 g (8 oz) each young green beans, zucchini, pattypan squash and button mushrooms	freshly ground pepper
	chopped fresh herbs (a choice of parsley, chives, marjoram, oregano)
2 tablespoons olive oil	2 hard-boiled eggs, chopped
juice of ½ lemon	1 lemon, quartered, to garnish
salt	

Top and tail the beans; thickly slice the zucchini; trim the squash and cut the mushroom stems level with the caps. Cook each vegetable separately in 1 cup boiling salted water, without a lid, until just tender-crisp. As each is cooked, refresh under cold running water; this stops cooking and sets the colour. Drain well and pat dry.

Arrange the vegetables on a platter. Combine the oil and lemon juice, season with salt and pepper and beat with a whisk or fork until thick and creamy. Spoon over the vegetables. Sprinkle the herbs over and spoon the chopped egg in a line down the middle of the vegetables. Garnish the platter with lemon wedges. Serve at room temperature, do not refrigerate. If you are making this dish a little ahead, cover loosely with plastic wrap. *Serves 6 as a first course, 8 as an accompaniment.*

Crostini di Provatura

Fresh Fish for the Family

Fish fresh from sea or river is one of the great natural delicacies. If you have a fisherman in the family you can taste fish at its absolute best. However, modern handling and transportation methods get fish to markets and suburban fish shops in double-quick time these days. If you have to shop for fish, buy from a place that's always busy, with a good turnover. This is the best guarantee of freshness. Be adventurous in your buying, too. Some of the lesser-known fish are as delicious as the old favourites, and often a more economical purchase. In fact, like your butcher, the fish shop proprietor can be a useful guide to 'what's the best buy today?'. Show him you're interested, and with his guidance it will be almost like having a fisherman in the family anyway!

Baked Sole with Oysters

Sole or flounder fillets are wrapped around an oyster filling and served in a creamy sauce. It's special enough for a celebration dinner, but delightfully easy to prepare. Bottled or canned oysters are quite suitable.

60 g (2 oz) butter	$\frac{1}{2}$ cup dry white wine
2 sticks celery, finely chopped	$\frac{1}{2}$ cup oyster liquor or water
2 tablespoons chopped parsley	freshly ground pepper
1 tablespoon chopped onion	chopped parsley or spring onions, to garnish
12 oysters	CREAM SAUCE:
$\frac{1}{2}$ cup soft white breadcrumbs	30 g (1 oz) butter
salt	1 tablespoon flour
8 small sole or flounder fillets	pan juices from fish
	$\frac{1}{2}$ cup cream

Heat the butter and sauté the celery, parsley and onion until soft. Chop the oysters. If using bottled oysters, drain them and reserve the liquor. Add the oysters and breadcrumbs to the vegetables and stir over a moderate heat for 30 seconds.

Salt the fillets lightly and divide the stuffing equally among them. Roll up and secure the ends with toothpicks. Arrange the rolls in a greased shallow baking dish and pour the wine and reserved oyster liquor or water over them. Cover and bake in a moderate oven (180°C/350°F) for 20 minutes, or until the fish is white and flakes when touched with a fork. Sprinkle lightly with pepper and remove to a warm platter.

Keep the cooking liquor to make the cream sauce. Melt the butter in a pan, add the flour and cook for 1 minute. Stir in the pan juices from the fish and the cream, and cook over a gentle heat for another minute. Check for seasoning and spoon over the rolls.

Serve at once, sprinkled with parsley or chopped spring onions.
Serves 4 to 6

Filleting Large Fish

1 Slit the fish down the back instead of the belly, and ease the top fillet off the backbone with the knife on a slant.

2 Open the fish out flat and cut off the fillet at the tail.

Filleting Flat Fish
Fish weighing approximately 500 g (1 lb) or more are usually filleted into 4 pieces.

1 Place the cleaned fish on a board with the tail facing you and cut down the centre on the backbone. Insert a thin knife between the flesh and the bone on the left of the backbone, and ease the flesh off. Turn the fish with the head facing you and remove another fillet in the same way.

2 Turn the fish over and repeat the process. Trim the fillets neatly and wash under cold running water. If desired, use the head, bones and skin to make fish stock. (Simmer in salted boiling water with a bouquet garni, sliced carrot and onion. Use for fish soup or sauces.)

3 Small flat fish are cut into 2 fillets. Place the fish on a board, tail towards you, and make a semi-circular cut below the head. Insert the knife between the flesh and the backbone and, working downwards, ease the flesh off in one wide fillet. Turn the fish over and repeat on the other side.

Poached Fish with Mushroom Sauce

Mushrooms have a natural affinity for fish, and the sauce for this recipe is an especially good one with its addition of egg yolk and cream.

1 bay leaf	*2 spring onions, chopped*
1 onion, sliced	*30 g (1 oz) butter*
6 peppercorns	*1 tablespoon chopped parsley*
2 teaspoons salt	*1 egg yolk*
2 cups water	*⅔ cup cream*
4 large or 8 small fish fillets	*salt*
MUSHROOM SAUCE:	*freshly ground pepper*
125 g (4 oz) mushrooms, sliced	

Place the bay leaf, onion, peppercorns, salt and water in a large frying pan. Bring to the boil and simmer for 5 minutes. Add the fish fillets and gently poach until cooked, about 6 to 8 minutes, depending on the thickness of the fish. Remove the fish to a heated platter and keep warm while making the mushroom sauce.

Sauté the mushrooms and onions in the butter for 3 to 4 minutes, remove from the heat and stir in the parsley. Mix the egg yolk with the cream and add to the mushrooms. Return to a low heat and stir until the sauce thickens. Season to taste with salt and freshly ground pepper. Spoon over the fish and serve at once. *Serves 4*

Variation

Reduce the quantity of water to 1 cup and add 1 cup white wine. Poach the fish in this, then drain and keep warm.

Strain the liquid and reduce a little by boiling. Combine ½ cup cream and 1 egg yolk and pour on a little of the reduced cooking liquid. Mix well, then add to ½ cup of the cooking liquid and heat gently, stirring until the sauce thickens. Season with salt and white pepper and serve instead of the mushroom sauce.

Fish Fillets Parmigiana

An Italian dish that's full of flavour and suitable for any kind of fish fillets or steaks. 'Parmigiana' in the title means, of course, that it contains Parmesan cheese.

4 fish fillets or steaks	*½ cup grated Parmesan cheese*
salt	*½ teaspoon dried oregano*
freshly ground pepper	*or basil*
1 × 425 g can tomatoes	*60 g (2 oz) butter, melted*

Place the fish in a greased shallow baking dish and season with salt and pepper. Chop the tomatoes and pour over the fish with the juice from the can. Sprinkle with the cheese and oregano or basil and pour the butter over. Bake in a preheated hot oven (200°C/400°F) for 15 to 20 minutes, or until the fish flakes easily when tested with a fork. *Serves 4*

Curried Fish Fillets

For this quick dish, fish fillets are coated in a spicy flour mixture, then quickly fried. Serve with rice and a few refreshing side dishes such as cucumbers with yogurt, tomato and onion salad, and bananas dipped in lemon juice and tossed in coconut. Little touches like these make a family meal special.

4 large fish fillets or cutlets	*1 teaspoon paprika*
3 tablespoons lemon juice	*oil for shallow frying*
1 teaspoon turmeric	*snipped chives or chopped*
2 teaspoons curry powder	*spring onions, to garnish*
½ cup flour	

Marinate the fish in the lemon juice for 10 minutes. Combine the turmeric, curry powder, flour and paprika in a flat dish. Dip the fish fillets in the flour mixture. Heat the oil and fry the fish for 4 to 5 minutes on each side, or until white and cooked through. Sprinkle with chives or spring onions to serve. *Serves 4*

With a pointed knife, ease the backbone off the other fillet and remove with the tail attached. If the 2 fillets are very large, each one can be cut diagonally in half to make conveniently sized portions.

Filleting Round Fish
1 Cut the head off (except with trout, where the head is often left on) and trim the fins with kitchen scissors. Slit the cleaned fish down the belly and open it out.

2 Spread the fish out flat on a board, skin side up, and press down firmly along the backbone to loosen it.

3 Turn the fish over and with a sharp pointed knife ease off the backbone, working from the head downwards. Lift the backbone off and the tail will come with it. Remove any other small bones and cut the fish down the centre into 2 fillets.

Pot Roasting for Tenderness

Pot roasting is a method of cooking large pieces of meat very slowly in a tightly covered pot until the meat is succulent and tender. It is very successful with the less tender and therefore relatively cheaper cuts of meat.

The meat is first browned all over in hot butter or oil to seal in the juices and give a rich colour, then a little stock or wine is added with seasonings and vegetables if desired. The pot is tightly covered and the meat cooked over a low heat in its own steam, allowing about 45 minutes per 500 g (1 lb).

The lovely juices that remain in the pot are served as a gravy, so a pot roast is a very simple dish to cook and a complete meal in itself if you have added vegetables.

When choosing a cut for pot roasting, try to buy a minimum of 1.5 kg (3 lb). Ask the butcher to tie it into shape, if necessary, or to cut a pocket if you wish to stuff it.

To Pot Roast Poultry

Pot roasting is an excellent way to tenderize a less than youthful bird, and also ensures tenderness in duck if you are not absolutely sure it is suitable for roasting. Truss the bird first into a good shape, then brown all over in a little hot oil, butter or bacon drippings. Turn the bird on its back and add a glass of wine, a cup of chicken stock, a chopped carrot and onion, and a bouquet garni. Season with salt and freshly ground pepper. Cover tightly, and cook over a low heat (or in a moderate oven) for 2 to 4 hours, until the bird is fork-tender. Serve with the juices poured over, or thicken them a little if desired.

Be Creative with your Pot Roasts

You can be as imaginative as you wish in your approach to pot roasting. The liquid can be wine, stock, canned consommé, tomato juice or a mixture. For pork and veal roasts, orange juice adds lovely flavour (and you can add grated orange rind as well). If you have fresh herbs in your garden, use them lavishly – but use a light hand with dried herbs. If the gravy seems too thin after cooking, stir in a little thick sour cream for thickening and extra flavour.

Pot-Roasted Vegetables

Vegetables can also be 'pot roasted' in the oven while the meat cooks to succulent tenderness. The general method is the same: sauté the vegetables of your choice in a little butter or oil, add seasonings and a small amount of liquid and cover tightly. Whole carrots, halved turnips, whole potatoes and sticks of celery are all delicious cooked this way. The liquid can be water, stock, wine or a mixture. Add snipped chives, fresh herbs or a little chopped ham as desired.

Suitable cuts for pot roasting include boned and rolled shoulder of lamb, forequarter joint of pork, rolled chuck steak, boned and rolled breast of lamb, boned and rolled fresh brisket of beef, fresh silverside of beef, boned and rolled breast of veal and topside of beef in the piece.

Rabbit Pot-Roasted in Cream

Rabbit is economical for a family meal, and this is a marvellously simple, but succulent, way of treating it.

1 rabbit
flour, seasoned with salt,
* pepper and paprika*
90 g (3 oz) butter

4 onions, thinly sliced
1 × 300 ml carton light sour
* cream*

Cut the rabbit into joints and dredge with seasoned flour. Heat the butter in a heavy flameproof casserole and brown the joints well on all sides. Add the onions and cream to the casserole, stir to get up the brown bits and cover tightly. Bake in a slow oven (150°C/300°F) for 1 hour, or until very tender. *Serves 4*

Pot-Roasted Beef with Vegetables

3 onions
6 medium carrots
2 tablespoons oil
1.5 kg (3 lb) beef topside,
* rolled fresh silverside or*
* flank*
1 clove garlic, crushed
½ cup red wine or beef stock

bouquet garni (3 sprigs of
* parsley, bay leaf, sprig of*
* thyme or rosemary, tied*
* inside a stick of celery)*
1 teaspoon salt
8 peppercorns
750 g (1½ lb) old potatoes
a little extra stock, if necessary

To prepare and cook, see step-by-step pictures at right. *Serves 6*

Pot-Roasted Beef with Vegetables

1 Peel and quarter the onions and scrape the carrots. Heat the oil in a heavy casserole or saucepan and brown the meat well on all sides, turning carefully to avoid piercing the flesh. Add the onions, garlic and carrots to the pan and turn over in the hot oil until lightly brown.

2 Add the wine or stock, bouquet garni, salt and peppercorns to the pan. Cover tightly, and cook over a very low heat for 1¼ hours. Peel the potatoes thinly and cut into halves or quarters if large. Arrange around the meat, replace the lid, and continue cooking for another 30 to 45 minutes until the meat is very tender. During this time, add a little more stock if the liquid has evaporated, but be sparing – there should never be more than half a cup. When the meat is cooked, place it on a heated platter and arrange the vegetables around it. Blot up any fat on the gravy with paper towels. Add extra seasoning if necessary, heat, and strain into a gravy boat.

Pot-Roasted Beef with Vegetables

Pot-Roasted Lamb

Use a boned leg of lamb for this dish, or the more economical boned shoulder. If you own an electric slow cooker you can put it on low before you leave for work and come home to a superb main course all ready to serve.

2 kg (4 lb) boned leg or shoulder of lamb	½ cup white wine or chicken stock
2 tablespoons oil	STUFFING:
1 onion, sliced	250 g (8 oz) sausage mince
2 sticks celery, sliced	1 onion, chopped
4 carrots, scraped	1 tablespoon chopped parsley
750 g (1½ lb) new potatoes, scrubbed	2 teaspoons chopped fresh oregano or ½ teaspoon dried
salt	1 clove garlic, crushed
freshly ground pepper	

Trim excess fat from the lamb. To make the stuffing, combine the sausage mince, onion, parsley, oregano and garlic and stuff the lamb with the mixture. Secure in place with string or skewers.

To cook the lamb, heat the oil in a heavy flameproof casserole or saucepan and brown the lamb all over. Add the vegetables to the pan, season with salt and pepper, and pour in the wine or stock. Cover tightly and cook over a low heat for 2 hours, or until the lamb is very tender. The lamb may also be cooked for 2 hours in a moderate oven (180°C/350°F) or in a slow cooker set at the lowest heat for 7 to 8 hours. Serve the lamb sliced, with the cooking juices poured over and accompanied by the vegetables. *Serves 6*

Pot-Roasted Stuffed Beef

2 kg (4 lb) topside in the piece	1 onion, sliced
250 g (8 oz) sausage mince	2 sticks celery, sliced
1 onion, chopped	4 carrots, scraped
1 tablespoon chopped parsley	1 kg (2 lb) new potatoes, scrubbed
1 tablespoon chopped fresh marjoram or ½ teaspoon dried	1 cup red wine
2 tablespoons oil	salt
1 clove garlic, crushed	freshly ground pepper

Cut a pocket in the meat. Mix the mince, chopped onion, parsley and marjoram together and stuff into the pocket. Secure the roast with string or skewers. Heat the oil in a large flameproof casserole and brown the meat on all sides. Add the garlic, sliced onion, celery, carrots, potatoes and wine, and season to taste with salt and pepper. Cover tightly and bake in a moderate oven (180°C/350°F) or simmer for 2 to 2½ hours, until the meat is tender. Serve with the pan juices. *Serves 6 to 8*

Pot-Roasted Duck in Burgundy

1 duckling, about 2.5 kg (5 lb)	freshly ground pepper
60 g (2 oz) butter	1 cup burgundy
1 large onion, finely chopped	2 tablespoons redcurrant jelly
salt	

Cut the duckling into quarters and pat dry. Heat the butter in a flameproof casserole and brown the pieces slowly on all sides. Add the onion, salt and pepper to taste, and the burgundy. Stir

well to get the brown bits up from the bottom. Cover the casserole tightly and bake in a moderate oven (180°C/350°F) for 1 hour, or until the duck is tender. Remove the duck to a warm platter. Stir the redcurrant jelly into the cooking liquid and reduce by rapid boiling, if necessary, until the sauce is the right consistency. Strain the sauce over the duck. *Serves 4*

Pot-Roasted Veal

1.5–2 kg (3–4 lb) breast of veal	½ cup grated, well-flavoured cheese
salt	¼ cup fine breadcrumbs
freshly ground pepper	90 g (3 oz) butter, melted
4 spring onions, finely chopped	½ cup chicken stock or dry white wine
1 cup chopped ham	

Ask your butcher to remove the bones from the veal. Spread the meat out flat, skin side down, and season with salt and pepper. Sprinkle with the spring onions, ham, cheese and breadcrumbs. Pour half the melted butter over the stuffing, then roll the veal up tightly and tie securely with string.

Heat the remaining butter in a heavy flameproof casserole and brown the veal on all sides. Pour in the stock or wine, cover the casserole tightly and cook over a low heat for 2 to 2½ hours, or until the meat is very tender. It may also be cooked for the same time in a moderate oven (180°C/350°F). During the cooking time, check now and again to make sure the liquid hasn't evaporated. Add a little more stock or wine, if necessary.

Remove the meat to a wooden board, cut away the string and slice thickly. Place on a heated serving platter and keep warm. Blot up any excess fat from the gravy with absorbent paper towels; taste for seasoning, and reheat. Pour over the meat to serve. *Serves 6 to 8*

Pot-Roasted Veal Shanks

Veal shanks are an economical buy for a family meal. Have them sawn in half if you don't have a pot big enough to take them; and don't forget the turnips, they add lovely flavour.

3 tablespoons oil (olive for preference)	2 bay leaves
6 veal shanks	6 medium potatoes, peeled
6 small carrots, scraped	3 turnips, peeled and cut into quarters
6 small onions, peeled	1 cup dry white wine
2 cloves garlic, crushed	salt
2 sticks celery, thinly sliced	freshly ground pepper
4 ripe tomatoes, peeled, seeded and chopped	chopped parsley, to garnish
1 tablespoon chopped fresh thyme or 1 teaspoon dried	

Heat the oil in a large heavy casserole or saucepan. Brown the shanks slowly on all sides (you will have to do this in batches). Add the remaining ingredients to the pan except the parsley, seasoning well with salt and pepper. Cover tightly and cook over a low heat for 1½ to 2 hours, until the meat is very tender. Remove the shanks and vegetables to a heated serving platter, discarding the bay leaves. Spoon off any fat that is on the surface of the liquid, or blot with absorbent paper towels. If the gravy seems too thin, reduce by rapid boiling to a good consistency, then pour over the meat. Sprinkle with chopped parsley and serve. *Serves 6*

Pot-Roasted Lamb

Pot-Roasted Pork with Madeira

Serve this for a special occasion. A hand of pork is richly flavoured and tender cooked with vegetables and fruity Madeira wine.

1 hand of pork, skinned and boned	*½ teaspoon thyme*
60 g (2 oz) butter	*1 bay leaf*
2 onions, finely chopped	*salt*
2 carrots, finely chopped	*freshly ground pepper*
4 sticks celery, finely chopped	*1 cup Madeira*
125 g (4 oz) mushrooms, finely sliced (including stalks)	*chopped parsley, to garnish*

Ask the butcher to skin and bone the hand of pork. Remove any fat from the pork. Heat the butter in a heavy saucepan or flameproof casserole and add the onions, carrots, celery and mushrooms. Cook over a medium heat until the vegetables are soft but not brown, stirring often. Place the pork on top of the vegetables, add the thyme and bay leaf to the pan, and season with salt and pepper. Pour in the Madeira, cover tightly, and cook over a low heat for 2 hours, or until the meat is very tender.

Remove the meat and keep warm. Discard the bay leaf and purée the sauce and vegetables in a blender, or push through a sieve. Slice the meat and arrange on a heated platter. Reheat the sauce to boiling, taste for seasoning and adjust if necessary, and pour over the meat. Sprinkle with parsley to serve. *Serves 4 to 6*
NOTE: Tiny new potatoes steamed in their skins would be good with this, or your family might like buttered rice or noodles.

Heart-Warming Stews and Casseroles

There is something about the aroma of a stew rich with meat and vegetables, or a savoury brown casserole, that says 'welcome home'. Our mothers and grandmothers made these dishes beautifully, understanding that time was the key to success. Stews and casseroles are not to be rushed; they need long, slow cooking to produce fork-tender meat and a perfect blend of flavours.

Today, we have automatic oven timers, electric slow cookers and heating elements that can be adjusted to the gentlest simmer – it's not necessary for us to be there all the time to supervise the bubbling pot! Instead, stews and casseroles are good friends to the busy cook. They can be prepared ahead and reheated – and often taste better for it.

Opposite: Flemish Carbonnade of Beef
Below: Many cuts are suitable for stewing. Starting from the top clockwise, suggestions are breast of lamb, best lamb neck chops, scrag end chops, neck of pork on the bone, pork belly, blade steak and gravy beef, breast of veal, knuckle of veal and veal cut from leg.

Most recipes for these lovely slow-cooked dishes are interchangeable and can be cooked on top of the stove or in the oven. However, unlike pot roasts, the meat for stews and casseroles is not left in one piece but is cut into bite-size portions and completely covered with the liquid. It is usually browned first and seasonings and vegetables added with wine or stock.

A flameproof casserole dish with a tight-fitting lid is ideal for stews and casseroles. The meat can be browned in it, the cooking can be done on top of the stove or in the oven; and finally, the casserole can be taken straight to the dining table for serving. No pans to clean!

Old-Fashioned Steak and Mushrooms

This is delicious on its own with creamy mashed potatoes and a green vegetable, or can be used as a pie filling. For a pie, allow it to cool before enclosing in pastry.

1 kg (2 lb) stewing steak	*freshly ground pepper*
2–3 tablespoons flour	*1 tablespoon chopped fresh*
60 g (2 oz) butter	*herbs or ½ teaspoon dried*
1 onion, chopped	*beef stock or water to cover*
250 g (8 oz) mushrooms	*chopped parsley, to garnish*
salt	

Remove any fat and gristle from the meat and cut into bite-size squares. Toss in the flour, shaking off any surplus. Heat the butter in a heavy flameproof casserole or saucepan and fry the onion until soft. Add the meat and stir over a medium heat until brown. Add the mushrooms and cook for 1 minute. Season with salt and pepper to taste, add the herbs and pour in enough stock or water to come just to the top of the meat. Cover tightly and simmer until the meat is very tender, about 1½ to 2 hours.

Turn into a heated serving dish and sprinkle with chopped parsley. *Serves 6*

Kidney and Beer Stew

Kidneys make a superb stew to serve over rice or noodles.

2 small ox kidneys	*½ cup beer*
lemon juice	*2 tablespoons tomato paste*
60 g (2 oz) butter	*salt*
2 tablespoons flour	*freshly ground pepper*
½ cup beef stock or canned	*chopped parsley, to garnish*
consommé	

Skin the kidneys and cut out the central core. Cover with cold water, add a good squeeze of lemon juice and leave for 30 minutes. Drain and pat dry, then cut into wafer thin slices.

Sauté the kidneys in hot butter for 3 to 4 minutes, stirring, just until the pink tinge has gone. Remove with a slotted spoon. Stir the flour into the pan drippings, then pour in the stock and beer and stir until smooth. Add the tomato paste, and salt and pepper to taste. Return the kidneys to the pan and stir until heated through. Sprinkle with parsley to serve. *Serves 6*

Some Hints on Marinating

A marinade is an aromatic liquid in which meat is soaked before cooking. The actual soaking is called 'marinating'. A marinade adds flavour to food and helps to give a good colour, and to tenderize tougher meats.

As a general rule, meat cut into pieces for stews or casseroles should be soaked only for 2 or 3 hours; left too long, it may absorb too much of the pungent liquid and lose some of its own character.

Cooking marinated meat: After marinating the meat for the specified time, drain and pat dry with absorbent paper towels; then brown the meat in a little butter or oil. Add vegetables and seasonings as desired, and enough liquid barely to cover the meat. Simmer on top of the stove or bake in a moderate oven, tightly covered, until the meat is tender. The liquid used can be stock or wine, or a mixture of stock or wine and the marinade. Before serving, it can be thickened if necessary with cream, sour cream or beurre manié (equal quantities of flour and butter mixed together).

As a marinade almost always contains an acid ingredient (to help in tenderizing) use a glass, stainless steel, plastic or enamel dish for marinating and stir with a wooden spoon.

Flemish Carbonnade of Beef

The beer and mustard give a unique flavour to this international favourite, with its crusty French bread topping.

750 g (1½ lb) topside or round	*salt*
steak, cut into thin slices	*freshly ground pepper*
2 tablespoons oil	*bouquet garni (3 sprigs*
4 onions, sliced	*parsley, 1 bay leaf, sprig of*
125 g (4 oz) mushrooms, sliced	*thyme, tied together)*
2 tablespoons flour	*butter for spreading*
2 teaspoons brown sugar	*6 thick slices French bread*
1 cup beer	*Dijon-style mustard*
about 1 cup beef stock	

Trim the fat from the meat and cut into strips about 4 × 5 cm (1½ × 2 inches). Heat the oil in a heavy flameproof casserole and fry the beef strips over a fairly high heat until browned on both sides. Remove the meat from the casserole with a slotted spoon. Turn the heat to medium and fry the onions and mushrooms until the onions are soft. Remove the casserole from the heat and stir in the flour and sugar. Return to the stove, stir for 1 minute, then gradually add the beer. Bring to the boil, add the meat strips and enough stock to come just to the top of the meat. Season to taste with salt and pepper and add the bouquet garni. Cover the casserole and cook in a moderately slow oven (160°C/325°F) for 1½ hours.

Spread butter generously on one side of the bread slices and mustard on the other. Arrange the slices, buttered side up, on top of the meat and return to the oven for a further 20 or 30 minutes, or until the meat is very tender and the bread crusty on top. (Don't cover the casserole this time.)

Serve from the dish, with green vegetables. *Serves 4 to 6*

Italian Lamb Stew

Lamb flavoured with bacon, tomatoes and herbs and cooked in a little red wine makes a fine main course (casks make cooking with wine an everyday affair). Serve with noodles, crusty bread and a crisp green salad for an Italian-style family meal.

1 kg (2 lb) boneless lamb, cut from leg or shoulder	1 teaspoon chopped fresh marjoram or ½ teaspoon dried
2 tablespoons oil	
250 g (8 oz) bacon, diced	1 teaspoon chopped fresh rosemary or ¼ teaspoon dried
1 onion, sliced	
2 cloves garlic, crushed	½ cup red wine
salt	2 tablespoons tomato paste
freshly ground pepper	extra 2 tablespoons red wine

Trim excess fat from the lamb and cut into bite-size squares. Heat the oil in a large heavy frying pan. Add the bacon, onion and garlic and sauté until golden. Remove with a slotted spoon and set aside. Add half the meat and brown on all sides, then remove from the pan and repeat with the remaining meat. Return the meat to the pan and season with salt, pepper, marjoram and rosemary. Stir in the red wine and cook gently until the wine reduces to half its original quantity. Add the bacon mixture, tomato paste and enough water to cover the meat. Cover and simmer slowly for about 1½ hours or until tender. Add the 2 tablespoons red wine just before serving for extra flavour. Serve with flat ribbon noodles or fluffy boiled rice. *Serves 4 to 6*

Casseroled Whole Fish

If there is a fisherman in the family, or you live near a fish market, you may get the opportunity to cook a whole snapper or jewfish now and again. This is a change from the usual stuffed baked fish, giving you a delectable sauce to enjoy with crusty bread and butter, rice or noodles.

1 whole fish, about 2 kg (4 lb), head and tail removed	1 sprig parsley
	1 bay leaf
lemon juice	sprig of fresh thyme or pinch of dried
1 onion, finely sliced	
1 carrot, finely sliced	1 cup fish stock or water
125 g (4 oz) mushrooms, sliced (including stalks)	½ cup dry white wine
	1 cup cream
salt	watercress sprigs or chopped spring onions, to garnish
freshly ground pepper	

Wipe the fish inside and out with a cloth dipped in lemon juice. Arrange the onion, carrot and mushrooms in the bottom of a shallow flameproof casserole. Place the fish on top of the vegetables, season well with salt and pepper and add the parsley, bay leaf, thyme, fish stock or water and wine. Cover tightly and bake in a moderately hot oven (190°C/375°F) for 40 to 60 minutes, or until the fish is white and opaque all the way through at the thickest part.

Transfer the fish carefully to a heated serving platter, remove the skin and keep warm. Cook the liquid in the baking dish over a high heat until it is reduced by two-thirds. Stir in the cream, taste for seasoning, and reheat but do not boil. Strain the sauce over the fish and serve at once, garnished with watercress sprigs or chopped spring onions. *Serves 4 to 6*
NOTE: The head and tail are usually left on for baking but are normally removed for casseroling. Leave them on if you prefer the splendid look of the fish intact.

Peruvian-Style Roast Pork

Pork is often combined with fresh or dried fruits, as in this interesting dish from South America. The same marinade could also be used for cubed veal.

6 pork chops, forequarter or large loin	1 cup seeded raisins
	2 tablespoons fresh breadcrumbs
1 tablespoon salt	
60 g (2 oz) butter, melted	MARINADE:
½ cup milk	¼ cup dry white wine
½ teaspoon cinnamon	4 whole cloves
½ teaspoon nutmeg	2½ tablespoons brown sugar

Rub the chops all over with salt and allow to stand for 20 minutes. Combine the marinade ingredients in a shallow dish and add the meat. Leave in the refrigerator for 24 hours, covered with foil, spooning the marinade over now and again.

Remove the meat and pat dry with absorbent paper towels. Add the melted butter, milk, spices and raisins to the marinade and mix well together. Place the chops in a baking dish or casserole just large enough to hold them comfortably, and cover with the marinade mixture. Sprinkle with the breadcrumbs and bake in a moderate oven (180°C/350°F) for 2 hours, tightly covered with a lid or aluminium foil. From time to time, lift the lid and spoon some of the juices over the meat. Serve with the pan gravy spooned over the pork. *Serves 4 to 6*
NOTE: The meat is not browned after marinating, as it is cooked in milk and should be a creamy-pale colour when finished.

Turlu

This is a rich stew from Turkey, brimming over with vegetables. Okra, or ladies' fingers, are an optional addition. These intriguingly shaped vegetables are making their way into some greengrocers and are also available in cans.

750 g (1½ lb) boneless lamb, cut from leg or shoulder	250 g (8 oz) okra (ladies' fingers), optional
2 onions	2 tablespoons olive oil
1 large eggplant	about 2 cups chicken stock (or stock cubes and water)
1 green and 1 red pepper	
4 zucchini	salt
250 g (8 oz) green beans	freshly ground pepper
4 ripe tomatoes	

Remove excess fat from the lamb and cut into bite-size pieces. Prepare the vegetables: peel and slice the onions; cut the unpeeled eggplant into cubes; seed the peppers and cut into squares; top and tail the zucchini and beans and cut into slices; peel and seed the tomatoes and roughly chop; and trim the okra by removing the top stem, but leave whole. (If using canned okra, rinse in cold water.)

Heat the oil in a large, heavy flameproof casserole or saucepan and slowly brown the meat on all sides. Add the onions and brown them, stirring constantly. Pour in enough stock to come just to the top of the meat, cover, and simmer until the meat is almost tender, about 50 minutes. Add all the vegetables to the meat with the remaining stock; taste the liquid and season well with salt and pepper to taste. Replace the lid and simmer until the vegetables are cooked and the meat is very tender, about another 40 minutes. Serve with boiled rice. *Serves 4*

Italian Lamb Stew

Honey-Ginger Lamb

A Roast makes a Meal Special

For most families, the sight and smell of a roast leg of lamb or a glistening brown sirloin of beef is all that's needed to make a meal very special indeed. However, with the climbing prices of meat, a roast is becoming more and more of a treat these days; so it is worthwhile knowing how to get the best from the meat you buy.

A plain roasted, juicy joint of meat has its own delicious natural flavour which is hard to surpass; but there are cheaper cuts which achieve distinction with stuffings or added flavourings. Served with the traditional gravy and vegetables, these cheaper cuts have the special appeal of a roast and are economical enough to be served more often.

On these pages you will find advice and recipes for roasting the traditional cuts of meat, and ideas for some of these useful budget roasts as well.

To Roast Meat

Cooking times for roast meat may vary a little; use the times given here as a guide unless a recipe states otherwise. The times in the following recipes are for medium-done meat. To check how well the meat is cooked, insert a fine skewer into the thickest part and note the colour of the juice that comes out. If red, the meat is rare; if pink, medium; if clear, well-done.

Place the meat to be roasted on a greased rack set in a greased roasting dish and roast, uncovered, in the centre of the oven. Set the meat with the fattest side up so that the fat runs over the rest of the joint.

Meat which has a good layer of fat does not need basting while it roasts, as its own fat is sufficient. Leaner meat should be rubbed with butter and basted with the buttery pan juices at regular intervals to keep it moist. Another method is to place strips of streaky bacon over the top of the meat as it roasts – this is particularly good with veal or rabbit.

When meat is done, rest it in a warm place for 10 to 20 minutes (the larger the joint, the longer the resting time) before carving. This is not just a frill, it makes all the difference to juiciness, ease of carving and evenness of cooking throughout the meat.

Roast Beef Allow 20 minutes per 500 g (1 lb) plus 20 minutes extra. Temperature: 220°C/425°F for 20 minutes, then reduce to 180°C/350°F. Baste with the pan juices every 20 minutes.

Roast Lamb Allow 25 minutes per 500 g (1 lb) plus 25 minutes extra. Temperature: 220°C/425°F for 20 minutes, then reduce to 180°C/350°F. Baste with the pan juices every 20 minutes.

Roast Pork Allow 25 minutes per 500 g (1 lb) plus 25 to 30 minutes extra. Temperature: 230°C/450°F for 25 to 30 minutes (until rind blisters) then reduce to 190°C/375°F. Rub a little salt into the rind, which should be well scored, before roasting. Do not baste if you want crisp crackling.

Roast Veal Allow 45 minutes per 500 g (1 lb). Temperature: 160°C/325°F for the whole cooking time. As veal has little fat of its own, spread with a little butter or margarine or cover with bacon before roasting, and baste every 10 minutes with the pan juices.

To Roast Frozen Meat

To time meat accurately, it should preferably be at room temperature before placing in the oven, and the oven should be preheated to the required temperature. Always defrost frozen meat in the original wrapping and, if possible, on the refrigerator shelf. Allow 5 hours defrosting for each 500 g (1 lb) for thick cuts, and about half that time if defrosting at room temperature. If you wish to cook large unthawed cuts of meat, allow approximately one and a half times the usual cooking time for fresh meat.

Orange-Glazed Lamb

Ask the butcher to remove excess fat from a boned shoulder, and to roll and tie it. Mix together $\frac{1}{2}$ cup orange juice, $\frac{1}{2}$ cup orange marmalade and 1 tablespoon lemon juice and put in a roasting dish. Baste the lamb with this mixture two or three times during roasting, and serve with the pan juices poured over (first blotting up surface fat with paper towels).
NOTE: It may be necessary to add a little water to the pan if the liquid has evaporated too much. Don't neglect to scrape up the good brown crusty bits on the bottom and to correct the seasoning.

Honey-Ginger Lamb

Roast a boned and rolled shoulder of lamb for 45 minutes. Meanwhile, mix together $\frac{1}{2}$ cup honey, 2 tablespoons lemon juice, 1 tablespoon soy sauce, a pinch of ground cloves and 1 teaspoon ground ginger (it is easier to mix if you warm the honey first). Brush the lamb with this mixture frequently during the rest of the cooking time, turning it over and brushing all sides. Remove the fat from the pan juices and add stock or vegetable water to make a gravy. Sweet potatoes would be an excellent accompaniment.

Persian Lamb with Yogurt

Ask your butcher to bone the shoulder and to score the surface fat in a diamond pattern. Combine 2 tablespoons lemon juice, $\frac{1}{4}$ teaspoon ground cardamom, $\frac{1}{2}$ teaspoon ground coriander and $\frac{1}{2}$ cup natural yogurt. Spread the lamb out flat and pat the mixture into it on both sides. Allow to stand for an hour or so, then roll up, tie firmly and roast for 1 hour.

Heat 30 g (1 oz) butter in a small frying pan and fry 1 chopped onion and $\frac{1}{4}$ teaspoon ground ginger, until the onion is soft and golden. Spread over the surface of the meat and continue to roast, basting with the pan juices, until the meat is cooked.

Skim the fat from the pan juices and add enough milk to make a gravy, scraping up the brown bits from the bottom and seasoning to taste with salt and pepper.

French Farmer's Lamb

A leg of lamb baked in chicken stock with lots of garlic is the kind of hearty dish French families have enjoyed for generations. Try it on your family as an exciting change from the usual roast lamb with mint sauce.

30 g (1 oz) butter, for greasing
1 leg of lamb, about 2.5 kg (5 lb)
4 cloves garlic, peeled and cut into thin slivers
6 large potatoes, peeled and cut into thick slices
salt
freshly ground pepper
2 large onions, sliced
1 cup chopped parsley
2 cups rich chicken stock, or use canned consommé

Generously butter a shallow casserole just wide enough to take the leg of lamb comfortably. Make tiny incisions all over the skin of the lamb and insert half the slivers of garlic.

Arrange the potatoes in overlapping rows on the bottom of the dish, season well with salt and pepper, add the onions and the remaining garlic, and season again. Sprinkle with the chopped parsley.

Place the lamb on top of the vegetables and pour over the stock. Roast, uncovered, in a moderately slow oven (160°C/325°F) for 2 hours for tender pink lamb or about $2\frac{1}{2}$ hours for well done. Baste every 20 minutes with the pan juices while the lamb is cooking.

Remove the lamb to a platter when cooked to your liking, and allow to rest for 20 minutes before carving. (Keep the casserole warm in a slow oven.)

Serve the lamb cut in slices, with the vegetables and pan juices. *Serves 6*

Variation

Instead of potatoes, the lamb can be placed on a bed of butter beans, with the onions and garlic. Use 2 × 310 g cans, rinsed in cold water and drained.

Fresh Silverside in Foil

Fresh silverside is a budget cut which makes a delicious roast. This is also an excellent way to cook a piece of bolar blade. Ask your butcher which he recommends on the day. There is no waste with either cut and leftovers are delicious for school lunches.

2 kg (4 lb) fresh silverside
1 clove garlic, crushed
1 packet French onion soup
a little dry mustard

Place the meat on a piece of aluminium foil large enough to wrap around it. Spread the top with half the garlic and sprinkle with half the soup mix and a little mustard, patting the flavourings in with a broad-bladed knife. Turn over and repeat on the other side.

Wrap the meat loosely in the foil, sealing the edges well, and place in a baking dish. Roast in a preheated moderately hot oven (190°C/375°F) for 1 hour 40 minutes. Carefully unwrap the meat and remove to a heated platter. Pour the juices that have collected back into the baking dish and add enough hot water to give a nice gravy consistency. Reheat, taste for seasoning, and pour into a sauce boat. Carve the meat in thin slices and serve with gravy, jacket-baked potatoes and green peas. *Serves 6 to 8*

Apple Sauce Beef Loaf

Economical minced beef makes a special family roast when it's topped with apple sauce and baked in a round container. The sauce can be homemade, or use a 130 g can baby apple sauce.

$1\frac{1}{2}$ cups soft white breadcrumbs
2 eggs, beaten
$\frac{1}{2}$ cup apple sauce
1 small onion, finely chopped
3 tender sticks celery, finely chopped
1 tablespoon Dijon-style mustard
salt
freshly ground pepper
750 g ($1\frac{1}{2}$ lb) lean minced beef

TOPPING:
$\frac{1}{2}$ cup apple sauce
$1\frac{1}{2}$ tablespoons brown sugar
1 teaspoon Dijon-style mustard
2 teaspoons vinegar

Combine all the ingredients for the meat loaf and mix thoroughly. Pat into a round shape and place in a shallow baking dish. Roast in a moderate oven (180°C/350°F) for 30 minutes, then turn over to brown the other side, using an egg slice or wide spatula. Pour off any excess fat from the dish and roast for a further 20 minutes. Meanwhile, mix the topping ingredients together and spoon over the top of the loaf. Bake for a further 10 minutes, then remove the dish from the oven and allow to rest for 5 minutes before cutting into wedges to serve. *Serves 6*

Little Pork Roasts

Forequarter pork chops are 'sandwiched' with a savoury stuffing for extra flavour. This dish is economical and easy to serve.

4 forequarter pork chops, cut fairly thin	15 g (½ oz) butter, melted
salt	1 tablespoon chopped fresh herbs or ½ teaspoon dried (thyme, basil, oregano)
freshly ground pepper	1 cup soft white breadcrumbs
1 small onion, finely chopped	1 teaspoon sugar
2 sticks celery, finely chopped	
8 soft dessert prunes, pitted and chopped	

Trim excess fat from the chops and snip round the edges two or three times with kitchen scissors to prevent them curling during roasting. Sprinkle the chops with a little salt and pepper.

Mix all the remaining ingredients together to make a stuffing, seasoning with salt and pepper. Divide the stuffing between two of the chops, then put the other two chops on top to make 'sandwiches'. Place the stuffed chops in a roasting pan, add 1 cup water and roast in a moderate oven (180°C/350°F) for 30 minutes. Using a spatula or egg slice, carefully turn the chops over and continue roasting for another 30 minutes. Cut each 'sandwich' in two. Serve at once with jacket-baked potatoes and a green vegetable. *Serves 4*
NOTE: This recipe also works well with large forequarter lamb chops. Add a little chopped mint to the stuffing and a chopped apple instead of prunes.

Stuffed Roast Pork

Pork belly stuffed and roasted has all the flavour of a more expensive cut and lots of crunchy crackling.

1.25 kg (2½ lb) pork belly in one piece	2 teaspoons chopped fresh sage or ¼ teaspoon dried
salt	1 egg, beaten
STUFFING:	1½ teaspoons salt
250 g (8 oz) veal and pork mince or sausage mince	freshly ground pepper
4 cups fresh white breadcrumbs	GRAVY:
1 small onion, finely chopped	1 tablespoon flour
8 prunes, pitted and chopped	1½ cups stock, vegetable water or water
1 teaspoon grated lemon rind	salt
	freshly ground pepper

Ask your butcher to bone the pork and score the rind. With a sharp knife, carefully cut a slit right through the centre of the meat to form a tunnel for the stuffing. This is easier to do if you start cutting from both ends, meeting in the middle.

Place all the stuffing ingredients in a bowl and mix well. Fill the cavity in the pork with the stuffing mixture and close each end with a skewer. Rub the rind with a little salt.

Grease a roasting pan large enough to take the pork lying flat, and put the meat in skin side up. Roast in a preheated very hot oven (230°C/450°F) for 25 to 30 minutes, until the skin has blistered. Reduce the heat to moderately hot (190°C/375°F) and continue cooking for 45 minutes. Remove the meat and keep warm while making the gravy. Pour off all but 1½ tablespoons of the fat from the pan, add the flour and stir over a moderate heat until brown. Pour in the stock or water and bring to the boil, stirring constantly until thick. Season to taste with salt and pepper and strain into a sauce boat. Remove the skewers from the pork and serve with the hot gravy. *Serves 6 to 8*

Beef Stuffed with Pork

A piece of topside steak is stuffed with pork mince and baked. Easy to carve, not too expensive and special enough for a family celebration.

1.5 kg (3 lb) topside steak, in one piece	½ teaspoon salt
250 g (8 oz) pork mince	½ teaspoon dried thyme
1 clove garlic, crushed	freshly ground pepper
1 medium onion, finely chopped	1 egg
½ cup sliced stuffed olives	3 slices wholemeal bread, soaked in ¼ cup milk
	2 tablespoons olive oil

Cut the steak in two, almost through, and butterfly (open up). Mix the remaining ingredients, except the oil, and spread over the steak. Reshape the meat and sew up with heavy thread. Rub all over with the oil and place in a greased roasting pan. Roast in a moderate oven (180°C/350°F) for about 1¾ hours, or until the meat is tender and the stuffing is cooked. Remove the thread before carving and pour the skimmed pan drippings over. *Serves 6*

Roast Stuffed Rabbit

Many butcher shops and delicatessens stock rabbit. It's as delicious as chicken when stuffed and roasted; but it can be a dry meat, so don't neglect the bacon and the frequent basting if you want tender, juicy flesh.

1 rabbit	1 onion, finely chopped
30 g (1 oz) butter	1 stick celery, finely chopped
3 rashers bacon	¼ teaspoon dried thyme
1 cup or more red wine or stock	¼ teaspoon dried sage
STUFFING:	salt
1 rasher bacon, chopped	freshly ground pepper
30 g (1 oz) butter, melted	

Wipe the rabbit over with damp paper towels. Place all the stuffing ingredients in a bowl and mix well. Fill the body cavity with the stuffing mixture and close with skewers.

Heat the butter in a flameproof casserole (just big enough to hold the rabbit comfortably) and brown the rabbit slowly on all sides. Cut the bacon rashers in halves and place over the rabbit. Pour the wine or stock into the casserole and cover tightly with a lid or aluminium foil. Roast the rabbit in a preheated moderate oven (180°C/350°F) until tender, about 1½ hours. (A fine skewer should slide easily into the thickest part of the leg and the juices run clear.) While the rabbit is cooking, baste frequently with the pan juices, adding more wine or stock if necessary.

Remove the rabbit and keep warm. Strain the juices into a small saucepan and reduce to gravy consistency by rapid boiling. Taste and adjust the seasoning and, if desired, add the bacon rashers (rind removed and finely chopped). Serve the rabbit with gravy, creamy mashed potatoes and green beans. *Serves 4*
Variation
Like pork, chicken and veal, rabbit also takes very well to fruity flavours. When making the gravy, you might like to add a sharp-sweet touch by stirring 2 tablespoons plum jam, 1 tablespoon brown sugar and 1 tablespoon lemon juice into the pan juices. Bring to the boil, stirring, then continue cooking over a high heat until it is the right consistency. Taste for seasoning before straining into a sauce boat.

Stuffed Roast Pork

Roast Veal with Vegetables

Cooked this way, veal makes its own lovely gravy.

90 g (3 oz) butter	2 kg (4 lb) shoulder of veal,
1 tablespoon chopped fresh	boned
thyme or ½ teaspoon dried	12 small onions, peeled
pinch of ground cloves	2 tablespoons flour
salt	hot water
freshly ground pepper	6 small carrots, scraped
3 tablespoons lemon juice	6 small potatoes, scrubbed

Mix together half the butter, the thyme, cloves, salt and pepper
to taste, and the lemon juice. Rub this mixture all over the veal,
then roll up and tie into a neat shape.

Melt the remaining butter in a flameproof baking dish. Add
the onions and gently brown them; then add the veal and brown
on all sides. Sprinkle the veal with flour, pour in 1 cup hot water
and roast in a moderately slow oven (160°C/325°F) for 1 hour,
basting frequently with the pan drippings. Add the carrots and
potatoes and continue cooking and basting, adding more hot
water if necessary.

When the veal is cooked (about 3 hours altogether), remove
the meat and vegetables and keep warm. Add enough hot water
to the baking dish to make about a cup of gravy, scraping up the
brown bits from the bottom. Check the seasoning and strain into
a sauce boat. Remove the string from the meat and serve cut in
slices. *Serves 6*

Loin of Veal with Rosemary

1 loin of veal, about	90 g (3 oz) butter, softened
2.5 kg (5 lb)	1 cup dry white wine
salt	
freshly ground pepper	
1 tablespoon crumbled fresh	
rosemary or 2 teaspoons	
dried	

Ask your butcher to bone and trim the veal. Season generously
with salt and pepper, then rub on both sides with the rosemary
and butter. Roll up and tie into a neat shape with white string.
Place in a baking dish, pour the wine over, and roast in a
moderate oven (180°C/350°F), allowing 30 minutes per
500 g (1 lb) or until done to your liking. Baste with the pan juices
every 20 minutes. Remove the string and serve cut in slices with
the juices poured over. *Serves 6*

Favourite Family Pies

Steak and Kidney Pie

1 Roll the pastry out to 5 mm (¼ inch) thick. Cut an oval about 2.5 cm (1 inch) larger than the top of the pie plate. Cut a strip from the outside edge, dampen it and press into position around the edge of the plate. Also dampen the ends of the strip and join together.

2 Put a pie funnel in the centre of the dish, to prevent pastry becoming soggy. Pack the cold filling around it. Moisten the top of the pastry strip. Roll the pastry lid over a rolling pin, then unroll it to cover the filling.

3 Press the pastry lid firmly in place, making sure it is joined to the strip underneath. If necessary, trim any overlap with a sharp knife.

4 Press the pastry lid out towards the edges of the pie dish with a finger. At the same time, holding a knife horizontally, lightly tap the cut edges of the pastry. This will give a flaky, attractive finish to the edge of the finished pie and is called 'knocking up' the pastry.

5 Flute the edge by pressing down with the thumb and pulling the pastry back towards the dish with the back of a knife held vertically in the other hand. Pull the pastry with the knife, do not cut it.

6 Pierce a hole through the centre of the pastry into the pie funnel, so the steam can escape. Also cut a small slit in the pastry on each side of the funnel. Brush the top with beaten egg, but not the flaked edges (if brushed with egg they won't rise).

Steak and Kidney Pie

875 g (1¾ lb) lean stewing steak (chuck or blade)
5 lambs' kidneys or ½ an ox kidney
3 tablespoons flour
60 g (2 oz) butter
1 large onion, chopped
good pinch of nutmeg
1 tablespoon Worcestershire sauce
beef stock to cover
salt
freshly ground pepper
250 g (8 oz) frozen puff pastry, thawed (this is half the usual 500 g/1 lb packet)
parsley sprigs, to garnish

Remove any fat and gristle from the meat and cut into bite-size cubes. Skin the kidneys, cut out the fatty core and slice thinly or dice. Place the flour in a paper bag and toss the steak and kidney until coated, then shake off any excess.

Melt the butter in a large heavy frying pan or flameproof casserole and fry the onion until soft and golden. Add the steak and kidney and fry until brown, stirring frequently. Season with nutmeg and Worcestershire sauce and add enough stock to cover the meat. Cover the pan and simmer gently until the meat is tender, about 1½ to 2 hours. Taste, and add salt and freshly ground pepper as required. Allow to cool, then refrigerate. The fat on the surface can easily be lifted off before making the pie.

Place a pie funnel in the centre of a 5-cup pie dish. This is to make a vent so the steam can escape during baking. Pack the cold filling around the funnel and follow the step-by-step instructions which show you how to cover the pie with pastry and add the decorations.

Place the pie on a baking sheet and bake in a preheated hot oven (220°C/425°F) for 10 minutes, until the pastry is well risen and turning brown. Reduce the heat to moderate (180°C/350°F) and bake for a further 30 minutes, until the pastry is cooked through. If the top is browning too fast, cover with aluminium foil. Serve the pie hot, garnished with parsley. *Serves 6*

Shepherd's Pie Supreme

2 tablespoons olive oil
1 large onion, finely chopped
500 g (1 lb) roast beef, minced
1 cup beef gravy (or use a stock cube and water)
2 teaspoons Worcestershire sauce
2 tablespoons chopped parsley
1 tablespoon chopped fresh herbs or ½ teaspoon dried
salt
freshly ground pepper
750 g (1½ lb) freshly cooked mashed potatoes
6 tablespoons cream
1 egg, lightly beaten
60 g (2 oz) butter, melted
grated Parmesan cheese

Heat the oil and gently fry the onion until soft. Mix in the beef, gravy, Worcestershire sauce and herbs with salt and pepper to taste. Spoon into a well-buttered deep casserole dish.

Blend the potatoes with the cream, egg and half the melted butter and spread over the meat mixture. Brush with the remaining butter and sprinkle with grated cheese. Bake in a hot oven (200°C/400°F) until the filling is piping hot and the potatoes are golden brown, about 20 minutes. *Serves 6*

Lamb and Vegetable Pie

500 g (1 lb) boneless lamb, cut from shoulder or leg	*6 small carrots, scraped and halved, or 3 large carrots, quartered*
60 g (2 oz) butter	*1 large turnip, peeled and diced*
2 tablespoons flour	
stock or water to cover	*1 cup shelled green peas*
salt	*1 tablespoon finely chopped fresh mint*
freshly ground pepper	
2 large tomatoes, peeled, seeded and chopped	*2 tablespoons chopped parsley*
12 small whole onions, peeled	

Remove any fat from the meat and cut into bite-size squares. Heat the butter in a heavy flameproof casserole or large frying pan and gently brown the meat. Sprinkle with flour, stir up the brown bits from the bottom, and cover the meat with stock or water. Season with salt and pepper, cover the pan, and simmer for 1 hour. Add the remaining ingredients, except the peas, mint and parsley. Replace the lid and continue cooking over a low heat until the meat and vegetables are tender, about 40 minutes. During the last 10 minutes of cooking time, add the peas, mint and parsley to the pot. Cool, then refrigerate and remove any fat that has risen to the surface. Use as a pie filling according to the step-by-step instructions for steak and kidney pie. *Serves 4 to 6*

Quick Chicken or Turkey Pie

2 cups cooked turkey or chicken, cut into small cubes	*1 cup milk*
	salt
	freshly ground pepper
1 cup cream	*4 spring onions, chopped*
60 g (2 oz) butter	*2 tablespoons grated Parmesan cheese*
2 tablespoons flour	

Simmer the turkey or chicken pieces in the cream until the cream is reduced by half.

Make a white sauce by melting the butter and stirring in the flour off the heat. Gradually add the milk over a moderate heat, stirring until the mixture is smooth. Season with salt and pepper to taste and add the spring onions, cheese and chicken mixture. Cool, then refrigerate until ready to top with pastry. *Serves 4 to 6*

Tamale Pie

500 g (1 lb) minced beef	*1 teaspoon salt*
1 large onion, chopped	*2–3 teaspoons Mexican-style chilli powder*
1 green pepper, seeded and chopped	
	TOPPING:
3 ripe tomatoes, peeled, seeded and chopped	*¾ cup cornmeal (polenta)*
	½ teaspoon salt
1 × 310 g can corn niblets, drained	*2 cups cold water*
	30 g (1 oz) butter
1 tablespoon sugar	

Place the meat in a hot frying pan and fry until brown, breaking up lumps with a fork. Add the remaining ingredients, except the topping, cover and simmer for 20 minutes. Turn into a greased casserole dish.

Stir the cornmeal and salt into the cold water. Place over a medium heat and cook, stirring, until thick, about 10 to 15 minutes. Add the butter and spoon over the hot meat. Bake in a moderate oven (180°C/350°F) for 40 minutes, or until the topping is firm and golden. *Serves 6*

Decorating the Pie

1 It is easy to give your pie a very special look to delight the family. Roll out the trimmings and cut a strip 2.5 cm (1 inch) wide. Cut this into diamond shapes to form leaves and mark 'veins' with the back of a knife. Mark one down the centre and short ones on either side.

2 Brush each leaf with beaten egg. Hold the points at each end and twist slightly to give a good leaf shape. Place in position on top of the pie, making sure not to cover the slits that allow the steam to escape.

3 Now make the 'flower'. Roll out another strip of pastry 3.5 cm (1½ inches) wide and cut slits along one edge with a sharp knife. Brush with beaten egg and roll the pastry strip around a skewer with the fringed edges towards you and the point of the skewer protruding 2.5 cm (1 inch).

4 Insert the point of the skewer into the pie funnel and press the base of the flower firmly on to the pie. Remove the skewer and use the point to open out the fringed edges into petal shapes. A very professional touch and fun to do.

Poultry can be Plain or Fancy

The modern poultry industry has helped us work magic with family meals. First, we can buy exactly the pieces everyone enjoys, even drumsticks galore, if they're the current favourite. We can count on tenderness, so quick cooking methods like grilling and pan frying are at our command. And chicken is undoubtedly one of the most economical meats of all, making it a basic part of family meal planning instead of the luxury it used to be.

There is still nothing more welcome than the sight of a plain, beautifully roasted, golden-brown bird with a jug of gravy and a platter of fresh vegetables. That's family cooking at its simplest, and its best! But when you want to ring the changes, poultry is also deliciously adaptable as these recipes show.

To Roast Chicken

Allow approximately 375 g (12 oz) raw weight of chicken per serving. When cooking with frozen poultry, it is essential that it is completely defrosted before cooking starts. This is best done slowly in the refrigerator, and will take at least 24 hours.

Remove the giblets (if any) once the cavity is soft enough for them to come out.

Wipe the chicken with damp paper towels inside and out. Make a stuffing, if desired, and stuff the chicken; otherwise, sprinkle a little salt and pepper and chopped fresh herbs or dried herbs inside the body. Truss (see step-by-step pictures on opposite page). Brush with melted butter and cover the breast with bacon rashers, buttered greaseproof paper or foil.

Place the chicken, breast up, on a rack set in a greased roasting pan. Roast in the centre of a hot oven (200°C/400°F) for 20 minutes, turn down to moderate (180°C/350°F) and continue roasting, allowing about 25 minutes per 500 g (1 lb). Very small birds will take a little more and very large birds a little less than this time. Baste with the pan juices every 15 minutes and remove the bacon, paper or foil 20 minutes before the chicken is done to allow the breast to brown. Test for doneness by inserting a fine skewer into the thickest part of the thigh near the body. The juices will run clear with no tinge of pink when the chicken is cooked.

Remove the chicken from the roasting pan and rest in a warm place for at least 15 minutes before carving. Meanwhile, make the gravy.

Gravy

To make thickened gravy, pour off all but 2 tablespoons of the pan juices. Sprinkle in 1 scant tablespoon of flour and stir over a moderate heat until lightly browned. Skim the fat off the remaining juices and add stock, water or vegetable water to make 1¼ cups. Pour into the pan, bring to the boil, stirring constantly until thickened. Season with salt and pepper.

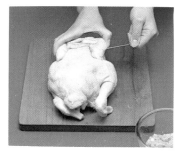

Stuffed Roast Turkey with Brussels Sprouts sautéed with Chestnuts and Bread Sauce

To make unthickened gravy, skim the fat off the pan juices and add enough stock or vegetable water to the pan to make about 1 cup. Stir over a moderate heat, scraping up all the good brown bits from the pan, until boiling. Season with salt and pepper and strain.

You may also like to serve bread sauce.

Bread Sauce

1 medium onion	*15 g (½ oz) butter*
2 whole cloves	*1 tablespoon cream*
1¼ cups milk	*1 tablespoon coarse*
½ bay leaf	*breadcrumbs fried in a little*
salt	*butter (optional)*
freshly ground pepper	
4 tablespoons fresh white	
breadcrumbs	

Peel the onion and stud it with the cloves; then put it into a small saucepan with the milk, bay leaf and salt and pepper. Bring slowly to simmering point, cover, and stand in a warm place for 20 minutes.

Add the fresh crumbs and leave for 20 minutes more. Remove the onion and bay leaf, whisk in the butter and cream, and adjust the seasoning. Reheat gently and pour into a warm sauce boat. Sprinkle the fried crumbs over the surface, if using.

Serves 4

Stuffing and Trussing

1 Draw back the neck flap of the bird and put some stuffing in through the opening over the breast. Do not pack too firmly; leave room for expansion. Replace the flap and shape the breast neatly with your hands.

2 Turn the bird over, back uppermost. Press the wings against the body and fold the wing tips over onto the flap. Pass a skewer through the right wing, through the end of the flap and out through the left wing.

3 Spoon the remaining stuffing through the rear vent into the body of the bird, again being careful not to pack firmly, to allow for expansion. Any remaining stuffing may be baked separately in a greased oven dish.

4 Turn the chicken over onto its back. Press the thighs against the side of the body, pass a skewer through the bird from one leg to the other. Tie the ends of the drumsticks and the parson's nose (tail stump) together with string.

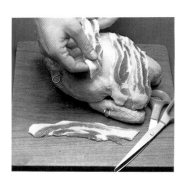

5 Brush all over with melted butter and cover the breast of the bird with rashers of bacon, rinds removed, or with buttered greaseproof paper or foil. This is to protect the breast, the driest part of the bird.

Frozen Chicken

It is essential that all whole birds are completely thawed before cooking. The usual method is to thaw them in their original wrappings, keeping in mind the following timetable:

If chicken is left in the refrigerator, allow 2 hours for every 500 g (1 lb) weight.

If chicken is left wrapped at room temperature, allow 1 hour for every 500 g (1 lb) weight.

To hasten the thawing process, the chicken may be placed in front of a fan, in which case you should allow 20 minutes per 500 g (1 lb).

To Roast Turkey

Allow approximately 375 g (12 oz) raw weight of turkey per person. If frozen, thaw it completely before cooking. This is best done slowly in the refrigerator, and will take from a day and a half to three days, depending on size.

It is a good idea to use a meat stuffing for the breast of a turkey, to keep it moist and give a good shape, and a bread or chestnut stuffing for the body.

Wipe the turkey inside and out with damp paper towels. Stuff and truss, following step-by-step pictures on page 99, but covering the tops of the legs as well as the breast with bacon.

Place the turkey on a rack in a large roasting pan and cover with oiled aluminium foil. Roast in a moderately slow oven (160°C/325°F), basting every 25 minutes. Remove the foil and bacon for the last 30 minutes to allow the turkey to brown. Allow approximately the following times:

2¾–4¼ kg (6–10 lb)	3–3¾ hours	8–12 servings
4½–6½ kg (10–14 lb)	3¾–4¼ hours	12–16 servings
6½–7¼ kg (14–16 lb)	4¼–4¾ hours	16–20 servings
9–10 kg (20–22 lb)	4¾–5 hours	28–30 servings

To test if the turkey is cooked, pierce the thickest part of the thigh near the body with a fine skewer; the juices should run clear. Remove to a warm serving platter or carving board and allow to rest in a warm place for at least 20 minutes before carving. Meanwhile, make the gravy as for chicken (page 98), making double the quantity. You may also like to serve bread sauce and garnish the bird with bacon rolls and chipolata sausages, baked separately. Roast potatoes and Brussels sprouts sautéed with chestnuts are a good choice of vegetables.

Brussels Sprouts Sautéed with Chestnuts

Choose 500 g (1 lb) small tight sprouts. Trim off the stalks and cut a cross in the base of each sprout. Cook in boiling salted water, without a lid, for 10 minutes and drain thoroughly.

Heat 60 g (2 oz) butter and, when foam subsides, put in the sprouts and 250 g (8 oz) canned, drained chestnuts, or fresh chestnuts, peeled and boiled until soft. Sauté briskly until they begin to turn golden. Season with freshly ground black pepper and a little freshly grated nutmeg. *Serves 6*

To Roast Duck and Goose

These birds have a large bony frame so you should allow 500–625 g (1–1¼ lb) raw weight per person. If frozen, thaw completely before cooking. This is best done slowly in the refrigerator, and will take 24 hours or more depending on size.

Pull out the loose fat round the neck and inside the body. Press the two little oil glands near the base of the tail to empty them. Wipe the bird with damp kitchen paper towels inside and out. Make the stuffing, if desired (see pages 102 to 104 for recipes), and stuff the bird; otherwise, sprinkle a little salt and pepper and chopped fresh herbs or dried herbs inside the body. Truss (see step-by-step pictures on page 99) but do not brush with melted butter or cover the breast. Duck and goose have a layer of fat beneath the skin of the breast so they do not need protection from dryness.

Place the bird, breast side up, on a rack set in a greased roasting pan. Roast in the centre of a moderately hot oven (190°C/375°F) for 10 minutes, turn down to moderate (180°C/350°F) and continue roasting, allowing about 25 minutes per 500 g (1 lb). Very small birds will take a little more and very

large birds a little less than this time. Baste with the pan juices every 15 minutes and, 20 minutes before the end of cooking time, prick the breast all over to allow extra fat to escape and make the skin crisp. Test for 'doneness' by inserting a fine skewer into the thickest part of the thigh near the body. The juices will run clear with no tinge of pink when the bird is cooked.

Baked Sherried Chicken

4 chicken Maryland joints	¼ teaspoon ground ginger
¼ cup dry sherry	½ teaspoon sugar
1 tablespoon soy sauce	60 g (2 oz) butter, melted
¼ teaspoon dry mustard	

Trim the chicken joints of any ragged edges, if necessary. Stir the sherry, soy sauce, mustard, ginger and sugar together in a large bowl. Put in the chicken pieces and turn them about until covered with the marinade. Cover and leave for 2 hours, turning the pieces occasionally.

Place the chicken pieces in a baking dish and pour over the remaining marinade, then the melted butter. Bake in a moderately hot oven (190°C/375°F), basting frequently with the pan juices, for 30 minutes or until the juice runs clear when a fine skewer is inserted in the thickest part. *Serves 4*

Chicken Pie

1 large roasting chicken	90 g (3 oz) butter
1 medium carrot, sliced	2 tablespoons flour
1 medium onion, sliced	salt
1 bay leaf	freshly ground pepper
1 teaspoon salt	½ cup cream
6 black peppercorns	1 × 375 g packet puff pastry
6 large mushrooms	1 egg yolk, beaten

Put the chicken into a large heavy saucepan with the carrot, onion, bay leaf, salt and peppercorns. Cover with water up to the top of the thighs and bring to the boil. Skim the surface, cover, and simmer gently for 20 minutes. Cool the chicken in the stock for 1 hour, then remove to a dish. Reserve the liquid.

Remove all flesh from the chicken. Skin the meat and cut into chunky pieces. Cover with a little cooking liquid to keep the flesh moist. Put the bones back into the saucepan with the remaining liquid and boil briskly for 10 to 15 minutes, without a lid, to reduce it. Strain and cool, then chill.

The preparation up to this point may be done the day before the pie is required.

Wipe the mushrooms with a damp cloth and cut each into quarters. Melt 30 g (1 oz) of the butter in a frying pan and toss the mushrooms over a high heat for a few minutes.

Place the chicken pieces in a deep buttered pie dish and spoon the mushrooms on top. Remove the fat from the chilled stock and measure 1½ cups stock. Melt the remaining butter, blend in the flour and cook for 1 minute. Add the stock gradually, stirring until boiling. Season to taste with salt and pepper and stir in the cream. Spoon this sauce over the chicken and mushrooms and mix gently. Place a pie funnel in the centre.

Roll out the pastry and cover the pie. For detailed instructions, see step-by-step pictures on page 96. Brush with beaten egg yolk (being careful to avoid cut edges) and bake in a hot oven (220°C/425°F) for 10 minutes, then reduce the heat to moderate (180°C/350°F) and bake for a further 20 minutes. *Serves 4 to 6*

Indian Chicken with Green Peppercorns

¼ cup peanut oil
4 onions, finely chopped
1 tablespoon green
 peppercorns, drained and
 chopped
2.5 cm (1 inch) piece fresh
 ginger, peeled and grated
½ teaspoon ground turmeric
½ teaspoon ground mace
¼ teaspoon ground coriander
¼ teaspoon ground cinnamon
10 small chicken thighs, cut in
 halves
2 teaspoons cornflour
2 cups chicken stock (or stock
 cubes and water)
2 apples, peeled, cored and
 cubed
2 tablespoons toasted
 desiccated coconut

Heat the oil in a large frying pan, add the onions and cook gently until golden. Add the green peppercorns, cook for 1 minute, then stir in the spices. Add the chicken pieces and brown all over.

Blend the cornflour with the chicken stock, pour into the frying pan and cook, stirring, until it boils and thickens. Turn the heat very low and simmer for 5 minutes. Add the apples, cover and simmer 10 minutes more or until the chicken is tender.

Serve on a bed of fluffy boiled rice with toasted coconut sprinkled over. *Serves 6*

Chicken Patties

Today you can buy chicken mince in most poultry shops. It makes quick, delicious meals.

½ cup fresh white breadcrumbs
½ cup evaporated milk
1 kg (2 lb) chicken mince
2 eggs
1 teaspoon grated lemon rind
1½ teaspoons salt
freshly ground pepper
2 tablespoons finely chopped
 fresh herbs, or 2
 tablespoons parsley sprigs
 chopped with 1 teaspoon
 mixed dried herbs
butter for frying
chutney

Place all the ingredients, except the butter for frying and the chutney, in a large bowl and mix lightly with a fork. Turn out onto a lightly floured board, shape into a round and cut into 12 even pieces. With wet hands, shape each piece into a flat patty.

Heat the butter in a frying pan. When the foam subsides, put in the patties (in batches if necessary, don't crowd the pan) and fry for about 5 minutes on each side. Serve with a dot of chutney on each patty. *Serves 6*

Chicken Pie

Stuffings and Dumplings add Savour

Mushroom Stuffing

A savoury stuffing is one of those added touches that make a family meal special. Don't save stuffings just for festive days and entertaining, make them part of your everyday meals. As well as adding interesting flavour, they can help the cook by holding the food in shape, keeping it moist and making it go further.

It is important to mix and handle stuffings lightly so as not to compact them, and to leave room for the stuffings to expand and stay light. If there is some over, cook it separately in a greased oven dish.

It is best to cook onion and garlic lightly before adding them to stuffing, as this improves the flavour and aids digestion. You should also precook pork or sausage mince until it changes colour, to make sure that it will cook through. The exception is sausage stuffing for the breast cavity of a turkey, when the stuffing is placed so close to the surface and is cooked for so long that pre-cooking is not necessary. Always stuff poultry just before cooking. This is a safety measure. Make fresh breadcrumbs, using bread 2 to 4 days old, by pulling it apart very lightly with your fingers or with two forks. Do not put bread through a mincer, as the stuffing will be too compact. Of course, if you have an electric blender or food processor, beautiful crumbs can be made in a trice.

Dumplings are also a traditional part of good family cooking, and are making a come-back in the light of rising meat prices. A stew or casserole takes on new interest (and goes much further!) with fluffy-light dumplings cooked in the gravy. The only 'secret' to success with dumplings is to leave the lid on the pot until the cooking time is up. Follow the recipes exactly and you'll be rewarded with perfect dumplings.

Mushroom Stuffing

Use for fish, tomatoes, peppers and marrow.

2 rashers rindless streaky bacon, chopped	1 tablespoon chopped parsley
30 g (1 oz) butter	2 tablespoons chopped mixed fresh herbs or 1 teaspoon dried
1 tablespoon finely chopped onion	salt
90 g (3 oz) mushrooms, finely chopped	freshly ground pepper
1 cup cooked rice	lemon juice

Gently fry the bacon over medium heat until the fat runs. Add the butter and fry the onion and mushrooms until soft. Stir in the rice, parsley and herbs, and season to taste with salt, pepper and lemon juice. *Makes enough to stuff 4 tomatoes or peppers, or 1 large fish or marrow.*

Apple, Prune and Nut Stuffing

Use for goose or large duckling.

90 g (3 oz) butter	$\frac{1}{4}$ cup chopped walnuts
1 onion, finely chopped	$\frac{1}{2}$ cup pine nuts
2 cooking apples, peeled, cored and cut into small dice	$\frac{1}{2}$ cup chopped parsley
4 cups day-old bread, cut into small cubes	1 teaspoon chopped fresh sage or pinch of dried
1 cup chopped pitted prunes	salt
	freshly ground pepper

Melt the butter in a heavy frying pan and sauté the onion until soft and golden. Add the apples to the pan and cook for 3 to 4 minutes, until the apple is soft. Meanwhile, lightly toast the bread cubes in a moderately slow oven (160°C/325°F) for 10 minutes, or until crisp.

Remove the apples and onion with a slotted spoon and place in a bowl with the prunes. In the same pan, lightly fry the walnuts and pine nuts until golden. Combine the apple mixture, bread cubes and nuts and fold through the parsley and sage. Season to taste with salt and pepper, and use at once.

Ham and Spinach Stuffing

This stuffing is superb with veal.

$\frac{1}{2}$ bunch spinach	1 cup finely chopped ham
salt	1 small onion, finely chopped
freshly ground pepper	30 g (1 oz) butter
pinch of nutmeg	1 cup soft breadcrumbs

Cut the spinach leaves away from the stalks and wash well. Place in a heavy saucepan with a little salt, pepper and nutmeg. Cover the pan and cook for 3 to 4 minutes until softened, shaking occasionally to prevent sticking. Drain well and, when cool enough to handle, squeeze out as much water as possible with your hands. Chop the spinach finely and place in a bowl with the ham. Season with salt and pepper.

While the spinach is cooking and cooling, cook the onion gently in the butter until soft and golden. Add to the spinach and ham, then add a pinch of nutmeg and the breadcrumbs and mix the ingredients lightly together with a fork. Correct the seasoning. *Enough to stuff a shoulder of veal for roasting or a breast of veal for braising.*

Rice and Watercress Stuffing

Use for chicken, duck, lamb and veal.

1 bunch watercress
1 cup cooked rice
2 sticks celery, finely chopped
1 tablespoon finely chopped onion
1 teaspoon salt
freshly ground pepper
60 g (2 oz) butter, melted
1 egg, beaten

Wash the watercress, discard any yellow leaves and long stalks and chop finely. Place in a bowl with the rice, celery, onion, salt, and pepper to taste. Stir in the melted butter and egg, mix well, and use immediately. *This is enough for a large chicken, duck or boned shoulder of veal.*

Sausage and Meat Stuffing

Use for turkey, chicken and veal.

500 g (1 lb) pork mince or sausage mince
1 medium onion, finely chopped
1 tablespoon chopped parsley
1 teaspoon dried sage
good pinch of ground mace
1 cup fresh white breadcrumbs
salt
freshly ground pepper

Break up the mince with a fork and lightly mix in the other ingredients. Use to stuff the breast cavity of a turkey about 6 kg (12 lb) in weight. For a chicken or boned shoulder of veal, halve the recipe.

Pork and Pineapple Stuffing

250 g (8 oz) pure pork mince
4 cups soft white breadcrumbs
1 cup crushed pineapple
1 cup sultanas
1 cup coarsely crushed walnuts
½ cup honey
salt
freshly ground pepper

Brown the pork in a heavy frying pan, using a fork to break up any lumps. Remove from the heat and stir in the remaining ingredients. *Makes about 7 cups of stuffing, enough for a 7 kg (14 lb) turkey.*

Apple, Prune and Nut Stuffing; Herb Stuffing (page 104)

Apple and Nut Stuffing

Use for duck or pork.

½ cup chopped, salted peanuts
60 g (2 oz) butter
1 cooking apple, peeled, cored and finely chopped
1 small onion, finely chopped
1 cup fresh white breadcrumbs
1 tablespoon chopped parsley
1 teaspoon dried savory
salt
freshly ground pepper
lemon juice

Gently fry the peanuts in butter until golden. Add the apple and onion and cook until soft. Stir in the remaining ingredients, adding enough lemon juice to give a good sharp flavour. *Enough for a duck or a boned loin of pork.*

Herb Stuffing

Use for fish, poultry or meat.

1 small onion, finely chopped	*1 tablespoon chopped parsley*
30 g (1 oz) butter	*1 teaspoon grated lemon rind*
2 cups fresh breadcrumbs	*½ teaspoon salt*
1 tablespoon chopped fresh	*freshly ground pepper*
herbs or 1 teaspoon dried	*1 egg, beaten*
(see below)	*stock or water, to moisten*

Cook the onion gently in the butter until golden. In a bowl, mix together the breadcrumbs, fresh or dried herbs, parsley, lemon rind, salt, and a generous amount of pepper. Add the onion and butter, egg, and enough stock or water to moisten the dressing very lightly. Do not over mix, just stir through with a fork. *This quantity is enough to stuff a chicken, a large whole fish, or a shoulder of lamb.*
NOTE: Use sage or savory for duck or goose; lemon thyme for fish, chicken, lamb or veal; mint for lamb.

Orange Stuffing

60 g (2 oz) butter	*2 oranges, peeled and diced*
4 sticks celery, finely sliced	*salt*
5 slices bread, cut in cubes	*freshly ground pepper*
2 teaspoons grated orange rind	*1 egg, beaten*

Heat the butter and sauté the celery until soft. Lightly stir in the remaining ingredients. *Makes enough to stuff a 2.5 kg (5 lb) duckling.*

Traditional Dumplings

These light, fluffy dumplings are delicious with any meat stew or casserole and are easily varied for extra flavour.

1 cup self-raising flour	*½ cup milk*
pinch of salt	*1 tablespoon chopped parsley*
30 g (1 oz) butter	*(optional)*
1 egg	

Sift the flour and salt into a bowl. Rub in the butter with the fingertips. Beat the egg and milk together, add to the flour mixture with the parsley, if using, and stir with a knife to form a soft dough. If you have a food processor, use the steel blade and put the flour, salt, butter and parsley (which need not be chopped) into the bowl. Process for 15 seconds then, with the motor running, pour in the beaten egg and milk.

Drop the dough by spoonfuls into boiling salted water or stock, or place on a stew or casserole. Cover tightly and simmer gently without lifting the lid for 15 minutes, until well risen and fluffy. *Makes 6 medium dumplings*

Variations

Cheese Dumplings Follow the recipe for dumplings, adding 2 tablespoons of grated cheese and a pinch of cayenne pepper to the dry ingredients. These are nice with a beef or chicken casserole. Alternatively, the mixture can be shaped into tiny balls and dropped into chicken or vegetable soup.
Roast Herb Dumplings Follow the recipe for dumplings, adding to the flour and butter mixture 1 tablespoon each of chopped fresh parsley and mint for lamb; lemon thyme for veal or chicken; sage or savory for pork or duck. If fresh herbs are not available, chop 1 teaspoon dried herbs with 1 tablespoon fresh parsley. Mix and shape the dumplings and place them in hot fat round a roasting joint for 20 to 30 minutes before the end of the cooking, turning once, until risen and golden brown. Drain on crumpled paper towels. Finely chopped onion or grated

lemon rind may be added to the flour and butter mixture for extra flavour. They make an imaginative change from baked potatoes, and children enjoy the difference as much as adults.

Cornmeal Dumplings

Interesting to serve with spicy meat dishes like Chilli con Carne.

$\frac{3}{4}$ *cup cornmeal*	*2 eggs*
$\frac{1}{2}$ *cup flour*	$\frac{1}{2}$ *cup milk*
1 teaspoon baking powder	*30 g (1 oz) butter, melted*
$\frac{1}{2}$ *teaspoon salt*	

Sift the cornmeal, flour, baking powder and salt together into a bowl. Beat the eggs and milk together, add to the dry ingredients with the melted butter and stir with a knife to make a soft dough.

Drop the dough by spoonfuls into boiling beef stock, consommé or any clear soup or water. Cover tightly and simmer without lifting the lid for 15 minutes until well risen and fluffy. *Makes 12 small dumplings*

Spinach and Cheese Dumplings

These beautifully flavoured dumplings, enriched with egg, are served as a dish in their own right. They are perfect as a first course before a light main dish or for a winter luncheon.

small bunch spinach	*5 tablespoons grated*
375 g (12 oz) Ricotta cheese	*Parmesan cheese*
1 teaspoon salt	*flour*
freshly ground pepper	*60 g (2 oz) butter, melted*
3 egg yolks	

Wash the spinach and chop the leaves finely, discarding the stalks. Cook the spinach until just tender, drain well, and process in a blender or food processor, or push through a sieve. Mix together the spinach, Ricotta cheese, salt and pepper, egg yolks and 3 tablespoons of the Parmesan cheese.

Drop the mixture by spoonfuls into a little flour spread on greaseproof paper. Shape into small balls. Bring a large

saucepan of lightly salted water to the boil, add the dumplings and cover tightly. Simmer for 5 minutes, then remove with a slotted spoon to a hot serving plate. Pour the melted butter over and sprinkle with the remaining Parmesan cheese. *Serves 4*

Semolina Dumplings

These Italian-style dumplings are very light, with a different texture to the usual flour dumplings.

2 cups milk	*2 eggs*
$\frac{1}{2}$ *cup semolina*	*boiling stock*
30 g (1 oz) butter	*30 g (1 oz) butter, melted*
$\frac{1}{2}$ *teaspoon salt*	*3 tablespoons grated*
$\frac{1}{2}$ *teaspoon paprika*	*Parmesan cheese*
good pinch of nutmeg	

Heat the milk to boiling point and add the semolina, butter, salt, paprika and nutmeg. Cook over a low heat until thick, then remove from the heat and beat in the eggs, one at a time. Drop into boiling stock from a teaspoon; cover the pan and steam for 2 to 3 minutes. Top with melted butter and cheese. *Serves 6*

Sweet Sultana Dumplings

An old-fashioned winter dessert for hearty appetites.

1 cup self-raising flour	*60 g (2 oz) butter*
pinch of salt	$\frac{1}{2}$ *cup sultanas*
2 tablespoons sugar	*1 egg, beaten with $\frac{1}{2}$ cup*
1$\frac{1}{2}$ teaspoons mixed spice	*orange juice*

Sift the flour, salt, sugar and spice into a bowl. Rub in the butter and stir in the sultanas. Bind together with the egg mixture. Drop by spoonfuls into boiling water, then cover tightly and steam for 15 minutes. Split open and serve with butter and golden syrup. *Makes 6 dumplings*

Opposite: Apple and Nut Stuffing (page 103); Sausage and Meat Stuffing (page 103); Rice and Watercress Stuffing (page 103)

Below: Traditional Dumplings; Herb Dumplings

Leftover Inspirations

When you are cooking for a family or any group of people, there are bound to be leftovers stored in the refrigerator or pantry: a few vegetables, perhaps a piece of roast meat, a couple of hard-boiled eggs, the remains of a chicken, some ends of cheese, a bowl of cooked rice or noodles.

Leftovers can stand for mundane repetition, or they can inspire the inventive cook! I often find them helpful in adding interest to a dish otherwise made from scratch. For instance, I sometimes use leftover vegetables in an omelette or soup, or turn cold noodles into a refreshing and pretty salad.

One secret is to think about contrasts of texture. When leftovers are soft, add chopped celery, nuts, crisp bacon or green peppers. Colours are important too: a touch of bright green herbs, red tomatoes or onion rings can spark up a bland-looking dish.

Cooked meat can be splendid the second time round cut into strips and tossed in a piquant dressing. Boiled rice can be dressed up a hundred ways! The syrup from fruits can go into a sauce, and even stale cake is a pleasant surprise flavoured and toasted and served with cream for dessert.

Here are some ideas to inspire your own thoughts about what to do with leftovers – they're budget-beaters as well as good to eat.

Meat Roll in a Cloak

This is a savoury, quickly made family main course, which makes excellent use of leftover meat. It is especially good with fresh tomato sauce.

1 × 375 g packet puff pastry	2 cups minced or finely
1 egg white, lightly beaten	chopped cooked meat (roast
FILLING:	lamb, beef, chicken, etc.)
2 tablespoons olive oil	½ cup leftover gravy, cream or
1 large onion, finely chopped	evaporated milk
1 tablespoon chopped	dash of Worcestershire sauce
gherkins, dill pickle or	salt
capers	freshly ground pepper
1 teaspoon dry mustard	

Heat the oil in a heavy frying pan and gently fry the onion until soft. Stir in the remaining filling ingredients and allow to cool. Taste, and add more seasoning if necessary; the mixture should be well flavoured.

Roll the pastry out thinly into a rectangle about 3 mm (⅛ inch) thick. Brush lightly with egg white around the edges. Spoon the meat mixture over half the pastry, leaving a rim of about 1 cm (½ inch). Fold over the pastry, pressing the edges together and sealing well. Make a few slashes in the top of the loaf with a sharp knife and brush with more egg white. Place on a greased baking tray and bake in a moderately hot oven (190°C/375°F) until the pastry is golden brown. This will take about 25 minutes. Serve cut into slices with fresh tomato sauce, if desired. *Serves 6*

NOTE: Other sauces can be served with this dish, depending on the kind of meat used. A lamb roll could be served with mint sauce, and a roast beef roll with horseradish sauce.

Fresh Tomato Sauce

2 teaspoons olive oil	1 tablespoon chopped fresh
4 ripe tomatoes, peeled,	herbs or ½ teaspoon dried
seeded and roughly chopped	⅔ cup chicken stock
1 clove garlic, crushed	salt
2 teaspoons tomato paste	freshly ground pepper

Heat the oil in a saucepan and cook the tomatoes and garlic until the tomatoes are soft, about 4 minutes. Add the tomato paste, herbs and stock and simmer for another minute. Taste, and add salt and pepper if necessary. Push the sauce through a strainer or purée in a blender. If it is too thin, reduce by rapidly boiling. *Makes about 2 cups*

Pork Chop Suey

Oriental-style dishes are always popular with the family. When you've enjoyed roast pork, here is a way of bringing back the leftover pork with a great new flavour.

2 tablespoons oil	1 cup fresh bean sprouts
4 tender sticks celery, with	1 cup chicken stock
leaves, cut in diagonal slices	1 tablespoon soy sauce
6 spring onions, sliced	2 teaspoons sugar
2 slices fresh ginger, finely	salt
chopped	freshly ground pepper
1 green pepper, seeded and	1 tablespoon cornflour mixed
sliced	with 2 tablespoons dry
6 mushrooms, sliced	sherry
2 cups cooked pork, cut in	
strips	

Heat the oil in a large frying pan. Quickly fry the celery, spring onions, ginger, pepper and mushrooms until tender-crisp, about 3 to 4 minutes. Stir in the pork and continue cooking and stirring for a couple of minutes, until the pork is heated through. Add the bean sprouts, stock, soy sauce and sugar, and bring to the boil. Taste for seasoning and, if necessary, add salt and pepper. Stir in the cornflour mixture and simmer for another minute, stirring all the time, until the gravy has thickened and is clear. Serve at once with boiled rice or noodles. *Serves 4 to 6*

Variation

Bamboo shoot and Chinese dried mushrooms can be added to the above mixture. Add some sliced bamboo shoot when frying the celery and add 6 soaked and sliced dried mushrooms with the pork. Omit the fresh mushrooms.

Ham and Rice Rolls

8 thin slices of cooked ham	SAUCE:
Dijon-style mustard	4 tablespoons grated Cheddar
1½ cups cooked rice	cheese
½ cup chopped seeded raisins	1 cup cream or evaporated
1 egg, beaten	milk
½ cup finely chopped celery	
½ teaspoon dried basil or	
oregano	

Pork Chop Suey

Spread the ham slices lightly with mustard. Combine the remaining ingredients and divide equally among the ham slices. Roll up, secure with toothpicks and place seam side down in a buttered baking dish.

To make the sauce, combine the cheese and cream or evaporated milk in a small saucepan, and heat gently until the cheese melts. Spoon the sauce over the ham and rice rolls and bake in a moderate oven (180°C/350°F) until heated through, about 20 minutes. *Serves 4*

Bubble and Squeak

This must be the great classic among leftovers – a savoury combination of potato, cabbage and meat that makes an appetizing bubbling sound as it cooks, hence the name. A great breakfast dish.

60 g (2 oz) butter or oil, or beef or bacon drippings	2 cups mashed potato
1 large onion, finely chopped	4 slices roast meat, finely chopped
2 cups cooked cabbage or any combination of cooked green vegetables (beans, peas, broccoli, zucchini)	salt
	freshly ground pepper

Heat the butter, oil or drippings in a large heavy frying pan. Fry the onion over medium heat until golden brown, then add the remaining ingredients. Stir well to combine and cook, without stirring, until a brown crust has formed on the bottom. Turn the bubble and squeak over with a spatula or egg slice (it will be easier to do if you cut it in half or quarters first) and cook the other side until crisp and brown. Serve very hot. *Serves 4*
NOTE: The traditional recipe contains meat, but you may omit it and serve the Bubble and Squeak simply as a vegetable or with grilled bacon as a main course.

Variation

When the Bubble and Squeak is cooked, top with a generous layer of grated cheese and pop under the grill until the cheese has melted.

Zippy Potted Cheese

Take a few odds and ends of leftover cheese, combine them with butter and seasonings, and you have an interesting spread. It's also fun to make, because you never quite know what the end flavour will be . . . though it's invariably delicious.

250 g (8 oz) grated cheese, any mixture you wish	pinch of pepper or cayenne
125 g (4 oz) butter	1 tablespoon snipped chives or fresh herbs (optional)
6 tablespoons port, sherry or brandy	

Place all the ingredients in a blender or food processor fitted with the steel blade and process until smooth. Alternatively, cream the butter and cheese together by hand with a wooden spoon, and gradually work in the wine and flavourings. Spoon into an attractive crockery bowl and store tightly covered in the refrigerator, where it will keep for weeks. *Makes about 1½ cups*

Good Things to do with Potatoes

Treated with respect, the potato is a package full of nutrition and flavour. A medium-size potato contains some high-quality protein, about the same amount of vitamin C as a glass of tomato juice, as much iron as an egg and no more joules (calories) than an apple the same size.

Nutrition
Vitamins and minerals lie just under the skin of the potato, so whenever possible cook them with their skins on and eat the skins, too. In any case, there is nothing more delicious than the crisp skin of a jacket-baked potato, or little steamed new potatoes in their skins.

Flavour
Be careful not to overcook potatoes. Their flavour is easily lost if they become watery and mushy. Boiled potatoes are done when they can be pierced easily with a fork. They should be cooked whole or in large pieces to avoid breaking up. Drain well when cooked and return to the pan to allow them to dry off a little. If they need to be kept for a short time before serving, cover the pan with a dry tea-towel.

Old or New?
Select the right potato for the way you want to serve it. Old, floury potatoes are best for mashing or baking in their skins, for making chips, and potato toppings for pies or creamed dishes. Smooth-skinned new potatoes are perfect just plain boiled or steamed, with a little butter and perhaps a seasoning of chopped mint, chives or parsley. Their waxy texture also makes them ideal for salads.

A Note on Storing Potatoes
Store potatoes in a cool dry place away from the light. Do not wash them. If you buy them in plastic bags, remove them from the bag and store loose in a vegetable bin or wire tray. Make sure there is air circulating around them. Don't use potatoes with greenish skins, as they are apt to be bitter, or sprouted or frost-bitten potatoes (these are watery with a black ring under the skin).

New Potatoes Maître d'Hôtel

When you want to give a special touch to the larger new potatoes, try this classic French way of treating them.

750 g (1½ lb) new potatoes
60 g (2 oz) butter
2 spring onions, finely chopped
2 tablespoons finely chopped parsley
salt
freshly ground pepper
4 tablespoons cream

Wash the potatoes and boil them in their skins until just tender. Peel and cut into fairly thick slices. Melt the butter in a flame-proof dish and add the potatoes in layers, seasoning each layer with chopped onion, parsley, salt and pepper. Heat the cream to boiling point and pour over the potatoes. Place the dish in a slow oven (150°C/300°F) until the potatoes are heated through. Serve from the dish. *Serves 4*

Sugar-Roasted New Potatoes

It may sound surprising to glaze potatoes with sugar, but they are excellent with ham, veal, lamb or pork – meats that would be good with a fruit sauce.

750 g (1½ lb) small new potatoes of even size
60 g (2 oz) butter
2 tablespoons sugar
1 teaspoon salt

Boil or steam the potatoes in their skins until tender, then peel. Melt the butter in a heavy frying pan and add the sugar, stirring to combine. Cook over gentle heat until golden brown, stirring constantly. Add the potatoes and turn until they are coated with the glaze. Turn into a heated bowl and sprinkle with the salt. *Serves 4 to 6*

New Potatoes Maître d'Hôtel; Pan-Roasted Potatoes

After potatoes have been boiled and drained, return to pan to dry off. To keep warm, cover with a dry tea-towel.

New potatoes are superb served in their skins; or peel them and return to pan with melted butter, shaking over low heat until coated.

Steamed New Potatoes

This is one of the simplest yet most perfect of all vegetable dishes. Enjoy it often while tiny new potatoes are in season.

1 kg (2 lb) small new potatoes   *salt*

Wash the potatoes and place them in a colander over a saucepan of boiling water, or in the top half of a steamer. Cover the pan and steam the potatoes for 20 minutes, or until they are tender when pierced with a fork. Transfer to a hot serving dish and sprinkle with a little salt. *Serves 6*

Variations
Toss the potatoes with a little melted butter or toss in butter, then sprinkle with snipped chives, chopped parsley or finely chopped fresh basil.

New Potatoes in a Bag

It's a pleasant change to serve the small new potatoes with a roast, especially when they can be cooked in the oven in this easy way.

750 g (1½ lb) small new   *60 g (2 oz) butter*
*   potatoes*   *salt*
4 mint leaves, finely chopped
1 tablespoon snipped chives or
*   finely chopped spring*
*   onions*

Wash the potatoes, place them in an oven bag and add the mint and chives or spring onions. Dot the butter over the potatoes and sprinkle with salt. Close the bag with its twist tie and make 3 or 4 holes in the top as directed. Place in a baking dish and cook in a moderately hot oven (190°C/375°F) for 30 to 40 minutes, or until tender. Transfer to a heated dish to serve. *Serves 4*

Pan-Roasted Potatoes

6 medium potatoes or large   *drippings from roast meat*
*   potatoes cut in half*   *salt*

Peel the potatoes thinly and dry with paper towels. Place around the roast for the last 50 to 60 minutes of cooking time, turning once or twice to brown all sides evenly. Drain on paper towels, sprinkle with a little salt and serve at once in a heated dish. *Serves 6*

Variation
Parboil the potatoes until they are almost cooked. There should be some resistance to a fork. Pat dry and put around the roast for the last 25 to 30 minutes, turning occasionally.

NOTE: If you are not roasting meat, the potatoes can be cooked in a mixture of butter and oil – enough to come to a depth of about 5 mm (¼ inch). Heat the oil and butter in a moderate oven (180°C/350°F) before adding the potatoes. Turn the potatoes in the fat to brown them evenly. Roast for 50 to 60 minutes, testing with a fork to see when they are done. Drain, sprinkle with salt, and serve.

Hashed Brown Potatoes

In American movies, especially Westerns, you often hear the hero asking for an order of hashed brown potatoes. This is the way they do them in Texas!

4–6 medium potatoes	1 teaspoon lemon juice
1 tablespoon grated onion	3 tablespoons oil or bacon
1 tablespoon chopped parsley	drippings
½ teaspoon salt	¼ cup cream
freshly ground pepper	

Wash the potatoes and boil them in their skins until tender. When cooked, peel the potatoes and cut them into small dice; there should be enough to give 3 cups. Combine all the ingredients, except the oil or bacon drippings and cream.

Heat the oil or bacon drippings in a large heavy frying pan and press the potato mixture into the pan, shaping it into a broad flat cake. Cook very gently over a low heat, shaking the pan from time to time to prevent sticking. When the bottom is brown, cut the potato cake in half and turn each half with two spatulas to avoid breaking. Pour the cream over the potatoes and continue cooking until the underside is brown. Cut into four pieces, slide onto a heated serving dish and serve at once. *Serves 4*

Stoved Potatoes with Garlic

The kitchen fills with the aroma of this hearty peasant dish – what a good way to welcome home the family on a cold night. 'Stoved' comes from the French word *étuver*, meaning 'to stew', and in this case potatoes stew in a small amount of water and butter on top of the stove. A heavy pan with a tight-fitting lid is essential, and you must be able to turn the heat down very low or the potatoes will stick.

750 g (1½ lb) new potatoes of	4 cloves garlic, finely chopped
even size	salt
2 tablespoons water	freshly ground pepper
60 g (2 oz) butter	

Scrub the potatoes well, rubbing off any loose skin. Arrange them in one layer in a large heavy frying pan. Add the water, dot the butter over the top and sprinkle with the garlic. Season well with salt and pepper. Place the lid on the pan and simmer very gently until the potatoes are cooked, about 30 to 40 minutes. Shake the pan often to prevent sticking, and add just a drop more water if you think it's necessary. Turn into a heated bowl and serve. *Serves 4 to 6*

Potatoes O'Brien

6 medium potatoes, boiled	dash of cayenne
1 green pepper, seeded and	¾ cup grated tasty cheese
chopped	1 cup hot milk
1 onion, finely chopped	½ cup dry breadcrumbs
1 tablespoon flour	extra ¼ cup grated cheese
salt	butter

Peel and slice the potatoes and mix with the pepper, onion, flour, salt, cayenne, cheese and milk. Pour into a greased baking dish, sprinkle the breadcrumbs and extra cheese over the top and dot generously with butter. Bake in a preheated moderate oven (180°C/350°F) until bubbly and brown on top. *Serves 8*

Creamy Mashed Potatoes

Here's the all-time favourite way of serving old potatoes. Never add cold milk to mashed potatoes or you won't get the light, fluffy texture that makes them so delicious.

4 medium-size old potatoes	½–¾ cup hot milk
salt	freshly ground pepper
30 g (1 oz) butter	

Scrub the potatoes well and place them in a saucepan with enough cold water to cover. Add salt to taste. Bring to the boil and cook with a lid on the pan until the potatoes are easily pierced with a fork, about 20 to 25 minutes. Drain thoroughly, then return to the pan and shake over a medium heat until all moisture has evaporated and the potatoes are dry.

Hold the potatoes on a fork, and strip off the skins with a sharp knife. Return to the pan and mash with a potato masher, or put through a potato ricer. Beat the potatoes with a wooden spoon until smooth, then add butter and hot milk, pouring in a little at a time and beating all the while. Use enough to make the potatoes light and fluffy. Season to taste with salt and pepper and serve at once in a heated dish. *Serves 4*

Mashed Potato Cakes

2 cups cold mashed potato	1 teaspoon celery seed
1 egg, beaten	salt
2 tablespoons chopped parsley	freshly ground pepper
2 tablespoons snipped chives	butter for frying

Blend the potato with the other ingredients, except the butter. Form into flat cakes about 7.5 cm (3 inches) wide. Brown on each side in hot butter. *Serves 4*

Potato Pancakes

These can be served as a vegetable with the main course, but don't limit them to this. Potato pancakes make a welcome supper snack spread with butter and jam or honey, and a substantial dessert after a light meal with stewed apples.

2 cups peeled and grated old	1¼ teaspoons salt
potatoes (about 3 medium)	¼ teaspoon nutmeg
3 eggs, lightly beaten	oil for frying
1½ tablespoons self-raising	
flour	

When the potatoes are grated, place them on a tea-towel and wring the towel to extract as much moisture as possible. Place the potatoes in a bowl and stir in the eggs. Sift the flour and salt together and add to the potatoes with the nutmeg. Blend well.

Heat enough oil in a heavy frying pan to give a depth of about 5 mm (¼ inch). Place spoonfuls of the potato mixture into the hot oil, using enough to make pancakes about 7.5 cm (3 inches) in diameter and about 1 cm (½ inch) thick. Cook over a medium heat until they are brown and crisp on the bottom, then turn and brown the other side. Drain on crumpled kitchen paper and serve at once. *Makes about 12 cakes*

From front to back: Mashed Potato Cakes; Potatoes O'Brien; Stoved Potatoes with Garlic

Root Vegetables can be Interesting too!

Vegetables are the new stars on the international cooking stage. It is now the sign of a good and knowledgeable cook to serve root vegetables often, and of course they contain vitamins and minerals essential to family health.

Basic Ways to Cook Root Vegetables

If the skins are thin, scrub them well but do not peel. Rinse in cold water and leave whole, slice or cut in quarters.

To Boil: Place the prepared root vegetables in a saucepan and barely cover with cold water, adding a teaspoon of salt for each 500 g (1 lb) of vegetable. Cover the pan and simmer gently for 20 minutes, or until tender. Drain, and toss the vegetables with a little butter, salt and pepper. Add chopped fresh herbs, if you like, or coat with a quick cheese sauce.

To make a cheese sauce, place 3 tablespoons of grated Cheddar cheese and 4 tablespoons of cream or evaporated milk in a small pan. Heat gently, stirring, until smooth and creamy. Season with salt and pepper to taste.

To Casserole: Melt enough butter to coat the bottom of a saucepan or flameproof casserole. Toss the prepared root vegetables in the butter, then add salt and freshly ground pepper and ½ cup of water or stock. Cover tightly and simmer for 20 to 30 minutes, or bake in a moderate oven.

To Cook Beetroot

Cut off the leafy tops, leaving about 4 cm (1½ inches) of stem.

Place the beetroot in cold water and remove any dirt gently, without scrubbing. Do not trim the thin root or break the skin or the beetroot will bleed and lose colour. Place in cold salted water to cover, add a teaspoon of sugar and simmer, covered, until the beetroot is tender (soft when pressed with the finger). An average beetroot takes about 45 minutes. Drain and slip the skins off.

Alternatively, you may bake beetroot. Cut the tops off, leaving about 4 cm (1½ inches) of stem, then wash gently. Bake in a moderately slow oven (160°C/325°F) until tender. Allow at least 30 minutes for small young beetroot and 1 hour for older ones.

Warm Beetroot Salad

Serve as a vegetable with hot meats, or as a salad with cold meats.

2 large, freshly cooked beetroot	*2 tablespoons olive oil*
½ teaspoon salt	*2 teaspoons wine vinegar*
freshly ground pepper	*2 tablespoons chopped*
good pinch of allspice	*parsley, to garnish*

Cut the skinned beetroot into cubes while warm and sprinkle with salt, pepper and allspice to taste. Whisk the oil little by little into the vinegar; pour over the beetroot and toss gently. Sprinkle with chopped parsley and serve immediately. *Serves 4 to 6*

Skirlie-Mirlie; Glazed Carrots

Buttered White Turnips with Mustard; Roast Parsnips

Skirlie-Mirlie

Root vegetables are delicious mashed together in almost any combination. Mashed parsnips and carrots are good, or carrots and turnips – or even all three. In this Scottish dish, turnips team up with potatoes for a subtle flavour and inviting colour.

500 g (1 lb) Swede turnips, peeled and diced	salt
500 g (1 lb) potatoes, peeled	freshly ground pepper
60 g (2 oz) butter or bacon drippings	1 tablespoon finely chopped parsley, to garnish
a little hot milk	

Cook the turnips and potatoes separately, drain well and mash. Heat the butter or bacon drippings in a saucepan; stir in the turnips and potatoes and enough hot milk to give a creamy texture. Season with salt and freshly ground pepper to taste. Spoon into a heated serving bowl and sprinkle with finely chopped parsley. *Serves 6*

Roast Parsnips

Parsnips are lovely baked around the roast, just as you would bake potatoes. Peel and wash them and leave whole if young and tender. Otherwise, cut them into quarters and remove any hard core. Boil parsnips for 5 minutes, then drain and pat dry and arrange around the meat. Cook for 45 minutes to 1 hour, turning once to brown evenly. Sprinkle with a little salt and serve piping hot with the roasted meat.

Glazed Carrots

500 g (1 lb) carrots, scraped	1½ tablespoons sugar
1 cup chicken stock (or use a stock cube and water)	salt
	freshly ground pepper
60 g (2 oz) butter	mint or parsley, to garnish

Cut the carrots into rounds or fingers, or leave them whole if tiny. Place in a pan with the stock, butter and sugar, and simmer gently with the lid on for 20 minutes. Remove the lid and continue cooking over a high heat until the liquid is thick and syrupy. Stir carefully from time to time to stop the carrots catching. When they are bright and glistening and the liquid has almost evaporated, remove from the heat. Season to taste with salt and pepper, pile into a hot serving dish and garnish with mint or parsley. *Serves 4*

Buttered White Turnips with Mustard

500 g (1 lb) young white turnips, peeled	1½ tablespoons Dijon-style mustard
60 g (2 oz) butter	2 tablespoons chopped parsley
½ teaspoon salt	

Cut the turnips into sticks like potato chips. Drop into boiling salted water and simmer for 15 minutes, or until barely tender. Drain thoroughly.

Heat the butter in a heavy saucepan and stir in the salt and mustard. Add the turnips and stir gently until they are coated. Fold the chopped parsley through and serve at once in a heated bowl. *Serves 4*

What would we do without Onions?

Onions were so prized by the ancient Egyptians they were worshipped! Whole books have been written about them, and there is not a cuisine that doesn't use them lavishly. Onions are always on family shopping lists, in every country in the world, and they're never out of season. They store well for long periods, and they're economical. No wonder we can't do without onions!

Here are some basic onion recipes and some new ideas to add interest to family meals.

Fried Onions

The other half of that all-time classic, Steak and Onions.

1 medium onion for each person	salt
	freshly ground pepper
oil to generously cover the base of a large frying pan	a pinch each of paprika and sugar (optional)

Peel the onions and slice them into rings. Heat the oil and add the onions to the pan. Cook over a gentle heat, stirring often, until they are golden brown and soft. This may take longer than you think: if you try to hasten the process by turning the heat up the onions could scorch.

When they are cooked, season with salt and pepper and add a pinch of paprika and sugar if you wish. The paprika intensifies the rich colour, and the sugar adds a subtle touch of sweetness. Serve piping hot.

A Quick Method of Frying Onions Chop the onions into small dice instead of rings. Melt enough butter in the frying pan to cover the base and stir the onions in the butter until well coated. Just cover with water and cook over high heat until all the water has evaporated. Reduce the heat and continue cooking and stirring in the butter until golden and tender. Season with salt and pepper and serve.

Onions Baked in their Skins

When you want baked onions with the roast, there is no need to peel them first. Simply top and tail them and place in the dish with the meat. Medium-size onions will take 1 hour to cook, larger ones 1½ to 2 hours. When they are tender if pierced with a fork, remove them to a heated serving dish and slip off the skins. Open up the centre a little with a knife and season with salt and pepper. To serve, top each onion with a knob of butter and a sprig of parsley.
NOTE: If you boil the onions for 10 or 15 minutes first, the cooking time will be reduced. For baked onions when you're not having a roast, just arrange them in a shallow greased baking dish.

Glazed Onions

Smaller onions look and taste especially inviting with a golden-brown glaze.

500 g (1 lb) small onions	30 g (1 oz) butter
salt	1 tablespoon brown sugar

Cook the onions in boiling salted water for 20 minutes or until tender. Drain well and dry on absorbent paper towels.

Heat the butter in a heavy frying pan and, when it has melted, stir in the brown sugar. Add the onions to the pan and continue cooking over a gentle heat until the onions are glazed. Shake the pan frequently, or turn the onions with a spoon so they are coated on all sides with the syrup. Turn into a heated serving bowl and serve. Serves 4

Onion Sandwiches

The mild Spanish onions with their pretty purple skins make superb sandwiches. Cut them into paper-thin slices and place between slices of buttered bread, with salt and freshly ground pepper to taste. For a gourmet touch, add a few leaves of watercress or finely chopped fresh herbs.

Crispy Onion Rings; Onions Baked in their Skins; Glazed Onions; Boiled Onions with Quick Parsley Sauce

Boiled Onions with Quick Parsley Sauce

Serve with corned beef, hot pickled pork or boiled beef.

6 large onions
30 g (1 oz) butter
1 tablespoon flour
½ cup evaporated milk or
  cream

salt
freshly ground pepper
1 tablespoon finely chopped
  parsley

Cook the onions in boiling salted water until tender, about 45 minutes. Drain, and reserve ½ cup of the cooking liquid. Arrange the onions in a serving dish and keep warm.

Melt the butter in a saucepan and blend in the flour off the heat. Return to the heat and add the reserved cooking liquid, stirring constantly. Cook for 1 minute, then stir in the milk or cream. Heat the sauce until boiling. Season with salt and pepper to taste, stir in the parsley, and pour over the onions. *Serves 6*

Scalloped Onions

750 g (1½ lb) onions
1 teaspoon salt
freshly ground pepper
2 tablespoons poppy seeds

1 × 125 g packet Philadelphia
  cream cheese
½ cup milk
chopped parsley, to garnish

Peel the onions and cut them into thin slices. Arrange in a shallow baking dish or casserole. Sprinkle with salt, pepper and poppy seeds. Put the cheese and milk in a small saucepan and stir over a low heat until it becomes a smooth sauce. Pour over the onions, cover the dish, and bake in a moderate oven (180°C/350°F) for 1 hour. Garnish with the chopped parsley to serve. *Serves 6 to 8*

Crispy Onion Rings

3 large onions
about 2 cups milk
salt
freshly ground pepper

1 teaspoon paprika
1 cup flour
oil for deep frying

Peel the onions. Cut them into slices about 3 mm (⅛ inch) thick and push out into rings. Combine the milk with 1 teaspoon of salt in a shallow dish. Add the onion rings and soak for 20 minutes. Add another teaspoon of salt, some pepper and the paprika to the flour and shake together in a plastic bag. Drain a few onion rings at a time and dip in the seasoned flour. Shake off excess flour, then deep fry the rings in oil until crisp and brown. Spread them out on a baking tray and keep warm in a slow oven while you fry the remainder. *Serves 4 to 6*
NOTE: To test if the oil is hot enough, drop one prepared onion ring into the oil. It should rise to the surface and turn crisp and golden in about 30 seconds. Take care that the oil does not overheat. The rings should be golden, not dark brown.

Spiced Baked Onions

24 small white onions
90 g (3 oz) butter
1½ tablespoons brown sugar
1 teaspoon salt
¼ teaspoon nutmeg

6 whole cloves
dash each of cayenne and
  white pepper
¼ cup slivered toasted almonds

Peel the onions and cook them in boiling salted water for 5 minutes. Drain. Melt the butter in a shallow flameproof dish and stir in the remaining ingredients, except the almonds. Add the onions to the dish, and turn over in the butter mixture so they are well coated. Cover and bake in a moderate oven (180°C/350°F) for 45 minutes, stirring once or twice. Before serving, remove the cloves and sprinkle with toasted almonds. *Serves 4 to 6*

Popular Peas and Beans

If you took a poll of favourite green vegetables, I'm inclined to think the overwhelming vote would be for peas and beans. They are certainly delicious when young and tender, and producers seem to be getting them to the markets earlier these days.

Peas and beans are very high in food value as well as flavour. Ideally they should be eaten absolutely fresh. They provide energy and vegetable protein and are a useful source of B vitamins as well as containing vitamin C. They are valuable in your family's diet.

When you serve peas and beans often, it's perhaps hard to think of them as exciting vegetables – they are more the 'old faithfuls' of the family production line. But with the smallest amount of extra time invested, they can be turned into international dishes, good enough to be served as separate courses on their own.

Don't neglect that popular pair, peas and beans – just change the way they look now and again and they'll never wear out their welcome.

Snow Peas

These are one of the delicacies of the vegetable world – a variety of peas called 'mange tout' (eat all) in France, 'snow peas' in China. The tender pods are eaten whole.

500 g (1 lb) snow peas	*knob of butter*
salt	*freshly ground pepper*
1 spring onion, finely chopped	

Top and tail the pods and remove any strings if necessary. Put them into enough boiling salted water to barely cover. Sprinkle with the spring onion, turn the heat down and simmer for 1 to 2 minutes, or until tender but still slightly crisp. Drain, toss with a knob of butter and season with extra salt, if required, and freshly ground pepper. *Serves 4*

Beans with Poulette Sauce

To Cook Peas

The peas we find in our greengrocers' shops these days are usually young and tender, and respond beautifully to a special method of cooking – in a small amount of liquid, with the lid on the pot. This liquid can be thickened with a teaspoon of cornflour mixed to a paste with cold water and served as a sauce with the peas, or saved for use in soups or gravies.

Minted Peas

750 g (1½ lb) peas in the pod	*pinch of sugar*
salt	*knob of butter*
freshly ground pepper	*extra chopped mint*
large sprig of mint	

Shell the peas. Put 1 cm (½ inch) of water in a saucepan with a little salt and pepper, the mint and sugar. Bring the water to the boil, add the peas and cover tightly. Leave over a medium heat for 6 to 8 minutes, or until the peas are tender.

Remove the mint and strain off any liquid. Taste peas for seasoning, and add extra salt and pepper if needed. Stir in a knob of butter and a little extra chopped mint and serve. *Serves 4*

Variations
Do not strain the peas, but thicken the liquid and serve as a sauce.
Strain the peas and add a few tablespoons of cream with a spoonful of chopped parsley.
While the peas are cooking, grill one or two rashers of bacon, chop or crumble it finely and stir through the cooked peas.

To Cook Green Beans

Top and tail the beans and remove the strings, if necessary. With young beans and the stringless variety, this won't be required. I like to leave young beans whole; older beans may be cut in half or sliced on the diagonal.

Bring enough lightly salted water to cover the beans to a rolling boil. Add the beans and boil rapidly, without a lid, until cooked (not covering helps to retain the bright green colour). Young beans will take only 6 to 8 minutes to become tender-crisp. Older beans may need a little longer, but shouldn't be cooked until too soft; a touch of crispness is desirable in a bean. Drain, then finish off in any of the following ways:
● Toss with a good knob of butter and a little finely chopped parsley. Add salt and pepper to taste.
● Instead of parsley, use a little fresh or dried savory, a herb that has a special affinity with beans.
● While the beans are cooking, saute a crushed clove of garlic and a few chopped spring onions in a little butter or oil. Toss into the drained beans with salt and pepper to taste.
● After seasoning the beans, sprinkle with slivered or flaked almonds that have been browned in a little butter.
● Combine the beans with lightly sautéed mushroom slices or crumbled crisp bacon.

Beans with Sour Cream

Top and tail the beans, remove the strings, and finely slice on the diagonal. Toss in hot butter, then add a good squeeze of lemon juice, salt and pepper, and enough beef stock to cover. Simmer gently until the beans are almost tender, then boil rapidly and reduce the liquid to a sauce. Serve topped with a spoonful of sour cream.

Beans with Poulette Sauce

For a special family occasion, you might like to serve beans with a creamy sauce. It is easily made while the beans are cooking.

500 g (1 lb) green beans	freshly ground pepper
2 tablespoons chopped parsley, to garnish	2 teaspoons chopped fresh herbs (e.g. savory or
POULETTE SAUCE:	marjoram) or ¼ teaspoon
30 g (1 oz) butter	dried
2 teaspoons flour	1 egg yolk
1 cup chicken stock	1½ tablespoons lemon juice
salt	

Top and tail the beans, and cook in boiling salted water until tender. While they are cooking, make the poulette sauce.

Melt the butter in a small saucepan. Remove the pan from the heat, stir in the flour and gradually blend in the chicken stock. Return to the heat and bring to the boil, stirring constantly. Add salt and pepper to taste and the herbs. Reduce the heat and simmer for 5 minutes.

Beat the egg yolk with the lemon juice. Remove the sauce from the heat, stir in the egg mixture and reheat without boiling. Taste, and add more salt and pepper if required.

Drain the beans and arrange in a heated serving dish. Pour the sauce over and sprinkle with the chopped parsley. *Serves 4*

Beans with Cheese and Herbs

Herbs, garlic and cheese add up to an Italian touch for green beans. Just the right accompaniment for roast seasoned veal, pork or lamb.

500 g (1 lb) green beans	1 clove garlic, crushed
30 g (1 oz) butter	salt
1 tablespoon oil	freshly ground pepper
2 tablespoons chopped	good pinch of nutmeg
parsley or 1 teaspoon	2 tablespoons freshly grated
chopped fresh sage	Parmesan cheese

Top and tail the beans. Leave whole if young, or cut in diagonal slices if larger. Cook in boiling salted water until just tender, then drain. Heat the butter and oil in a saucepan, stir in 1 tablespoon of the chopped parsley or ½ teaspoon of the sage and the garlic. Cook for a minute, stirring, then add the beans and season to taste with salt, pepper and nutmeg. Stir for another minute or two over a gentle heat until the beans are piping hot, then add the grated cheese and lightly stir through. Turn into a heated serving dish and sprinkle with remaining herbs. *Serves 4*

Ham, Bean and Potato Platter

This is a satisfying, substantial family main course, with meat and vegetables all in one. Instead of ham, you could use a whole clobassi sausage or two rookwurst.

1 × 680 g can ham or picnic	4 medium onions, peeled
shoulder	salt
water to cover	freshly ground pepper
500 g (1 lb) green beans	lemon wedges and mustard, to
4 potatoes	serve

Place the ham in a large pot, cover with water and simmer for 20 minutes. Top and tail the beans; peel the potatoes and cut in

Beans with Cheese and Herbs

halves if large. Add to the pot with the peeled onions. Cook until the vegetables are tender. Remove the meat and vegetables to a large platter, pour a little of the cooking liquid over and sprinkle with salt and black pepper to taste. Serve with lemon wedges and mustard. *Serves 4 to 6*
NOTE: The ham adds excellent flavour to the cooking liquid, so no extra seasonings are really necessary. However, if you like a spicy taste, you could add a few whole cloves, peppercorns and cardamom pods.

Beans Greek Style

1 kg (2 lb) green beans, topped	salt
and tailed	freshly ground pepper
½ cup olive oil	1 teaspoon sugar
2 medium onions, thinly sliced	1 teaspoon ground cumin
2 cloves garlic, crushed	(optional)
2 large ripe tomatoes, peeled,	extra chopped parsley, to
seeded and chopped	garnish
3 tablespoons chopped parsley	
2 teaspoons chopped fresh	
oregano or ¼ teaspoon dried	

Cut the beans in half if very long, leave whole if small and young. Heat the oil in a large saucepan and gently fry the onions and garlic until they soften and turn a pale golden colour. Place the beans on top of the onions, then the tomatoes and parsley. Sprinkle with the oregano, salt, pepper and sugar. Cover the pan tightly, and simmer over a gentle heat until the beans are tender, about 25 to 30 minutes. Check the liquid from time to time, and add a little water if it seems to be evaporating too much. You should have a thick sauce at the end of the cooking time. Stir in the cumin just before serving and sprinkle with a little extra chopped parsley. *Serves 6*
NOTE: This bean dish is also excellent served cold, with sliced meats or poached fish. Allow to cool, then chill in a covered container in the refrigerator.

Variation
Beans done this way are often cooked with lamb, for a complete meal in a pot. Cut 1 kg (2 lb) of lean shoulder lamb into small squares, brown in the olive oil, then follow the recipe for Beans Greek Style. Serve with lemon wedges and boiled rice.

Green Peas à la Française

Green Peas à la Française

This is a lovely dish made with small young peas, but succeeds with older peas as it helps to tenderize them. It also adds flavour to frozen peas; there is no need to thaw, just put them straight from the packet on top of the bed of lettuce and cook for a little longer than fresh peas.

1 kg (2 lb) peas in the pod or 500 g (1 lb) frozen peas	*½ lettuce or 6–8 outside lettuce leaves*
60 g (2 oz) butter	*few sprigs of mint*
1 rasher rindless streaky bacon, finely chopped	*1 teaspoon sugar*
	salt
6 spring onions, finely chopped (including green tops)	*freshly ground pepper*
	2 tablespoons water

To prepare and cook, see step-by-step pictures, below. *Serves 4*

Green Peas à la Française
1 Shell the peas. Melt the butter in a flameproof casserole and gently fry the bacon and onion until the onion is soft but not brown. Wash the lettuce and shred finely. Add to the casserole, and stir over a low heat until the lettuce is bright green and juicy.

2 Add the peas to the casserole with one or two sprigs of mint, the sugar and salt and pepper to taste. Pour in the water, cover the casserole tightly and cook over a gentle heat for 25 to 30 minutes, or until the peas are tender. To serve, remove the sprigs of mint, garnish with fresh mint, and serve from the casserole with the pan juices and lettuce.

Adding Zest to Frozen Peas

No wonder frozen peas are so popular. Busy family cooks appreciate the convenience of having them already shelled and the quality is controlled, so they are always tender. Here are ways to give these useful standbys a new look and a new flavour, based on the 500 g (1 lb) packet size which serves 4 people.
Purée of Peas Cook the peas as usual; then drain. Whirl them in an electric blender with 2 tablespoons of the cooking liquid, salt and pepper to taste, and a chopped sprig of mint if desired. Return to the saucepan, add a little cream, evaporated milk or a tablespoon of butter and stir over a gentle heat until piping hot.
Curried Peas and Ham Cook the peas as usual; then drain. Melt 60 g (2 oz) butter in the same saucepan and stir in 1 teaspoon (or more to taste) of curry powder, with 1 crushed clove of garlic. Return the peas to the pan and gently stir until heated through and coated with the curry mixture. Taste, and add extra salt and a pinch of sugar if needed. Sprinkle with finely chopped ham to serve.
Peas with Sour Cream and Mushrooms Cook the peas as usual; then drain. Sauté 125 g (4 oz) of sliced mushrooms in 30 g (1 oz) butter until tender. Add the peas to the mushrooms in the pan, stir to combine, and season with salt and freshly ground pepper to taste. Stir in ½ cup of light sour cream and bring just to boiling point.

Stir-Fried Beans with Almonds

This quick method of cooking beans is suited to young tender beans and also to sliced frozen beans. Keep an eye on them to see that they're not overcooked; you may have to adjust the cooking times suggested to ensure that nice touch of crispness.

500 g (1 lb) fresh or frozen sliced green beans	*1 teaspoon cornflour mixed with 3 teaspoons soy sauce*
1½ tablespoons oil	*salt*
1 teaspoon sugar	*freshly ground pepper*
4 tablespoons chicken stock (or use ½ stock cube and water)	*½ cup toasted almonds*

Top and tail the fresh beans, if using, and cut in two or into diagonal slices. Heat the oil in a heavy frying pan and add the beans. (There is no need to thaw frozen beans; add them to the pan and break them up with a fork as they soften.) Stir and cook over a medium heat for 3 minutes, then add the sugar and stock. Simmer for another 2 minutes and stir in the cornflour-soy sauce mixture. When the sauce thickens, taste and add salt and pepper if necessary. Gently stir until the beans are lightly coated with the sauce. Add the almonds and serve at once. *Serves 4*

Lazy Day Pea Purée

Try this interesting purée based on pea soup – so quick, yet it looks and tastes like a Middle Eastern specialty.

1 medium onion, finely chopped	*½ cup cream*
	1½ teaspoons ground cumin
90 g (3 oz) butter	*dash of cayenne*
1 × 690 g can condensed green pea soup or 2 smaller cans	

Sauté the onion in butter until soft. Gradually stir in the remaining ingredients and heat, stirring, until smooth and hot. *Serves 4 to 6*

Nutritious Pulses and Grains

When you are cooking for a family, and sticking to a budget, it isn't always easy to plan meals that are satisfying and nutritious but still have a little excitement to them. That's the time to think of grains and pulses!

Pulses, which are the seeds of leguminous plants, are all rich in protein and have happily remained low in cost compared to many other high-protein foods.

They include red and brown lentils, chick peas, soy beans, haricot, lima and kidney beans, black-eyed peas and beans of many other colours. We are lucky that in our supermarkets and health food stores today there is an international selection to choose from. The Cassoulet of France, the Frijoles of Mexico and the Pease Pudding of England are all based on pulses.

Grains are also protein-rich, relatively low-cost and offer good variety. Cornmeal or polenta is beloved of the Italians, who treat it in a host of savoury ways. Cracked wheat, often called 'burghul', is a Middle East favourite for salads and as a hot accompaniment to main courses. Barley is popular in many countries as a course in itself, as well as an interesting addition to soups and stews.

I think you will enjoy the ideas on the following pages.

Boston Baked Beans (page 120); Frijoles (page 120)

To Cook Pulses

Pulses are usually soaked overnight in cold water to restore the moisture content and hasten the cooking process next day. Use about 3 to 4 times as much water as beans, as they swell. Remove any beans that float.

Next day, drain the beans, cover with fresh cold water and bring to the boil. Turn the heat down and simmer until they begin to soften before adding salt. (If you add salt at the beginning it slows down the softening process.)

Continue cooking until the beans are tender. How long this will take depends on the type of bean, the length of soaking, how long they have been stored and even where they were grown. Lima beans may take only 30 minutes, while chick peas may take 3 hours to soften. Test for yourself from time to time, and add more boiling water if required.

Handy Tips

Buying: Buy pulses where there is a frequent turnover of stock, as old beans tend to remain hard even after long cooking. Buy only the amount you will use fairly quickly.

Quantities: Peas, beans and lentils expand to twice their bulk or more during cooking. For an average appetite, a serving of 60 g (2 oz) dry weight is sufficient.

Quick Tenderizing: If you have forgotten to pre-soak the beans, cover them with cold water and bring to the boil, then simmer for 2 minutes. Remove from the heat and allow to stand, tightly covered, for 1 hour. Drain, cover with fresh cold water and cook until tender. (The preliminary blanching is equal to 8 hours' soaking.)

Cooking Red Lentils: Cover with cold water, bring to the boil and simmer until tender, about 25 minutes. No need to pre-soak. Add salt during the last 10 minutes.

Frijoles (Fried Mexican Beans)

Frijoles are one of the staples of Mexican cuisine, served as often as we serve potatoes. Try them with spicy meatballs, grilled sausages, beef stew or hamburgers.

250 g (8 oz) red kidney beans, soaked overnight	4 tablespoons oil, olive for preference
2 onions, chopped	2 teaspoons (or more)
2 cloves garlic, crushed	Mexican-style chilli powder
1 × 225 g can peeled tomatoes	
salt	

Drain the beans and place in a heavy saucepan with the onions and garlic. Add enough cold water to come just to the top of the beans and simmer until they start to soften, about 1 hour. Add the tomatoes and juice, salt to taste and 2 tablespoons of the oil. Continue cooking for a further 30 minutes, or until the beans are completely soft, stirring from time to time as the liquid is absorbed.

Heat the remaining 2 tablespoons of oil in a heavy frying pan. Gradually add the cooked beans, mashing them as you go with a potato masher. Stir in the chilli powder, taste, and add more if you like it hotter and spicier. Continue stirring over a low heat until the mixture is thick, then spoon into a heated serving bowl. *Serves 6*

NOTE: For a shortcut, use 2 × 450 g cans of kidney beans, with their liquid. Cook with the onions, garlic and tomatoes until the vegetables are soft (adding extra liquid if necessary), then proceed as above.

Boston Baked Beans

Baked beans in cans are a useful standby, but the flavour is deliciously different when you make your own.

250 g (8 oz) haricot beans, soaked overnight	2 tablespoons tomato paste
2 onions, chopped	1 tablespoon vinegar
125 g (4 oz) pickled pork, cut into small cubes	1 teaspoon dry mustard
2 tablespoons brown sugar	1 teaspoon salt
	freshly ground pepper

Drain the soaked beans and cover with fresh water. Simmer for 1 to 1½ hours or until tender. Drain them, reserving the liquid. Put the beans in a deep, greased casserole and mix the remaining ingredients with just enough of the reserved cooking liquid to cover the beans. Cover tightly with a lid or aluminium foil and bake in a slow oven (150°C/300°F) for 7 to 8 hours, until the beans are very tender and have absorbed the flavourings. Stir occasionally while they cook, adding a little more liquid as necessary. Leave uncovered for the last hour of cooking. Serve hot from the casserole. *Serves 6 to 8*

Chilled Butter Bean Casserole

Butter beans cooked in a spicy tomato sauce are delicious served cold and make an unusual light dish for a warm day. For big appetites, add cold sliced meat or chicken and a green salad.

¾ cup olive oil	2 tablespoons wine vinegar
2 cloves garlic, crushed	salt
1 onion, finely chopped	freshly ground pepper
2 ripe tomatoes, peeled, seeded and chopped	4 spring onions (including green tops), finely chopped
¼ cup finely chopped parsley	
1 teaspoon sugar	
4 cups cooked butter beans or baby lima beans	

Heat half the oil in a saucepan and gently fry the garlic and onion until soft, stirring often. Do not let them brown. Add the tomatoes, parsley and sugar to the pan and continue cooking and stirring until the tomatoes are soft, about 5 minutes.

Mix the beans with the tomato mixture, turn into a serving bowl and chill. Just before serving add the remaining oil and the vinegar to the bowl, with salt and pepper to taste. Sprinkle with the chopped spring onions to serve. *Serves 6 to 8*

Sweet-Sour Cracked Wheat or Barley

Cracked wheat and barley make welcome changes from rice or potatoes.

1 cup cracked wheat (burghul) or pearl barley	good pinch of nutmeg
2 cups beef or chicken stock (or use stock cubes and water)	2 tablespoons each oil, vinegar and brown sugar
1 bay leaf	chopped parsley or spring onions, to garnish
1 teaspoon salt	
2 cloves garlic, crushed	

Rinse the wheat or barley in a colander and drain. Bring the stock to the boil with the bay leaf, salt and garlic. Add the wheat or barley, turn the heat to low and simmer for 25 to 30 minutes. Add the remaining ingredients, except the garnish, and cook for another 10 minutes or so, stirring often, until quite tender. Turn into a heated serving bowl and sprinkle with chopped parsley or spring onions. *Serves 4*

For nutrition and variety look to the colourful family of lentils and pulses.

Pease Pudding; Lentils with Parsley Butter

Pease Pudding

This old-English specialty is very good served with hot pickled pork or corned beef, ham, meat loaf or sausages.

2 cups yellow split peas, soaked overnight	*freshly ground pepper*
	water or stock to cover
1 large onion, sliced	*1 teaspoon Worcestershire*
2 rashers of bacon, chopped, or a ham bone	*sauce*
	30 g (1 oz) butter
salt	

Drain the peas, then put in a large saucepan with the onion, bacon or ham bone, and salt and pepper to taste. Add enough water or stock to come 5 cm (2 inches) above the top of the peas. Bring to the boil and simmer, covered, for about 2 hours, or until the peas are very soft and almost all the liquid has been absorbed. Stir now and again to prevent sticking. Remove the ham bone, if used. Taste for seasoning, then stir in the Worcestershire sauce and butter. Serve hot. *Serves 6*
NOTE: Leftover pease pudding reheats well, but will need thinning down with a little more liquid or stock, as it thickens when cold. The purée can also be made into a delicious soup with the addition of extra stock, milk, or a mixture of both.

Lentils with Parsley Butter

¼ cup olive oil	*3½ cups boiling water*
1 clove garlic, crushed	*salt*
1 large onion, finely chopped	*freshly ground pepper*
1 cup brown lentils	*parsley butter (see right)*

Heat the oil in a large heavy saucepan and fry the garlic and onion over a medium heat until golden brown. Stir in the lentils, continuing to stir until they have absorbed the oil. Pour the boiling water over them and simmer for 1½ hours, or until the lentils are soft. Season with salt and freshly ground pepper. Stir in a little parsley butter and serve with a good knob on top as a garnish. *Serves 4*
Parsley Butter Cream 60 g (2 oz) butter with a wooden spoon and beat in 1 tablespoon finely chopped parsley, a squeeze of lemon juice and a little salt to taste. This can be rolled and chilled, then cut into slices to top grilled steak or used at once for the lentil dish, or other hot vegetable dishes.

Corn and Bean Dinner in a Dish

1 × 440 g can corn niblets, drained	*salt*
	freshly ground pepper
1 × 675 g can 3-bean mix, drained and rinsed, or 3 cups cooked beans of your choice	*1 medium onion, finely chopped*
	1 tablespoon brown sugar
	1 cup finely chopped unsalted peanuts
1 × 425 g can tomatoes, undrained	*1 cup grated tasty cheese*

Mix all the ingredients together, except the cheese, and spoon into a greased baking dish. Sprinkle with cheese and bake in a moderate oven (180°C/350°F) for 45 minutes. Serve with warmed French bread (which can go into the oven, wrapped in foil, for the last 10 minutes) and a green salad. *Serves 6*

Fruits make Perfect Desserts

Most families look forward to something sweet to finish the main meal of the day. Fruits are not only nutritious, but offer endless variety, fresh or cooked. Even when the fresh fruit basket is running low, we can turn to canned or frozen fruits to produce a lovely dessert with little effort.

Plum Crisp

This simple dessert tastes wonderful – the secret is the contrast of the crispy bread with the sweet, juicy plums.

8–10 large ripe plums	½ cup brown sugar
6 slices well-buttered bread, crusts removed	30 g (1 oz) butter
	caster sugar and cinnamon

Wash the plums, halve and stone them. Place the bread, buttered side down, in a greased shallow casserole and sprinkle with half the brown sugar. Arrange the plums on top and sprinkle with the rest of the brown sugar. Dot with butter.

Cover the dish with buttered aluminium foil and bake in a moderately hot oven (190°C/375°F) for 25 to 30 minutes, until the bread is crisp and the plums soft. Sprinkle with sugar and cinnamon, and serve hot with cream or ice-cream. *Serves 4 to 6*

Fruity Baked Apples

4 Granny Smith apples	1 tablespoon chopped nuts
4 tablespoons seeded raisins, mixed fruit or sultanas, chopped	2 teaspoons lemon juice
	60 g (2 oz) butter
½ teaspoon cinnamon	2–3 tablespoons brown sugar
	water or apple cider

To prepare and cook, see step-by-step pictures below. *Serves 4*

Baked Peaches Flambé

Canned peach halves are an excellent standby in your cupboard for interesting desserts – use them for this dish when fresh peaches are out of season.

4 large ripe peaches or 8 canned peach halves, drained	60 g (2 oz) unsalted butter
	1 cup crushed macaroons or cake crumbs
½ cup rum or brandy, to flambé	1 egg yolk, beaten with 1 tablespoon lemon juice
STUFFING:	
1 tablespoon sugar	

If using fresh peaches, pour boiling water over them to cover, allow to stand for 2 minutes, then slip off the skins. Halve carefully and remove the stones. Arrange them, hollow-side up, in a greased shallow casserole.

Mix the stuffing ingredients together and fill the peach halves, rounding into a dome shape. Cover the peaches with buttered aluminium foil and bake in a moderate oven (180°C/350°F) for 20 minutes, or until heated through (don't overcook). Heat the rum or brandy in a small saucepan, set alight and pour flaming over the peaches. Serve immediately with whipped cream or ice-cream. *Serves 4 as a substantial dessert after a light meal or 8 as a lighter dessert.*

Banana Rum Freeze

4 ripe bananas, mashed	2 tablespoons dark rum
½ cup sugar	1 cup cream, whipped
pinch of salt	2 tablespoons chopped toasted almonds
½ cup pineapple juice	
2 tablespoons lemon juice	

Place the mashed bananas in a bowl and combine well with the sugar and salt. Stir in the pineapple and lemon juices and rum. Fold in the cream. Spoon into a freezer tray and freeze until firm, about 3 hours. Turn out into the bowl again, break up with a fork and beat with a rotary beater or electric mixer until light and frothy. Fold in the chopped almonds, return to the tray and freeze until set. Serve in slices with a crisp sweet biscuit. *Serves 8*

Fruity Baked Apples
1 Preheat the oven to moderate (180°C/350°F). Core the apples with an apple corer, then use a small sharp knife to cut away any pieces of remaining core. Make a slit around the centre of the apples to prevent them bursting as they cook.

2 Mix together the fruit, cinnamon, nuts and lemon juice and stuff the apples with the mixture. You could also use dates, chopped prunes or dried apricots and a little brandy instead of lemon juice. Arrange the apples in a buttered ovenproof dish.

3 Top each apple with a knob of butter and sprinkle with brown sugar. Pour in enough water or apple cider to cover the bottom of the dish. Cover the tops of the apples with a piece of buttered brown paper or foil. (This will stop the stuffing browning too quickly.)

4 Bake the apples for 40 to 60 minutes, or until they are soft when tested with a fine skewer. If the liquid seems to be evaporating too much as they cook, add a little more. Serve the apples warm, with cream, custard or ice-cream.

Pears in Red Wine

Choose firm pears for this classic dessert; if they are too ripe they won't keep their shape. If necessary, trim the bottoms level so they stand up straight in the baking dish.

4 pears of even size	1 long sliver of lemon rind
1 cup red wine	$\frac{1}{2}$–1 cup water
$\frac{1}{2}$ cup caster sugar	

Choose a deep casserole just large enough to hold the pears standing up. Peel the pears, leaving on the stalks, and arrange them in the casserole. Bring the wine, sugar and lemon rind to the boil in a small saucepan and stir until the sugar has dissolved. Pour over the pears and add enough water to come just level with the stalks.

Cover the dish and bake in a moderately slow oven (160°C/325°F) for 1½ hours, or until the pears are tender when tested with a fine skewer. Allow to cool, then chill in the refrigerator, spooning the syrup over the pears now and again. Serve with cream, if desired, or a crisp sweet biscuit. *Serves 4*

Macaroons

These are lovely to pass around with fruit desserts or with coffee afterwards.

3 egg whites	$\frac{3}{4}$ cup caster sugar
1 cup ground almonds	

Beat the egg whites until stiff but not dry, then fold in the almonds and sugar. Grease a baking sheet and cover it with greased foil. Pipe or spoon the mixture into small mounds and allow to stand for 4 hours. Bake in a moderate oven (180°C/350°F) for 12 to 15 minutes until delicately browned. Cool, and store in an airtight tin. *Makes about 24*

Apricot Trifle

1 × 822 g can whole apricots	2 eggs
1 single layer sponge cake	1 cup crumbled macaroons
$\frac{1}{2}$ cup Marsala	(about 8–10)
2 tablespoons cornflour	1½ cups cream
3 tablespoons sugar	1 teaspoon vanilla
1½ cups hot milk	glacé fruits, to decorate

Drain the apricots, remove the stones, and purée in a blender. Cut the sponge cake in half horizontally, spread half the apricot purée between the layers and reassemble. Slice the cake into strips about 5 × 2.5 cm (2 × 1 inch) and use to line the bottom of a large serving bowl, preferably glass. Sprinkle Marsala over the cake and spread with the remaining apricot purée.

Mix the cornflour and 2 tablespoons sugar to a smooth paste with a little hot milk. Stir in the remaining milk, then place over a low heat and stir constantly until the mixture thickens. Remove from the heat and beat in the eggs, one by one. Return to low heat and cook for 5 minutes, stirring. Add the crumbled macaroons to the custard, mixing well, and allow to cool.

Spoon the cooled custard over the trifle and chill until serving time. Just before serving, whip the cream with the vanilla and the remaining sugar and spoon over the custard. Decorate with glacé fruits. *Serves 10*

Pears in Red Wine

Fresh Pineapple Tart

This recipe from the West Indies has an interesting twist – the pineapple isn't cooked, but quickly glazed under the grill.

1 fresh ripe pineapple, or	*¼ teaspoon salt*
1 × 850 g can pineapple	*125 g (4 oz) butter*
rings	*1 egg yolk, lightly beaten*
¾ cup plain flour	*2–3 tablespoons iced water*
¾ cup self-raising flour	*¼ cup icing sugar*
1 tablespoon sugar	

If using fresh pineapple, peel, core and cut into slices about 1 cm (½ inch) thick. Drain canned pineapple.

Combine the flours, sugar and salt in a bowl. Cut the butter into small pieces, then quickly blend into the flour with the fingertips until the consistency of coarse breadcrumbs. Add the egg yolk and mix to a dough with iced water. Roll out on a lightly floured board to a rectangle about 30 × 10 cm (12 × 4 inches). Crimp the edges up with the fingers to give a rim about 2 cm (¾ inch) high and chill for 20 minutes. Prick all over with a fork and bake in a moderately hot oven (190°C/375°F) for 20 minutes, or until cooked and golden brown.

Arrange the pineapple in overlapping slices in lengthwise rows on the pastry. Sprinkle with the icing sugar and place under a preheated grill for 2 to 3 minutes or until lightly browned. Serve warm, cut in squares, with whipped cream or ice-cream. *Serves 6*

NOTE: If desired, soak the pineapple slices in Kirsch or rum while you cook the pastry, then drain and pat dry before arranging on the pastry. A little of the Kirsch or rum could also be sprinkled over the finished tart.

Bananas Rio

Bananas are beautifully flavoured with citrus juices and coconut for a dessert all age groups will enjoy. Serve with coffee ice-cream if you want to be even more South American!

6 medium-ripe bananas	*pinch of salt*
½ cup orange juice	*60 g (2 oz) butter*
1 tablespoon lemon juice	*1 cup grated fresh coconut or*
¼ cup brown sugar	*flaked coconut*

Peel the bananas and arrange them in a buttered shallow casserole. Combine the orange and lemon juices, brown sugar and salt and pour over the bananas. Dot with butter and bake for 10 to 15 minutes in a hot oven (200°C/400°F). The bananas should be cooked through but not too soft. Serve hot or warm, sprinkled with coconut. *Serves 6*

NOTE: The health food store sells flaked coconut.

Pear Crumble

6 medium-ripe pears	CRUMBLE TOPPING:
3 tablespoons lemon juice	*½ cup flour*
½ cup sugar	*¼ cup sugar*
2 tablespoons cornflour	*½ teaspoon each ground ginger*
1 teaspoon grated lemon rind	*and cinnamon*
	60 g (2 oz) butter

First make the crumble topping. Stir the flour, sugar and spices together and mix in the butter with the fingertips until the mixture is crumbly. Set aside.

Peel, core and slice the pears. Toss with the lemon juice, sugar, cornflour and lemon rind. Place in a greased casserole dish and sprinkle with the topping. Bake in a hot oven (200°C/400°F) for 45 minutes, or until the pears are tender and the topping is crisp. Serve with custard, cream or ice-cream. *Serves 6 to 8*

Apple and Walnut Delight

1 cup self-raising flour	*¼ cup chopped dates*
60 g (2 oz) butter, melted	*2 tablespoons chopped*
1 egg	*walnuts*
1 teaspoon vanilla	*4 medium cooking apples,*
2 teaspoons grated lemon rind	*washed, cored and diced*
1 cup brown sugar	

Sift the flour into a bowl, make a well in the centre and add the melted butter, egg, vanilla and grated lemon rind. Mix well with a wooden spoon, then add the remaining ingredients and stir thoroughly. Spread the mixture in a well-greased shallow ovenproof dish and bake in a hot oven (200°C/400°F) for 50 to 60 minutes, until puffy and well browned. Cut into squares and serve hot with whipped cream, custard or ice-cream. *Serves 6*

Frozen Lemon Cream

1 cup milk	*grated rind and juice of 2*
1 cup cream	*medium juicy lemons*
1 cup sugar	*6 whole large lemons*
	small leaves, to garnish

Place the milk, cream and sugar in a bowl and stir until the sugar is dissolved. Pour the mixture into a freezer tray and freeze until it is beginning to set, about 1½ to 2 hours.

Spoon the mixture into a deep bowl, add the lemon rind and juice and beat until smooth. Return to the freezer tray and freeze for a further 2 hours, then beat again. Freeze until firm.

Slice the tops from the lemons and carefully remove all the pulp (save for other uses or discard). Cut a slice from the bottom of each lemon so it will stand up straight. Fill the shells with the lemon cream, piling it high. Garnish with a green leaf. *Serves 6*

Fruit Fondue

a selection of fruits,	*2 tablespoons sieved apricot*
to serve	*jam*
SAUCE:	*2 teaspoons finely chopped*
1 cup thick sour cream	*preserved ginger*
¼ cup desiccated coconut	
2 tablespoons chopped	
walnuts	

Combine all the ingredients for the sauce and divide among 4 small bowls. Arrange a selection of fruits on 4 individual plates for dipping. Choose any of the following fruits or use fresh fruits in season: pineapple, apples, bananas, melon, grapes, cherries, strawberries or oranges. Slice or cut the fruit prettily. Place a bowl of sauce in the centre of the fruit. Chill before serving. *Serves 4*

Fruit Fondue

Steamed Puddings are Special

Some of the warmest family memories centre around old-fashioned puddings – especially steamed puddings with cream or velvety custard.

The method of cooking puddings in a basin over boiling water produces a beautifully light texture which can't be duplicated in any other way. Steamed puddings may be filling, but they should never be stodgy!

Here is a selection of old favourites and a couple of new ideas as well.

Hints on Steaming Puddings

A crockery pudding basin can be used for steaming, or the aluminium type with a snap-on lid. If you are using a crockery basin, seal the top with two layers of buttered greaseproof paper or a single layer of greased aluminium foil, tied securely in place with string.

The pudding basin must be well greased as well as the underside of the lid or foil. Never fill the basin more than two-thirds full with the mixture, to allow for expansion as the pudding cooks.

If you don't have a steamer, it is possible to improvise using an ordinary saucepan. Place an old saucer in the saucepan, rounded side up, and sit the basin on top of this. Add enough boiling water to reach halfway up the pudding basin, and cover the pan with a tight-fitting lid. Check the pan from time to time and top up with more boiling water to keep it at the required level.

Individual puddings look charming and are especially enjoyed by children. Small light metal moulds are available everywhere today, and are not expensive. (You will find them at kitchen shops, department stores and probably your local hardware store.) Butter well and tie down with a double thickness of buttered paper or aluminium foil. An electric frypan half-filled with water makes an excellent steamer for these small puddings.

Light Fruit Pudding

1½ cups self-raising flour	⅔ cup soft brown sugar
pinch of salt	2 eggs
1 teaspoon mixed spice	1 teaspoon grated lemon rind
125 g (4 oz) butter or margarine	½ cup mixed fruit
	3 tablespoons milk

Sift the flour with the salt and spice. Cream the butter and brown sugar until light and fluffy, then beat in the eggs and lemon rind. (If beating by hand, the eggs should be beaten first.) Stir in the fruit, then fold in the flour alternately with the milk.

Spoon into a well-buttered 4–5 cup pudding basin. Cover with a double thickness of buttered greaseproof paper or aluminium foil, or a snap-on lid, and steam for 2 hours. Add extra boiling water when necessary. When cooked, remove the paper or lid and turn out onto a hot dish. Serve hot with custard, cream, ice-cream or jam. *Serves 4 to 6*

Chocolate Steamed Pudding

125 g (4 oz) butter or margarine	2 eggs
¾ cup caster sugar	1½ cups self-raising flour
1 tablespoon golden syrup or honey	2 tablespoons cocoa
	pinch of salt
	¼ cup milk

Cream the butter or margarine and caster sugar together, beating thoroughly, then stir in the syrup or honey. Add the eggs, one at a time, and beat well. Sift the flour with the cocoa and salt and fold into the egg mixture alternately with the milk.

Spoon into a well-greased 4–5 cup pudding basin. Cover with a double thickness of greased greaseproof paper or aluminium foil, or a snap-on lid, and steam for 2 hours. Remove the cover and turn out onto a heated serving dish. Serve hot with custard or cream, or with chocolate ice-cream. *Serves 4 to 6*

Sauces to Serve with Puddings

Prepared dairy custard, available in refrigerated cabinets at your food market, is very good and keeps well. The custard can be heated, but cold custard is nice on hot puddings. If you wish, flavour it with a little extra vanilla, a pinch of nutmeg or a nip of brandy. Custard is also delicious mixed half and half with softened ice-cream (this should be done at the last moment, so the ice-cream doesn't melt too much).

Leftover syrup from stewed or canned fruit is good, thickened with a little cornflour mixed to a paste with some of the syrup, and sharpened with lemon juice. For a quick sauce, you can push a good fruit jam through a sieve (apricot, plum, raspberry, strawberry or peach) and heat it to pouring consistency with water and a dash of lemon juice. Sour cream is a change from fresh cream – try it lightly sweetened with brown sugar – and cold ice-cream on hot pudding is a special favourite with children.

Pineapple Fluff Sauce

¼ cup sugar	¾ cup pineapple juice
1 tablespoon cornflour	½ cup orange juice
1 egg, lightly beaten with 3 tablespoons cold water	1 cup cream, whipped with 2 tablespoons sugar

Combine the sugar and cornflour in a small bowl. Add the beaten egg and blend well. Heat the juices in a saucepan and stir a little into the egg mixture. Tip the mixture into the hot juice, and stir until clear and thick. Chill in the refrigerator, then combine with the whipped cream. *Makes about 3 cups (6 servings)*

Light Fruit Pudding

Sago Plum Pudding

This old favourite has a light texture and lovely flavour.

2 tablespoons sago	pinch of salt
1 cup milk	1 cup fine breadcrumbs
60 g (2 oz) butter	1 cup mixed fruit
¾ cup sugar	2 teaspoons grated lemon rind
1 teaspoon bicarbonate of soda	1 teaspoon mixed spice

Soak the sago in the milk overnight. Cream the butter and sugar and stir in the sago, bicarbonate of soda and salt. Add the remaining ingredients and mix well. Spoon into a well-greased 4-cup pudding basin. Cover with a double thickness of greased greaseproof paper or aluminium foil, or a snap-on lid, and steam for 2 hours. Serve hot with boiled custard or cream. *Serves 6*

Date Pudding

60 g (2 oz) butter	1 cup boiling water
½ cup brown sugar	1 egg, beaten
1 cup chopped dates	1 cup self-raising flour
½ cup sultanas	1 teaspoon cinnamon
1 teaspoon vanilla	pinch of salt
1 teaspoon bicarbonate of soda	

Place the butter, sugar, dates, sultanas, vanilla and bicarbonate of soda in a large bowl and pour boiling water over. Stir well to mix and allow to cool. Stir in the egg. Sift in the flour, cinnamon and salt and combine lightly. Pour into a well-greased 7-cup pudding basin. Cover with greased greaseproof paper or aluminium foil, or a snap-on lid, and steam for 2 hours. *Serves 6*

Almond Caramel Pudding

A most distinctive pudding with ground almonds replacing most of the flour. The texture is rich but light, the flavour superb.

⅓ cup sugar	1 cup ground almonds
¾ cup hot milk	butter and sugar for lining basin
60 g (2 oz) butter, softened	whipped cream or Eggnog Sauce (see below), to serve
5 eggs, separated	
1 teaspoon vanilla	
1½ tablespoons flour	

Place the sugar in a heavy frying pan and stir over a medium heat until it melts and is light brown. Stir in the hot milk very slowly off the heat, then allow to cool. Place the softened butter in a bowl and beat in the egg yolks, one at a time. Add the caramel milk, vanilla, flour and ground almonds and mix well until smooth.

Whip the egg whites until stiff but not dry and lightly fold them through the yolk mixture. Grease a 5-cup pudding basin generously with butter and sprinkle with sugar. Spoon the batter in, cover with a double thickness of greased greaseproof paper or greased aluminium foil, or a snap-on lid, and steam for 1 hour. Turn out onto a serving dish and serve hot with whipped cream or Eggnog Sauce. *Serves 6*

Eggnog Sauce Beat 2 egg yolks until light and frothy, then beat in 1 cup sifted icing sugar. Add 2 tablespoons dark rum and 2 tablespoons sweet sherry and mix well. Stir in 1 cup cream, whipped until stiff. *Makes 6 servings*

Cherry Castle Puddings

Cherry Castle Puddings

Cherry jam is available in most supermarkets today, but if you are unable to find it use strawberry, raspberry or blackcurrant.

125 g (4 oz) butter	1½ cups self-raising flour
½ cup caster sugar	pinch of salt
½ teaspoon vanilla	3–4 tablespoons milk
2 eggs, beaten	cherry jam

Cream the butter, sugar and vanilla. Gradually beat in the eggs, about a tablespoon at a time. Sift the flour with the salt and fold into the egg mixture. Add enough milk to give a soft dropping consistency. Grease 6 small moulds and put a spoonful of jam in the bottom of each. Fill each mould two-thirds full with the pudding mixture and tie a circle of buttered aluminium foil over the top.

Place the moulds in a baking tin with enough boiling water to come halfway up the sides (or arrange them in an electric frypan). Cover, and bake in a preheated moderate oven (180°C/350°F) for about 50 minutes or the same time in a frypan with the control set at Moderate.

Test with a skewer when the time is almost up; if it comes out clean the puddings are cooked. Allow the puddings to stand for a moment before turning out and, if necessary, trim the tops with a sharp knife so they will stand up straight on the serving dish. Serve with pouring cream or custard. *Serves 6*

Light Jam Sauce

2 tablespoons jam	1 teaspoon cornflour blended
½ cup water	with 2 teaspoons water
1 tablespoon lemon juice	1 tablespoon fruit liqueur
	(optional)

Place the jam, water and lemon juice in a saucepan and heat gently, stirring. Add the blended cornflour, bring to the boil and simmer for 3 minutes. Stir in the liqueur, if using. *Serves 4*

Custard Sauce

1½ tablespoons sugar	1 egg, beaten
2 tablespoons custard powder	3 cups milk
pinch of salt	1 teaspoon vanilla

Combine the sugar, custard powder, salt and egg. Mix to a smooth paste with a little of the milk. Bring the remaining milk almost to boiling point, then stir in the custard powder mixture. Bring to the boil and simmer, stirring constantly, for 3 minutes. Stir in the vanilla. *Serves 6 to 8*

Lemon Passionfruit Sauce

½ cup sugar	1 cup water or syrup from
pinch of salt	stewed fruit
1 tablespoon cornflour	3 tablespoons lemon juice
1 teaspoon grated lemon rind	pulp of 2 passionfruit
	15 g (½ oz) butter

Blend the sugar, salt, cornflour and lemon rind to a smooth paste with the water or syrup. Bring to the boil, stirring constantly, and simmer for 3 minutes. Stir in the remaining ingredients over a low heat. *Serves 4 to 6*
NOTE: If using syrup from canned or stewed fruit, reduce sugar to 2 tablespoons.

Golden Orange Sponge

Golden syrup puddings bring back lovely memories of leisurely Sunday dinners. Serve with custard or Lemon Passionfruit Sauce.

30 g (1 oz) butter, softened	2 eggs, beaten
1 medium orange	1½ cups self-raising flour
3 tablespoons golden syrup	pinch of salt
SPONGE:	reserved orange juice, made up
125 g (4 oz) butter	to 2 tablespoons with water
½ cup brown sugar	if necessary
grated rind of 1 orange	

To prepare and cook, see step-by-step pictures opposite. *Serves 4 to 6*

Spiced Apple Pudding

A light, economical, one-egg pudding with lovely flavour.

60 g (2 oz) butter	1 teaspoon each ground
½ cup brown sugar, firmly	ginger, nutmeg and
packed	cinnamon
1 egg, beaten	½ cup buttermilk or milk
½ cup golden syrup	soured with a little lemon
1 tablespoon finely grated	juice
orange rind	1 cup chopped unpeeled
1½ cups sifted flour	apples
½ teaspoon bicarbonate of soda	Spicy Hard Sauce (see below –
	optional)

Cream the butter and sugar until light and fluffy. Beat in the egg, golden syrup and orange rind. Sift the flour with the bicarbonate of soda and spices and add to the creamed mixture alternately with the buttermilk. Fold in the chopped apples. Spoon into a greased 6-cup mould, cover with a double thickness of greased greaseproof paper or foil, or a snap-on lid, and steam for 1½ hours. Turn out onto a serving dish and serve with Spicy Hard Sauce. *Serves 6*
Spicy Hard Sauce Cream 60 g (2 oz) butter with ¾ cup icing sugar. Add a pinch of salt, 1 tablespoon lemon juice, 1 teaspoon vanilla and 2 teaspoons mixed spice. Beat until light and fluffy, then chill. Serve cold on a hot pudding. *Serves 6*

Golden Orange Sponge

1 Grease a 4–5 cup pudding basin with the softened butter. Finely grate the rind of the orange and reserve for the sponge. Remove the pith with a sharp knife. Cut to the centre on either side of each membrane and remove flesh, catching the juice in a bowl. Spread the golden syrup over the bottom of the basin and arrange the orange segments on top.

2 Cream the butter and sugar together until light and fluffy, then stir in the grated rind.

3 Gradually add the eggs, about a tablespoon at a time, beating well between each addition.

4 Sift the flour and salt together and fold into the egg mixture quickly and lightly. Add the reserved orange juice, or orange juice and water, and fold in. Spoon the mixture into the bowl on top of the orange segments. Cover tightly with greased greaseproof paper or aluminium foil, or a snap-on lid, and steam for $1\frac{1}{2}$ hours, until cooked when tested with a fine skewer.

Golden Orange Sponge

Old-Fashioned Roly-Poly Puddings

Roly-poly puddings are made of a pastry crust rolled around a sweet filling and either steamed or baked. The crust traditionally contains suet, but butter or margarine gives a nice light crust and is always handy in the refrigerator.

Fillings can be as varied as you wish. A well-flavoured jam like raspberry or plum makes a simple but delicious filling, and you can have almost any combination of fresh or dried fruits.

Spread filling over pastry, leaving border. Fold edges in, then roll up. Moisten edges to seal.

Basic Roly-Poly

2 cups self-raising flour	4–5 tablespoons iced water
good pinch of salt	filling (see suggestions below)
60 g (2 oz) butter	
60 g (2 oz) lard	

Sift the flour and salt into a bowl. Add the butter and lard, cut into small pieces, and mix lightly through the flour until the mixture resembles coarse breadcrumbs. Add enough cold water to bind into a soft dough.

Roll the pastry out on a floured board to a rectangle about 25 × 20 cm (10 × 8 inches). Spread with chosen filling, leaving a border about 1 cm (½ inch) around the edges. Fold this border in (see picture), then roll up. Bake or steam as directed.
To Steam Roly-Poly Place the roly-poly, seam side down, on a sheet of greased aluminium foil and wrap loosely. Seal the foil at each end by pressing the edges together and folding over. Put the roll in a steamer over boiling water, cover with a lid, and steam for 2 hours. (Have a look at the water level now and again and add more water as necessary.)

If you don't have a steamer, place a wire cake rack inside a deep baking dish or saucepan. Put the foil-wrapped pudding on the cake rack with the water level coming about 5 cm (2 inches) below it. Cover the pan tightly and steam for 2 hours.
To Bake Roly-Poly Place the roly-poly, seam side down, on a greased baking tray. Cut a few slits in the top to allow the steam to escape, brush with milk and sprinkle with sugar. Bake in a preheated hot oven (200°C/400°F) for 30 minutes or until the pastry is crisp and golden brown.

For steaming, pudding is wrapped loosely in foil, leaving a little room for pastry to expand. To serve, open foil and roll pudding onto serving dish.

Roly-Poly Fillings

Jam Filling 1 cup jam sprinkled with 1 tablespoon lemon juice.
Fruit and Nut Filling ¾ cup mixed fruit; ¼ cup crushed nuts; 1 tablespoon honey; 1 teaspoon cinnamon; 1 tablespoon lemon juice. Mix all together and spread over the pastry.
Apple and Date Filling 1 cup finely chopped cooking apple; ½ cup chopped dates; 2 tablespoons brown sugar; 1 tablespoon lemon juice. Mix all together and spread over the pastry.
Caramel-Banana Filling 3 ripe bananas; 2 tablespoons softened butter; ½ cup brown sugar; 1 tablespoon lemon juice. Peel the bananas and slice. Spread the pastry with the softened butter and sprinkle evenly with brown sugar. Arrange the banana slices on top, sprinkle with lemon juice and roll up.

Lemon Currant Roly-Poly

This makes a roly-poly with a lovely sponge-like bottom layer and a crispy top crust. This is due to the syrup being absorbed as the roly-poly bakes.

1 quantity Basic Roly-Poly (see this page)	SYRUP:
	1½ cups water
1½ cups currants	3 tablespoons lemon juice
2 tablespoons brown sugar	½ cup sugar
2 teaspoons grated lemon rind	

Roll out the pastry to a rectangle. Mix the currants, sugar and lemon rind together and spread over the pastry. Roll up, moistening the edges and pressing well to seal them together. Cut two or three slashes in the top of the pastry to allow the steam to escape. Arrange the roly-poly, seam side down, in a baking dish.

Heat the water, lemon juice and sugar to boiling point and stir until the sugar has dissolved. Pour around the roly-poly while still boiling, (don't pour it over the top, but around the base), and place at once in a preheated hot oven (200°C/400°F). The syrup should come only halfway up the sides of the roly-poly, so choose a baking dish or casserole that will give the correct

Baked Roly-Poly and Steamed Roly-Poly

depth. Bake for 30 minutes, or until the top crust is golden brown and the bottom has absorbed most of the syrup and is light and spongy. Serve hot with custard or ice-cream. *Serves 4 to 6*

Walnut-Cinnamon Roly-Poly with Brandy Sauce

This is a rich combination, so small servings are in order. However, you might also like to add a spoonful of ice-cream before pouring on the hot sauce . . . a real feast for the sweet tooths in the family.

1 quantity Basic Roly-Poly (see opposite)	*60 g (2 oz) butter, softened*
1 cup crushed walnuts or hazelnuts	*1 large cooking apple, peeled, cored and chopped*
2 teaspoons cinnamon	*Brandy Sauce, to serve (see right)*
½ cup brown sugar	

Roll the pastry out to a rectangle. Mix the remaining ingredients together and spread over the pastry. Roll up, moistening the edges and pressing well to seal them together. Wrap the roly-poly loosely in greased aluminium foil, leaving enough room for the pastry to swell during cooking. Place in a steamer or on a rack over boiling water and steam for 2 hours, adding more water if necessary. Lift out carefully, unwrap the foil and roll onto a heated serving dish.

Cut in slices and serve with hot Brandy Sauce and ice-cream if desired. *Serves 6*

Brandy Sauce Blend 2 tablespoons cornflour or custard powder with a little milk. Place 1¼ cups milk in a saucepan with 2 tablespoons sugar. Heat almost to boiling point, then stir in the blended mixture and simmer for 4 minutes over a low heat, stirring. Add ¼ cup brandy or sweet sherry and serve. *Makes about 1½ cups*

Barbecues for Family Get-togethers

Barbecues are perfect for family gatherings. They can be simple sausage and chop get-togethers or gourmet feasts, depending on the occasion and the budget. But whatever you cook, here are a few simple guidelines:

Get the heat right before you start to cook. A charcoal or wood fire should look ash grey, with a few red gleams by day or glowing red at night.

• Grease the hot grill with oil (or a piece of beef fat on a long fork) just before cooking. Move each piece of food a little as you place it on the grill and it won't stick.

• Have all foods at room temperature. Use square or flat skewers for kebabs, as food tends to slip about on round ones. If using wooden skewers, soak for 30 minutes in hot water to prevent scorching.

Buy an 8 cm (3 inch) brush at the hardware store for basting. It is easier to use than a pastry brush.

To Barbecue Chicken

Cook chicken over a medium heat. If you can't easily adjust the heat, raise the grill; or place two flat stones on the grill, rest a rack on the stones and cook the chicken on that. Allow about 20 minutes for drumsticks (turning now and again) and more for larger pieces. Juices should run clear when tested with a fine skewer.

To Barbecue Fish

The double-sided folding grills with long handles are perfect for whole fish, as you can turn them over without breaking the fish. Baste well with melted butter and lemon juice to keep the flesh juicy. As a safeguard against sticking when cooking directly on the grill bars, cover them with well-greased aluminium foil, and pierce a few holes in it.

Chicken Liver Appetizers

Barbecued Butterfly Lamb

One large piece of meat needs less attention than small pieces and is impressive when you invite friends for a barbecue. This recipe uses a 'butterflied' leg of lamb, which you could order from your butcher the day before.

1 large leg of lamb, about 2.5 kg (4 lb), butterflied	*2 teaspoons garam masala*
MARINADE:	*2 teaspoons turmeric*
1 medium onion, chopped	*½ cup oil*
4 slices fresh ginger, chopped	*2½ teaspoons salt*
5 cloves garlic, chopped	*freshly ground pepper*
½ cup lemon juice	*½ teaspoon orange food*
1 tablespoon ground coriander	*colouring (optional, but*
2 teaspoons ground cumin	*adds rich colour)*

Prepare the marinade first. Place the onion, ginger and garlic in an electric blender with 4 tablespoons of the lemon juice. Blend at high speed to a smooth paste, adding more lemon juice if necessary. Place in a large bowl and stir in the remaining marinade ingredients.

Remove any skin and gristle from the lamb and pierce all over on both sides with a sharp-pointed knife. Rub the marinade well in over the entire surface. Put the meat in the marinade bowl, cover, and refrigerate for 24 hours, turning now and again. Remove from the refrigerator 4 hours before serving time. One hour before serving, lift the meat from the marinade and place in a double-sided hinged grill. Sear on both sides over high heat for 5 minutes each side. Adjust the heat to medium and cook for 20 minutes longer on each side, brushing frequently with the marinade. If you can't adjust the heat, use flat stones to raise the grill further away. The lamb is cooked when it is dark brown outside and the juices run faintly pink when the meat is pierced with a fine skewer. Rest off the heat for 15 minutes before serving.

To serve, place the meat on a carving board and slice downward on the diagonal into thin slices. Serve with crisp salad vegetables (radishes, onion rings and celery sticks) or place the sliced meat and vegetables inside pockets of flat Lebanese bread. *Serves 8*

Chicken Liver Appetizers

1 × 230 g can water chestnuts	DRESSING:
500 g (1 lb) chicken livers	*1 tablespoon wine vinegar*
250 g (8 oz) bacon rashers	*½ teaspoon salt*
	freshly ground pepper
	3 tablespoons vegetable oil

Drain the water chestnuts, cut in halves if large, and place in a small bowl. Mix the vinegar with salt and pepper and beat in the oil with a fork or whisk. Pour the dressing over the chestnuts and set aside.

Trim the membrane and any dark parts from the livers and cut in halves if large. Remove the rind from the bacon and cut into pieces 8–10 cm (3–4 inches) long.

Wrap a chicken liver and a water chestnut in each piece of bacon and secure with a toothpick. Cook under a preheated grill, at medium heat, for 3 to 4 minutes on each side. Brush with dressing once or twice each side. *Makes about 20 appetizers*

Variation

If water chestnuts are unavailable, bamboo shoot can be substituted. Drain well, then cut into slices about 1 cm (½ inch) thick.

Peachy Sausages

Peachy Sausages

A sharp-sweet fruit glaze gives sausages added flavour and
colour. This can also be used with tender cubes of beef or lamb.

1 kg (2 lb) thick sausages	*½ teaspoon Worcestershire*
1 tablespoon oil	*sauce*
1 tablespoon vinegar	*¼ teaspoon salt*
½ cup peach nectar	*2 teaspoons chopped fresh*
¼ cup tomato sauce	*oregano or ½ teaspoon dried*
1 tablespoon brown sugar	*dash of Tabasco or chilli sauce*
1 tablespoon grated onion	

Prick the sausages in several places, place in a frying pan with
water to cover and simmer for 5 minutes, then drain. Parboiled
in this way, the sausages will cook through without scorching
or bursting on the barbecue.

Place the remaining ingredients in a saucepan and simmer for
5 minutes, stirring now and again. Pour over the sausages and
allow to stand for 30 minutes. Thread the sausages onto long
skewers or simply place on grill bars and barbecue until crisp
and brown on all sides, brushing frequently with the glaze.
Spoon remaining glaze over the sausages to serve. *Serves 6 to 8*

Barbecued Spareribs

Spareribs are real 'finger licking' food and especially good
basted with a soy-honey marinade. The preliminary baking
melts away excess fat – this can be done the day before if you
wish and the ribs marinated overnight. Try to get the American
cut spareribs from your butcher, or ask for them at a specialty
pork shop.

1.5 kg (3 lb) pork spareribs, in	*2 cloves garlic, crushed*
two whole pieces	*2 tablespoons honey*
½ cup soy sauce	*2 tablespoons dry sherry*

Wipe the ribs with damp paper towels and place on a rack in a
shallow roasting pan. Bake in a moderate oven (180°C/350°F)
for 45 minutes, when excess fat will have cooked away. Pour the
fat away and place the ribs in the pan. Mix the remaining
ingredients, pour over the ribs and allow to marinate for 1 hour
or so, or refrigerate overnight. Turn the ribs several times.

When ready to barbecue, place the ribs on a grill over a
moderate heat and cook until brown and crisp on both sides,
basting with the marinade. Cut into serving pieces and eat in the
fingers – don't forget plenty of paper napkins! *Serves 6*

Gingered Beef

Ginger-marinated beef, threaded 'snake fashion' in thin strips on skewers, makes a change from the usual steak and also goes much further. It is delicious inside buttered bread rolls or Lebanese bread, with chopped celery or bean sprouts.

750 g (1½ lb) rump, boneless sirloin or good blade steak (see note), cut 4 cm (1½ inches) thick ½ cup soy sauce	2 tablespoons vegetable oil 3 tablespoons honey 1 clove garlic, crushed 1 tablespoon grated fresh ginger

Slice the beef across the grain into 5 mm (¼ inch) strips and place in a bowl. Mix the remaining ingredients and pour over, turning the meat about to coat evenly. Leave to marinate for 1 hour, turning the meat several times.

Remove the meat strips from the marinade and thread onto skewers, concertina or 'snake fashion'. Grill over a very hot fire for about 3 minutes, turning once and brushing with the marinade. The meat should be rare on the inside. *Serves 4 to 6* NOTE: If you are buying blade steak for barbecuing, ask your butcher to recommend his best cut on that day. Undercut, crosscut and oyster blade can all be satisfactory.

Ham and Pineapple Parcels

Ham and pineapple are perfect partners and children love the combination, too. In fact, this recipe is so easy the children can get the parcels ready while you relax.

6 ham steaks prepared mustard 1 tablespoon snipped chives or finely chopped spring onions	6 slices fresh or canned pineapple 2 tablespoons brown sugar mixed with 1 tablespoon vinegar

Cut 6 pieces of foil large enough to wrap loosely around the steaks. Place a ham steak on each piece of foil, spread with a little mustard and sprinkle with chives or spring onions. Top with a pineapple slice and drizzle a little of the brown sugar mixture over the top.

Make into neat parcels, sealing the edges well, and heat over a medium fire for about 8 minutes each side. Let the guests unwrap their own parcels. Serve with a jacket potato (parboiled, then baked in the ashes) and a crisp salad. *Serves 6*

Porkburgers with Pineapple

½ cup fresh white breadcrumbs ½ cup milk 1 kg (2 lb) pork mince 2 teaspoons chopped fresh sage or ½ teaspoon dried 1 small onion, grated 1 egg, beaten	1 teaspoon salt freshly ground pepper 1 fresh pineapple or 1 × 850 g can pineapple rings, drained 2 teaspoons French mustard 15 g (½ oz) butter, melted

Put the breadcrumbs into a large bowl, pour the milk over and leave to soak for a few minutes. Add the pork, sage, onion, egg, salt and a good grinding of pepper. Mix lightly with a fork. Turn out onto a lightly floured board, shape into a round and cut into 8 even-size pieces. With wetted hands, shape each piece into a flat cake.

If using a fresh pineapple, peel, then cut into 8 slices and core.

Mix together the French mustard and melted butter.

Grill the porkburgers over a high heat for about 5 minutes on each side. When the first side is done, brush the pineapple slices with the mustard and butter mixture and grill for about 2 minutes on each side while the porkburgers finish cooking. Serve a slice of pineapple topped with a porkburger. *Serves 4*

Sesame Drumsticks

Chicken is flavoured with a teriyaki-type marinade and rolled in toasted sesame seeds after cooking. Just as nice cold as hot, though it's unlikely there will be any left over!

8 chicken drumsticks ½ cup soy sauce 2 teaspoons sugar 1 teaspoon salt	2 slices fresh ginger, finely chopped 30 g (1 oz) butter, melted 3 tablespoons toasted sesame seeds

Wipe the chicken with damp paper towels. Mix the soy sauce, sugar, salt and ginger and marinate the chicken in the mixture for 2 to 3 hours.

Remove the chicken from the marinade and barbecue over glowing coals until tender, about 10 to 15 minutes each side. (A hinged, double-sided grill will make it easy to turn the chicken.) Mix the melted butter with the remaining marinade and brush the cooked chicken with the mixture, then roll in the toasted sesame seeds. *Serves 4 to 6* NOTE: To toast the sesame seeds, spread out in a baking tray and leave in a moderate oven until lightly browned; or toast in a frying pan over a medium heat, shaking the pan to prevent scorching.

Barbecued Vegetables

You can also cook vegetables while the meat is barbecuing:
Cheesy Spuds
Scrub old potatoes and peel thinly. Cut into chips and place individual servings on squares of foil. Sprinkle each serving with onion salt, celery salt, pepper, and 1 tablespoon grated Parmesan cheese, making sure all the chips are well seasoned. Bring the edges of the foil together and seal tightly, leaving a little room for steam. Cook the potatoes on a rack over glowing coals, turning the packages several times. They will take about 30 minutes.
Vegetables in Foil
Take frozen vegetables directly from the freezer, remove from the pack and place a whole block on a large square of foil. Season with salt and pepper, fresh herbs or chopped onions and add a knob of butter. Seal securely, leaving room for expansion, and cook over hot coals for 15 minutes, turning occasionally.

Cheese and Onion Bread

Hot bread is always a favourite at barbecues, and there are many ways of adding interesting flavours.

1 crusty Italian loaf butter or margarine for spreading 8–10 slices cheese (processed cheese, Mozzarella, Edam, Gouda, etc.)	2 medium onions, thinly sliced salt freshly ground pepper

Cut the loaf across into slices almost through to the bottom crust. Butter in between the slices and over the top of the loaf. Insert a slice of cheese and a couple of onion slices in between each bread slice and season with salt and pepper. Wrap the loaf tightly in aluminium foil and heat over glowing coals for about 10 minutes each side; the cheese will be melted, the onions soft and the bread crisp. *Serves 8 to 10*

Fresh Herb Bread

This is really best with fresh herbs, but dried herbs will do at a pinch; use 2 teaspoons mixed with 1 cup chopped parsley.

1 long loaf French bread	*salt*
90 g (3 oz) butter, softened	*freshly ground pepper*
1 cup chopped fresh herbs	*2 tablespoons lemon juice*
(marjoram, oregano,	
parsley, chives, basil)	

Cut the bread into thick slices almost through to the bottom crust. Combine the butter with the herbs and salt and pepper to taste. Work in the lemon juice. Butter the bread between the slices and over the top with the herb mixture and wrap tightly in foil. Heat over glowing coals for 10 minutes each side. *Serves 8*

Barbecue Desserts

No need to miss out on something sweet when the barbecue's going. Here are some delicious desserts to cook over glowing coals:

Cake Kabobs
Cut a plain butter cake into 2.5 cm (1 inch) cubes. Dip in melted redcurrant jelly or sweetened condensed milk, then roll in

Fresh Herb Bread

desiccated coconut. Thread cubes on skewers and grill over hot coals, turning often, until the coconut is toasted.

Marshmallow Surprises
This is a favourite American confection. You need a packet of marshmallows, squares of milk chocolate and plain cracker biscuits. Toast the marshmallows on a long fork until runny, then sandwich 2 hot marshmallows and a square of chocolate between 2 crackers. The hot marshmallow partially melts the chocolate, and the whole thing – though it sounds odd – is absolutely delicious.

Skewered Fruits
Thread any combination of fruits on long skewers, dip in lemon juice and honey and toast until heated through. Serve plain or with ice-cream.

Spirited Fruits

The rum flavour is great for grown-ups. For children, make a separate batch using extra fruit juice.

4 canned peach halves, drained and cut in halves	*½ cup brown sugar*
4 bananas, each cut in 4 pieces	*½ cup reserved syrup from fruit*
4 canned pineapple rings, drained, and each cut in 4 pieces	*¼ cup rum or brandy*
	2 tablespoons lemon juice

Place the fruit in a heavy frying pan or baking dish that can go over the glowing coals. Add the sugar and syrup and heat through. Stir in the rum or brandy and lemon juice. Serve plain or with ice-cream. *Serves 4*
NOTE: If you wish, you can flame the rum or brandy. Pour it into the pan, allow to warm, then light it and serve when the flames subside. You can also make the recipe with any combination of fresh fruits in season such as peaches, nectarines, apricots or plums.

Cooking for Special Occasions

Cooking for Special Occasions

There are many occasions that make life special and that seem to call for a touch of celebration about the food.

Weddings, births, birthdays and anniversaries are natural celebrations. So are housewarmings, promotions, passing exams and travelling overseas or returning.

Entertaining friends is an opportunity to present food with a difference, and it's exciting to plan a lovely picnic or a meal served in your own garden for a change, or a children's party . . . or perhaps a quiet dinner for two.

Even feeling good to be alive on a mellow autumn day, for no special reason at all, is just cause for a special occasion meal to celebrate!

Of course, food doesn't have to be expensive or elaborate to be special. A bouquet of bright watercress on a platter makes a simple cold meat salad look spring fresh. An interesting first course automatically makes a meal special and so does a pretty dessert or a table set with care.

There are many ideas here to help you enjoy your own special occasions. But don't wait for an excuse . . . lovely food makes an occasion special just by itself, and can give pleasure every single day!

Soup . . . The Great Classics

An exquisite soup is the perfect opener for an important dinner; it shows restraint and an understanding of the balance of a meal. Of course, the flavour must be just right and the garnish imaginative. Usually you will start with a good homemade stock, rich from long simmering with meat, bones and aromatics. There are exceptions, however, where the ingredients for a specific soup provide all the flavour.

When you are planning a more casual occasion, think of the robust classics that have warmed midnight revellers or graced alfresco luncheons in many countries. A soup like this can be a great beginning or the heart of the meal.

Basic Stocks

If you have an electric slow cooker, you will find it ideal for making stock; put it on at bedtime and let it simmer all night. If you don't have one, make the stock in a big heavy saucepan and cook over the lowest possible heat for only 2 to 3 hours.

Beef Stock

approximately 1 kg (2 lb) beef bones	*1 small onion, roughly chopped*
250 g (8 oz) chopped shin beef	*4 peppercorns*
2 sticks celery or celery leaves	*bouquet garni (bay leaf, sprig of thyme, and 4 parsley stalks, tied together)*
2 small pieces each of turnip and carrot	

Ask the butcher to crack the bones. Remove any meat and chop it finely. Wash the bones and place them in an electric slow cooker with the chopped meat, vegetables and seasonings. Fill the cooker two-thirds full with cold water (don't fill further or the stock may splutter over it when it comes to simmering point).

Put the lid on and cook overnight, 8 to 10 hours, on Low setting. If it is more convenient, cook at High setting for 4 to 6 hours only; this will give stock that is lighter in colour and less concentrated in flavour.

At the end of the cooking time, remove the bones and strain the stock into a bowl. Cool, then chill in the refrigerator and remove the solid fat from the top.

NOTE: Stock will keep for several days in the refrigerator; if you want to keep it longer, reboil every few days or freeze it in batches suitable for use – it will remain in good condition for months.

Variations

Brown Stock Use the same ingredients as for Beef Stock, but first put the vegetables into a greased, flameproof baking dish, place the bones and meat on top and brown them for 20 minutes in a hot oven (220°C/425°F). Transfer them to a slow cooker. Pour 2 cups of water into the baking dish and stir over a low heat for a minute or two to incorporate all the good brown bits from the dish into the liquid. Use as part of the water for the stock and proceed as in the recipe for Beef Stock.

Chicken Stock Use a chicken carcass, chicken pieces such as wings or backs, or a small boiling fowl instead of beef bones and meat, and follow the recipe for Beef Stock.
Veal Stock Use veal bones (knuckle and shin) and chopped stewing veal instead of beef bones and meat, and follow the recipe for Beef Stock.

Game Soup

When you're lucky enough to have game, make the most of it by using the carcasses and any leftover meat for this gourmet soup.

2–3 game bird carcasses (cooked)	*90g (3 oz) mushrooms, chopped*
6 cups beef stock (this page)	*½ cup flour*
2 teaspoons chopped, mixed fresh herbs or ½ teaspoon dried	*salt*
	freshly ground pepper
60 g (2 oz) butter	*¼ cup port or sherry*
60 g (2 oz) streaky bacon, chopped	*60–90 g (2–3 oz) cooked game bird meat, chopped*
1 onion, chopped	*lemon juice*
	small croûtons, to garnish (see page 199)

Simmer the carcasses, stock and herbs together for 1½ hours. Strain into a bowl and wash out the saucepan.

In the same saucepan, melt the butter and brown the bacon and vegetables. Stir in the flour, cook for 2 minutes, then stir in the stock and bring to the boil, stirring constantly. Season with salt and pepper, add the port or sherry and the meat. Cover, and simmer until the vegetables are tender, 20 to 30 minutes. Sharpen the flavour with lemon juice to taste. Serve garnished with croûtons. *Serves 6*

French Onion Soup, Gratinée

30 g (1 oz) butter
1 tablespoon olive oil
500 g (1 lb) onions, thinly
    sliced
large pinch of sugar
¼ cup flour
5 cups warm brown stock
    (see opposite)
¼ cup dry white wine or
    vermouth

salt
freshly ground pepper
3 tablespoons brandy
TOPPING:
4 thick slices French bread
1 clove garlic, cut in half
30 g (1 oz) butter
125 g (4 oz) Gruyère cheese,
    grated

Heat the butter and oil in a large heavy saucepan, add the onions, stir well and cover. Cook gently for 15 minutes, then remove the lid and sprinkle in the sugar. Continue to cook, stirring often, until the onions are deep golden brown.

Sprinkle in the flour, stir for 2 minutes, then remove from the heat and cool a little. Blend in the warm stock and wine or vermouth. Season with salt and pepper, cover the pan and simmer for 45 minutes.

Meanwhile, rub the bread with garlic, butter it and bake in a slow oven (150°C/300°F) until dried out and lightly browned. Sprinkle with about half the cheese and grill until it has melted.

Place the bread croûtes in 4 heated bowls or a tureen. Stir the brandy into the soup and pour over the croûtes. Serve immediately, handing the remaining cheese separately. *Serves 4*

Game Soup; French Onion Soup,
Gratinée

A Note on Stocks, Broths and Consommés

Strictly speaking, stock is not salted. Salt is added to the recipe in which it is used. The reason is that this gives the cook perfect control over the saltiness of the particular dish.

Broth is stock with seasonings added. It may be made from the basic stock, unstrained, or from strained stock with additional meat, vegetables or cereals.

Consommé is seasoned stock which has had all fat removed and has been clarified so that it is sparkling clear. The stock is simmered with egg whites which, as they cook, trap and hold the particles that cause cloudiness. (See Consommé Royale, page 145.)

Fish Stock

Unlike other stocks, fish stock is cooked for a short time only. If cooked with the bones for longer than about 20 minutes, the stock becomes sticky and the flavour less delicate. This recipe makes a light stock to use as the basis for soups. To make a more concentrated one for use in sauces, it is boiled down rapidly after straining.

approximately 750 g (1½ lb) fish trimmings (bones, skins, heads)	bouquet of 6 parsley stalks and a sprig of thyme or lemon thyme, tied together
1 medium onion, chopped	½ cup dry white wine or 1 tablespoon white wine vinegar
1 carrot, chopped	
10 cm (4 inch) piece of celery	7 cups water
6 peppercorns	

To prepare, see step-by-step pictures below. *Makes approximately 7 cups*

Fish Stock

1 Rinse the fish trimmings in cold water and put them into a large saucepan with the other ingredients. Heat until just simmering (when the surface of the liquid shivers and a few bubbles rise). If you allow it to boil, the stock will be clouded with white particles of overcooked protein shed by the fish.

2 Simmer for 5 minutes, then skim off any scum that has collected on the surface, using a large metal spoon or perforated skimmer. Continue to simmer for another 15 minutes, then strain through a fine-meshed sieve into a bowl. Use the stock for soups or return to the rinsed-out pan and reduce by rapid boiling if it is required for a sauce.

New England Fish Chowder

More than a soup, not quite a stew, chowder is a comforting, stick-to-the-ribs concoction just right for crisp winter nights. It comes to us from the United States, where each region has its own special recipe. Diced pickled pork or bacon are almost invariably used to flavour the chowder. Potatoes are added for hearty texture, and milk is included to give the traditional creamy colour. This is a great recipe for a crowd, because it doubles or even trebles successfully – and any kind of fish may be used.

500 g (1 lb) fish fillets	1 large onion, chopped
2½ cups fish stock (see this page) or water	60 g (2 oz) mushrooms, sliced
	2 tablespoons flour
salt	1½ cups milk
60 g (2 oz) diced pickled pork or streaky bacon	lemon juice
	freshly ground pepper
60 g (2 oz) butter	2 tablespoons chopped parsley
2 large potatoes, peeled	

Cut the fish into pieces. Bring the fish stock or water to the boil in a large heavy saucepan, add a pinch of salt and the fish and simmer gently for 10 minutes. Strain into a bowl, reserve the liquid and flake the fish roughly, discarding any skin or bones. Wash and dry the saucepan.

Put the diced pork or bacon into the saucepan and cook gently until the fat runs and the meat crisps, then add the butter. Cut the potatoes into cubes and add with the onion and mushrooms. Fry slowly for 5 minutes, stir in the flour and cook for 1 minute more.

Remove from the heat. Cool a little and blend in the warm cooking liquid, then the milk, stirring until smooth. Return to the heat and stir until simmering. Cook until the potatoes are soft, then add the fish and reheat. Sharpen the flavour with lemon juice to taste, season with salt and pepper and stir in the parsley. *Serves 6*

*New England Fish Chowder;
Fish and Lemon Soup*

Fish and Lemon Soup

1 large or 2 small fish heads	salt
5 cups fish stock (see opposite)	freshly ground pepper
2 tablespoons raw rice	(preferably white)
3 egg yolks, beaten	snipped chives, to garnish
4 tablespoons lemon juice	

Wash the fish head. Bring the stock to the boil and add the fish and rice. Reduce the heat and simmer for 20 minutes, then remove the head, flake off any flesh and discard the skin and bones. Remove the saucepan from the heat.

Put the egg yolks into a small bowl and gradually whisk in the lemon juice. Stir in 3 or 4 tablespoons of the hot soup, a spoonful at a time, then pour the mixture slowly back into the hot soup, stirring all the time. Return the saucepan to the heat. Add the flaked fish and reheat, still stirring continuously, until glossy and slightly thickened – but be very careful not to allow the soup to boil or it will curdle. Season with salt and pepper and serve immediately, garnished with snipped chives. *Serves 6*

Variation

Avgolemono The classic Greek 'egg and lemon' soup is made in the same way. Omit the fish head and use chicken stock in place of fish stock. You may add a little shredded cooked chicken after the egg and lemon mixture is stirred in, if you wish.

Matelote

90 g (3 oz) butter	1 bay leaf
12 tiny onions, peeled	2 cloves garlic, crushed
18 button mushrooms	1 teaspoon chopped fresh thyme
750 g (1½ lb) skinned fish fillets	½ cup chopped celery
2 tablespoons brandy	1 teaspoon salt
2 cups red wine	freshly ground pepper
4 cups fish stock (see opposite)	2½ tablespoons flour
2 teaspoons chopped parsley	500 g (1 lb) small peeled prawns

Heat 30 g (1 oz) of the butter and fry the onions and mushrooms for 3 minutes over high heat. Remove the mushrooms. Reduce the heat and add a little water to the pan; then cover the pan, and cook the onions until tender. Set aside.

Cut the fish into 2.5 cm (1 inch) slices and place in a large saucepan (preferably not aluminium). Heat the brandy, set alight, and pour over the fish. Add the wine, stock, herbs, celery, salt and pepper. Cover the pan and simmer for 10 minutes or until the fish is tender. Remove fish and keep warm.

Blend the remaining 60 g (2 oz) of butter with the flour to make a beurre manié for thickening. Pick up a little beurre manié on the end of a small whisk and whisk gently into the simmering soup. Repeat with the rest of the beurre manié. Taste the soup and correct the seasoning.

To serve, arrange the fish in 6 large heated bowls. Place the onions and mushrooms on top and divide the prawns evenly among the bowls. Ladle the piping hot soup over and serve at once with crusty bread. *Serves 6*

Consommé Royale

Cream of Lettuce Soup, Reform Club

In the heyday of London's great clubs, some of the most famous French chefs ruled over the kitchens and invented dishes that became stars of the *haute cuisine*. This is a soup of velvet texture and rich yet delicate flavour – worthy of the grandest occasion.

60 g (2 oz) butter	*1 medium head lettuce, finely*
1 thin slice garlic, finely	*shredded*
chopped	*1 cup finely chopped*
1 teaspoon finely chopped	*watercress (optional)*
fresh tarragon	*5 cups beef stock (page 140)*
1 tablespoon finely chopped	*salt*
parsley	*freshly ground pepper*
¼ teaspoon dried tarragon	*1 cup milk*
3 tablespoons finely chopped	*2 egg yolks*
onion	*1 cup cream*
2 tablespoons finely chopped	
green pepper	

Melt the butter in a large heavy saucepan, add the garlic and herbs and warm gently for a few minutes. Stir in the onion and green pepper and cook over a low heat for 3 minutes, stirring constantly. Add the lettuce and watercress and continue to cook gently for 3 or 4 minutes, still stirring. The vegetables should be soft but not even an edge must begin to brown or the flavour will be spoilt. Add the beef stock, cover the pan and cook for 20 minutes. Taste and season with salt and pepper, and continue cooking for 15 minutes more.

Scald the milk (heat gently until bubbles form round the edge). Remove the soup from the heat and stir in the milk; cover and stand aside until ready to serve. When required, reheat gently. Beat the egg yolks slightly, mix in the cream and pour slowly into the soup, stirring constantly. Heat, stirring, but do not allow to boil. The soup is ready when it becomes glossy and thickens very slightly. Check the seasoning, adjust if necessary and serve immediately. *Serves 8 to 10*

Zuppa alla Pavese

This soup is said to have been invented by an Italian farmer's wife to honour King Francis I after the Battle of Pavia.

6 cups chicken stock (page	*6 thick slices crusty bread*
140)	*(e.g. Italian or Vienna)*
salt	*½ cup grated Parmesan cheese*
freshly ground pepper	*6 eggs at room temperature*
90 g (3 oz) butter	

Place the stock in a saucepan, heat gently, and season to taste with salt and pepper. Heat the butter in a large frying pan and sauté the bread on both sides until golden. Place a slice in 6 heated soup bowls. Sprinkle with a little salt and the grated cheese. Break an egg into each bowl. Bring the stock to a rolling boil and carefully ladle over the eggs. (Keep the stock on the heat while working, so it remains hot enough to poach the eggs.) Serve at once. *Serves 6*

Chilled Herb Soup

A quick, light and healthy soup.

2 cups natural yogurt	*freshly ground pepper*
1 cup tomato juice	*1 large or 2 small green*
6–8 parsley sprigs	*cucumbers*
6–8 mint sprigs	*extra snipped chives, to*
2 tablespoons snipped chives	*garnish*
salt	

Put the yogurt, tomato juice, herbs and salt and pepper to taste in a blender or food processor fitted with the steel blade. Blend until well combined, then chill.

Peel the cucumber with a spiral peeler, leaving a few strips of green skin on. Halve lengthwise and scoop out the seeds. Chop finely and chill.

To serve, divide the cucumber among 4 soup bowls and ladle the chilled soup over. Garnish with finely snipped chives. *Serves 4*

Consommé Royale

Nothing can match a fine consommé for elegance, and it is the perfect choice when you want to serve another course that is rich or elaborate. Consommés take their names from the garnish; this one, Royale, consists of delicate little shapes cut from savoury baked custard.

8 cups brown stock (page 140)	1 egg yolk
2 egg whites and shells	2 tablespoons milk
250 g (8 oz) absolutely lean raw beef, finely minced	1/4 teaspoon salt
1/2 cup dry sherry	small pinch of white pepper
TO GARNISH:	pinch of nutmeg
1 egg	

Chill the stock and remove every speck of fat from the surface. Put the stock into a perfectly clean saucepan, not aluminium. If it is set to a jelly, warm it just enough to become liquid. Whip the egg whites to a froth, crush the egg shells and add the whites, shells, minced beef and sherry to the saucepan. Set over a moderate heat and whisk the whole steadily until the mixture comes to the boil.

As soon as the mixture boils, stop whisking, turn heat to low and simmer gently for 20 minutes. A white crust will form on the surface and this must not be broken as it holds all the impurities from the stock.

Have ready a clean tea-towel, some butter muslin or disposable cloths. Scald the cloth well by pouring boiling water through it, wring out and fold into a double layer to line a large sieve. Set the sieve over a large bowl.

Carefully lift the white crust from the saucepan into the sieve and pour the liquid slowly through it. Do not press or squeeze the crust or the cloth.

When the consommé is required, reheat, adjust the seasoning if necessary, and serve with the garnish. *Serves 6 to 8*
Royale Garnish Beat the egg and egg yolk together in a small bowl, add the remaining ingredients and combine well. Strain through a fine strainer into a greased 23 × 13 cm (9 × 5 inch) loaf tin. The custard mixture should be about 5 mm (1/4 inch) deep. Place the loaf tin in a pan of hot water and bake in a slow oven (150°C/300°F) for 20 minutes. To test the custard, insert a stainless knife into the centre. If it comes out clean, the custard is done. If not, cook 5 minutes more and test again.

Allow the custard to cool in the loaf tin, then cover and refrigerate until cold. With small fancy cutters, stamp out pieces of royale into such shapes as crescents, stars or fluted circles, or cut into diamond shapes with a knife. Lift out and place the shapes in serving cups, then pour the hot consommé over them.

Iced Apple-Curry Soup

Serve this delicious soup for a summer lunch. It's very special – and foolproof!

3 cups chicken stock (page 140)	2 large eating apples, peeled, cored and cut into small dice
1 cup apple juice	
1 cup cream	
3 teaspoons curry powder mixed to a paste with 1 tablespoon sherry	1 tablespoon lemon juice
	a few strips of unpeeled apple

Heat the chicken stock, juice and cream together but do not allow to boil. Stir in the curry powder and allow to cool, then chill. Sprinkle the apples with lemon juice and divide among 4 bowls, then ladle in the chilled soup. Garnish each bowl with a few strips of apple. *Serves 4*

Tomato Soup with Fresh Basil Paste

Make the basil paste in the summer when the fresh herb is available, and keep it, covered with oil, in the refrigerator for the winter months.

1 teaspoon olive oil	3 ripe tomatoes, chopped
1 medium carrot, scraped and sliced	1 tablespoon tomato paste
1 small sliced leek, white part only, or 8 spring onions, chopped	5 cups chicken stock (page 140)
	1 teaspoon salt
	freshly ground pepper
1 clove garlic, crushed	BASIL PASTE:
sprig of fresh thyme or small pinch dried	2 handfuls of basil leaves
1/2 bay leaf	2 teaspoons olive oil

Heat the olive oil in a large heavy saucepan, add the carrot, leek or spring onions and garlic and cook gently for 5 minutes. Stir in the thyme, bay leaf, tomatoes and tomato paste, then the chicken stock. Heat until simmering, add salt and pepper to taste and simmer, half covered, for 20 minutes.

Meanwhile, put the basil leaves and olive oil in a blender or food processor fitted with the steel blade and blend to a paste.

Rub the soup through a sieve and return to the saucepan (or purée in a blender or food processor and strain back into the saucepan). Reheat and serve, swirling a small dollop of the basil paste into each serving. *Serves 6*
NOTE: If fresh basil is unavailable, use the basil sauce called 'pesto', from good delicatessens.

Fresh Mushroom Soup

This soup has a stunningly different flavour from those which use cooked mushrooms. Here the raw mushrooms are puréed then merely reheated with the other ingredients, giving a true fresh mushroom taste.

5 cups chicken stock (page 140)	1 egg yolk
1 clove garlic, crushed	1/2 cup cream
250 g (8 oz) large open mushrooms	2 small button mushrooms, thinly sliced
60 g (2 oz) butter	croûtons, to serve (page 199)
salt	
freshly ground pepper	

In a large heavy saucepan, heat the stock with the garlic. Roughly chop the large mushrooms and put about one-third of them into a blender or food processor. Add the butter, pour in about one-third of the stock and process until smooth. Pour into a saucepan for reheating. Repeat twice with the remaining mushrooms and stock.

Heat the mushroom mixture gently until very hot, and season with salt and pepper to taste. Beat the egg yolk with the cream until well blended. Stir in a little of the hot soup, then pour this mixture back into the saucepan and stir until the soup becomes glossy and thickens slightly, but do not allow to boil. Serve immediately, garnished with mushroom slices. Hand croûtons separately. *Serves 6*

146

Sauces . . . Basic and Classic

The difference between everyday and 'special occasion' food is often no more than a good sauce. A simple vegetable coated in a Mornay Sauce or a delicate Poulette Sauce becomes a stylish first course. Eggs baked with a variation of the basic Béchamel Sauce are transformed into those French stars of little luncheons, Oeufs en Cocotte Soubise. The homely hamburger can be the hit of an informal party when served with a delicious red wine sauce. Poached or sautéed fish and chicken, chops and steaks, familiar roasts – all, with a fine sauce in support, become distinguished dishes worthy of the most important occasion.

The good news about sauce-making is that, though there are many, many individual sauces with a great variety of names and ingredients, there are only a few *kinds* of sauce. Anyone who likes to cook can become skilled at the basic techniques for making these, and after that you're at home with any sauce recipe you meet, because it's just a variation on a procedure you know well.

Roux-Based Sauces

The most common way to give a sauce its thickness or body is with a roux. This is a carefully cooked mixture of fat and flour. The longer the mixture cooks the darker it gets; a white roux or golden roux is for the lighter coloured sauces, a brown one for the dark sauces.

Making a roux-based sauce is quite easy as long as you watch a few vital points. A properly cooked roux gets you off to a good start; a poorly cooked one may be the reason why a finished sauce falls short of perfection. You must cook the mixture over a low heat, stirring. This cooking expands the flour grains and gives them a delicate flavour, but the heat must be gentle. Rapid cooking shrivels the grains, causing a grainy, less smooth sauce. Neglecting to stir results in uneven cooking and you may produce burnt spots which will affect both the flavour and texture.

The best way to guard against lumps is to cool the roux a little after cooking it; have the liquid for the sauce warm and, off the heat, stir the warm liquid into the warm roux until the mixture is perfectly smooth. Return the saucepan to a medium heat and cook, stirring constantly, until the sauce boils and thickens. Ideally, use a flat wooden spatula (like a spoon without a bowl) as a spoon may collect some of the mixture which will cook into a lump in the bowl.

All sauces of this type should be cooked gently for some time, stirring often, after they have thickened. This develops the flavour to its fullest.

Poulette Sauce coating chicken pieces; Sour Cream Sauce with fish steaks; Mornay Sauce poured over cooked leeks, sprinkled with grated cheese and browned under the grill.

1 Melt butter over moderate heat but do not allow to brown.

2 Remove pan from heat and stir in flour until smoothly blended.

3 Still off the heat, gradually stir in the milk and season to taste.

4 Return pan to heat and stir constantly until sauce thickens. Simmer for 3 minutes to finish cooking flour.

Béchamel (Coating) Sauce

Béchamel and its many variations enhance vegetables, fish, eggs, poultry and delicate meats.

This recipe makes a coating sauce – the right consistency for masking food. For a flowing or pouring sauce, use 30 g (1 oz) butter and 2 tablespoons flour to 2 cups milk.

2 cups milk	*pinch of nutmeg*
1 slice onion	*60 g (2 oz) butter*
1 small stick celery	*3 tablespoons flour*
8 peppercorns	*salt*
1 bay leaf	*white pepper*

In a small heavy saucepan, heat the milk with the vegetables and spices until bubbles form round the edge. Remove from the heat, stand for 20 minutes, then strain.

Wipe out the saucepan and melt the butter in it. Remove from the heat, blend in the flour and stir over a low heat for 1 minute. Cool a little, add the milk and stir until smooth. Season lightly with salt and pepper. Stir over a medium heat until boiling, then lower the heat and cook 3 minutes more. Adjust the seasoning.
Makes about 2 cups

Velouté Sauce

Velouté is made in the same way as Béchamel, but the roux is cooked longer until straw-coloured and stock is used instead of milk. Use chicken, veal or fish stock according to the dish.

For a richer Velouté, add egg and cream: for each 2 cups of sauce, beat 2 egg yolks with 2 tablespoons cream. Stir a little hot sauce into the mixture, then return to the pan and stir over a low heat until well blended and glossy. Do not allow to boil.

Sauces based on Béchamel or Velouté Sauce

Mornay Sauce   Add $\frac{1}{4}$ cup grated cheese, $\frac{1}{2}$ teaspoon dry mustard and $\frac{1}{4}$ teaspoon pepper to 2 cups of Béchamel Sauce. If browned on top, the dish is described as *au gratin*. Serve with vegetables, seafood or eggs.

Parsley Sauce   Add 2 tablespoons finely chopped parsley to 2 cups of Béchamel Sauce. Serve with boiled potatoes or other vegetables, fish or chicken.

Sour Cream Sauce   Add $\frac{1}{2}$ cup sour cream to 2 cups of Béchamel or Velouté Sauce. Excellent with fish or veal.

Poulette Sauce   To 2 cups of chicken Velouté with egg yolk and cream enrichment, add 1 teaspoon lemon juice and 2 teaspoons chopped parsley. Elegant on chicken, broad beans or other green vegetables.

Soubise Sauce   Simmer 1 cup chopped onion in water to cover for 1 minute. Drain off the water, add 30 g (1 oz) butter and cook gently until the onions are soft. Rub through a sieve or purée in a blender or food processor. Beat into 2 cups of Béchamel Sauce and add 2 tablespoons cream. Eggs baked in ramekins, with this sauce above and below, become Oeufs en Cocotte Soubise, a first course or luncheon dish. Use also with veal or lamb.

Brown Sauces

Brown roux-based sauces are made by the same method as Béchamel and Velouté, but the roux is cooked until it is nut-brown, and brown stock is used for the liquid. They also have additional flavourings and are cooked for longer to give depth and richness. Cool stock is added two or three times to help the fat to rise to the surface and help clear the sauce.

Other brown sauces and gravies, more quickly made, are lightly thickened with arrowroot or cream or are given slight 'body' with butter. These depend for their savour on the use of really well-flavoured stock, wine or the good brown bits that are left in a pan after roasting or sautéing.

Brown Sauce

1 Chop the onion and carrot; wash the celery, wipe the mushrooms and chop them finely. Remove the rind from the bacon and dice it. In a heavy saucepan, heat the clarified butter or oil and fry the vegetables and bacon (called a 'mirepoix') until golden.

2 Remove the saucepan from the heat, blend in the flour, return to medium-low heat and fry, stirring constantly, until the roux is hazelnut brown. Remove the saucepan from the heat and cool a little.

3 Blend in the tomato juice and half the stock. Add the bouquet garni and peppercorns, return to a medium heat and stir until boiling. Half cover and simmer for 25 minutes. Skim the surface, add half remaining stock, boil and skim again. Simmer 5 minutes, add remaining stock and sherry; boil and skim, simmer 5 minutes more.

4 Strain the sauce through a sieve, pressing the vegetables to extract the juice. Reheat, taste and season with salt and pepper. If you wish, add a nut of butter to the hot sauce at serving time and swirl it in by swinging the saucepan in a circular motion. Do not stir. If preferred, the sauce may be left unsieved.

Brown Sauce (Simple Sauce Espagnole)

This sauce is simple compared to the two-day marathon of making the Sauce Espagnole of Escoffier's time, but it is still a fine classic sauce.

1 small onion, peeled	*1 tablespoon flour*
1 small carrot, scraped	*½ cup tomato juice*
10 cm (4 inch) piece of celery	*2 cups brown stock (page 140)*
60 g (2 oz) mushrooms	*bouquet garni*
2 rashers streaky bacon	*6 peppercorns*
60 g (2 oz) clarified butter (ghee) or 3 tablespoons vegetable oil	*¼ cup dry sherry*
	salt
	freshly ground pepper

To prepare, see step-by-step pictures at left, below.

Sauces Based on Brown Sauce

Burgundy Sauce Substitute ½ cup dry red wine for the sherry in the recipe for Brown Sauce, and reduce the tomato juice to ¼ cup. Serve with steak, roast beef and game.

Madeira or Marsala Sauce Substitute ¼ cup Madeira or Marsala for the sherry in the recipe for Brown Sauce. Good with ham, or with grilled or sautéed kidneys or liver.

Bigarade Sauce Make Burgundy Sauce and add the grated rind and juice of 2 oranges and 1 small lemon, 2 tablespoons redcurrant jelly and ¼ cup port. Cook until the jelly has melted and the sauce is slightly reduced. Serve with duck, goose, hare or venison.

Sauce Robert Fry 2 tablespoons finely chopped onion gently in 1 tablespoon melted butter until softened. Add ½ cup dry white wine and 2 teaspoons wine vinegar and boil briskly until reduced by half. Add this reduction to 2 cups of Brown Sauce and stir in 1 tablespoon Dijon-style mustard and a pinch or two of sugar, to taste. Piquant with lamb or pork.

Variations of Brown Sauce, from the left: Sauce Robert; Bigarade Sauce; Madeira Sauce

Gravies

A simple gravy, a kind of pan sauce, can be made for meat and poultry in the roasting pan. It should enhance the meat, never concealing it or blanketing it heavily.

Keep the gravy light and clear by making it in one of the following ways. Allow about 3 tablespoons ($\frac{1}{4}$ cup) of gravy per person to allow for second helpings.

Pan or Brown Gravy

The French describe meat served with this gravy as *au jus*. The process for making this simple and delicious gravy is called 'deglazing'.

For a rich-flavoured gravy, spread the meat for roasting with a little dripping (or butter, for a more delicate flavour for chicken gravy) and put a few slices of onion and carrot in the roasting pan. Baste the meat with the fat during roasting and, if there seems any chance of the fat and juices scorching, add a very little water to the pan. When the meat is done, remove and keep warm. Discard the onion and carrot and pour the fat off slowly, without disturbing the sediment. Add water, wine, stock or vegetable cooking water (or a mixture) to the pan and boil briskly for about 5 minutes on top of the stove, stirring and scraping in all the brown crustiness with a wooden spoon. Season with salt and pepper and swirl in a tablespoon of butter, then strain into a heated sauceboat. When the meat is carved, add any juices that escape to the gravy.

Thickened Gravy (Jus Lié)

When you want a gravy that will cling to the meat yet allow it to show through, make it in the same way as Pan or Brown Gravy but thicken it, after boiling down, with arrowroot (which becomes clear when boiled). Use 2 teaspoons of arrowroot per cup of gravy; mix with a little cold water, stir into the simmering liquid and cook for 5 minutes. If you wish, add a tablespoon of Madeira, port or brandy per cup of gravy and simmer for a further 2 to 3 minutes.

Vegetable-Thickened Gravy

For a thickened gravy in today's health-conscious style, prepare Pan or Brown Gravy and stir in 2 tablespoons of puréed vegetables per cup after the gravy is strained. For the purée, cook mixed vegetables with a few chopped herbs in a little seasoned stock until soft and then purée in a blender.

Pan Sauce

If steaks or hamburgers have been sautéed, you can make an excellent little sauce in the same pan.

$\frac{3}{4}$ cup stock, red wine, dry white wine or dry vermouth salt	freshly ground pepper 45 g ($1\frac{1}{2}$ oz) butter, softened

Sauté the steaks or hamburgers in a little butter and oil. When cooked, remove the meat to a hot serving dish and pour off the fat. Add the liquid to the pan and place over a high heat, stirring and scraping with a wooden spoon to collect the brown bits. When the liquid is reduced by about half, season, then remove from the heat and add the butter, swirling it in by swinging the pan in a circular motion. *Makes a little over $\frac{1}{2}$ cup, enough for 4 to 6 steaks or hamburgers.*

Traditional British Sauces

These are the special sauces that have time-hallowed associations with certain dishes.

Apple Sauce

500 g (1 lb) cooking apples
3 tablespoons water
30 g (1 oz) butter
sugar to taste

Peel, core and slice the apples. Put into a small heavy saucepan with the water; cover and cook gently until soft. Remove the lid, beat the apples with a wooden spoon until smooth and continue cooking over a very low heat until thickened. Add the butter and sugar to taste and beat until melted.

Serve hot or cold with roast duck, roast pork or pork sausages. *Serves 4*

Cumberland Sauce

3 spring onions, finely
  chopped
1 medium orange
1 small lemon
pinch of ground ginger
½ teaspoon English mustard
6 tablespoons redcurrant jelly,
  melted
5 tablespoons port

Cover the spring onions with water in a small saucepan and boil for 1 minute. Drain into a sieve and run cold water through until cool.

Put about 1 cm (½ inch) cold water into the saucepan. Peel the orange and lemon very thinly with a rotary peeler and cut the thin peel (zest) into fine strips, dropping them immediately into the cold water as they are cut. Boil for 3 minutes, then drain.

Squeeze the orange and lemon and stir the juices, rind, spring onions and remaining ingredients together.

Serve cold with ham or other cold meats, grilled ham steaks, roast venison or cold duck. *Serves 4*

Gooseberry Sauce

250 g (8 oz) fresh or frozen
  gooseberries
3 tablespoons water
30 g (1 oz) butter
sugar to taste

Top and tail the gooseberries. Put them into a small heavy saucepan with the water; cover and cook gently until soft. Remove the lid, beat with a wooden spoon until smooth and continue cooking over a very low heat until they form a thick purée. Stir in the butter and sugar to taste.

Traditionally, this sauce is served hot or cold with grilled mackerel; it is also good with other grilled oily fish such as mullet, and with pork chops. *Serves 4*

Bread Sauce

1 medium onion, peeled
2 cloves
1¼ cups milk
salt
freshly ground pepper
4 slices white bread (without
  crust), diced
30 g (1 oz) butter

Put the onion stuck with the cloves, the milk, salt and pepper into a small heavy saucepan. Bring slowly to the boil, remove from the heat, cover, and leave in a warm place for 20 minutes to allow the flavours to develop. Stir in the bread, stand for a further 20 minutes, then remove the onion and add the butter. Beat with a fork until fairly smooth – the texture should be like porridge.

Serve warm with roast chicken, turkey and game birds. It is also good with grilled sausages. *Serves 4*

Mint Sauce

$\frac{1}{4}$ cup fresh mint leaves	3 tablespoons wine vinegar or
1 tablespoon sugar	cider vinegar
2 tablespoons boiling water	pinch of salt

Chop the mint leaves finely with the sugar. Put them into a bowl or sauceboat and add the boiling water. This will set the colour. Stir until the sugar is dissolved, add the vinegar and salt and stand for 1 hour to infuse. The sauce should be bright green and quite thick.

Serve cold, with hot or cold roast lamb, or lamb chops. It is also good on sliced tomato for a salad. *Serves 4*

Horseradish Cream

2 tablespoons grated	1 teaspoon caster sugar
horseradish	salt
$\frac{1}{2}$ cup sour cream	freshly ground pepper
1 teaspoon Dijon-style	
mustard	

Mix all the ingredients together. Serve cold with roast and boiled (fresh) beef, smoked trout, mackerel and eel. *Serves 4*

English Onion Sauce

2 large onions	salt
30 g (1 oz) butter	freshly ground pepper
2 tablespoons flour	pinch of nutmeg
$\frac{1}{2}$ cup warm milk	

Peel and chop the onions. Simmer in salted water to cover until tender. Drain, reserving the liquid.

Melt the butter, remove from the heat and stir in the flour. Return to a low heat and stir for 1 minute. Remove from the heat, cool a little, then blend in the milk and $\frac{1}{4}$ cup of the cooking liquid. Season with salt, pepper and nutmeg. Return to the heat, stir until boiling, and add the onion.

Serve with boiled mutton, corned beef, fresh beef, or on boiled potatoes. *Serves 4*

Hard Sauce

125 g (4 oz) unsalted butter	4 tablespoons brandy, rum,
125 g (4 oz) caster sugar or soft	Grand Marnier or
brown sugar	Cointreau, or 1 teaspoon
	vanilla essence

Beat the butter until creamy and add the sugar and liquor by degrees, beating until fluffy. Chill.

Serve with Christmas pudding and other steamed puddings, and mince pies. It is also good on baked apples. *Serves 4 to 6*

'Instant' Dessert Sauces

Both these sauces take about a minute to make, but they are so good that you'll have guests asking for the recipes. Whether you tell or not is up to you!

Crème Caribbean

1 cup heavy sour cream
approximately 1 tablespoon
soft brown sugar

Stir the cream to soften the texture, then add sugar to taste, a little at a time, stirring well to melt it in. Chill. Sublime with fresh, poached or baked fruits. *Serves 6 to 8*

Chocolate Mint Sauce

16 chocolate peppermint	4 tablespoons cream
creams (after-dinner mints)	

Put the chocolate creams into a pottery or heatproof glass bowl that will fit over a saucepan. Melt over simmering water and stir in the cream. Serve warm on coffee ice-cream or poached pears. *Serves 4*

At the back: Cumberland Sauce; Bread Sauce
In front: Gooseberry Sauce; Horseradish Cream; Mint Sauce

Classic Salad Sauces

Vinaigrette (French Dressing)

1 tablespoon wine or cider vinegar or lemon juice *large pinch of salt* *¼ teaspoon dry mustard*	*freshly ground pepper* *¼ cup olive, walnut, pumpkin seed or other good oil*

Mix the vinegar, salt, mustard and pepper together in a small bowl or cup. Add the oil slowly, beating with a fork or whisk.

For flavour variations, a few herbs or a little garlic, crushed with the salt, may be added. *Makes about ¼ cup, enough for a tossed salad for 4 to 6.*

Mayonnaise

Infinitely better than most bottled products, and not hard to make if you follow these pictures and instructions. Have all the ingredients at room temperature.

2 egg yolks *½ teaspoon salt* *pinch of white pepper* *½ teaspoon dry mustard*	*2 teaspoons wine or cider vinegar or lemon juice* *1 cup olive oil, other vegetable oil or a mixture*

To prepare by hand, see step-by-step pictures below. *Makes about 1 cup*

Blender or Food Processor Mayonnaise

Place the egg yolks, seasonings and 1 teaspoon vinegar or lemon juice in the container and process for a few seconds. With the motor running, pour the oil in little by little, checking that each addition is absorbed before adding the next; then add the remaining vinegar or lemon juice.

Tartare Sauce

Mix 2 teaspoons drained, chopped capers, 1 tablespoon chopped gherkin or dill pickle, 3 finely chopped green or black olives and 2 teaspoons chopped fresh herbs into 1 cup of Mayonnaise. Use for fried or grilled fish, cold fish and shellfish.

Egg and Butter Sauces

Hollandaise Sauce

This is lovely over fish, vegetables, chicken or eggs.

125 g (4 oz) unsalted butter *2 egg yolks* *1 tablespoon water*	*small pinch of salt* *½ teaspoon lemon juice*

To prepare by hand, see step-by-step pictures opposite. *Makes about ¾ cup*

Blender or Food Processor Hollandaise

Place 3 egg yolks, 1 teaspoon lemon juice and 1 tablespoon water into the container and blend briefly. Heat 125 g (4 oz) butter until foaming hot, but not brown. With the motor at high speed, pour the butter very slowly into the container. Season with salt and pepper. *Makes about ¾ cup*

Béarnaise Sauce

Put ¼ cup white wine vinegar, 1 chopped spring onion, 4 peppercorns, 1 bay leaf, ¼ teaspoon dried tarragon and a sprig of thyme or a pinch of dried thyme into a small saucepan. Boil until reduced to 1 tablespoon liquid. Strain. Use this liquid instead of water in the recipe for Hollandaise Sauce and make in the same way, but omit the lemon juice at the end.

Mayonnaise
1 Rinse a small bowl in hot water, dry it and wrap the base in a damp cloth to keep it steady. Add the egg yolks, seasonings and 1 teaspoon vinegar or lemon juice.

2 Beat these ingredients together, then add the oil, drop by drop, from a teaspoon at first, then trickle by trickle from a jug. Stir vigorously and constantly in one direction.

3 Incorporate each addition thoroughly before adding the next. If the mixture shows signs of separating, beat in a teaspoon of boiling water before adding more oil

4 When all the oil is incorporated, beat in the remaining vinegar or lemon juice. Adjust the seasoning.

At the back: Tartare Sauce; Mayonnaise
In front: Hollandaise Sauce poured over asparagus

Hollandaise Sauce

1 Cut the butter into small pieces. Put the egg yolks and water into a bowl over a saucepan of simmering water. Be sure the water does not touch the bottom of the bowl. Beat egg yolks and water together until they thicken slightly. This stage is reached when you begin to see the bottom of the bowl between strokes. Now add the butter, piece by piece, slipping it through your fingers to soften it slightly. Beat all the time, incorporating each piece of butter before adding the next. Have a teaspoon and a little cold water ready.

2 If there is any sign of 'scrambling' (lumping), lift the bowl off the saucepan and stir in a teaspoon of cold water, then add the next piece of butter off the heat. Return to the saucepan and continue until all the butter is in. Remove from heat and add salt and lemon juice to taste.
NOTE: If the sauce separates, don't worry, there is a cure. Rinse another bowl with hot water, dry it and put in a teaspoon of lemon juice and a tablespoon of sauce. Whisk together with a fork or wire whisk until they thicken, then gradually whisk in the remaining sauce.

Sensational First Courses

A first course sets the mood for a special occasion, so it is nice if it has a special talking point about it. It might only be the garnish, or the way it's arranged on the plate, or an unusual combination of flavours or textures. It only takes a small touch to add excitement, yet by doing so you add so much to the enjoyment and importance of the occasion itself.

There are many first courses here to inspire you, from the light to the substantial. Choose a suitable one according to the main dish that's to follow.

Scallops Sous le Toit

Scallops in a creamy wine sauce have a 'roof' of crisp puff pastry.

750 g (1½ lb) scallops	60 g (2 oz) butter
2 spring onions, finely chopped	2 tablespoons flour
bouquet garni (2 sprigs parsley, 2 sprigs thyme, 1 bay leaf, tied together)	¼ cup cream
	1 teaspoon grated lemon rind
	1 × 375 g packet frozen puff pastry
½ teaspoon salt	1 egg, beaten
freshly ground pepper	
½ cup dry white wine	

Trim the dark beards from the scallops. Place in a saucepan with the spring onions, bouquet garni, salt and pepper and wine. Add enough water to come just to the top of the scallops and simmer for 2 minutes. Drain, and reserve ¾ cup of the cooking liquid. If the scallops are large, halve them.

Melt the butter, stir in the flour, and cook for 1 minute over a low heat. Remove from the heat and cool a little, then add the warm scallop liquid and stir until smooth. Return to a medium heat and bring just to the boil, stirring constantly. Stir in the cream and lemon rind, taste for seasoning and fold in the scallops. Divide the mixture among 6 scallop shells or small ovenproof dishes, cover with foil, and chill.

Roll out the pastry thinly and cut 6 lids large enough to cover the shells, with an overlap of about 1 cm (½ inch) all round. Remove the foil from the shells and brush the edges with beaten egg. Fit the pastry lids over the top and cut off surplus pastry. Press the edges down firmly to seal, cut 2 small slits in the top of each lid, and chill for 30 minutes. Brush with beaten egg, place the shells on an oven slide, and bake in a very hot oven (230°C/450°F) for 10 minutes, or until the pastry is crisp and golden brown. Serves 6
NOTE: Although this dish sounds a little complicated, it is suitable for a dinner party, as much of the preparation can be done in advance. The scallop mixture can be chilled overnight, and the pastry shapes cut ready for baking.

From front to back: Yakitori (page 156); Precious Jade Cocktail served with Fresh Tomato Sauce and Curried Mayonnaise; Scallops Sous le Toit.

Smoked Trout with Horseradish Sauce

Look for smoked trout in good delicatessens and supermarkets as well as fish shops.

3 smoked trout, about 375 g (12 oz) each	TO SERVE:
¾ cup cream	6 slices freshly made toast, crusts removed
1½ tablespoons prepared horseradish	6 crisp lettuce leaves
salt	6 ripe black olives, halved and pitted
freshly ground pepper	6 lemon wedges
	chopped parsley

Skin the trout, run a knife down the centre of each side and lift the two halves off the bone; turn over and repeat on the other side. You will have 12 fillets altogether.

Whip the cream until stiff, then fold in the horseradish. Taste, and add just enough salt and pepper to suit your palate, taking into account the smoky taste of the trout.

At serving time, make the toast and cut each slice into 2 triangles. Serve 2 triangles of toast per person with 2 trout fillets, arranged on a crisp lettuce leaf and garnished with olives and lemon wedges. Sprinkle with chopped parsley and serve the horseradish sauce in individual bowls or pass around for guests to serve themselves. *Serves 6*

Precious Jade Cocktail

Fascinating presentation makes this seafood cocktail the highlight of the meal. Offer a choice of two interesting sauces.

2 cucumbers	3 tablespoons oil
375 g (12 oz) cooked prawns	fresh dill, parsley or watercress, to garnish
250 g (8 oz) scallops	
¼ cup dry white wine	TO SERVE:
¼ cup water	Fresh Tomato Sauce (see below)
salt	
freshly ground pepper	Curried Mayonnaise (see below)
1 tablespoon lemon juice	

Lightly peel the cucumbers, leaving a little pale green; then, with a swivel-bladed potato peeler, shave off thin ribbons of flesh. Drop them into iced water, which will make them curl into pretty shapes.

Shell the prawns, leaving the tails intact, and remove the dark veins. Trim the dark beards from the scallops and poach for 2 minutes in the wine and water seasoned with a little salt and pepper. Drain.

Whisk together the lemon juice, oil and salt and pepper to taste and pour over the scallops, turning to coat them with the dressing. Drain the cucumber and arrange in the middle of 6 individual serving plates. Arrange the prawns on one side and scallops on the other. Garnish with dill, parsley or watercress and pass the sauces separately, so each guest may choose which he or she prefers. Or even a little of both! *Serves 6*
Fresh Tomato Sauce Skin and seed 2 ripe tomatoes and chop finely. Fold into ¾ cup of lightly whipped cream, with 2 tablespoons horseradish and salt and pepper to taste. Serve at once.
Curried Mayonnaise Place 1 cup mayonnaise in a small bowl and add 2 spring onions, finely chopped, 2 teaspoons chutney, 2 teaspoons curry powder and salt and pepper to taste. Just before serving, fold in 1 egg white beaten until it forms soft peaks.

Yakitori

Squares of beautifully seasoned chicken and chicken livers are threaded onto small bamboo skewers and grilled for this stunning Japanese first course.

2 whole chicken breasts	1½ teaspoons sugar
8 chicken livers	4 slices fresh ginger, finely
8 spring onions, cut into short	chopped
lengths	TERIYAKI SAUCE:
MARINADE:	½ cup bottled teriyaki sauce
2½ tablespoons saké or sherry	2 tablespoons saké or sherry
2½ teaspoons soy sauce	½ cup chicken stock (page 140)
1 clove garlic, crushed	

Combine the marinade ingredients in a small bowl, and the teriyaki sauce ingredients in a flat dish. Bone and skin the chicken breasts and cut into bite-size squares. Trim the livers, and cut each one in half. Add the livers to the marinade and leave, covered, in the refrigerator for an hour or so.

Thread 4 chicken pieces and 3 lengths of spring onion alternately onto skewers, beginning and ending with chicken. Thread the chicken livers onto skewers, 4 pieces each. Turn the filled skewers around in the teriyaki mixture, coating all sides. Leave for several hours or overnight in teriyaki, turning once or twice.

Preheat the grill and line the grill rack with foil. Grill the yakitori for 3 minutes on one side, brushing with teriyaki sauce. Turn and grill the other side, brushing again with teriyaki sauce. Serve at once on individual plates, each person receiving two chicken skewers and one of liver. Garnish with a pretty garden leaf if desired. Serves 4

NOTE: This recipe is the traditional way of preparing yakitori, but there is a shortcut method which still produces delicious results. Make a double quantity of the marinade and place in two separate bowls. Prepare the chicken breasts and livers according to the recipe and marinate separately for several hours or overnight. Fill skewers as directed and grill until golden brown on both sides, brushing several times with the marinade.

Galloping Horses

Thailand is the home of this very different salad; it is a combination of hot and cold with a sweet-sour flavour.

4 large navel oranges	2 teaspoons sugar
1 small lettuce	1½ tablespoons soy sauce
1 tablespoon oil	1 tablespoon water
1 clove garlic, crushed	salt
250 g (8 oz) minced raw pork	dash of cayenne
2 tablespoons finely chopped	coriander or parsley sprigs, to
peanuts	garnish

Peel the oranges, removing the rind and white membrane, and cut into thin slices. Wash and dry the lettuce, and line 6 individual plates with lettuce leaves. Arrange the orange slices over the lettuce and chill.

Heat the oil in a frying pan and fry the garlic until golden. Add the pork mince and stir until brown, breaking up any lumps with a fork. Add the peanuts, sugar, soy sauce, water, salt and cayenne to the pan and mix well. Pour the hot pork mixture over the oranges and serve at once, garnished with sprigs of coriander or parsley. Serves 6

NOTE: If your butcher doesn't have minced pork, buy a pork steak or 2 pork chops and put the flesh through a mincer, or chop finely in a food processor.

Caviar Roulade

This sumptuous first course is not difficult to make, because, unlike the classic high soufflé, a roulade can be prepared in advance.

ROULADE:	CAVIAR FILLING:
90 g (3 oz) butter	1 × 175 g packet Philadelphia
½ cup flour	cream cheese
2 cups warm milk	1 tablespoon lemon juice
1 teaspoon salt	2 tablespoons thick sour
¾ teaspoon pepper	cream
1 tablespoon brandy	freshly ground pepper
1 tablespoon sour cream	½ cup cream, whipped
4 eggs, separated	90 g (3 oz) red caviar or
extra sour cream and caviar,	lumpfish roe
to garnish	

Preheat the oven to moderately slow (160°C/325°F). Oil a large Swiss roll pan, approximately 25 × 38 × 2.5 cm (10 × 15 × 1 inch). Line the pan with greaseproof paper, leaving a couple of inches overhang at each end. Brush the paper with oil and dust with flour, shaking out excess.

Melt the butter in a large saucepan and stir in the flour over a low heat. Cook for 1 minute, stirring all the time. Remove from the heat, cool a little, and add the milk all at once. Stir until smooth, then return to a medium heat and continue stirring constantly until the sauce boils. Remove from the heat and stir in the salt, pepper, brandy and sour cream. Whisk in the egg yolks, one at a time.

Beat the egg whites until they stand in soft peaks and fold into the yolk mixture. Pour into the prepared pan, spreading evenly with a rubber spatula. Bake for 40 minutes, or until golden on top.

Remove the roll from the oven and, using the overhanging paper ends to help, turn it out onto a damp tea-towel lined with greaseproof paper. Gently peel the paper off, and trim the crusty edges. Roll the roulade up loosely in the tea-towel and paper, like a Swiss roll, and allow to cool.

To make the filling, soften the cream cheese and beat in the lemon juice and sour cream. Season to taste with pepper, and fold in the whipped cream and caviar. At serving time, unroll the roulade, spread with filling, and roll up again. Serve cut in thin slices, garnished with a spoonful of sour cream and a teaspoon of caviar. Serves 8

Tomatoes Stuffed with Rice and Crab

8 ripe tomatoes	1 teaspoon curry powder
salt	1 tablespoon lemon juice
freshly ground pepper	1 × 200 g can crabmeat
3 cups freshly cooked, long-	4 tender sticks celery, finely
grain rice (1 cup raw)	chopped
½ cup French dressing	sprays of parsley or
½ cup mayonnaise	watercress, to garnish

Cut the tops from the tomatoes and scoop out the seeds. Season with salt and pepper and invert onto a plate to drain. Combine the rice, while still warm, with the French dressing, mayonnaise, curry powder and lemon juice. Pick over the crabmeat for any cartilage, separate into chunks, and add to the rice mixture with the finely chopped celery. Lightly spoon into the tomato cases and chill for 30 minutes or so before serving, garnished with sprays of parsley or watercress. Serves 8

Prawn and Vegetable Tempura

From Japan comes one of the great first courses – fresh prawns and tender vegetables coated in a light batter and quickly fried to golden crispness. Each person receives three or four prawns and a taste of the different vegetables, with an individual bowl of sauce for dipping. The following quantities serve 6.

24 *medium green prawns*	*oil for deep frying*
½ *small cauliflower, separated into florets*	*Dipping Sauce (see below)*
	BATTER:
4 *green peppers, seeded and cut into bite-size squares*	*1 egg*
	1¼ cups ice-cold water
2 *medium zucchini, cut into diagonal slices*	*2 cups sifted flour*
250 g (8 oz) *button mushrooms*	
2 *onions, thinly sliced and separated into rings*	

Peel the prawns, leaving the tails intact. Parboil the cauliflower for 2 minutes; prepare the other vegetables and pat dry with paper towels.

To prepare the batter, beat the egg thoroughly with a whisk or rotary beater, then stir in the water. Sprinkle the flour all at once over the liquid. With the same whisk or beater, stir in the flour just until it is moistened and large lumps disappear – it will still have small lumps in it. Do not stir the batter again.

Pour enough vegetable oil into a wok, electric frypan or deep frying pan to give a depth of at least 10 cm (4 inches). When it is hot, drop in a little batter. If the oil is the right temperature the batter will rise immediately to the surface and little bubbles appear around it. It should turn golden in about 20 seconds; if it browns too quickly the oil is too hot and the heat should be adjusted.

Fry only a few pieces of food at a time to keep the temperature constant.

Hold one prawn at a time by the tail and dip into the batter. Allow excess batter to drain off, then slide the prawn gently into the hot oil. Repeat with 3 or 4 more prawns. Fry for 1 minute, then turn over and brown the other side. As the prawns are cooked, drain on absorbent paper towels or on a wire rack over a cake pan. Keep warm on a rack placed in a slow oven.

Dip and fry the vegetables as for prawns, skimming off any pieces of cooked batter from the oil with a wire strainer. The tempura may be cooked at the table in an electric frypan, and each guest served with prawns and vegetables as they are cooked. Or the cooking may be done in the kitchen, and the tempura served on a large platter for guests to help themselves. (Keep each ingredient separate, as in the picture.) *Serves 6*

Dipping Sauce Mix together 1½ cups hot water, ½ cup soy sauce (Japanese if possible), ¼ teaspoon grated fresh ginger, and a dash of monosodium glutamate (optional). Pour into 6 individual bowls to serve.

Blue Cheese Mousse

This elegant first course can be moulded in a decorative shape (in a jelly mould, for instance) and crowned with a spray of watercress or fresh herbs. Place it in the centre of a large platter, and surround with melba toast, lightly toasted French bread or plain crackers.

6 egg yolks, lightly beaten	375 g (12 oz) blue cheese
6 tablespoons cream	1½ cups cream, whipped
1¼ tablespoons gelatine, softened in 4 tablespoons cold water	3 egg whites, stiffly beaten watercress or sprays of fresh herbs, to garnish

Combine the egg yolks and the 6 tablespoons of cream in a saucepan over a low heat, and stir constantly until the mixture is creamy. Remove from the heat. Dissolve the gelatine over hot water and stir into the eggs. Whirr the blue cheese in a blender until very creamy, or force through a sieve, and add to the mixture. When it is cool, fold in the whipped cream and then the egg whites.

Spoon the mousse into an oiled mould (a small pudding basin will do if you don't have a jelly mould) and chill for at least 3 hours. Unmould carefully to serve and garnish with watercress or herbs. *Makes 20 appetizer servings*

Spiced Onions and Raisins

These tiny onions in a sweet-sour sauce can be made well ahead of time as they are served chilled. A perfect first course before spicy kebabs or spareribs.

1 kg (2 lb) small white onions	2 tablespoons wine vinegar
1 cup dry white wine	1 tablespoon lemon juice
½ cup sugar	1 teaspoon ground cumin
½ cup raisins	salt
2 tablespoons tomato paste	pinch of cayenne
4 tablespoons olive oil	chopped parsley, to garnish

Peel the onions. Combine all the other ingredients in a saucepan and bring to the boil. Add the onions, turn the heat down, and simmer for 15 minutes or until the onions are tender but still firm. Cool, then chill until serving time. Serve in individual bowls, sprinkled with chopped parsley and accompanied by crusty bread or Lebanese flat bread. *Serves 6*

Vermouth Carrots with Grapes

Brightly glazed orange carrots and black grapes make a dazzling colour display, and the textures complement each other beautifully. It's a dish for gourmet friends.

1 kg (2 lb) tender young carrots	½ cup water salt
90 g (3 oz) butter	freshly ground pepper
2 tablespoons sugar	1 cup dark grapes, seeded
¼ cup dry vermouth	

Scrape the carrots, if necessary, and cut into diagonal slices. Heat the butter in a heavy frying pan and stir the slices until well coated, then sprinkle with sugar. Add the vermouth and water and simmer the carrots until almost tender, stirring all the time. Season with salt and freshly ground pepper and lightly stir in the grapes. Cook 30 seconds longer, until the grapes are heated through, then spoon into a heated serving dish. *Serves 6*

Chilled Dolmades

18 pickled grape leaves	½ cup chopped parsley
½ cup olive oil	6 spring onions, chopped
2 medium onions, finely chopped	(including green tops)
½ cup long-grain rice	2 tablespoons pine nuts
3 tablespoons chopped fresh herbs (dill, marjoram, rosemary, thyme) or 2 teaspoons dried	4 tablespoons lemon juice
	1¼ cups water
	salt
	freshly ground pepper
	lemon wedges, to serve

Rinse the grape leaves in cold water and drain well. Heat half the olive oil in a large saucepan and gently fry the onions until golden. Stir in the rice, and continue stirring over a low heat for 5 minutes. Add the herbs, spring onions, nuts, 2 tablespoons lemon juice, ½ cup water and salt and pepper to taste. Simmer the mixture for 15 minutes, or until the water is absorbed and the rice is tender. Allow to cool.

Place the grape leaves on a board, shiny side down, and put 1 teaspoon of rice mixture in the centre of each. Fold the sides to the centre, then roll them up tightly starting from the stem ends. Arrange the rolls in tightly packed layers in a saucepan, then gently pour in the remaining water, oil and lemon juice. Place a plate over the rolls to prevent them coming apart, bring the mixture to the boil and cook for 5 minutes. Remove the plate and simmer the rolls for about 45 minutes, or until the liquid is absorbed. Cool, then carefully lift onto a serving plate and chill until required. Serve with lemon wedges. *Serves 6*

Ham and Prawn Jambalaya

In New Orleans, rice is combined with savoury ingredients to make the exotic-sounding dish called Jambalaya.

90 g (3 oz) butter	salt
1 green pepper, seeded and finely chopped	freshly ground pepper
	1 cup cooked diced ham
4 tender sticks celery, finely chopped	250 g (8 oz) medium peeled prawns
1 onion, finely chopped	3 cups hot cooked rice (1 cup raw)
1 clove garlic, crushed	
1 × 425 g can peeled tomatoes	2 tablespoons chopped parsley, to garnish
1 tablespoon chopped fresh oregano or ½ teaspoon dried	

Heat the butter in a chafing dish or a heavy frying pan over medium heat. Sauté the pepper, celery, onion and garlic until soft but not brown, about 3 minutes. Stir in the tomatoes with their juice and heat to boiling point. Add the oregano, salt and pepper to taste, ham and prawns. Add the rice and heat through, stirring gently. Sprinkle with parsley and serve. *Serves 6*

Lettuce Leaves with Roquefort

A gourmet nibble that's ready in minutes!

8 Cos lettuce leaves	2 teaspoons brandy
250 g (8 oz) Roquefort or blue cheese	

Wash the lettuce leaves, pat them dry, and cut in two. Crumble the Roquefort and mix well with the brandy. Spread the lettuce leaves with the cheese mixture and roll up. *Serves 6 to 8*

Chicken Liver in Little Pots

Here is an exciting change from the usual pâté. A creamy liver and mushroom mixture is cooked in small ramekins, to be served hot or cold.

500 g (1 lb) chicken livers	30 g (1 oz) butter, melted
125 g (4 oz) mushrooms, finely chopped	salt
4 egg yolks, beaten	pinch of cayenne
4 tablespoons cream	triangles of hot wholegrain toast
3 tablespoons chopped parsley	

Pick over the chicken livers and remove any sinews or discoloured parts. Chop finely in a food processor fitted with the steel blade, or chop very finely by hand. Combine with the remaining ingredients except toast.

Butter 6 small ramekins or soufflé dishes and spoon in the liver mixture. Cover the ramekins with buttered aluminium foil and arrange in a baking dish. Pour in enough cold water to come halfway up the sides of the moulds, and bake in a moderate oven (180°C/350°F) for 40 minutes, or until a knife inserted in the centre comes out clean. Serve hot or cold, with hot wholegrain toast. *Serves 6*

Steak Tartare and Walnut Balls

Steak tartare made from raw minced beef is a famous first course. In this recipe, the meat is moulded into small balls and rolled in crushed walnuts – an idea that looks very inviting and appetizing.

500 g (1 lb) very finely minced raw lean beef (e.g., Scotch fillet, rump or topside)	1 teaspoon Worcestershire sauce
1 tablespoon grated onion	1 teaspoon Dijon-style mustard
1 tablespoon finely chopped parsley	salt
1 tablespoon anchovy paste	freshly ground pepper
	1 cup chopped walnuts
	lettuce leaves, to serve

Combine all the ingredients, except the walnuts, mixing well. Form into about 40 small balls, and roll each in chopped walnuts. Chill for at least a few hours, and serve on a bed of lettuce leaves. *Makes 10 to 20 servings*

Vermouth Carrots with Grapes

The Gentle Art of Poaching Fish

Poaching is one of the most basic yet classic ways to cook fish. The fish is cooked very gently in a flavoured liquid, the surface of which should just shudder with an occasional bubble rising.

Any kind of fish can be poached, but for best results choose those with firm, fine-grained flesh such as whiting, sole or bream, snapper, cod or trout. Large fish, like snapper, may be poached whole and served hot with a sauce, or allowed to cool in the poaching liquid and presented cold with a suitable sauce and garnish. Rainbow trout are delicious poached and are equally good served hot or cold. Frozen fillets of fish, which might otherwise be insipid, take on character when poached with care in a flavoursome liquid.

To Poach Smoked Fish

Smoked cod is always filleted; finnan haddock and kipper are usually split and left on the bone. Serve with melted butter or a simple sauce such as Parsley Butter (page 199).

Put the fish into cold water in a frying pan, bring to a simmer, reduce the heat and cook gently for 10 minutes. Lift out with a fish slice and drain.

To Poach White Fish

Since fillets are flat they do not require a deep pan; a frying pan or flameproof baking dish is a good choice. Whole large fish naturally require a larger dish. Spread the pan with a little butter, sprinkle with chopped spring onion or a small onion and any vegetables that are being used in the dish, like mushroom stalks or trimmings or chopped tomatoes. The seasoned fish is arranged on these. Whole fish, or very large pieces, are started in cold liquid and brought up to simmering point so that the inside will have time to cook through before the outside is over done. Unless otherwise stated, fillets and small pieces are started in hot liquid; this seals the fish and keeps in the natural juices. The liquid may be: Court Bouillon (this page); or half white wine, half water, with a bay leaf, a few sprigs of parsley, thyme and 3 to 4 peppercorns; or Fish Stock (page 142).

On no account should the liquid more than barely reach the top of the fish. In the case of fish fillets, when only a very small amount of liquid is required, drizzle it over the fish.

Butter a piece of white paper cut big enough to cover the pan and lay it on the fish. Make a tiny hole in the centre to allow a little steam to escape and prevent the paper bouncing up and down.

Place the pan over the heat and bring to simmering point. Cover with a lid or foil, reduce the heat and allow to poach. As the liquid barely simmers, the flavoursome steam helps to cook the fish in the sealed-in container.

Small whole fish weighing about 375 g (12 oz) should cook in 15 to 20 minutes or less; a large whole fish of 1–1.5 kg (2–3 lb) should take 30 to 45 minutes. Flat fillets take about 8 to 10 minutes, steaks or cutlets of fish 10 to 15 minutes.

Be careful not to over cook. When the flesh loses its translucency, becomes milky and flakes at the touch of a fork, it is done. Test the flesh of a large fish close to the bone.

Lift the fish onto a warm serving plate and keep warm. The strained cooking liquid is then used to make a sauce.

Sauce for Fish

If you have more than 1 cup of poaching liquid, boil it down to 1 cup; this concentrates the flavour. If you have less, add water to make up to 1 cup. In a small saucepan, melt 15 g ($\frac{1}{2}$ oz) of butter and blend in 1 tablespoon of flour. Add the liquid, stirring over a gentle heat until the sauce thickens. Season and enrich it with oysters, mussels, chopped parsley or an egg yolk mixed with a few spoonfuls of cream. Allow to heat through, but do not let it boil again. Spoon the sauce over the fish to mask, and serve.

Court Bouillon

Whole fish or large pieces are often cooked in a liquid called a Court Bouillon, which is prepared ahead.

1 litre water	1 tablespoon salt
1 carrot, sliced	2 tablespoons vinegar
2 spring onions	6 parsley stalks
1 onion	6 peppercorns
1 small bay leaf	

Put all the ingredients except the peppercorns into a saucepan. Simmer for 45 minutes, add the peppercorns and simmer for 10 minutes more. Strain and cool.

Court Bouillon may be used several times, provided it is strained and chilled. It will keep, refrigerated, for about 1 week.

Seafood Poulette

Fish fillets, scallops and mushrooms are coated in a classically simple sauce.

750 g ($1\frac{1}{2}$ lb) fish fillets (gemfish, snapper)	6 parsley stalks
500 g (1 lb) scallops	$\frac{3}{4}$ cup hot water
250 g (8 oz) mushrooms	$\frac{1}{4}$ cup dry white wine
30 g (1 oz) butter	1 cup cream
2 spring onions, chopped	2 egg yolks
	1 tablespoon snipped chives

Cut the fillets into 6 even-size portions. Remove any brown beards from the scallops. Trim the stalks off the mushrooms and slice them.

Butter a flameproof baking dish and layer in the onions and parsley, then the fillets, then the scallops and mushrooms. Add the water and drizzle the wine over. Cover with buttered paper with a tiny hole in the centre. Bring just to simmering point, cover and cook slowly for 8 to 10 minutes.

Lift the fish, scallops and mushrooms onto a hot serving dish and keep warm. Discard the parsley stalks and boil the liquid in the pan until reduced by one-third. Add the cream and cook for a few minutes more. Beat 3 tablespoons of this liquid with the egg yolks, then pour back into the pan and reheat gently, stirring until thickened. Do not let the sauce boil. Spoon over the fish and serve sprinkled with chives. *Serves 6*

Seafood Poulette

Turbans of Sole Véronique

1½ cups fish stock (page 142)	250 g (8 oz) green grapes,
2 sole or flounder, skinned	preferably seedless
and filleted (8 fillets)	½ cup dry white wine
juice of 1 lemon	2 egg yolks
salt	¼ cup cream
freshly ground pepper	
30 g (1 oz) butter	

To prepare and cook, see step-by-step pictures below. *Serves 4 as a main course, 8 as a first course.*

Poached Trout with Cucumber

3–4 trout, about 375 g (12 oz)	30 g (1 oz) butter
each	2 tablespoons snipped dill or
2 cups Court Bouillon (page	2 teaspoons dried
160) or 1½ cups water and	salt
½ cup white wine	white pepper
½ bay leaf	TO GARNISH:
3 spring onions, chopped	lemon or lime wedges
2 cucumbers	fresh dill or parsley

Wash the trout and dry with an absorbent paper towel. Trim the fins and tail. Put the court bouillon or water and wine into a flameproof baking dish and add the bay leaf and onions. Add the trout, and cover with buttered paper with a tiny hole in the centre. Bring just to simmering point, reduce the heat, cover (foil will do) and poach for about 5 minutes.

Skin the cucumbers, leaving a touch of green, and cut into small, even cubes, discarding the seeds (for very special occasions, scoop into balls with a melon baller or cut into little olive shapes). Heat the butter in a pan and stir the cucumbers until well coated.

Cover and cook slowly for 5 to 6 minutes. Remove from the heat and add the dill. Season with salt and white pepper.

To serve, remove part of the skin of the trout, revealing the pale pink flesh but leaving the heads and tails intact. Arrange on a warm serving dish and decorate with lemon or lime wedges and fresh dill or parsley. Accompany with cucumber. *Serves 3 to 4 as a main course, 6 to 8 as a first course.*

Fish Fillets with Mushrooms

Fish cooked this way is often called 'Bonne Femme' – in the style of the 'good woman'. It is one of the classics. I have given a choice of two sauces, one very simple, the other a richer version.

2 sole or 6–8 skinless fillets of	SIMPLE SAUCE:
sole or other fish	1 cup poaching liquor
30 g (1 oz) butter	15 g (½ oz) butter
3 spring onions, chopped	1 tablespoon flour
12 small mushrooms, sliced	RICH SAUCE:
salt	1 cup poaching liquor
white pepper	1 egg yolk
1½ cups Court Bouillon (page	¼ cup cream
160) or 1 cup water and	
½ cup white wine	

Skin and fillet the sole if using whole fish. Lightly butter a flameproof dish, sprinkle with the chopped spring onions and half the sliced mushrooms and arrange the fish on top. Cover with the remaining mushrooms and season with salt and pepper. Pour over the court bouillon or water and wine. Cover with a sheet of buttered paper with a small hole in the centre. Bring the liquid to simmering point, cover the pan, reduce the heat and poach for 8 to 10 minutes.

Using a broad spatula, remove the fish and vegetables to a warm serving plate and keep warm while making the sauce.

To make the simple sauce, reduce the liquid in the pan to about 1 cup and swirl in beurre manié, made by creaming the butter and flour to a smooth paste. Correct the seasoning with salt and spoon the sauce over the fish.

Alternatively make a rich sauce by reducing the fish cooking liquid to ¾ cup by rapid boiling and then thickening it by adding the egg yolk beaten lightly with the cream. Heat, stirring, but do not allow it to boil. Spoon the sauce over the fish. *Serves 6*

 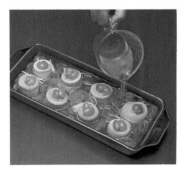  

Turbans of Sole Véronique
1 Use the heads, skins and bones of the sole to make about 1½ cups of fish stock. Preheat the oven to 180°C/350°F. Trim and wash the fillets, rub with lemon juice and season with salt and pepper. Roll each fillet around your index finger, starting from the tail end, skinned side in and fleshy side out (the membrane on the skin side

contracts when heated, helping the turbans to stay rolled). Tie with heavy thread if you wish.

2 Spread a shallow baking dish with the butter. Arrange the turbans in the dish, packing close together (if not tied with thread) so that they will not unroll while cooking. Seed the grapes, if necessary, (use a bobby pin

with the ends pushed into a cork, and hook the seeds out). Fill the centre of each turban with grapes; put the remainder in the dish. Add wine and fish stock to come almost to the tops of the turbans.

3 Cover the dish with buttered white paper with a tiny hole in the centre, then loosely with foil. Place in the oven and poach for about 20

minutes. The fish is done when it turns white and offers almost no resistance to a toothpick. Lift the turbans and grapes onto a heated serving dish and keep warm. Boil the liquid rapidly until reduced by half. Strain.

4 Beat the egg yolks and cream together in a bowl and gradually stir in ½ cup of the reduced cooking liquid.

Fish Mould

Don't wait for summer to serve this attractive fish mould. Cold fish features in Scandinavian meals throughout the coldest weather.

1 kg (2 lb) fish fillets (gemfish, sole, snapper)	*salt*
	white pepper
1½ cups Court Bouillon (page 160) or 1 cup water and ½ cup white wine	*1 lemon*
	TO GARNISH:
1 onion, sliced	*2 tomatoes, cut in wedges*
1 bay leaf	*6–8 onion rings*
1½ teaspoons gelatine	*1 tablespoon olive oil*
3 tablespoons cold water	*1 teaspoon vinegar*
⅔ cup white wine	*chopped parsley*
	sprays of watercress or parsley

Poach the fish fillets gently in court bouillon with the sliced onion and bay leaf (read the instructions for poaching, page 160). When cooked, lift the fillets onto a clean plate. Strain and reserve the liquor. Cut or break the fish into chunks.

Sprinkle the gelatine over the cold water and allow to sponge. Heat 2 cups of the fish liquor, which should be strained through several thicknesses of muslin (face tissues may be used if muslin isn't available). Add the gelatine to the hot liquor and heat gently to dissolve.

Add the white wine and season to taste. Peel the rind from the lemon and cut into julienne (matchstick) lengths.

Pour a little gelatine liquid into a 23 cm (9 inch) ring mould, to a depth of 5 mm (¼ inch). Allow to set until firm. Cool the remaining gelatine liquid.

When the gelatine base is firm, arrange half the fish pieces over it with half the lemon rind. Spoon a little of the gelatine liquid over and allow to set. When firm, add more fish and rind and a little more liquid which should be just on the point of firming, but not set. Allow to set.

Leave the mould in the refrigerator. Turn out onto a serving dish and fill the centre with tomato wedges and onion rings, seasoned with a little oil and vinegar. Sprinkle chopped parsley over and garnish with sprays of watercress or parsley. *Serves 6*

Mussels in Sauce Vin Blanc

Why leave this great dish until you go to an expensive restaurant? It's one of the simplest dishes to prepare with style.

1.5 kg (3 lb) fresh mussels	*2 cups dry white wine*
6 spring onions	*1 tablespoon flour*
6 parsley stalks	*½ cup cream*
sprig of thyme	*2 egg yolks*
freshly ground pepper	*chopped parsley, to garnish*
60 g (2 oz) butter	

Thoroughly scrub the mussels, one by one, to remove mud or seaweed. Use a good stiff brush and plenty of water. Pull off the beard that clings around the edges. Soak them in water – they should disgorge any sand. Discard any that are not shut tightly.

Put the mussels in a large wide pan with the spring onions, herbs, pepper, half the butter and the wine. Cover the pan and cook over a high heat for 5 minutes, shaking the pan now and then. Remove the mussels as soon as they open, discarding half of each shell.

Arrange the mussels in their half shells in a large bowl (or individual, warm soup plates). Keep warm while making the sauce.

Strain the liquid and bring to the boil in a clean saucepan. Mix the remaining butter with the flour and stir into the liquid, bit by bit, until slightly thickened. Beat the cream with the egg yolks and add to the sauce. Heat, stirring constantly, until it thickens slightly. Do not let the sauce boil. Pour over the mussels and sprinkle with chopped parsley.

Serve at once with crusty bread. A glass of dry white wine is the perfect accompaniment. *Serves 4*

Variation

Mussels with Pernod Prepare as for Mussels in Sauce Vin Blanc, adding 2 tablespoons Pernod with the cream and egg yolks.

Turbans of Sole Véronique

Place the bowl over a saucepan of simmering water (about 4 cm (1½ inches) water).

5 Stir constantly with a wooden spoon until the sauce thickens, coating the back of the spoon thinly. Remove from the heat and season to taste with lemon juice, salt and pepper. Serve the turbans with sauce poured round them.

Memorable Meat Dishes

A meat dish needn't be expensive to be memorable, but there should be something about it that shows a little extra care and imagination. It's always a thrill, even for the most experienced cook, when guests ask, 'How did you do that?' or comment, 'Doesn't it look wonderful!'.

These meat dishes have been carefully chosen to bring that touch of excitement to the main course, without too much effort for the busy cook!

Only a few ingredients are needed to make the memorable dish below.

Pâté-Stuffed Veal Chops in Port

Buy a good quality, firm pâté from the delicatessen for this dish.

6 veal chops, cut double thickness	250 g (8 oz) pâté in one piece
salt	flour for dusting
freshly ground pepper	3 tablespoons oil
a few fresh sage leaves, chopped, or a good pinch of dried sage	60 g (2 oz) clarified butter (ghee)
	¾ cup port wine

Ask the butcher to 'butterfly' the chops for you, by splitting almost in two and opening out. Sprinkle with salt, pepper and sage. Cut the pâté into 6 squares about 2.5 cm (1 inch) square and 1 cm (½ inch) thick. Place a square of pâté inside each chop and press the sides firmly together. Dust the chops on both sides with flour.

Heat the oil and butter in a large frying pan and brown the chops over a low heat on both sides, 10 minutes each side. Remove to a serving plate and keep warm. Pour off any fat from the pan and add the port. Heat to boiling, scraping up any brown bits on the bottom of the pan, and boil rapidly for a minute or two until reduced to a thin syrup consistency. Taste for seasoning, strain over the chops and serve. *Serves 6*

Beef Salad with Piquant Sauce

1 kg (2 lb) rump steak or Scotch fillet (or use leftover rare roast beef)	1 large white onion, thinly sliced
a little oil	¼ cup finely chopped parsley
freshly ground pepper	PIQUANT SAUCE:
salt	2 hard-boiled eggs
4 medium potatoes, cooked and thickly sliced	½ teaspoon dry mustard
500 g (1 lb) green beans, cooked until tender-crisp and cut into 5 cm (2 inch) lengths	¼ teaspoon salt
	freshly ground pepper
	¾ cup olive oil
	¼ cup vinegar
4 medium tomatoes, peeled and thickly sliced	2 tablespoons chopped pickled cucumber
2 hard-boiled eggs, cut into quarters	1 tablespoon chopped mixed fresh herbs (chives, oregano, thyme, marjoram, tarragon, etc.)

Have the rump cut in one thick slice, or buy Scotch fillet in the piece. Preheat the grill until very hot and brush the grill bars and meat with oil. Grind black pepper over the meat and grill at high heat for 7 to 10 minutes on each side, or until the outside is crusty brown and the inside still rare. Cool, slice thinly on the diagonal, and salt lightly. Overlap the slices of beef down the centre of a long platter and arrange the potatoes, beans, tomatoes and eggs around them. Separate the onion slices into rings, soak in iced water for 5 minutes, then drain and scatter over the beef. Sprinkle with chopped parsley.

To prepare the piquant sauce, cut the eggs in half, then place the yolks in a bowl and mash them with the mustard, salt and pepper. Add the olive oil and vinegar alternately, being careful to add just a few drops at a time. Whisk well with a fork all the time to combine. Chop the egg whites finely and stir in with the chopped cucumber and herbs.

Spoon half the sauce over the meat and vegetables and pass the remainder in a separate bowl. *Serves 6*

Flambéed Veal Kidneys in Calvados

Calvados is the rich apple brandy of France. If you have a chafing dish, make this recipe at the table; it's a dazzler in every sense of the word!

2 teaspoons olive oil	½ teaspoon freshly ground pepper
60 g (2 oz) clarified butter (ghee)	4 spring onions, finely chopped
4 veal kidneys	3 tablespoons Calvados
½ teaspoon coarse salt (sea salt if possible)	½ cup Brown Sauce (page 148)
	chopped parsley, to garnish

Heat the oil and butter in a chafing dish or heavy frying pan. Have the kidneys skinned and cut into thin slices (after removing the fatty core). Add the kidneys to the pan with the salt, pepper and spring onions, and cook gently for 3 to 4 minutes until brown outside but still slightly pink inside. Heat the Calvados, pour over the kidneys, and set alight. Shake the pan until the flames die down. Stir in the brown sauce, heat through, and sprinkle with chopped parsley to serve. *Serves 6*
NOTE: Buttered rice is the only accompaniment required, or you might like to add sautéed apple slices glazed with a little brown sugar. If veal kidneys are scarce, substitute 10 lamb kidneys.

Lamb in White Wine and Cream

Many lamb stews have brown gravy, but this one is elegantly different, with its creamy sauce and bright vegetable garnish.

1 kg (2 lb) boned leg or shoulder of lamb, trimmed of all fat	*salt*
	white pepper
3 tablespoons oil	*½ cup cream*
1 carrot, sliced	*3 egg yolks, beaten*
1 small onion, chopped	*2 teaspoons lemon juice*
1 stick celery, sliced	TO GARNISH:
3 tablespoons flour	*1 large carrot cut in julienne*
1 cup dry white wine	*strips (matchstick strips)*
2 cups chicken stock (or stock cubes and water)	*and cooked until tender-crisp*
1 bay leaf	*1 cup green peas, cooked*
2 sprigs thyme or pinch of dried	

Cut the meat into bite-size squares, discarding any sinew or gristle. Heat the oil in a heavy saucepan and gently brown the lamb for a few minutes. Add the carrot, onion and celery and cook until the vegetables begin to soften, stirring so they don't stick. Add the flour and mix well, then stir in the wine and chicken stock. Add the bay leaf and thyme with salt and pepper to taste. Put a tight-fitting lid on the pan, and simmer gently for 1¼ hours, or until the meat is very tender.

Remove meat from the liquid with a slotted spoon, arrange in a serving dish and keep warm. Combine the cream, egg yolks and lemon juice and stir into the cooking liquid. Simmer for 3 minutes, then strain over the lamb. Sprinkle with the freshly cooked carrot and peas and serve at once. *Serves 4*

Breast of Veal Samarkand

Economical breast of veal simmers to tenderness in an intriguingly flavoured stock. Sour cream adds the rich finishing touch.

1.5 kg (3 lb) breast of veal	*2 tablespoons redcurrant jelly*
3 tablespoons oil	*1 teaspoon salt*
3 tablespoons flour	*pinch of cayenne*
3 tablespoons dry sherry	*2 teaspoons ground cumin*
½ cup sultanas	*1 cup sour cream*
1 tablespoon tomato paste	*chopped parsley, to garnish*
1½ cups beef stock (or use canned consommé or stock cubes and water)	

Remove the meat from the bones and cut into bite-size squares. Heat the oil in a wide heavy saucepan and quickly brown the meat on all sides. Sprinkle the flour over the meat and cook gently for a few minutes, stirring. Pour the sherry into the pan and stir well, getting up any brown bits from the bottom. Add the sultanas and tomato paste and mix in, then pour in the stock. Bring the mixture to the boil and add the redcurrant jelly, salt, cayenne and cumin. Cover the pan tightly, turn the heat down, and simmer gently for 1 hour or until the veal is tender. Stir in the sour cream and heat through. Taste and adjust the seasoning. Spoon into a heated serving bowl and serve sprinkled with chopped parsley. *Serves 6 to 8*
NOTE: Tiny new potatoes steamed in their jackets would be perfect with this dish.

Breast of Veal Samarkand

Beef with Celery and Walnuts

Here is a fresh twist on the great classic, Beef Stew.

2 tablespoons oil	*1 clove garlic, crushed*
90 g (3 oz) butter	*salt*
1 kg (2 lb) round or topside	*freshly ground pepper*
steak, cut into bite-size	*2 cups beef stock or canned*
squares	*consommé*
12 small white onions	*8 tender sticks celery*
1 tablespoon flour	*¾ cup walnut halves*
¾ cup dry red wine	*rind of 1 small orange,*
bouquet garni (1 bay leaf,	*shredded and blanched, to*
1 sprig thyme, 2 sprigs	*garnish*
parsley, tied together)	

Heat the oil and 30 g (1 oz) butter in a large saucepan and brown the meat well on all sides. Remove the meat with a slotted spoon and brown the onions. Take the pan from the heat and stir in the flour. Return to the heat and add the browned meat, wine, bouquet garni, garlic, salt and pepper to taste, and the stock or consommé. Bring slowly to the boil, cover the pot, and simmer for 1½ hours, or until the beef is tender.

Ten minutes before the end of cooking time, cut the celery in diagonal slices and toss in half the remaining butter until golden. Add to the meat. Heat the remaining butter in the same pan and when it foams brown the walnuts, shaking the pan to prevent them burning. Sprinkle lightly with salt and add to the meat. Turn into a heated serving bowl and sprinkle with orange rind. *Serves 4 to 6*

Chinese Steamboat

This spectacular main dish – in fact, it's a feast! – is also called a Mongolian Hotpot. It's a marvellous way of entertaining guests, as well as feeding them, because everyone does his or her own cooking, and the procedure is relaxed and good fun. The pot of simmering stock is set in the centre of the table with foods and sauces arranged around it, so a circular table is ideal. Small strainers are used to lift the food, or the experienced can use chopsticks. The cooked food is transferred to individual small bowls to be eaten, and the rich broth which results after cooking is ladled into the bowls to be drunk as the finale to the meal.

If you are using a traditional steamboat (available from Chinese grocery shops), make sure to place an asbestos mat under it and a thick wooden chopping board or piece of marble under that, to protect your table.

A useful alternative is an electric frypan – not quite as spectacular, but less trouble, and good for practising your first attempt.

10 cups chicken stock (page	*1 small bunch young spinach*
140)	*1 bunch Chinese cabbage*
2 whole chicken breasts,	*250 g (8 oz) Chinese*
skinned and boned and cut	*transparent noodles, known*
into thin slices	*as rice vermicelli*
500 g (1 lb) lean pork, cut into	*250 g (8 oz) snow peas, if*
thin slices	*available*
500 g (1 lb) rump steak or	*a few squares of bean curd*
Scotch fillet, cut into thin	*(optional)*
slices	*sauces for dipping (see right)*

Heat the chicken stock in your steamboat or frypan. Meanwhile, arrange the sliced meats separately in overlapping rows on one or two platters. Wash the spinach and cabbage, remove most of white stalk from spinach, and slice vegetables thinly. Cover the noodles with boiling water, leave to soak for 1 minute, then drain and cut into 8 cm (3 inch) lengths. Arrange on a platter with the sliced vegetables, snow peas and bean curd (if using).

When the stock boils, each guest picks up a piece of meat in his strainer and holds it for a minute or so in the stock to cook it; it is then transferred to the bowl and the desired sauce added. When all the meat has been eaten, the noodles and vegetables are dropped into the pot and eaten, then the soup is finally drunk. Towards the end of the cooking time, it may be necessary to add a little more stock so there's enough lovely soup to go around. *Serves 6 to 8*

Sauces for Dipping Choose one or all of the following, which should be poured into small individual bowls so each guest has his own dips at hand:

Plain soy sauce; hoisin sauce or lemon sauce; soy sauce mixed with a little dry sherry, sugar and chilli sauce; grated fresh ginger mixed with sugar, dry sherry and soy sauce; melted butter mixed with sesame seeds, a dash of dry sherry and sugar, and a little soy sauce.

NOTE: The meats should be sliced paper thin, so they cook very quickly. This is easier to do if they are partially frozen first. Vermicelli noodles and interesting sauces are available at all Chinese grocery shops, and most delicatessens and supermarkets.

Mousse of Ham in Peaches

500 g (1 lb) leg of ham, thickly	*1 tablespoon port or brandy*
sliced	*6 large ripe peaches or 12*
⅓ cup mayonnaise	*canned peach halves*
salt	*lettuce leaves*
cayenne	*fresh mint leaves, to garnish*
60 g (2 oz) butter, softened	

Cut the ham into small pieces, place in a blender or food processor fitted with the steel blade and process until smooth. Place in a bowl and stir in the mayonnaise, salt and cayenne to taste, the softened butter and port or brandy. Beat until smooth and chill for 1 hour.

Peel the fresh peaches by plunging into boiling water for 2 minutes, when the skins will slip off easily. Cut in half, and remove the stones. Spoon the ham mousse into the cavities in the peaches, mounding it up. Line 6 plates with lettuce, arrange 2 peach halves in each and garnish with mint leaves. *Serves 6*

Pork Steaks with Green Peppercorns

If pork steaks aren't available, use well-trimmed loin chops for this succulent French dish.

4 pork steaks or chops	SAUCE:
salt	*2 teaspoons green peppercorns*
freshly ground pepper	*1 tablespoon Dijon-style*
1 tablespoon oil	*mustard*
watercress or parsley, to	*⅔ cup cream*
garnish	

Season the pork with salt and pepper, and fry in the oil for 5 minutes on each side. Remove to a heated platter and keep warm. Pour off excess fat, add the peppercorns to the pan and stir for 1 minute, then add the mustard and cream. Stir well to pick up the brown bits from the bottom and continue cooking until the sauce thickens. Spoon over the pork and serve garnished with a spray of watercress or parsley. *Serves 4*

When loin chops are boned and rolled they become 'noisettes' of lamb. Recipe on right.

Stuffed Beef Roulades in Wine

An interesting dinner party dish that's richly flavoured but easy on the budget.

1 clove garlic, crushed	*60 g (2 oz) butter*
4 slices topside steak, pounded very thin	*1 cup red wine*
salt	*1 tablespoon tomato paste*
freshly ground pepper	*1 tablespoon Worcestershire sauce*
250 g (8 oz) sausage mince	*1 tablespoon vinegar*
1 onion, finely chopped	*1 tablespoon brown sugar*
½ teaspoon dried thyme or oregano	*2 tablespoons chopped parsley, sliced olives or sliced dill pickle*
1 carrot, cut into quarters	

Spread a little garlic on each steak and season with salt and freshly ground pepper. Mix the sausage mince with the onion and thyme or oregano, and spread a layer of mince over each steak. Place a piece of carrot in the middle, and roll the steaks into neat rolls, tucking in the ends to give a good shape.

Melt the butter in a flameproof casserole and gently brown the rolls on all sides. Combine the wine, tomato paste, sauce, vinegar and sugar and pour over the meat. Cover the casserole tightly with a lid or aluminium foil and bake in a moderate oven (180°C/350°F) for 1¼ hours, or until the rolls are very tender. Stir in the parsley, olives or pickles, and taste for seasoning. *Serves 4*

Noisettes of Lamb with Bacon and Lettuce

A simple dish, but the presentation makes it memorable. Serve with mashed potatoes, buttered rice or a purée of lentils.

6 double thickness lamb loin chops, boned	*90 g (3 oz) butter*
salt	*12 lettuce leaves*
freshly ground pepper	*½ cup chicken stock*
12 rashers bacon, rind removed	*¼ cup cream*

Trim excess fat from the chops, and curl each one into a round shape. Season well with salt and pepper. Wrap a strip of bacon around each chop and keep in place with a toothpick or tie with string.

Heat the butter in a large flameproof casserole and gently brown the chops on both sides, about 4 minutes each side. Take the chops from the casserole and remove the toothpicks, leaving the bacon in place. Blanch the lettuce leaves, one at a time, by dipping into boiling water for 3 seconds then into cold water. Dry gently with absorbent paper towels. Wrap each chop in two leaves of lettuce and replace in the casserole.

Pour the chicken stock over, cover tightly, and bake in a preheated hot oven (200°C/400°F) for 20 minutes. Remove the chops to a heated serving platter and stir the cream into the liquid left in the casserole. Bring to boiling point, taste for seasoning, and spoon over the chops. *Serves 6*

Marmalade-Glazed Corned Beef

Corned beef looks special enough for a party when it's finished with a golden glaze. The garnish is golden too – tart-sweet orange wedges.

2–2.5 kg (4–5 lb) corned silverside	1 carrot, scraped
1 large onion	1 bay leaf
6 cloves	2 tablespoons brown sugar
1 tablespoon lemon juice	GLAZE:
12 peppercorns	1 tablespoon Dijon-style mustard
1 blade mace	8–10 cloves
1 stick celery	3 tablespoons marmalade

Place the meat in a large saucepan with all the ingredients, except the glaze, and add cold water to cover. Simmer with the lid on until tender, approximately 2½ hours from the time the liquid reaches simmering point.

Lift the meat carefully from the saucepan and place on a rack (a cake rack that fits your baking dish is ideal). Spread the mustard over the top fatty surface, stud with cloves, and then spread with marmalade. If the marmalade is thick, heat it slightly to make a spreading consistency.

Place the meat in a preheated hot oven (200°C/400°F) for 20 to 30 minutes, or until the glaze is golden and bubbly and has caramelized a little. Watch carefully though, it mustn't burn.

Serve with Spiced Oranges (page 184) and also offer hot English mustard or Dijon-style French mustard. Suitable vegetables are parsleyed potatoes, buttered Brussels sprouts, or that great old-time partner, buttered wedges of cabbage. *Serves 8*

Pork Fillet en Croûte

This is one wonderful French way with pork. Each guest is served with his own glamorous little package.

500 g (1 lb) pork fillet in one piece or two smaller fillets	30 g (1 oz) butter
2 tablespoons brandy	1 tablespoon oil
1 tablespoon Dijon-style mustard	2 teaspoons chopped fresh herbs (chives, parsley, thyme)
salt	1 × 250 g packet puff pastry
freshly ground pepper	1 egg, lightly beaten

Cut the pork fillet into 4 portions, or cut smaller fillets in half. Trim the edges. Mix together the brandy, mustard and salt and pepper to taste in a shallow dish. Marinate the pork in this mixture for several hours in the refrigerator, turning often. Remove and pat dry.

Heat the butter and oil in a heavy frying pan and quickly fry the fillets until golden on both sides. Cool completely and sprinkle with herbs. Roll out the pastry thinly and cut into 4 portions. Wrap each fillet neatly in pastry, sealing the joins with a little beaten egg. Use the trimmings to make decorative shapes and attach to the pastry with egg. Chill the packages for at least 1 hour, then glaze the tops with the remaining egg and bake in a moderately hot oven (190°C/375°F) for 20 minutes. Reduce the heat to moderately slow (160°C/325°F) and bake for a further 15 minutes. *Serves 4*
NOTE: A crisp green salad is all that's required to accompany this memorable main course, though if you really want to gild the lily you could add a sauce of fresh mushrooms sliced and simmered in a little cream and seasoned with salt and pepper.

Peruvian Lamb

A leg of lamb takes on a whole new dimension when it's cooked on a bed of vegetables and subtly flavoured with coffee.

2–2.5 kg (4–5 lb) leg of lamb	1½ cups hot, strong black coffee
salt	
freshly ground pepper	1 tablespoon sugar
3 onions, sliced	½ cup cream
3 carrots, sliced	
1 cup hot beef stock (or use canned consommé)	

Trim excess fat from the lamb and season well with salt and pepper. Place the vegetables in a greased baking dish, put the lamb on top, and bake in a hot oven (200°C/400°F) for 30 minutes. Mix together the stock, coffee and sugar and pour over the lamb. Reduce the heat to moderate (180°C/350°F) and continue roasting the lamb for 1 hour, or until done to your taste. One hour gives you meat that is tender but still pink, but you will probably need 1½ hours for well-done meat. While the lamb is cooking, baste frequently with the pan juices.

Transfer the lamb to a warm platter, and allow to rest for 10 to 15 minutes before carving. This allows the juices to settle back into the meat and makes it easier to carve.

Meanwhile, rub the contents of the roasting pan through a sieve or purée in a blender. Reheat to boiling point, stir in the cream, and serve in a sauceboat with the lamb. *Serves 6 to 8*
NOTE: Sweet potatoes glazed with a little butter and brown sugar would be delicious with this dish.

Fricadelles Suprême

Horseradish adds an intriguing flavour to these moist, light beef patties with a lemony cream sauce.

1 kg (2 lb) lean minced beef	3 tablespoons snipped chives
salt	a little oil
freshly ground pepper	chopped parsley, to garnish
1 cup soft breadcrumbs	SAUCE:
60 g (2 oz) butter, softened	2 tablespoons lemon juice
3 tablespoons prepared, grated horseradish	1 cup beef stock
	½ cup light sour cream

Place the meat in a large bowl, season with salt and pepper, and blend in the breadcrumbs with a fork. Cream together the butter, horseradish and chives and combine gently with the meat. Be sure to handle the mixture lightly or the fricadelles will be compact instead of moist and fluffy. Shape the meat into 6 patties.

Heat enough oil in a heavy-based frying pan to give just a thin film over the base. Cook the fricadelles over a high heat for about 3 minutes each side, or until well browned outside but still a little pink inside. Transfer to a heated platter and keep warm while you make the sauce.

Pour the lemon juice and stock into the same pan used to cook the fricadelles. Stir well to get up the brown bits from the bottom, then cook over a high heat until reduced by about half. Remove the pan from the heat, stir in the sour cream and heat gently, but do not boil. Taste for seasoning, spoon over the patties and sprinkle with chopped parsley. Serve with creamy mashed potatoes or buttered noodles and a green salad. *Serves 6*

Marmalade-Glazed Corned Beef

Poultry to serve with Pride

Chicken and duck can be served in many varied and interesting ways in addition to the usual roasting, grilling and sautéing. The French have utilized their knowledge of sauces to produce a great number of excellent poultry dishes and have inspired the rest of the world to follow suit.

Wine is used as a choice flavouring agent and herbs play an important part – certain herbs belonging with certain dishes. Vegetables like mushrooms, spring onions and tomatoes are indispensable. Butter lends its own good flavour; and some sauces are finished off with a fortified wine or cream, which gives them a rich but smooth character.

These are recipes that have stood the test of time: they come from provincial France, Middle Europe and Italy, and are dishes that thousands of housewives have served with pride to family and friends.

Viennese Chicken Schnitzels

Now that chicken breasts are readily available, dishes like this, although special, can be an everyday affair.

6 half breasts of chicken
salt
freshly ground pepper
6 tablespoons flour
2 eggs, beaten
1 cup fresh white breadcrumbs
125 g (4 oz) butter

TO GARNISH:
lemon slices
rolled, stuffed anchovy fillets
chopped parsley

Remove the skin and bones from the chicken breasts. Place between two sheets of plastic food wrap and pound until thin.

Sprinkle each chicken schnitzel with salt and pepper and dredge lightly with flour. Coat with egg and breadcrumbs, patting lightly to make the crumbs cling. Chill for 20 minutes.

Heat the butter in a large frying pan (or use two pans) and fry the chicken until brown on both sides, about 6 to 8 minutes.

Arrange on a warm serving plate and garnish each schnitzel with lemon slices, anchovy fillets and a sprinkling of parsley. Serve with boiled potatoes. *Serves 6*

Viennese Chicken Schnitzels

Chicken with Citrus Cream Sauce

The fresh flavour of orange and lemon goes particularly well with chicken; the tang is mellowed by the smooth softness of cream.

6 chicken pieces, breasts or legs	salt
2 tablespoons flour	freshly ground pepper
90 g (3 oz) butter	$\frac{3}{4}$ cup cream
1 orange	2 tablespoons grated cheese (Gruyère or Emmenthal)
1 lemon	TO FINISH:
1½ cups white wine or chicken stock	lemon slices
	a little butter

Dust the chicken lightly with flour. Heat the butter in a large frying pan and brown the chicken pieces on all sides. Cover and continue to cook for about 20 to 25 minutes until nearly cooked. Remove to a warm plate.

Grate the rind of the orange and lemon. Stir the white wine or stock, grated rinds and 1 tablespoon lemon juice into the pan and season with salt and pepper. Turn up the heat and stir in the cream slowly. Return the chicken and cook in the cream sauce for a few minutes, turning the chicken to coat well. Arrange on a serving dish, spoon the sauce over and sprinkle with the cheese.

To finish, put a slice of lemon on top of each piece of chicken, top with a few pieces of butter and brown under a preheated grill. *Serves 6*

Chicken Sauté Maintenon

A dish for a special occasion, served in the traditional style on little rounds of fried bread, and containing mushrooms and tongue. A good green salad would be a perfect accompaniment.

2 × 1 kg (2 lb) chickens	½ teaspoon chopped fresh thyme or pinch of dried
salt	
freshly ground pepper	8 slices white bread
olive oil	chopped parsley, to garnish
4 chicken livers	GRAVY:
8 mushrooms, sliced	3 tablespoons white wine
4 slices cooked tongue or ham	3 tablespoons water
	3 tablespoons cream

Split the chickens in two and season with salt and freshly ground pepper. Brush with a little olive oil and grill the chickens under a preheated grill, skin side up first, then underside, and finally skin side to give a good colour. Brush several times with the pan juices while grilling. Allow about 30 minutes.

Meanwhile, prepare the garnish. Sauté the chicken livers very quickly in 1 tablespoon olive oil, remove and add the mushrooms to the pan. Shred the cooked tongue and add to the pan. Season with salt, pepper and thyme and keep warm.

Cut the slices of white bread into large rounds, fry in olive oil until golden, and drain on absorbent paper towels.

To assemble the dish, cut the grilled chicken halves in two, trimming off any bone ends (rib cage or neck). Place the fried bread on a large serving dish or individual plates, top each with the mushroom and tongue mixture, and arrange a piece of grilled chicken on each. Garnish with slices of chicken liver and sprinkle with chopped parsley.

Add the white wine, water and cream to the grilling pan. Bring to the boil, stirring in the brown bits until smooth. Season to taste and spoon over the chicken. *Serves 8*

Suprême of Chicken Auvergne

The French province of Auvergne produces exquisite mushrooms which are dried for use throughout the year. Look for European dried mushrooms at any good delicatessen.

4 half breasts of chicken	2 tablespoons sherry
3 tablespoons flour	salt
2 tablespoons chopped dried mushrooms	freshly ground pepper
	1 medium eggplant
½ cup dry white wine	2 medium tomatoes
30 g (1 oz) butter	nut of butter
4 tablespoons olive oil	

Dust the chicken breasts with flour. Put the mushrooms to soak in the wine.

In a large frying pan, brown the chicken on each side in butter and a tablespoon of olive oil. Heat the sherry and pour over the chicken. Cover, reduce the heat and cook very slowly for about 25 minutes, or until the chicken is tender. Add a little of the liquid from the soaking mushrooms to the pan if necessary. Season with salt and pepper. Remove the chicken and keep warm. Do not rinse out the pan – keep it for making the gravy.

Meanwhile, cut the eggplant in slices, sprinkle with salt and let stand for half an hour. Rinse, dry well and fry until golden in the remaining 3 tablespoons oil. It may be necessary to add a little more oil, but do not overdo it.

Arrange the eggplant slices on a hot serving dish and keep warm. Thickly slice the tomatoes and sauté in the same pan, slip off the skins and arrange over the eggplant. Place the chicken on top. Keep warm while making the gravy.

Using the pan the chicken was cooked in, add the soaked, dried mushrooms and the wine and boil up, stirring the brown bits from the bottom of the pan. Swirl in a little butter, taste for seasoning, and spoon over the chicken. *Serves 4*

Chicken Pojarski

Minced chicken is available from most poultry shops. Alternatively, buy 1 kg (2 lb) chicken breasts or thighs and make your own, using a mincer or food processor. These little chicken cakes are Russian in origin—note the vodka!

750 g (1½ lb) minced chicken	4 tablespoons vodka or dry sherry
salt	
pinch of nutmeg	4 tablespoons flour
4 slices white bread	60 g (2 oz) butter
¼ cup milk	6–8 mushrooms, sliced
	1 cup cream

Place the chicken mince in a bowl and season with salt and a good pinch of freshly grated nutmeg. Trim crusts from bread, pour the milk over and beat in. Add to the chicken along with 2 tablespoons vodka or sherry. Mix lightly but well. Shape into 6 patties and dust lightly with flour. Heat the butter in a large frying pan and cook the patties for 3 to 4 minutes on each side. Transfer to a warm serving plate.

Sauté the mushrooms in the same pan, adding a little more butter if necessary. Stir in the remaining 2 tablespoons vodka or sherry and heat through. Add the cream and stir well to pick up the brown bits; the sauce will take on 'body' and thicken slightly. Spoon over the patties. *Serves 6*

NOTE: A simple dish of plain boiled potatoes would be a classic accompaniment, or little new potatoes steamed in their jackets. You could also serve noodles tossed in butter and sprinkled with poppy seeds, or boiled rice.

White Chicken with Tarragon

6 half breasts of chicken	SAUCE:
½ medium onion, sliced	90 g (3 oz) butter
½ medium carrot, sliced	3 tablespoons flour
½ stick celery, sliced	2 cups chicken cooking liquid
2 tablespoons chopped fresh	1 tablespoon fresh tarragon or
tarragon or 1 teaspoon	½ teaspoon dried
dried	pinch of cayenne
¼ cup white wine	salt
salt	white pepper
freshly ground pepper	1 egg yolk
4½ cups hot, boiled buttered	2 tablespoons cream
rice (1½ cups raw)	TO GARNISH:
	paprika
	tarragon or parsley sprigs

Remove the skin from the chicken and trim the bones neatly. Place in a saucepan with the onion, carrot, celery, tarragon and wine. Season with salt and pepper, cover with hot water and simmer with a lid on for 15 minutes or until tender.

Meanwhile, place the rice in an ovenproof serving dish. Drain the chicken, reserving the liquid, and arrange on the rice. Cover loosely with foil and keep warm in a low oven (120°C/250°F).

Strain the cooking liquid. Melt 60 g (2 oz) butter in a small heavy saucepan, add the flour and cook gently, stirring, for 1 minute. Remove from the heat, cool slightly and stir in 2 cups warm cooking liquid and the tarragon. Add the cayenne, salt and pepper to taste. When smoothly blended, return to the heat and stir until boiling. Beat the egg yolk and cream together, stir in a little hot sauce, return to the saucepan and stir until the sauce thickens a little. Do not allow to boil. Remove from the heat and swirl in the remaining butter.

Spoon the sauce over the chicken and garnish each breast with paprika and a tarragon or parsley sprig. *Serves 6*

Chicken with Walnut Sauce

The chicken is cooked by a method perfected by the Chinese, which keeps all the natural juices in.

1 × 1.5–2 kg (3–4 lb) chicken	¼ cup chopped walnuts, to
1 medium onion, sliced	garnish
1 medium carrot, sliced	SAUCE:
10 cm (4 inch) piece celery,	½ cup diced white bread
sliced	(crustless)
3 sprigs parsley	1 cup chicken cooking liquid
½ bay leaf	1 cup walnut pieces
salt	salt
8 peppercorns	

Place the chicken in a large saucepan and almost cover with cold water. Remove the chicken (now that you have determined the quantity of water) and add the onion, carrot, celery, parsley, bay leaf, salt and peppercorns to the saucepan. Bring to the boil, replace the chicken, bring to the boil again and cover. Reduce the heat and simmer for 10 minutes, then turn off the heat and leave to cool in the liquor.

When cold, remove the chicken from the saucepan, skin and cut into joints. Arrange on a serving platter. Strain the cooking liquid. Put the bread and 1 cup of cooking liquid into a blender or food processor fitted with the steel blade and blend at high speed, gradually adding the walnut pieces, until smooth. Add salt to taste. Spoon the sauce over the chicken and sprinkle with chopped walnuts. *Serves 6*

Chicken with Cat's Teeth

'Poulet aux Dents du Chat' is a popular French sauté chicken dish. The cat's teeth are slivered almonds!

1 × 2 kg (4 lb) chicken or 6	1½ cups chicken stock
chicken pieces	1 bay leaf
90 g (3 oz) butter	salt
3 tablespoons dry sherry	freshly ground pepper
1 clove garlic, chopped	¼ cup slivered almonds
1 small onion, finely chopped	¼ cup light sour cream
4 tomatoes, peeled and sliced	2 tablespoons grated Gruyère
1 tablespoon tomato paste	cheese
2 tablespoons flour	nut of butter

Joint the chicken and pat dry with absorbent paper towels. Heat the butter in a large frying pan and sauté the pieces, turning with 2 spoons so they brown on all sides. Do not crowd the pan or they will steam. Heat the sherry and pour over the chicken, then remove the chicken to a plate. Place the garlic and onion in the pan and cook gently for a few minutes. Add two of the sliced tomatoes and cook for 2 to 3 minutes. Remove from the heat and stir in the tomato paste, flour, stock, bay leaf, salt and pepper. Return the chicken to the pan, skin side down. Cover and cook slowly for 45 minutes, turning the chicken pieces once or twice during cooking.

Arrange the chicken pieces on a flameproof serving dish. Add the slivered almonds, sour cream and the remaining sliced tomatoes to the pan, simmer a few minutes and spoon over the chicken. Sprinkle with the grated cheese, dot with butter and brown under a preheated grill. Serve with boiled noodles. *Serves 6*

Braised Duck with Port

Duck does not give as many servings as a chicken of similar weight and because it is awkward to carve this is best done in the kitchen – or, as with this recipe, before cooking.

1 large duck about 2 kg (4 lb)	freshly ground pepper
3 tablespoons flour	1 bay leaf
60 g (2 oz) butter	sprig of thyme or pinch of
250 g (8 oz) mushrooms, sliced	dried
5–6 spring onions, chopped	½ cup port
2 cups chicken stock	½ cup chopped parsley
1½ teaspoons salt	

First joint the duck. With a sharp, heavy knife, cut straight down through the breast bone and back; kitchen scissors help cut through the bone. Lay each half on a board and make a slanting cut between the ribs to separate the wings and legs, giving 4 good portions. The portions should be 2 wings and 2 legs, with a piece of breast on each. Trim away any unnecessary bone.

Dust the duck with flour. Heat the butter in a frying pan and brown the duck on all sides, then transfer it to a large flameproof casserole or pot. Add the mushrooms and chopped spring onions to the frying pan and cook for 5 minutes. Stir in the stock and bring to the boil. Season with salt and pepper and add the bay leaf and thyme. Pour over the duck, cover and simmer very gently for 1 to 1½ hours or until tender, or bake in a moderate oven (180°C/350°F). Discard the bay leaf and thyme, add the port and heat through. Sprinkle with chopped parsley and serve with boiled long-grain rice. *Serves 4*

Chicken with Cat's Teeth

Vol-au-Vents are Versatile

Small, crisp pastry cases with creamy fillings are always popular. They make an exciting first course, or can be handed round with drinks at a party. The pastry illustrated is not quite as rich as puff pastry, but is very light and flaky, and quite easy to make if you follow the step-by-step instructions.

Once you have mastered the easy art of making these little pastry cases, there is virtually no end to the possible fillings. Simply start with a well-flavoured Béchamel (Coating) Sauce and add ingredients to suit your taste and your budget. Or add lovely sweet fillings. There are suggestions on the opposite page.

Just a few tips to keep in mind:
● Keep the board and rolling pin clean and dry and well floured to prevent sticking.
● If the dough becomes sticky at any stage, chill it before rolling again.
● Put the prepared pastry in a plastic bag and chill for at least 30 minutes, until it is cool and firm, before rolling out and cutting the vol-au-vents.
● As the pastry contains a high percentage of fat, there is no need to grease the baking trays; just dampen them lightly to provide a firm base for the vol-au-vents.

Rich Flaky Pastry

2 cups flour	1 teaspoon lemon juice
pinch of salt	1 cup iced water
90 g (3 oz) butter	(approximately)
90 g (3 oz) lard	beaten egg, to glaze

Sift the flour and salt into a mixing bowl. Allow the butter and lard to soften at room temperature, then mix well together. Pat into a round shape, chill, then divide into four.

Rub one portion of the butter-lard mixture into the flour until it resembles coarse breadcrumbs. Mix together the lemon juice and water, and add enough to the flour to bind it into a soft but not sticky dough.

Knead the dough lightly on a floured board, then roll out into a rectangle about 38 × 18 cm (15 × 7 inches). Mark the rectangle lightly with a knife into three equal parts. Take the second portion of the butter-lard mixture and dot it over the top two-thirds of the pastry, leaving a margin of about 1 cm (½ inch). Fold the bottom third of pastry up, sealing the edges, then fold the top portion down and seal the edges again (a rolling pin does this effectively). Give the dough a quarter turn, then roll out again into a rectangle the same size as before. Repeat the whole process twice more, with the remaining portions of fat, but leave folded after the final addition instead of rolling into a rectangle. Wrap in plastic film or place in a bag, and chill in the refrigerator for 30 minutes before rolling out.

The step-by-step pictures opposite will help you. *Makes 8 vol-au-vents*

Fillings for Vol-au-Vents

Prawn and Mushroom Filling

60 g (2 oz) button mushrooms, sliced	1 tablespoon chopped parsley
250 g (8 oz) prawns, peeled and coarsely chopped (or leave whole if very small)	2–3 teaspoons lemon juice
	salt
	freshly ground pepper
45 g (1½ oz) butter	watercress or parsley, to garnish
1 cup hot Coating Sauce (page 147)	

Gently fry the mushrooms and prawns in butter until heated through. Add to the hot sauce with the parsley, lemon juice, salt and pepper to taste. Spoon into the prepared cases and garnish with watercress or parsley.

Ham and Egg Filling

1 cup diced cooked ham	1 cup hot Coating Sauce (page 147)
2 hard-boiled eggs, chopped	
2 spring onions, finely chopped	1 teaspoon Dijon-style mustard
1 tablespoon finely chopped green pepper	salt
45 g (1½ oz) butter	freshly ground pepper

Gently fry the ham, eggs, spring onions and green pepper in butter until heated through. Stir into the hot sauce with mustard and salt and pepper to taste. Spoon into the prepared cases.

Chicken Filling

1 cup chopped cooked chicken	1 cup hot Coating Sauce (page 147)
6–8 button mushrooms, sliced	
45 g (1½ oz) butter	salt
½ teaspoon Worcestershire sauce	freshly ground pepper
	2 tablespoons toasted slivered almonds, to garnish
2 tablespoons finely chopped pickled cucumbers	

Gently fry the chicken and mushrooms in butter until heated through. Stir the chicken, mushrooms, Worcestershire sauce and pickles into the hot sauce and add salt and pepper to taste. Spoon into the prepared pastry cases and sprinkle the tops with toasted almonds.

Salmon Filling

1 × 220 g can red salmon	1 tablespoon grated Parmesan cheese
2 spring onions, chopped	
45 g (1½ oz) butter	1 tablespoon finely chopped parsley
1 cup hot Coating Sauce (page 147)	salt
2 teaspoons lemon juice	freshly ground pepper

Drain the salmon, remove the skin and bones, and separate into flakes. Toss the salmon and spring onions lightly in hot butter until heated through. Fold into the sauce with the lemon juice, cheese, parsley and salt and pepper to taste. Spoon into the prepared pastry cases.

Cream and Fruit Filling

Sweet fillings are also delicious in vol-au-vents. In this case, the pastry cases are served cold

1 × 225 g can apricots or peaches
2 tablespoons brandy

1 cup cream, whipped
1 bar Flake chocolate, or ½ cup grated chocolate

Drain the fruit well and chop coarsely. Soak in brandy for an hour or so. Spoon a little cream into the bottom of each pastry case, top with brandied fruit, and spoon more cream on top. Decorate with crumbled Flake chocolate or grated chocolate. NOTE: Crisp the pastry cases in the oven and cool before using. Fill the vol-au-vents just before serving so the pastry doesn't become soggy.

Rich Flaky Pastry
1 Only one-quarter of the butter-lard mixture is rubbed into the flour. The remainder is added in three separate portions, and rolled into the pastry. This method gives the lovely flaky texture to the pastry and makes it rise during cooking. Use your fingertips to rub in the first portion of butter-lard, and work in a large bowl – much more convenient than a small one.

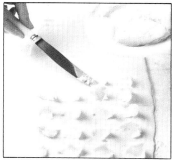

3 The second portion of butter-lard is flaked in small pieces over two-thirds of the pastry, leaving a margin at the sides so the pastry edges can be sealed together. It is quite easy to flake fat with a round-bladed knife.

5 Fold this top third of pastry down to meet the part you have just folded up – like making a parcel. Seal all the edges with a firm pressure of the floured rolling pin, then give the pastry a quarter turn to the left or right.

6 Flour the board and rolling pin and roll out the folded pastry to the same size as before. Mark into three once again, and flake the third portion of butter mixture over the top two-thirds of the pastry. Fold one third to the middle, then the second third over it as before. Seal the edges, give a quarter turn, and roll out again. Repeat the process with the last portion of butter, folding the two sides over. Wrap the folded pastry in plastic film and chill.

to about 5 mm (¼ inch) thick. Cut into rounds with a floured, 7.5 cm (3 inch) pastry cutter and arrange half the rounds on a dampened baking tray. Cut the centre out of the remaining rounds with a 4.5 cm (1¾ inch) cutter, leaving rings. Gather the trimmings together (do not knead) and re-roll to make more vol-au-vents.

8 Prick the large rounds on the tray with a fork, and dampen the edges. Place a pastry ring on each round and press to seal. Mark a criss-cross pattern with a knife around the tops of the rings and brush with a little beaten egg. Brush the small circles cut from the rings with egg and place on a separate tray, as they will cook quickly and need to be removed from the oven first. (They make the lids for the vol-au-vents.) Bake the pastry on the upper shelf of the oven for 10 minutes, or until crisp and golden. Remove any soft dough from the inside and cool on a wire rack. Place on a warm serving dish, fill with the desired filling, and top with pastry lids.
NOTE: Pastry cases can be made beforehand and stored in an airtight tin. Reheat for 5 to 6 minutes in a moderate oven (180°C/350°F) when required.

4 Lift the bottom edge of the pastry up with floured fingers, to prevent sticking, and fold it over the middle third of the pastry, pressing the side edges firmly together. You will then have one-third of the buttered pastry exposed.

2 When the dough has formed a soft ball after adding the lemon juice and water, turn it out onto a floured board and knead lightly. Then roll it out with long, smooth strokes into a rectangle about 38 × 18 cm (15 × 7 inches). Keep the edges and corners neat, and don't forget to flour your rolling pin to prevent sticking.

To Cook Vol-au-Vents
7 Preheat oven to very hot (230°C/450°F). Roll the folded, chilled pastry out

Special Occasion Vegetables

Beautifully cooked vegetables can build your reputation as a cook who really understands good eating. Fortunately, it is easier to cook them right than to ruin them. The watchword is to take a light approach, sautéing them quickly in butter or oil, or cooking them in water or stock only until tender-crisp.

It often just takes an imaginative eye to give drama to a routine vegetable. Cucumber, carrots, turnips and parsnips look sensationally new when they are cut into fine curling ribbons with a rotary peeler, and they have a beautiful new texture, too. Zucchini, when grated and tossed through hot butter with a touch of nutmeg, is a conversation piece.

Create a fresh feeling by combining vegetables with each other or with other foods: nuts, bean sprouts, burghul and toasted seeds for crunch; cheese, chopped egg, orange or lemon zest for a pretty colour and texture contrast. Robust or delicate sauces and, of course, the addition of spices and herbs all add the touch that says 'special'.

Sauté Potatoes

500 g (1 lb) small or medium-size old potatoes	*salt*
1 tablespoon oil	*freshly ground pepper*
30 g (1 oz) butter	*1 tablespoon snipped chives or chopped parsley*

To prepare and cook, see step-by-step pictures below.

Sauté Potatoes

1 Scrub the potatoes and boil them in salted water to cover for 10 to 15 minutes or until beginning to get tender. Drain, peel and cut into 5 mm (¼ inch) slices. Heat a frying pan, add the oil and, when hot, add the butter. When foaming, put in the potatoes.

2 Cook briskly, turning the potatoes often to give the crusty outside that is a characteristic of sauté potatoes. They should not be left to fry. When tender and golden brown, turn the contents of the pan into a hot serving dish (do not drain). Sprinkle with salt and pepper and chopped herbs.

Sauté Vegetables 1

This way of cooking makes it easy to achieve just the right balance of tenderness and crunch, and adds a lovely flavour and gloss.

Carrots, parsnips, turnips, Brussels sprouts and broccoli are all sautéed in the same way – parboiled first, then shaken in butter and oil over a brisk heat until golden.

500 g (1 lb) of the chosen vegetable	*30 g (1 oz) butter*
	salt
1 tablespoon oil	*freshly ground pepper*

Scrape carrots, peel parsnips or turnips thinly, and cut them into 5 mm (¼ inch) slices. Divide broccoli into florets and peel the tough stalks. Drop into boiling salted water and cook without a lid until just slightly softened, 7 to 10 minutes.

Heat a sauté pan or large frying pan, put in the oil and, when hot, add the butter. When foaming, add the vegetables and spread out gently in a layer. Cook briskly for 5 to 10 minutes, shaking the pan often to prevent sticking and turning the vegetables carefully once or twice with a fish slice. When tender and golden, season lightly with salt and pepper plus a touch of nutmeg for sprouts. Turn into a hot serving dish (do not drain). *Serves 4 to 6*

A colourful selection of sauté vegetables: Brussels sprouts, carrots, potatoes, zucchini, onions, cabbage and peppers.

Sauté Vegetables 2

Tender vegetables such as zucchini, eggplant, onions, green or red peppers, mushrooms and cabbage do not need parboiling before being sautéed.

500 g (1 lb) of the chosen vegetable	*30 g (1 oz) butter*
	salt
1 tablespoon oil	*freshly ground pepper*

Trim zucchini or eggplant, cut them into 5 mm (¼ inch) slices and salt lightly; stand for 20 minutes, then rinse and dry. Peel and slice onions. Slice peppers and discard the membrane and seeds. Trim and wipe mushrooms; slice if large. Cut cabbage into fine shreds, discarding tough outer leaves and heavy stems.

Heat a sauté pan or large frying pan, put in the oil and, when hot, add the butter. When foaming, add the vegetables and spread out gently into a layer. Cook briskly for 4 to 10 minutes, shaking the pan often to prevent sticking and turning the vegetables carefully with a fish slice once or twice. Eggplant may need a little more butter to prevent scorching. When tender, season with salt and pepper and turn into a hot serving dish. If you wish, sprinkle with herbs. *Serves 4 to 6*

Aïgroissade in Bread Pockets

This splendid vegetable dish from the Mediterranean could be served as the main dish for a casual luncheon. Make double or treble the quantity for a crowd and set out in a big pot with a pile of Lebanese bread pockets; then let guests help themselves.

250 g (8 oz) beans	*1 cup Aïoli (see below)*
250 g (8 oz) zucchini	*2 hard-boiled eggs, chopped*
250 g (8 oz) carrots	*4–6 rounds of flat Lebanese*
250 g (8 oz) peas	*bread*
1 × 310 g can chick peas, drained	

String the beans if necessary and trim them. Trim the zucchini. Scrape the carrots and cut into slices. Shell the peas. Cook all the vegetables separately in boiling water until just tender, then drain. Combine the vegetables with the chick peas and reheat.

Turn into a heated serving dish, fold the Aïoli through and sprinkle with chopped egg. Serve at once, accompanied by Lebanese bread cut in two and pulled apart to make pockets. At the table, fill the bread pockets with the Aïgroissade. *Serves 4*

Aïoli

6–8 cloves garlic	*1 cup olive oil*
¼ teaspoon salt	*1 tablespoon lemon juice*
2 egg yolks	

Crush the garlic with the salt. Place in a small bowl and beat well with the egg yolks. Add the oil gradually, drop by drop at first, then trickle by trickle, being sure to incorporate each addition thoroughly before adding the next. The sauce should be thick and creamy. When all the oil is incorporated, beat in the lemon juice.

This may also be made in a blender or food processor. Put the garlic, salt and egg yolks into the container, blend for a few seconds, then, with the motor running, add the oil and lemon juice. Serve as a sauce with raw or cooked vegetables.

Grated Buttered Zucchini

Zucchini tastes and looks quite different when it is grated and heated through in foaming butter. If you wish, the watercress or lettuce may be left out and the quantity of zucchini increased to 750 g (1½ lb). Leave the green skins on for colour.

500 g (1 lb) zucchini	60 g (2 oz) butter
salt	freshly ground pepper
2 cups shredded watercress or lettuce	pinch of nutmeg

Wash and trim the zucchini and grate on the coarsest side of a hand grater, or with the coarse grating attachment of a food processor. Toss with a little salt and stand for 30 minutes in a colander or sieve to drain, then rinse under cold water. Fold the watercress or lettuce through the zucchini.

Heat the butter and, when it is foaming, put in the vegetables and toss with two forks over a medium heat. When very hot, season with salt, pepper and nutmeg. Serve immediately. *Serves 4 to 6*

Braised Celery

This is an interesting accompaniment to roast veal or other roast or grilled meats. The celery is blanched in boiling water to set the colour, then cooked slowly on top of the stove, or in the oven, in chicken stock and butter.

6 tender sticks celery	salt
15 g (½ oz) butter	freshly ground pepper
1 cup chicken stock	beurre manié (see below)

Wash the celery, trim and cut into 10 cm (4 inch) lengths. Tie into 4 bundles with string. Drop into boiling water and boil for 5 minutes, then drain.

Melt the butter in the same saucepan (or in a flameproof casserole if you are going to complete the cooking in the oven). Put the celery bundles in and turn about gently to coat them. Add the chicken stock, salt and pepper. Cover the pan and cook on a low heat or in a moderately slow oven (160°C/325°F) for about 1 hour, until tender.

When the celery is cooked, arrange it in a heated serving dish, remove the strings and keep warm. Bring the liquid in the saucepan or casserole to the boil and whisk in beurre manié on the end of a whisk, a small piece at a time, until the sauce is the consistency of pouring cream. Simmer for 3 minutes, taste and adjust the seasoning and pour over the celery. *Serves 4*
Beurre Manié Mix together 30 g (1 oz) butter and 2 tablespoons flour.

Spiced Green Beans

Nice to serve with grilled meat or chicken.

750 g (1½ lb) green beans	pinch of cayenne
2 cloves garlic, chopped	½ cup vegetable oil
1 tablespoon lemon juice	½ teaspoon cumin seed
1 teaspoon salt	

Top and tail the beans, string if necessary, and cut into 4 cm (1½ inch) lengths. Combine the garlic, lemon juice, salt and cayenne in a small bowl.

Heat the oil in a frying pan, add the cumin seeds and fry for a few seconds. Add the beans and sauté briskly for 1 minute. Stir in the garlic mixture, cover tightly, and cook over a low heat for 10 minutes or until just tender, stirring two or three times. Increase the heat, remove the cover and stir constantly until the liquid has evaporated. *Serves 4 to 6*

Belgian Endive and Ham au Gratin

An interesting first course or luncheon dish.

4 heads Belgian endive (witloof)	1 cup Mornay Sauce (page 147)
2 teaspoons lemon juice	3 tablespoons grated cheese
salt	2 tablespoons fresh breadcrumbs
4 slices cooked ham	15 g (½ oz) butter, melted

Remove any damaged leaves from the endives, trim the bases and dig out the bottom of the cores with a pointed knife. Wash them and cover with cold water in a saucepan. Add the lemon juice and a little salt, and bring to the boil. Boil for 5 minutes and drain.

Roll each head of endive in a slice of ham and arrange in a buttered shallow ovenproof dish. Pour the mornay sauce over and sprinkle with cheese. Toss the crumbs in melted butter and scatter over. Bake in a moderate oven (180°C/350°F) for 20 to 30 minutes, until the endive is tender and the top is golden. *Serves 4*

Carrot Ribbons

500 g (1 lb) firm carrots
60 g (2 oz) butter
½ teaspoon sugar
1 tablespoon water
salt

freshly ground pepper
1 tablespoon chopped parsley,
mint or thyme, to garnish

Have the carrots chilled. Scrape them and cut lengthwise into thin ribbons with a vegetable peeler with a swivel blade. Melt the butter in a heavy saucepan and add the sugar. Put the carrot ribbons in and toss gently to coat with the butter. Add the water, place a piece of greaseproof paper over the saucepan and put the lid on tightly.

Cook on a high heat for 2 minutes, then turn the heat to low and cook a few minutes more, shaking the saucepan frequently, until the ribbons are tender-crisp. Season with salt and pepper and sprinkle with herbs. *Serves 4 to 6*
Turnip Ribbons or Parsnip Ribbons Peel chilled, firm turnips or parsnips and prepare in the same way as Carrot Ribbons.

Ambrosial Onions with Nuts

3 large onions, peeled
1 cup chicken stock
30 g (1 oz) butter
2 teaspoons honey

1 teaspoon grated lemon rind
1 teaspoon salt
½ teaspoon paprika
½ cup chopped pecans

Cut the onions downward into halves and arrange, cut side up, in a baking dish. Combine the remaining ingredients except nuts in a small saucepan and bring to a simmer. Pour over the onions, cover and bake in a moderate oven (180°C/350°F) for 50 minutes to 1 hour until tender. Sprinkle with nuts and bake uncovered for 10 minutes. *Serves 6*

Leeks with Poulette Sauce

Prepare 8 small leeks as illustrated in the step-by-step pictures below, arrange in a hot serving dish and pour 1 cup hot Poulette Sauce (page 147) over them. *Serves 4*

1 Choose small to medium leeks with crisp tops. Trim off the roots but leave joined at the root end. Cut off the tops to leave about 5 cm (2 inches) of green. Remove the tough, damaged or discoloured leaves.

2 Cut two slits at right angles to each other through the green tops down to the white part.

3 Holding the root ends, plunge them up and down in cold water to remove grit. In a wide pan, bring water to boiling point. Salt lightly and lay leeks in the pan.

4 Boil uncovered for 15 to 25 minutes, according to size, until tender when tested with a fine skewer. Drain on a cloth or absorbent paper towels, or, if not using immediately, cool quickly under cold running water.

Braised Celery; Belgian Endive and Ham au Gratin; Leeks with Poulette Sauce

Festive Fruits

Fresh, canned and dried fruits are easily turned into something special to complete a meal, but the festive feeling doesn't stop there. They also appear in preserves, chutneys, garnishes, and as accompaniments to meats and salads – those finishing touches that add a special note to even the simplest meal.

Fruit Salad

Any combination of fruits can be used to make fruit salad. The one illustrated combines orange segments with bananas, grapes and slices of unpeeled apple. Here are just a few handy tips to keep in mind:

● Dip banana, apple and pear slices in lemon juice before adding to the fruit salad and they won't turn brown.

● Cut the fruit in fairly large chunks or slices, so its density isn't lost. Fruit salad shouldn't look like confetti!

● Sprinkle the fruit salad with sugar to taste, but don't use too much – the fruits themselves are naturally sweet, of course. Add lemon juice for a fresh tang, or you might like to pour a little orange juice, apricot nectar, brandy or Kirsch over the fruit.

Interesting Combinations

Fruit salad needn't have a lot of ingredients. Some of the simplest combinations are also the most exciting.

Golden Salad   Orange segments, halved apricots (fresh or canned) and rock melon chunks. Sprinkle with sugar and lemon or lime juice.

Tropicana Salad   Pineapple wedges, passionfruit and pawpaw. Add canned guavas or jackfruit, with some of their juice, or fresh or canned mango slices.

Red and White Salad   Strawberries, canned lychees and slices of red-skinned apple. Add a little lychee juice and a squeeze of lemon.

Pear and Walnut Salad   Peel, core and slice ripe pears and sprinkle with lemon juice. Pour over a little pear brandy if available, or Kirsch or white rum. At serving time, sprinkle with chopped walnuts.

Gala Fruit Salad with Champagne

A spectacular presentation of fresh fruits for a birthday party.

1 medium-size ripe pineapple	*500 g (1 lb) seedless grapes*
4 pears	*½ cup icing sugar*
2 tablespoons lemon juice	*½ cup Kirsch or brandy*
4 medium oranges	*½ bottle champagne*
1 punnet strawberries	

Peel and core the pineapple and cut into wedges, reserving the frond. Peel, core and slice the pears and toss in lemon juice. Peel and slice the oranges. Wash and hull the strawberries and wash the grapes.

Combine all the fruits in a large bowl with the icing sugar and Kirsch or brandy. Just before serving, place an upturned glass or small dish in the middle of the serving bowl, and place the pineapple frond on it. Pour the champagne around the fruits and serve at once. *Serves 8*

Compote of Plums

1 kg (2 lb) plums in season	*2 thin slivers of lemon rind*
1 cup sugar	*1 vanilla pod or 1 teaspoon*
2 cups water	*vanilla essence (optional)*

Wash the fruit and remove the stalks. Cut the fruit crosswise, twist the two halves in opposite directions, and the fruit will split, making it easy to remove the stones.

Meanwhile, make the syrup. Place the sugar, water, lemon rind and vanilla pod or essence (if using) in a pan and bring slowly to the boil, stirring to dissolve the sugar. Boil briskly without a lid for 5 minutes, or until syrupy.

Place the prepared plums in the syrup and simmer gently until they are tender but still hold their shape, about 5 minutes (test with a fine skewer or toothpick). Serve the plums chilled, or at room temperature, with cream or ice-cream. *Serves 6*
NOTE: The same method is used for other fresh fruits such as peaches, nectarines and apricots. Cooking them in syrup helps to keep their shape and fresh colour, and prevents them going mushy or watery.

If not using apples immediately, place slices in cold water with a little lemon juice added and they won't turn brown.

Plum stones are easy to remove if you slice the plum around the middle and twist the sides in opposite directions.

To remove grape pips, cut in half and hook seeds out with the end of a paper clip.

Make sure all white pith is removed from oranges. When separating into segments, hold orange over a bowl so no juice is wasted.

Peel and core pineapple before cutting into wedges. Store unused pineapple in the refrigerator, covered with plastic wrap.

Melon balls are spectacular for a special occasion dessert. They are easy to make with the special cutter available everywhere.

Tropical Cream

4 ripe bananas	*2 tablespoons lemon juice*
pulp of 2 large passionfruit	*1 cup cream, whipped*
¼ cup sugar	*¼ cup chopped walnuts*
pinch of salt	*extra cream and passionfruit*
⅔ cup pineapple juice	*pulp, to serve*

Peel the bananas and mash with a fork. Combine with the passionfruit pulp, sugar, salt and juices. Fold in the whipped cream. Spoon into a freezer tray and freeze until firm, about 3 hours. Turn into a bowl and break up with a fork, then beat with a rotary or electric beater until frothy. Fold in the walnuts and return to the freezer until firm. Decorate with extra whipped cream and passionfruit to serve. *Serves 6 to 8*

Kish Mish with Rum

This luscious Middle-Eastern compote is made from dried fruit and traditionally served warm.

250 g (8 oz) large prunes	2 tablespoons lemon juice
1–2 cups cold tea	3/4 cup raisins
250 g (8 oz) dried figs	1/4 cup dark rum
250 g (8 oz) dried apples	2 tablespoons blanched
125 g (4 oz) dried apricots	slivered almonds
1/4 cup brown sugar	thick sour cream, to serve

Soak the prunes overnight in cold tea to cover. Soak the figs, apples and apricots in cold water to cover. Place all the fruits in a pan with the soaking liquid, brown sugar and lemon juice and simmer for 10 minutes or until soft and plump.

Remove the fruits to a bowl with a slotted spoon. Soak the raisins in boiling water for 5 minutes to plump them, and add to the fruit. Reduce the cooking liquid by rapid boiling until it becomes syrupy, then remove from the fire and stir in the rum. Pour over the fruit. Scatter the almonds over the top and serve warm with a spoonful of thick sour cream. *Serves 8*

Figs Paradiso

500 g (1 lb) fresh ripe figs	1/2 cup honey
1 slice fresh ginger	1 cup cream, lightly whipped
dry white wine to cover	1 tablespoon slivered almonds

Wash the figs and place in a saucepan with the ginger. Add enough wine to come to the top of the figs and bring to the boil. Stir in the honey, and cook gently until the figs are tender, about 20 minutes. Chill, and serve topped with cream and a sprinkle of almonds. *Serves 4*
NOTE: When fresh figs are out of season, use the plump preserved figs sold in plastic packets at the supermarket.

Glazed Butterscotch Apples

Children love this dessert of juicy apples cooked until tender in butter and brown sugar. Use a heavy pan with a tight-fitting lid, and cook over a very low heat so the apples don't scorch.

6 Granny Smith apples	3/4 teaspoon cinnamon
90 g (3 oz) butter	whipped cream or ice-cream,
pinch of salt	to serve
4 tablespoons brown sugar	

Peel and core the apples and cut each one into 8 wedges. Heat the butter in a frying pan and add the apples. Cover the pan and cook over a very low heat (turning now and again) until the apples begin to soften, about 10 minutes. Sprinkle with salt, sugar and cinnamon and continue cooking and turning until the apples are quite soft, a further 10 to 15 minutes. Serve warm with cream or ice-cream.
NOTE: If wished, a little dark rum may be heated, poured over the cooked apples, and set alight. This is not for children, of course. For them, a special treat would be to serve the apples with butterscotch ripple ice-cream.

Danish Apple Crunch; Raspberry Fool

Strawberry Peaches with Chilled Zabaglione

An absolutely stunning dessert for a very special occasion.

6 large ripe freestone peaches	1/2 cup caster sugar
2 tablespoons lemon juice	1/2 cup orange juice
2 punnets ripe strawberries	Chilled Zabaglione
1/4 cup Kirsch or cherry brandy	(see below)

Peel the peaches by plunging into boiling water for 2 minutes, then into cold, and slipping off the skins. Cut in half, remove the stones, and sprinkle with lemon juice. Finely slice half the peaches. Wash and hull the strawberries and purée in a blender or push through a sieve. Mix the berries with the Kirsch, sugar, orange juice and sliced peaches.

At serving time, divide the strawberry mixture among 6 individual glass bowls. Top each with a peach half, cut side up, and fill with chilled zabaglione. Pass extra zabaglione separately so guests may help themselves. *Serves 6*

Chilled Zabaglione

6 egg yolks	2 teaspoons grated lemon rind
3/4 cup caster sugar	pinch of cinnamon
1 cup sweet Marsala wine	1 cup cream, whipped and
1/2 teaspoon vanilla essence	chilled

Place the egg yolks, sugar and 1 tablespoon Marsala in the top of a double boiler. (If you don't have one, use a heatproof bowl that will fit in the top of a saucepan.) Place over hot, not boiling water, making sure the bottom of the container doesn't touch the water. Beat with a wire whisk until the mixture starts to foam, then gradually add the remaining Marsala in a trickle, beating all the time. Continue beating, scraping the sides and bottom of the bowl, until the mixture forms soft mounds. Remove at once from the stove and beat with the whisk – or you may now use an electric beater – until cool.

Add the vanilla, lemon rind and cinnamon and place the bowl in a larger one filled with cracked ice. Continue beating until chilled, then fold in the chilled whipped cream. *Serves 6 to 8*

Plum Sherbet

12 ripe plums	*½ cup sugar*
¼ cup lemon juice	*strawberries, plum slices and*
grated rind of 1 lemon	*kiwi fruit or pineapple*
2¼ cups buttermilk	*slices, to decorate*
pinch of salt	

Turn the freezer to the coldest setting. Wash the fruit, then halve and remove the stones. Mash with a fork or purée in a blender. Stir in the lemon juice and rind, buttermilk, salt and sugar. Pour into freezer trays and freeze until solid around the edges and almost set in the middle, about 3 hours. Turn into a bowl and whip until light and foamy. Return to the trays and freeze until set. Spoon into individual bowls and decorate with fruit. *Serves 6*

Danish Apple Crunch

This famous dessert combines apple purée with crisp buttered crumbs, cream and chocolate. Try it also with puréed peaches or plums or stewed rhubarb.

8 large cooking apples	*1 cup cream, whipped*
sugar to taste (about ¼ cup)	*1 bar Flake chocolate,*
125 g (4 oz) butter	*crumbled, or ½ cup grated*
2 cups soft white breadcrumbs	*dark chocolate*
¾ cup brown sugar	

Peel and core the apples and cut into slices. Grease a heavy saucepan with butter and add 3 tablespoons of water. Put the apples in the pan, cover tightly, and cook gently until the juices begin to flow, about 4 minutes. Remove the lid and continue cooking slowly, stirring often, until the apples are very soft. Beat with a wooden spoon until smooth and stir in sugar to taste. Don't add too much, because the crumb mixture is sweet.

Heat the butter in a frying pan, stir in the breadcrumbs and cook over medium heat until crumbs are golden brown, stirring all the time. Add the brown sugar and continue cooking and stirring until the crumbs are crisp. Remove the pan from the heat and allow the crumbs to cool, stirring now and again. Put alternate layers of crumbs and apple purée in a glass bowl, finishing with crumbs. Swirl the whipped cream over the top, sprinkle with chocolate, and chill until serving time. *Serves 6 to 8*

Peaches and Cream

Here is a lovely new version of an old favourite.

6 large ripe peaches	*1½ cups light sour cream*
¾ cup brown sugar	

Pour boiling water over the fruit, leave for 2 minutes, then slip off the skins. Cut into halves, remove stones and slice thinly. Combine the brown sugar with the cream, and arrange alternate layers of peaches and cream in a glass serving bowl. Cover tightly with plastic wrap and chill until serving time. *Serves 6*

Strawberry or Raspberry Fool

'Fools' are made of fruit purée combined with custard and cream, and are a traditional English dessert. Raspberry Fool is perhaps the most famous of all, and within the reach of some of us now that fresh raspberries are beginning to appear in fruit shops for a brief season at least.

2 punnets fresh strawberries or	*1 cup cream, whipped*
raspberries	*blanched flaked almonds, to*
a little sugar to taste	*decorate*
1 tablespoon lemon juice	
1 cup thick cold custard (see note)	

Wash the berries (hull strawberries if using) and whirr in a blender until smooth, or rub through a sieve. Sweeten to taste with a little sugar, and stir in the lemon juice. Combine with cold custard, blending well, then fold in the whipped cream. Spoon into individual glasses and decorate with flaked almonds. *Serves 6*
NOTE: Packet custard powder may be used to make the custard. Use 1 cup milk and 1½ tablespoons custard powder, following the cooking directions on the packet.

184

Busy-Day Strawberry Tart

Sometimes a special occasion comes up when you least expect it! (Even a happy mood is cause for celebration.) When you want a beautiful dessert in a hurry, just buy a cooked pie shell from the supermarket and add this luscious filling.

1 baked 20 cm (8 inch) pie shell	3–4 tablespoons icing sugar
2 punnets strawberries	2 teaspoons grated orange rind
6 tablespoons Kirsch or Grand Marnier	1 egg white, stiffly beaten
	1 cup cream, whipped

Leave the pie shell at room temperature. Wash and hull the strawberries and cut into slices. Combine in a bowl with the Kirsch or Grand Marnier, icing sugar to taste, and grated orange rind. Marinate in the refrigerator for 30 minutes or more. Just before ready to serve, fold the egg white and cream together, then add the strawberries to the mixture and combine lightly. Pile into the pie shell and serve at once. *Serves 6 to 8*
NOTE: Save a few whole strawberries for decoration if you wish, or decorate with a little extra grated orange rind. And if there's not even time to go to the supermarket, just serve the strawberry cream by itself, spooned into individual glasses.

Honeyed Apricots with Brandy

A simple but luscious idea using fresh apricots.

18 ripe apricots	¼ cup water
1 cup honey	¼ cup brandy
¼ cup lemon juice	

Plunge the apricots into boiling water, leave them for a minute, then rinse in cold water. The skins should slip off easily. Cut the peeled apricots in half and remove the stones.

Place the honey, lemon juice and water in a saucepan and bring to the boil. Add the apricots, reduce the heat and simmer very gently for 8 to 10 minutes, or until the fruit is tender when pierced with a fine skewer.

Cool the apricots in the syrup, then stir in the brandy. Chill until serving time and serve with pouring cream or whipped cream. *Serves 6*
NOTE: When fresh apricots aren't in season you may use canned fruit. Add ¼ cup of the syrup instead of water, but reduce the honey to ¾ cup.

Fruits with Meat

In many countries, fruits are traditional accompaniments to meat dishes. Here are ideas old and new for your own kitchen.

Baked Rhubarb

The sweet-tart flavour of rhubarb is wonderful with pork.

1 large bunch rhubarb, about 1 kg (2 lb)	½ cup sugar
grated rind and juice of 1 medium orange	pinch of ground ginger

Wash the rhubarb, but do not peel the stalks or the rosy colour will be lost. Cut into 5 cm (2 inch) lengths. Mix the rhubarb with the remaining ingredients and place in a buttered baking dish. Bake in a moderate oven (180°C/350°F) for 20 minutes or until tender. *Serves 6*

Spiced Oranges

Serve these spicy orange wedges with cold or hot roast pork or pickled pork. Leftovers store well in the refrigerator in a covered container.

4 large oranges, unpeeled	½ cup white vinegar
¾ teaspoon bicarbonate of soda	12 whole cloves
2 cups sugar	1 stick cinnamon
1¼ cups water	6 cardamom pods

Cover the oranges with water, add the bicarbonate of soda and bring to the boil. Cook uncovered for 20 minutes or until the oranges are tender when tested with a skewer. Drain, then cut each orange into 8 wedges.

Combine the sugar, water, vinegar and spices. Stir over a low heat until the sugar has dissolved and boil for 5 minutes. Add the orange wedges and simmer for 20 minutes. Cool, then spoon into a serving bowl and refrigerate, covered, until ready to serve. *Serves 8*

Fresh Plum Sauce

Bottled plum sauce makes an excellent dip for barbecued pork, chicken and meatballs. But it's easy to make your own sauce – and there's a lovely freshness to the flavour that unmistakably says 'homemade and very special'.

500 g (1 lb) dark plums	2 tablespoons vinegar
½ cup sugar	1 tablespoon soy sauce
1 tablespoon oil	½–1 teaspoon Chinese chilli sauce
2 slices fresh ginger, chopped	
1 clove garlic, crushed	salt

Wash the plums, place them in a pan and add the sugar and a few tablespoons of water. Stir over a low heat until the sugar has dissolved. Simmer covered until the plums are tender, stirring now and again to prevent sticking.

In another pan, heat the oil and fry the ginger and garlic until soft. Stir in the vinegar and soy sauce. Add this mixture to the plums, then push through a sieve. Taste, and add chilli sauce to suit your palate, and salt if required. Store in a covered jar or bowl in the refrigerator. *Makes about 3 cups*

Hot Buttered Pawpaw

For a change from fresh pawpaw, try this interesting hot dish. Serve it with ice-cream as a dessert, or as an accompaniment to roast pork or veal instead of potatoes.

1 large or 2 medium pawpaw	½ cup brown sugar
90 g (3 oz) butter, softened	cinnamon, to serve
3 tablespoons lemon juice	

Preheat the oven to moderate (180°C/350°F). Peel the pawpaw, cut in half and remove the seeds. Combine the butter with lemon juice and brown sugar and dot the mixture over the top of the pawpaw. Bake until tender, about 45 minutes, and sprinkle with a little cinnamon to serve. *Serves 6*

Fruits as Accompaniments

Everyone enjoys the delicious difference when you serve homemade jam, relish or chutney. They add a special touch to the simplest meal.

Sweet Pickled Lemons

These take 6 months to mature, but are worth it! They give a gourmet touch to cold meats and make an intriguing garnish for hot roast meats and grilled or fried fish.

12 small lemons	2 tablespoons olive oil
6½ cups sugar	

Wash the fruit but do not peel. Cut into quarters and pack into an earthenware crock in layers, sprinkling each layer with sugar. Cover the jar and keep in a cool place until a liquid fills the jar and fermentation starts. Remove the scum and pour the olive oil on top, making sure the lemons are covered with oil. Leave for 6 months before eating. *Makes approximately 10 cups*

Quick Apricot-Pineapple Preserves

Make this any time of the year from ingredients in your pantry cupboard. It is lovely spooned over waffles, sponge cake, or as a filling for pancakes as well as your breakfast toast and afternoon scones.

300 g (10 oz) dried apricots	1 × 850 g can crushed
1 cup water	pineapple
1½ cups sugar	2 tablespoons lemon juice

Soak the dried apricots in water overnight. Place the apricots and water in a wide-bottomed pan and simmer until they are pulpy, stirring often, about 20 minutes. Add the sugar and stir until dissolved, then add the crushed pineapple and lemon juice. Bring the mixture to the boil, and boil for 1 minute. Allow to cool a little, spoon into sterile jars, and seal. Store in the refrigerator. *Makes approximately 8 cups*

Strawberry and Pineapple Jam

A fascinating combination of flavours, and very easy to make.

2 cups ripe firm strawberries (about 3 punnets), washed and hulled	1 cup canned crushed pineapple
4 cups sugar	grated rind and juice of ½ large lemon

Place all the ingredients in a large saucepan, and bring very slowly to the boil, stirring gently. Simmer for 20 to 25 minutes, stirring often, or until the jam has thickened. Allow to cool a little, then spoon into sterile jars. Cover, and store in the refrigerator. *Makes approximately 7 cups*

Fresh Apple Chutney

Apple Chutney

Serve with curries or any cold sliced meats, or try it on one of my favourite sandwiches – wholegrain bread, lettuce, cheese and chutney.

1 lemon	1½ teaspoons salt
1 clove garlic, finely chopped	¼ teaspoon cayenne
5 cups peeled, chopped Granny Smith apples (about 5 large apples)	2 cups white vinegar
	1 red pepper, seeded and chopped
2¼ cups brown sugar	1 green pepper, seeded and chopped
1 cup raisins	
½ cup currants	
90 g (3 oz) chopped crystallized ginger	

Cut the lemon in half, remove the seeds and core, but do not peel. Chop finely. Combine with all the other ingredients in a large saucepan. Bring to the boil, then turn the heat down and simmer for 45 minutes, or until the fruit is very tender. Cool a little, spoon into sterile jars and seal. Store in the refrigerator. *Makes approximately 12 cups*

Fresh Apple Chutney

When time is short, you can make this in 10 minutes.

4 green apples, peeled and finely chopped	1 medium onion, finely chopped
1 teaspoon salt	2 tablespoons lemon juice
¼ cup cold water	2 tablespoons sugar
½ cup desiccated coconut	

Combine the apples with the salt and water; allow to stand for 5 minutes and drain. Combine with the remaining ingredients and chill until serving time.

Salute to Custards!

How to end a dinner with a flourish, or on a note of assured simplicity? Look to the custard family. Delicate, silken . . . these lovely desserts and sauces have one thing in common – ninety-nine out of a hundred people adore them.

Orange Spanish Flan

The Spanish love their smooth custard flan which may be cooked with fruit underneath and gently spiced. It's served everywhere from top restaurants to little cafés and, of course, in the home.

CARAMEL:	10 cm (4 inch) piece cinnamon
1/3 cup water	stick
1 cup sugar	4 eggs
CUSTARD:	3 egg yolks
2 small seedless oranges	3/4 cup sugar
3 cups milk	pinch of salt
1 vanilla bean or 1/2 teaspoon	
vanilla essence	

Make a caramel syrup and line a shallow 23cm (9 inch) cake tin in the same manner as for Crème Caramel (opposite).

Peel the oranges thinly and set rind aside. Remove all the pith and outside membrane. Separate the segments by cutting down between the dividing membranes and arrange them in a decorative pattern on the bottom of the mould.

Heat the milk slowly with the orange peel, vanilla bean if using, and cinnamon stick, until bubbles form round the edge. Strain into a jug.

Beat the eggs and egg yolks with 3/4 cup sugar and the salt. Add the milk slowly, stirring constantly. Add vanilla essence, if using. Pour gently into the mould, without disturbing the orange segments.

Set the cake tin in a pan of hot water and bake in a preheated moderately slow oven (160°C/325°F) for 55 minutes, or until a knife inserted in the centre comes out clean. Chill and unmould as for Crème Caramel. *Serves 6 to 8*

Grand Marnier Sauce

Custard's grand relation, superb over fresh fruits.

5 eggs	1/4 cup Grand Marnier
1/2 cup plus 2 tablespoons caster	1 cup cream
sugar	

Using a wire whisk or hand-held electric beater, whisk the eggs and 1/2 cup sugar together in a bowl set over simmering water. Be sure that the water does not touch the bottom of the bowl. Whisk until the mixture is very fluffy and pale lemon in colour, then remove from the heat and stir in half the Grand Marnier. Cover the bowl with plastic film and chill.

Shortly before serving time, whip the cream with the remaining sugar until it just holds a shape. Turn into the bowl with the egg mixture, drizzle the remaining Grand Marnier round the sides and fold all together until well blended. *Makes about 3 cups, sufficient for 10 to 12 servings.*

Caramel Queen of Puddings

Our grandmothers loved this pudding. Today it is revived as a special party dessert.

2 1/2 cups milk	MERINGUE:
3 tablespoons sugar	2 egg whites
1 cup fresh brown	pinch of cream of tartar
breadcrumbs	3 tablespoons caster sugar
2 egg yolks, beaten	extra caster sugar for
3 tablespoons sieved apricot	dredging
jam	

Heat the milk until bubbles form round the edge, then set aside. Spread the sugar in an even layer in a heavy-bottomed, medium-size saucepan and heat very gently until it has melted. Continue to cook, watching closely, until it turns golden brown (once it starts to colour, it can turn dark and bitter between one moment and the next). Take off the heat and slowly pour in half the milk, being careful not to have your pouring hand over the sugar – it bubbles up fiercely with a burst of steam. Return to a low heat and stir until the caramel is completely dissolved, then add the remaining milk. Pour the caramel milk over the breadcrumbs in a bowl and leave for 30 minutes for the bread to soften and swell, then stir in the beaten egg yolks.

Pour the mixture into a buttered 5-cup pie dish or soufflé dish, and bake in a preheated moderate oven (180°C/350°F) for 30 minutes or until set. Remove the pudding from the oven and reduce the heat to 160°C/325°F. Warm the apricot jam and spread it over the pudding.

Beat the egg whites until frothy, add the cream of tartar and continue to beat, adding the sugar gradually. When stiff and glossy, spoon onto the top of the pudding, starting round the edge, then filling in the centre. Swirl the top into little peaks with the back of a spoon and dredge with caster sugar. Return the pudding to the oven and cook until the meringue is crisp and golden, about 30 minutes. Serve hot or cold. *Serves 8*

Lemon Cheese Custard Sauce

When you blend lemon cheese into custard you get the perfect blend of creamy texture and fresh, tangy flavour. Serve it warm over a plain steamed pudding for a great winter dessert; or chilled, over an old-fashioned flummery or homemade meringues joined together in pairs with whipped cream; or just enjoy it plain, with a crisp biscuit.

LEMON CHEESE:	CUSTARD:
2 teaspoons butter	1 large egg
1/2 cup sugar	2 tablespoons sugar
juice and grated rind of	1 cup milk
1 lemon	1 vanilla bean or a few drops of
1 large egg	vanilla essence
1/2 teaspoon cornflour	

For the lemon cheese, stir the butter, sugar and a little of the lemon juice over a low heat until melted. Remove from the heat. Beat the egg, cornflour and remaining juice together. Stir in a little of the sugar mixture, then add to the mixture in the saucepan. Add the rind, and stir until boiling. Set aside.

To make the custard, cream the egg and sugar together in a small bowl. Heat the milk with the vanilla bean if using, until bubbles form round the edge. Whisk a little hot milk into the egg mixture, then stir this back into the saucepan.

Stir with a wooden spoon over a low heat until it coats the

back of the spoon. Add the vanilla essence, if using, and strain into a bowl.

Add the lemon cheese to the custard and stir until blended. To serve cold, cover and chill. To serve warm for later use, cover and chill, then when required place the bowl over a saucepan with a little simmering water in the bottom and warm gently, stirring. *Makes approximately 1½ cups, sufficient for 6 people.*

Variation

Orange-Passionfruit Custard Instead of lemon in the cheese mixture, use the grated rind and juice of 1 small orange and pulp of 1 passionfruit. Serve in pretty glass bowls topped with extra passionfruit and a spoonful of whipped cream.

Crème Caramel

A classic that's never out of style.

CARAMEL:	2.5 cm (1 inch) piece vanilla bean
¼ cup water	
1 cup sugar	3 eggs
CUSTARD:	2 egg yolks
1 cup milk	¼ cup sugar
1 cup cream	

To prepare and cook, see step-by-step pictures below. *Makes 6 individual crèmes in ½ cup moulds.*

Crème Caramel
1 Have oven gloves and a large bowl or sink of cold water ready. Warm 6 individual ¼-cup moulds. Put the water and sugar for the caramel into a small heavy-based saucepan and stir over a low heat until the sugar is dissolved, then remove the spoon and wash down the sides of the saucepan with a wet pastry brush.

2 Boil without stirring until the syrup is golden brown, watching closely as it can become too dark in a moment or two. As soon as it is the right colour, dip the base of the pan in the cold water to stop cooking. Hold a mould in a gloved hand and pour in the caramel to about 2 cm (¾ inch) deep.

3 With both hands gloved, turn the mould round so that the caramel coats it evenly. Pour in a little more if needed. Repeat with other moulds.

Preheat the oven to moderately slow (160°C/325°F). Heat the milk and cream together with the vanilla bean until bubbles appear round the edge. Discard vanilla bean.

4 Beat eggs and sugar together, and add cream mixture slowly, stirring.
5 Strain, then pour into the moulds. Put into a roasting pan and pour in boiling water to come halfway up the moulds. Place in centre of oven and bake for 45 minutes, until a knife inserted near the centre comes out clean. Do not allow the water to boil or custards will be grainy.

Chill the cremes thoroughly. To unmould, run a knife carefully between custard and edge of mould, place a serving plate upside down over the top of the mould, hold together firmly and invert. Give a slight shake and carefully lift the mould. The caramel will run down the crème as a sauce. Serve with cream, if desired.

Cooking for Parties

It's so lovely to eat out of doors, it's a celebration in itself. We can picnic at the beach or in the bush, or in our own garden; serve food in the sunroom or sun-deck; arrange a wedding buffet under a bright awning in the garden; have a housewarming party that spreads from indoors to out.

Food for such alfresco meals has to carry easily as well as look and taste delicious. It should be simple to serve and eat. In other words, a portable feast!

Portable Hot Foods

Smoked Haddock in Filo Pastry

A quiche-type tart with a beautifully flavoured filling.

8 sheets filo pastry	2 tablespoons chopped parsley
60 g (2 oz) butter, melted	½ teaspoon salt
FILLING:	freshly ground pepper and
1½ cups milk	nutmeg
250 g (8 oz) smoked haddock	2 tablespoons toasted slivered
2 eggs	almonds
1 cup light sour cream	
2 hard-boiled eggs, chopped	

Brush a 20 cm (8 inch) metal flan tin or pie dish with melted butter. Brush one sheet of filo pastry with melted butter and fit it into the tin. Repeat with the remaining pastry, brushing each sheet with butter. Trim the edges.

Heat 1 cup of the milk and poach the haddock for 10 minutes. Drain, remove skin and bones, and separate into flakes. Beat the eggs, add the remaining ½ cup milk and sour cream. Fold in the chopped eggs, parsley and haddock. Season with salt, pepper and nutmeg to taste.

Spoon the filling into the pastry shell and sprinkle with toasted almonds. Bake in a moderately hot oven (190°C/375°F) for 15 minutes, then reduce the heat to moderate (180°C/350°F) and cook a further 25 minutes, or until the filling is set and golden. (Cover the pastry edges with foil if it is getting too brown.)

To take on a picnic or serve outdoors, leave the pie in the plate and wrap in two sheets of foil. It will stay deliciously warm for half an hour or so. *Serves 4 to 6*
NOTE: The pie is also good cold.

Frankfurts in Pea Soup

Carry to the picnic in wide-mouthed thermos flasks. Filling and delicious, it makes a good cold weather idea.

2 × 445 g cans pea soup	6 Continental frankfurts

Make up pea soup according to packet directions. Simmer the frankfurts in water until heated through, then cut into diagonal slices about 2.5 cm (1 inch) long. Pour the soup into thermos flasks, filling three-quarters full, and add the frankfurts. With bread and butter and fruit you have a complete meal. *Serves 8*

Cornish Pasties

In Cornwall, everyone really does eat Cornish pasties, out of doors as well as in. They carry so well because the filling is succulent without having gravy that could spill. Wrap freshly baked pasties in foil, then in kitchen paper or tea-towels, and pack in an insulated container. The foam type is cheap and effective, and will keep your pasties hot for hours.

PASTRY:	1 large potato
4 cups flour	1 medium turnip
pinch of salt	1 large onion
½ teaspoon baking powder	salt
375 g (12 oz) butter	freshly ground pepper
2 egg yolks, beaten with 2	2 tablespoons water
tablespoons cold water	beaten egg or milk, to glaze
FILLING:	
375 g (12 oz) topside, oyster	
blade or rump steak	

Sift the flour, salt and baking powder. Rub in the butter until the mixture resembles coarse breadcrumbs. Make a well in the centre and add the egg yolks, blending with a knife to form a dough. Knead lightly and form into a ball. Wrap in plastic wrap or foil and chill for 1 hour before rolling out.

Trim the steak, removing any fat, and cut into small dice. Peel the vegetables and cut into small dice. Add to steak, season well with salt and pepper, and stir in the water.

Roll out the pastry and cut into 15 cm (6 inch) circles. Spoon a little filling down the centre of each circle, dampen the pastry edges, and bring up to meet in the middle, twisting together to join. The pasties will stand up like cock's combs. Make a small slit in each pasty to allow steam to escape; arrange on a greased baking tray, and brush with beaten egg or milk. Bake in a preheated hot oven (200°C/400°F) for 10 minutes, then reduce the temperature to moderate (180°C/350°F) and bake for a further 35 minutes, until the pastry is cooked and filling tender. *Makes 6 to 8 pasties*

Chilli-Cheese Macaroni

Bake this in a square dish or casserole. When cooked, wrap in foil and then in several thicknesses of paper. It will keep warm for several hours to enjoy on a picnic. Cut into squares and serve with crisp salad vegetables and a glass of beer, wine or fruit juice.

Paper plates and napkins and plastic throw-away forks make clearing up a breeze!

90 g (3 oz) butter	4 cups cooked and drained
1 medium onion, finely	macaroni (1 × 250 g packet)
chopped	250 g (8 oz) mature Cheddar
2 sticks celery, finely	cheese, cut into small cubes
chopped	salt
1 green pepper, seeded and	freshly ground pepper
chopped	3 eggs
2 teaspoons Mexican-style	2½ cups milk
chilli powder	

Melt the butter in a heavy frying pan and sauté the onion, celery and pepper until soft but not brown. Stir in the chilli powder, then add the cooked macaroni, cheese and salt and pepper to taste. Spoon into a greased baking dish. Beat the eggs and milk together and pour over the macaroni. Bake in a moderate oven (180°C/350°F) for 45 minutes, or until firm and golden brown on top. *Serves 6*

Picnic Herb and Bacon Bread

Sometimes it takes just one exciting hot touch to make an outdoor meal special. Serve this delicious savoury bread sliced and buttered, with stuffed eggs and a tossed green salad.

250 g (8 oz) streaky bacon, rind removed	3 tablespoons chopped mixed fresh herbs or 1 teaspoon dried
2 cups flour	
⅓ cup sugar	2 eggs, beaten
1 tablespoon baking powder	1 cup light sour cream
1 teaspoon salt	⅓ cup milk
½ teaspoon bicarbonate of soda	

Cut the bacon in small pieces (easy with kitchen scissors) and fry gently until crisp. Drain in a sieve, then spread on absorbent paper towels to cool. Sift together the flour, sugar, baking powder, salt and bicarbonate of soda. Stir in the herbs. Combine the eggs, sour cream and milk, and pour this mixture into the dry ingredients. Sprinkle the bacon bits over the top. Stir lightly with a wooden spoon just enough to moisten the flour. Don't over mix; the mixture will still be lumpy.

Turn into a well-greased loaf pan, about 21×11 cm ($8\frac{1}{2} \times 4\frac{1}{2}$ inches), and bake in a moderate oven ($180°C/350°F$) for 55 minutes, or until a toothpick inserted in the centre comes out clean. Turn the loaf out of the tin to allow steam to escape. To carry, replace the loaf in the tin and wrap in foil, then in several thicknesses of paper or a tea-towel. *Serves 6 to 8*

Seafood Wrap-Ups

Seafood cooks in buttery juices inside foil parcels so easy to take outdoors in a basket, ready to serve and piping hot. Or you can make up the packages at home, carry them to the picnic and cook over glowing coals on the spot.

8 fish fillets (e.g., bream, flathead, gemfish, flounder)	4 tablespoons chopped spring onions
125 g (4 oz) butter	2 teaspoons dried dill weed
4 tablespoons lemon juice	salt
	freshly ground pepper

Use two thicknesses of foil for each fillet and cut into squares big enough to wrap around the fish. Grease the foil with a little butter, place a fillet in the middle, and season with lemon juice, spring onions, dill, salt and pepper. Dot more butter over the top, seal the foil parcels tightly, and grill over hot coals or under a hot grill for 4 to 5 minutes each side. Serve the fish wrapped in the parcels, so guests can open their own. *Serves 4*

Hot Cheese and Anchovy Bread

The loaf is filled at home, wrapped in foil, and heated at the picnic. A glass of red wine is optional but delicious!

1 loaf crusty Italian bread	125 g (4 oz) Mozzarella or Provolone cheese, cut into shreds
4 tablespoons olive oil	
90 g (3 oz) butter, softened	2 tablespoons drained, chopped capers
1 clove garlic, crushed	
1 small can flat anchovies, drained	

Slice the loaf in half lengthwise. Combine the olive oil, butter, garlic and anchovies in a small bowl, mashing to a smooth paste. Spread on both halves of bread, and sprinkle one half with shredded cheese and capers. Join the halves together and wrap tightly in foil. Heat on the barbecue or among the coals for 5 minutes. *Serves 4 to 6*

Smoked Haddock in Filo Pastry

A Portable Cold Feast

You can serve this menu for an informal wedding reception in the garden, for a housewarming, birthday party or anniversary. It's simple to prepare, with memorable little touches that make it special.

Quantities given are for 25, and can easily be increased to serve extra guests.

MENU
Bratwurst Rolls
Herb and Cream Cheese Sandwiches   Chicken Sandwiches
Stuffed Celery   Stuffed Mushrooms
Lovers' Knots

Bratwurst Rolls

Bratwurst are small uncooked Continental sausages sold by most delicatessens.

---

25 long soft bread rolls (the little ones called 'twins' that come in pairs are the perfect size)
250 g (8 oz) butter, melted
12 spring onions, finely chopped

½ cup chopped mixed fresh herbs, or 1 tablespoon mixed dried herbs chopped with ½ cup parsley sprigs
25 bratwurst sausages
Dijon-style mustard
salt
freshly ground pepper

Cut the rolls in half lengthwise and pull out some of the crumb from each half. Brush the insides with melted butter and sprinkle with chopped onions and herbs. Grill the sausages on both sides until brown and cooked through, split in half and spread generously with mustard. Put the sausages back together and place a sausage inside each bread roll, seasoning with salt and pepper.

Wrap 6 to 8 rolls at a time in aluminium foil, and store the packages overnight in the refrigerator. When the rolls are required, heat the packages straight from the refrigerator for 20 minutes in a moderate oven (180°C/350°F). Unwrap and pile in baskets to serve. *Serves 25*

Herb and Cream Cheese Sandwiches

---

2 × 250 g packets Philadelphia cream cheese
juice of 1 large lemon
freshly ground pepper
½ cup chopped mixed fresh herbs (chives, thyme, marjoram, oregano)

1 cup finely chopped parsley
8 spring onions, finely chopped (use less if including chives)
2 loaves sliced sandwich bread (1 brown and 1 white)
softened butter for spreading

Soften the cream cheese in a bowl, and mash with the lemon juice and a good grinding of pepper. Mix in the fresh herbs, parsley and spring onions.

Spread the bread with a thin layer of butter. Spread herbed cheese on top of the white slices and top with the brown slices.

Remove the crusts from the sandwiches and cut each one into 4 triangles or 3 finger lengths. Wrap in plastic wrap, then pack into airtight containers and store in the refrigerator. *Serves 25*

Chicken Sandwiches

The chicken roll available from delicatessens is ideal for sandwiches. If you prefer fresh chicken, buy 1 kg (2 lb) of chicken breasts and poach in seasoned water to cover. Allow to cool in the water before skinning and boning and cutting into thin slices.

---

1 loaf white sandwich bread
softened butter for spreading
750 g (1½ lb) chicken roll, thinly sliced
salt

freshly ground pepper
Mayonnaise (page 152)
fresh herbs or parsley, to garnish

Butter the bread slices and place the chicken in overlapping slices on half of them. Season with salt and pepper to taste and spread thinly with mayonnaise. Top with the remaining bread slices and trim the crusts. Cut each sandwich into 4 triangles or into 3 finger lengths. (If wrapped tightly in plastic film and then in foil, the sandwiches will stay fresh overnight in the refrigerator.) Serve garnished with herbs. *Serves 25*

Stuffed Mushrooms and Celery

---

250 g (8 oz) small firm mushrooms
lemon juice
5 tender sticks celery
FILLING:
2 cooked half-breasts of chicken
¾ cup Mayonnaise (page 152)
¼ cup finely chopped parsley

¼ cup snipped chives
salt
freshly ground pepper
TO GARNISH:
finely chopped nuts
paprika
sprays of watercress or parsley

To prepare the filling, skin and bone the chicken and chop very finely. Combine with the mayonnaise, parsley and chives, and season with salt and pepper to taste. Remove the stalks from the mushrooms and wipe over with a cloth dipped in lemon juice. Wash the celery, pat dry, and remove any strings.

Spoon the filling into the hollow sides of the mushrooms and celery, cover with plastic wrap, and store in the refrigerator. When ready to serve, sprinkle the mushroom caps with chopped nuts and the celery with paprika. Cut the celery into finger lengths. Garnish with parsley or watercress. *Serves 25*

Lovers' Knots

A delicate romantic biscuit for a wedding.

---

250 g (8 oz) butter
4 tablespoons caster sugar
2 teaspoons vanilla essence
3 eggs

3 cups flour
¼ teaspoon salt
6 tablespoons ground almonds
icing sugar for dredging

Soften the butter and cream with the sugar. Add the vanilla essence, then beat in the eggs, one at a time, beating well between each addition. Sift the flour and salt together and fold in the ground almonds. Work into the creamed mixture to form a dough, then knead lightly, and wrap in plastic wrap. Chill for 1 hour.

Divide the dough into pieces about the size of a walnut. Lightly flour a board, and roll out each little piece of dough into a sausage shape. It should be about 20 cm (8 inches) long and the thickness of your little finger in the middle, but thinner at each end. Twist each piece into a pretzel shape, like a loose knot, and press the ends firmly together to make a double ring.

Arrange the biscuits on greased baking sheets and bake in a hot oven (200°C/400°F) for 10 to 12 minutes, or until pale golden. Place on wire racks and dredge thickly with icing sugar while still hot. Cool, and store in an airtight tin. Just before serving, sift more icing sugar over the biscuits. *Makes about 50*

A Portable Cold Feast. At the back: Bratwurst Rolls; Left: Lovers' Knots; Right, from the back: Herb and Cream Cheese Sandwiches; Chicken Sandwiches; Stuffed Celery and Mushrooms.

A Wedding Buffet for 50

Many of today's brides look forward to having the reception at home. This needn't be an overwhelming task for the cook (who is probably mother!) if the dishes are chosen for simplicity as well as style. Everything on this menu can be made ahead of time, so all that's required is a friend or two willing to offer refrigeration space, and help set the table and serve on the day itself.

MENU

Chicken Sandwiches (page 191) Stuffed Mushrooms and Celery (page 191) (make double quantities)

Paradise Cocktail
Wedding Chicken with Rice Salad
Cider-Glazed Ham   Green Salad

Kish Mish with Rum (page 182) (make in larger quantities)
Sherried Chocolate Gâteau (make 2)

Lovers' Knots (page 191)

Paradise Cocktail

6 × 425 g cans grapefruit segments	4 × 425 g cans pineapple pieces
6 × 283 g cans mandarin segments	2 teaspoons Angostura bitters
2 × 227 g cans maraschino cherries in syrup	50 mint sprigs

Drain the fruits, reserving the liquid from the grapefruit and cherries. Gently mix the fruits together with the grapefruit and cherry syrups and bitters. Cover and chill. Wash the mint and store it, covered, in the refrigerator. At serving time, spoon the cocktail into small glass coupes and top with a sprig of mint. *Serves 50*

Wedding Chicken

The chicken and sauce are cooked ahead (2 or 3 days, if necessary) and assembled on the wedding day.

TO COOK THE CHICKEN:	4 carrots
2 onions, halved	1 teaspoon salt
6 cloves	1 cup white wine
8 peppercorns	5 kg (10 lb) half breasts of
4 sticks celery	chicken

Cooking this large quantity of chicken is easier if done in several batches. Place all the ingredients, except the chicken, in a large wide saucepan or baking dish and add one layer of chicken breasts. Pour in enough water to cover the chicken (return remaining breasts to refrigerator). Cover the dish with a lid or foil, and simmer gently for 20 minutes.

Lift the chicken from the liquid as soon as it is cool enough to handle. Remove the bones and skin, place them in a clean

saucepan and set aside. Cut each chicken breast diagonally into 2 neat pieces. As soon as they are cool, store in the refrigerator in a covered container. Repeat the process with the remaining chicken, adding water as required.

To prepare the stock for the sauce, add the poaching liquid and 4 cups of water to the skin and bones saved from the chicken. Bring slowly to the boil, reduce the heat, and simmer for 1 hour. Strain, cool and refrigerate.
IMPORTANT: Take great care when cooking in bulk. Food should be cooled quickly to prevent bacteria multiplying, and then stored at once in the refrigerator.

SAUCE FOR THE CHICKEN:	12 dried apricots
2 onions, finely chopped	salt
4 tablespoons oil	freshly ground pepper
2 tablespoons ground cumin	5 cups Mayonnaise (page 152)
3 tablespoons tomato paste	TO GARNISH:
1½ cups white wine	watercress or parsley
2 cups stock	tomato slices
4 bay leaves	

Cook the onions gently in hot oil until soft but not brown, about 4 minutes. Add the cumin and cook for 3 minutes longer, stirring. Add the tomato paste, wine, stock, bay leaves and apricots. Bring to the boil, and add salt and pepper to taste. Simmer, uncovered, for 10 minutes. Strain and cool.

Gradually add the cooled sauce to the mayonnaise. Taste, and adjust the seasoning. Take the poached chicken pieces from the refrigerator and gently fold through enough sauce to moisten them lightly; you will need about one-third. Cover, and replace in the refrigerator. Also cover and chill the remaining sauce.
TO SERVE: Arrange the chicken pieces on a bed of rice salad on 2 or 3 long serving platters. Spoon a little sauce over each, and garnish with sprays of watercress or parsley and bright red tomato slices. Serve with ham and salad. *Serves 50*

Rice Salad

Cook the rice one or two days before the wedding for convenience, and mix some of the dressing through to keep the grains moist and separate.

8 cups raw Basmati or long-grain rice	2 green peppers, seeded and finely chopped
2 cups Vinaigrette (page 152)	6 tender sticks celery, sliced
1 kg (2 lb) frozen peas	

Cook the rice, 3 cups at a time, in plenty of boiling salted water. Drain, rinse with hot water to remove any trace of starch and drain again. When all the rice is cooked, moisten with 1 cup of the dressing and store, covered, in the refrigerator. The night before the wedding, cook the peas in boiling salted water until just tender. When cool, add to the rice with the peppers and celery and remaining vinaigrette. Keep refrigerated until ready to serve. *Serves 50*

Green Salad

You can give this salad an interesting look by using two kinds of lettuce.

10 lettuce (5 Iceberg and 5 Cos, if possible)	walnut halves or chopped parsley, to garnish
2 cups Vinaigrette (page 152)	

Cut the cores from the lettuce and wash under cold running water. Turn upside down to drain well. Separate Cos lettuce into leaves, if using, and set aside. Cut Iceberg lettuce into 2.5 cm (1 inch) strips, then cut across to make squares. This is an easy way to prepare lettuce in large quantities. Dry the Cos leaves, and the cut Iceberg lettuce on clean tea-towels, then place separately in large plastic bags (kitchen tidy bags are a useful size). Tie the tops of the bags and store in the refrigerator.

At serving time, sprinkle the vinaigrette into the bags of lettuce and, holding the tops firm, shake the bags gently to distribute the dressing. This is much easier to do than tossing lettuce in bowls. If using Cos, line salad bowls with upright Cos leaves and spoon the lettuce squares into the centre. Sprinkle with walnuts or parsley to serve. *Serves 50*

Cider-Glazed Leg of Ham

Ask a friend who is a good carver to carve the ham at the table – this looks more impressive than having it already sliced.

1 cooked leg of ham about 7.5 kg (15 lb)	*1 cup brown sugar*
24 cloves	*slices of unpeeled red apple dipped in lemon juice, to garnish*
2 teaspoons dry mustard	
1 bottle sweet cider (plain or alcoholic)	

Peel the skin from the ham, leaving a collar around the bone. Trim away excess fat, then score the fat diagonally with a sharp knife to form a diamond pattern. Stud alternate diamonds with cloves. Place the ham, fat side up, in a large baking dish. Mix the mustard to a paste with a little of the cider and rub into the cuts in the fat.

Pour the cider over and around the ham, and bake in a preheated moderate oven (180°C/350°F) for 1½ hours, spooning the cider over now and again. Sprinkle brown sugar over the top and return to the oven for a further 1 hour, basting often with the pan juices. If they seem to be evaporating too much, add a little water to the pan. Allow to cool, then refrigerate, but leave at room temperature for at least an hour before serving. Serve garnished with apple slices. *Serves 50*

Sherried Chocolate Gâteau

This is best made the day before the wedding, to allow the flavours to mellow.

2 packets Savoy finger biscuits (about 18)	TO DECORATE:
3 × 500 ml cartons cream	*1 cup cream, whipped*
3 tablespoons drinking chocolate	*1 thick bar milk chocolate or chocolate buttons*
1 teaspoon instant coffee	
1 cup sweet sherry	

Lightly oil a 28 cm (11 inch) springform tin. Cut the sponge fingers in half diagonally. Whip the cream with the drinking chocolate and instant coffee until it just holds its shape.

Pour the sherry into a shallow dish and dip one piece of biscuit at a time into the sherry, dipping one side only. As each one is dipped, arrange it in cartwheel fashion around the base of the tin. Be careful to dip lightly – just enough to moisten. When the base of the tin is covered with biscuits, spread one-third of the whipped cream over the top. Repeat with another two layers of biscuits and cream. Cover with foil and chill until serving time.

To serve, remove the clips from the springform pan and take off the sides. Leave the cake on the base and place on an attractive serving dish. Pipe rosettes of whipped cream on top and decorate with chocolate curls or buttons. (To make curls, have a bar of chocolate at room temperature and shave thin pieces from the side with a swivel-bladed vegetable peeler.) *Serves 25*

A Guide to Beverages

Coffee: 500 g (1 lb) finely ground coffee makes 60 cups.
Instant Coffee: 120 g instant coffee makes 60 cups.
Soft Drinks: 6 drinks to a 1-litre bottle.
Beer: 4 drinks to a bottle.
Wine: 6 glasses to a bottle.
Sherry or Port: 12–16 glasses to a bottle.
Liqueurs: 20–24 small liqueur glasses to a bottle.

Wedding Chicken

A Gala Picnic for 12

On a summer's day, pack a basket with elegant cold food and eat out of doors. Cold chicken, terrines, crusty bread, salads and cheese are popular, and so are little cold pork pies with their golden-glazed raised pastry.

MENU
Black and Green Olives
Chicken Liver and Pork Pâté
Sliced Tomatoes with Basil   Spicy Drumsticks
Miniature Pork Pies   Crusty Bread and Butter
Fresh Fruit   Cheese   Orange Cake

Chicken Liver and Pork Pâté

---

6 rashers streaky bacon, rind removed	2 tablespoons brandy
500 g (1 lb) chicken livers	1 clove garlic, crushed
500 g (1 lb) pork shoulder or pork steaks	salt
1 egg, beaten	pinch each of dried cloves, ginger, white pepper and nutmeg
2 cups fresh white breadcrumbs	bay leaves

Line a 6-cup mould or ovenproof dish with bacon strips, letting ends overhang on one side. Pick over the chicken livers and remove any sinews and discoloured parts. Dice the pork, then mince the livers and pork finely in a mincer or food processor fitted with the steel blade. Combine the meat with the egg, crumbs, brandy, garlic, salt to taste and spices. Turn into the mould, and fold bacon ends over. Top with a few bay leaves.

Cover with a lid or aluminium foil. Place in a baking dish with a little hot water and cook in a moderate oven (180°C/350°F) for 1½ hours. Cool, and refrigerate. (If possible, make a few days before so the flavours can mellow.) *Serves 12*

Sliced Tomatoes with Basil

---

4 large ripe tomatoes	salt
1 tablespoon wine vinegar	freshly ground pepper
3 tablespoons olive oil	1 tablespoon chopped fresh basil
¾ teaspoon Dijon-style mustard	

Wash the tomatoes. Combine the remaining ingredients in a screw-top jar. Pour over the tomatoes, which should be cut into wedges, just before serving. *Serves 12*

Spicy Drumsticks

---

1 tablespoon green masala paste (from curry shelf at delicatessens)	1 small onion, chopped
	1 × 275 g carton natural yogurt
	12 chicken drumsticks

Mix together the masala, onion and yogurt. Arrange the drumsticks in a glass dish and pour the mixture over, turning the drumsticks so they're well coated. Cover and refrigerate for several hours.

Oil a baking dish large enough to hold the drumsticks in one layer, pouring the yogurt mixture over them. Bake in a preheated hot oven (200°C/400°F) for 15 minutes, turning once or twice in the pan drippings. Cook a further 15 to 20 minutes, turning again, until the juices run clear and the flesh is very tender. Pack into a box with foil between layers and serve warm or cold. *Serves 12*

Miniature Pork Pies

These are substantial, so may be cut into halves or quarters for serving. It's fun to raise the pastry, and not at all difficult!

---

1 kg (2 lb) pork sausage meat or pork mince (or buy shoulder pork or steaks and mince your own)	4 hard-boiled eggs
	PASTRY:
	4 cups flour
6 sage leaves, finely chopped, or ¼ teaspoon ground sage	1 teaspoon salt
	185 g (6 oz) lard
salt	8 tablespoons water
freshly ground pepper	beaten egg, to glaze

Mix the meat with the sage and season lightly with salt and pepper. Divide into 4, and mould each piece around a boiled egg, using lightly floured hands. Leave in the refrigerator while making the pastry.

Sift the flour and salt into a bowl. Place the lard and water in a saucepan over a medium heat and bring to the boil, stirring. When boiling rapidly, pour at once into the centre of the flour. Beat well with a wooden spoon until the mixture clings together in a ball, leaving the basin clean.

Turn out onto a clean working surface and knead to a smooth dough. The pastry must be worked while warm and pliable, so set aside 4 small pieces for the lids and shape the remainder into 4 circles. Flatten out the centre of each to make the base and shape the edges of the pastry upwards to start the sides. Pinch the edge between the thumb and first finger, drawing it up to a round container shaped like a little money purse. Put the pork filling inside and continue drawing the pastry up until it is deep enough to enclose the filling.

Roll out the 4 reserved pieces to make lids to fit. Dampen the pastry edges and cover the pies; pinch the edges together and flute.

Make a small hole in the centre of each pie for the steam to escape, and fix a band of greased, double-thickness greaseproof paper around each to support it during baking. Tie with string. Brush the tops of the pies with beaten egg.

Bake in the centre of a preheated hot oven (200°C/400°F) for 20 minutes, then reduce the heat to moderate (180°C/350°F) and cook for 40 minutes. Remove the supporting paper after 30 minutes' cooking time, and glaze the sides of the pies with the remaining egg. Allow the pies to cool, then cut in halves or quarters to serve. *Makes 4 pies*

A Gala Picnic. From the back: Orange Cake; Spicy Drumsticks; Chicken Liver and Pork Pâté.

Orange Cake

125 g (4 oz) butter, softened
grated rind and juice of 1
   orange
¾ cup caster sugar
2 eggs

2 cups self-raising flour
pinch of salt
2–3 tablespoons milk
2 tablespoons candied peel

Grease and lightly flour a deep 20 cm (8 inch) round or square tin and line the base with greased greaseproof paper. Set the oven temperature at moderate (180°C/350°F).

Cream the butter with the orange rind until very smooth. Gradually add the sugar, beating well between each addition. The mixture should be very light and fluffy. Beat the eggs, and add a little at a time to the butter and sugar mixture, beating thoroughly to prevent curdling. Sift the flour with salt and, using a metal spoon, fold in the flour alternately with the orange juice. Add milk, if necessary, to make a soft dropping consistency.

Turn the mixture into the prepared tin and smooth the top. Sprinkle peel over the cake and bake in a moderate oven for 45 minutes, or until the cake is cooked when tested with a skewer. Remove from the tin and cool on a wire rack, then wrap in foil to carry.

A Wine Tasting Dinner Party for 8

The food itself is easy to make and serve, so the whole evening should be good fun and relaxing for the cook as well as the guests, with lots of talking points.

Bon appétit!

Add extra interest to a dinner party by combining delicious food with a wine tasting.

I am suggesting a choice of two aperitif wines, two dry whites, two reds, a choice of ports (if desired) and two dessert wines, with food to complement them. This works out at about a bottle for each guest, with one bottle providing eight small glasses.

Have the food ready before the guests arrive, and the wines at the required temperatures. I like aperitif wines well chilled, almost icy. Dry whites and dessert wines are chilled; red and fortified wines (like port) are usually served at room temperature. Remember to uncork red wines some time before serving, giving them a chance to 'breathe'.

If you set each place with four glasses, these can be rinsed and dried after the first four wines are tasted, leaving you only 32 glasses to find for the party. Most large hotel bottle departments or liquor stores will let you borrow glasses, or you can ask friends to help.

You will notice I am suggesting a cheese course before the dessert. This allows the choice of finishing off the red wines from the meat course, or going on to port if you wish.

MENU

Salted Nuts and Olives
Melon in Prosciutto
Choice of 2 aperitif wines
(sweet and dry vermouth or
medium and dry sherry)

Cold Prawns in Dill Sauce
Buttered rye bread
Choice of 2 dry white wines
(Riesling and Chablis)

Hot Noodles with Basil Sauce
Sliced Roast Beef
Choice of 2 dry red wines
(a claret and Burgundy or
wines from different areas)

Cheese Plate or Creamy Cheese Mould
Crusty bread and fruit, if desired
Continue with the red wines or offer
a choice of ports

Orange Spanish Flan (page 186), with a bowl of
fresh sugared strawberries
Choice of Sauternes

A Wine Tasting Dinner Party, above: Scotch Fillet; Noodles with Basil; Cold Prawns in Dill Sauce.

Melon in Prosciutto

Instead of melon, you could use pawpaw; and the spiced beef, called pastrami, is an interesting alternative to prosciutto.

1 large rock melon, honeydew melon or pawpaw	*250 g (8 oz) prosciutto or pastrami, sliced paper thin*
freshly ground pepper	

Peel the melon or pawpaw and cut into cubes. Grind a little black pepper over. Cut the prosciutto or pastrami into strips and wrap a strip around each melon cube, securing with a toothpick (the decorative toothpicks with frilly paper ends are ideal). Chill in the refrigerator and pass with nuts and olives as you sip the aperitif wines.
NOTE: Prosciutto is cured raw ham. It is available with pastrami at good delicatessens.

Cold Prawns in Dill Sauce

If you can buy green prawns for this dish, the flavour and texture will be better. Otherwise, use cooked prawns.

1 kg (2 lb) medium-size green prawns	*1 small onion, grated*
	2 teaspoons sugar
chopped fresh dill and dill sprigs, to garnish	*1 teaspoon salt*
	¼ teaspoon ground allspice
SAUCE:	TO SERVE:
¾ cup cooking liquid	*lemon wedges*
½ cup lemon juice	*thinly sliced, buttered rye*
1 teaspoon dried dill weed	*bread*

Cook the green prawns in boiling salted water to cover. As soon as they turn bright pink, remove them from the heat. Drain and reserve ¾ cup of the liquid for the sauce.

Mix the liquid with the lemon juice, dill, onion, sugar, salt and allspice. Peel the prawns, remove the dark veins, and pour the sauce over them. Cover and chill overnight. Arrange in a pretty bowl set in a bed of crushed ice and garnish with fresh dill. Serve with lemon wedges and pass buttered rye bread separately.
NOTE: If using cooked prawns, peel and reserve the shells and heads. Simmer for 2 minutes with 1 cup of water and a pinch of salt; strain, and use this liquid for the sauce.

Hot Noodles with Basil Sauce

The sauce for this dish can be made weeks ahead, as the flavour matures on keeping. Toss the sauce with freshly cooked noodles just before serving.

500 g (1 lb) flat tagliatelle noodles, or your favourite kind	*¼ cup chopped parsley*
	2 small cloves garlic, chopped
	⅔ cup olive oil
a good knob of butter	*¼ teaspoon nutmeg*
BASIL SAUCE:	*1 cup freshly grated Parmesan or Romano cheese*
1 cup chopped fresh basil or	
¼ cup dried basil leaves	*1 teaspoon salt*

Place the basil, parsley and garlic in a blender or food processor fitted with the steel blade. Process until pulpy, then add the olive oil little by little to form a smooth paste. Stir in the nutmeg, cheese and salt. Spoon into a jar, cover tightly with a lid or foil, and store in the refrigerator.

Cook the tagliatelle in plenty of boiling water about 10 minutes before ready to serve; bite a strand to test if it's cooked to your liking. Drain, then return to the saucepan and fork through the knob of butter. Add the basil sauce and toss lightly until the noodles are well coated. Serve at once. *Serves 8*

Roast Beef

1 Scotch fillet in the piece weighing about 1.5 kg (3 lb)	*3 tablespoons oil*
	salt
freshly ground pepper	

About an hour and a half before guests are due, preheat the oven to hot (200°C/400°F). Season the meat with plenty of freshly ground pepper. Heat the oil in a flameproof baking dish and brown the meat well until crusty on one side, then turn and brown the other side.

Place in the oven and roast for 45 minutes to 1 hour for medium-rare meat. Place the cooked meat on a sheet of foil, spoon the pan juices over, wrap tightly and leave at room temperature. The juices will set in the meat and make it easier to carve. Serve the meat at room temperature, cut in thin slices and seasoned with salt and a little extra pepper. *Serves 8*

Cheese Plate

It's fun preparing a cheese plate, and there are really no hard and fast rules. You might like just one kind of soft dessert cheese – for example, a Port Salut or Brie – served with plain water biscuits. Or you might offer a selection with crusty bread, pumpernickel, rye wafers or perhaps some Scottish oat cakes.

When I serve a selection of cheeses, I like to include a Cheddar for those who prefer a 'plain' cheese, a semi-firm one with a sweeter flavour like Gruyère or Emmenthal, a blue cheese such as Gorgonzola, Stilton or Roquefort, a soft dessert type and a Camembert almost at the 'runny' stage.

You will find your cheese shop helpful in selecting cheeses; and don't hesitate to ask the proprietor of the bottle shop or liquor store for his help with wines. The more information you have, the more interesting your party will be.

Creamy Cheese Mould

2 cups natural yogurt (goats' milk if possible)	*1 teaspoon orange flower water (from chemist or health food shop)*
1 cup cream	*fruits, to serve (see below)*

Combine the yogurt, cream and orange flower water in a bowl. Line a sieve with a double thickness of dampened cheesecloth, or a double layer of Chux cloth and set over a bowl. Pour the yogurt mixture into the sieve and allow to drain for 8 hours at room temperature, or until the whey has drained off and the curds are firm. Spoon into a small basin, cover, and chill in the refrigerator. Unmould, and serve with fruit and bread or biscuits. *Serves 8*
Fruits to Serve Ripe pears, peeled and quartered and sprinkled with a little lemon juice; sliced fresh apricots or peaches; plump, preserved figs or prunes; fresh dates; wedges of fresh pineapple; ripe cherries in season; halved, ripe plums.

Place the mould in the centre of a large platter and arrange the fruits around it. Serve water biscuits or crusty bread on a separate platter. If you are serving port you might also like to add some walnuts, a traditional accompaniment to port.

Little Touches make a Meal Special

Experienced cooks know that a simple detail can make all the difference to the taste and appearance of a dish.

I appreciate that some cooks like to be adventurous in their approach, and this helps make cooking creative and satisfying. But don't neglect the details! Even the simplest ingredient is there for a purpose, and when a garnish or accompaniment is suggested it really helps to complete the dish.

I am giving some of my own favourite 'little touches' and hints on these pages, and hope you will share them with me.

Bouquet Garni

In its simplest form, a bouquet garni consists of 1 bay leaf and 2 or 3 sprigs of parsley and thyme. They are usually tucked inside a stick of celery with a slice of carrot, and tied with a piece of string long enough to dangle over the side of the pot. It is then easy to remove the bouquet when it has imparted its flavour to the cooking liquid. Never neglect adding a bouquet garni when it's called for – it is at the heart of so much good cooking.

Spring Onions

Throughout this book I have referred to spring onions, which are the slender onions with a white base and a green top. Each one is separate, though they are sold in bunches. Spring onions are often called shallots, but true shallots have a root end with a bulbous base, and grow like garlic in a compact group of individual cloves attached to each other.

Wine in Cooking

Wine is added to food to complement the natural flavours, not to overshadow them.

Apart from dessert cooking (poaching fruit, making jellies, etc.) there are three major uses for wine. First, it often goes into a marinade, helping to season and tenderize meat. The marinade is frequently used in the cooking as well, becoming part of the sauce.

In cooking fish, wine is used for the poaching liquid and later for making the sauce. Cooking wine needn't be of expensive quality but should certainly be 'good enough to drink'. Our cask and flagon wines have brought wine cookery within everyone's reach.

Secondly, wine is used to make pan sauces, after sautéing or roasting meat, fish and poultry. It is poured into the pan or baking dish and swirled around as you scrape up the brown bits and juices that have collected on the bottom. This process of dissolving the flavoursome bits that cling to the pan is called 'deglazing'. The sauce is then reduced a little, seasoned, and poured over the food.

The third use of wine is as a last-minute flavouring, at the very end of the cooking process or just before serving, and only a small amount is used. Wines for this use are generally the fortified wines and include sherry, Madeira and port. Sherry is

often poured directly into soup, for instance, and port is stirred into a gravy after it is made.

Never use more wine than is specified on the theory that 'more is better'. Too much wine can spoil the flavour of a dish.

Chopping Parsley

Roughly chopped parsley is a traditional garnish for salads or hearty stews and casseroles, and can easily be chopped by hand or with a food processor.

Parsley with a light, mossy effect should be used on delicate poached fish dishes, sautéed poultry and for cold dishes on more formal occasions.

To get this fine parsley, first pull the stems of the parsley between your fingers, collecting the curly heads in a tight, compact bunch. Chop the heads as finely as possible with a very sharp knife.

When the parsley is chopped, roll it up in a tea-towel or piece of muslin and hold it under a cold running tap. Twist the cloth tightly to squeeze out as much moisture as possible, then spread the parsley out on absorbent paper towels and pat dry. Transfer to a plate, and cover until ready to use.

Croûtons

These are crisp little pieces of bread, usually fried, which can be made in all sizes. As coarse crumbs they are an attractive garnish for vegetables, noodles and dumplings. In small dice they add crunch and good looks to pea soups and other soups. Cut into rounds, they are an excellent base for canapés to serve with drinks or for snacks.

Croûtons can also add flavour and texture to salads. For the famous Caesar salad, bread is crisped in olive oil and flavoured with anchovy and perhaps a hint of garlic.

There are three ways of making croûtons. First, the bread is cut into dice or the shape required. They may be deep-fried in oil or sautéed in a frying pan in a little oil or butter. Alternatively they may be brushed with oil, or buttered on each side, and placed in a moderately hot oven (190°C/375°F) until crisp and golden.

Croûtons store well in an airtight container or in the freezer, and may be reheated in a moderate oven.

Bercy Butter

A lovely, light whipped butter to serve with grilled meats.

2 teaspoons finely chopped spring onions	2 teaspoons finely chopped parsley
¾ cup dry white wine	salt
60 g (2 oz) butter, softened	freshly ground white pepper

Place the onions and wine in a small saucepan and boil until the wine is reduced to 1 tablespoon. Strain and cool, then blend into the softened butter with the chopped parsley and salt and pepper to taste. Pile into a bowl to serve.

Parsley Butter

Serve on grilled meats, fish or vegetables.

60 g (2 oz) butter, softened	2 teaspoons lemon juice
1 tablespoon finely chopped parsley	salt
	freshly ground pepper

Combine all the ingredients, seasoning with salt and pepper to taste. Mould the butter into a roll, wrap in foil and chill in the refrigerator. To serve, cut into slices.

Garlic Butter

Spread on hot French bread, or use for garlic bread, or as a flavouring for meats and vegetables.

2 cloves garlic, peeled	salt
60 g (2 oz) butter, softened	freshly ground pepper

Cover the garlic cloves with water in a small saucepan, and simmer for 5 minutes. Drain, and crush. Combine with the butter, and season to taste with salt and pepper.

Oven Magic

Oven Magic

A generation or two ago it was the custom to put aside one day a week for baking, usually Friday, so there would be plenty of good things ready for the weekend.

They were the days when afternoon tea often included date and nut loaf and a mile-high sponge as well as hot scones and little sandwiches. It might have been hard work for the cook but it was also a labour of love, because no shop could match the good things from her own oven. 'Homemade' was the unswerving yardstick of quality in those days.

Today, good things from the oven have come into their own again. A new generation of creative cooks is discovering that home-baked bread has superb flavour and texture; that pastry you make yourself really does 'melt in the mouth'; and that cakes can be packed with healthy ingredients and still satisfy a sweet tooth.

On top of everything else, baking lets you explore new cooking skills. Making a good spaghetti sauce or tossing a crisp salad is one thing, but there's a special kind of satisfaction in turning out a great pie or a high, fluffy sponge cake.

In this book, I've tried to take the fuss out of baking. Steps are clearly explained, procedures are often simplified, and recipes are geared to today's busy cooks. At the same time, these recipes will fill your kitchen with old-time fragrance, and give old-time pleasure to your family and friends. That's real oven magic!

Traditional Cakes

There are some cakes that give double pleasure . . . enjoyment for their own sake plus the knowledge that you're one of a long line of cooks who have prepared that same recipe with love. Some are cakes for particular festivals, such as Simnel Cake for Mothering Sunday or Easter and Christmas Cake. Many are regional specialties, including Cornwall's Saffron Buns, Yorkshire's Parkin, America's Angel Cake, Australia's Lamingtons, and others. All have stood the test of time, remaining favourites to generation after generation of good cooks and enthusiastic eaters.

Victoria Sandwich

1 Grease two 18 cm (7 inch) sandwich tins and line the bases. Set the oven to moderately hot (190°C/375°F).

Cream the butter and add the sugar gradually, beating until fluffy. Add the eggs gradually, beating well between additions. If there are signs of curdling, stir in a spoonful of flour with each addition of egg.

Sift the flour and salt together and fold into the mixture with enough milk to give a soft dropping consistency – the mixture should drop freely off the spoon in 5 seconds.

2 Divide the mixture evenly between the tins and smooth the tops. Bake side by side in the oven for 20 minutes, or until the cakes are golden brown, with sides shrinking from the tins and centres that spring back when pressed lightly. Cool for a few minutes in the tins and turn out onto a rack.

When cool, spread one cake with jam, place the other on top and dredge with caster sugar.

Victoria Sandwich

This recipe is based on the time-honoured method of weighing the eggs and using the equivalent weight of butter, sugar and flour. With today's commercially graded eggs, this is not really necessary.

For the best results, have the butter and eggs at room temperature; the mixture will be easier to beat and less likely to curdle.

Cream the butter well before adding the sugar, and beat in the sugar a little at a time, scraping the sides of the bowl once or twice to bring in any loose sugar. (Sugar which is not dissolved gives the cake a speckled top.) When the mixture is quite smooth and looks like whipped cream, the eggs may be added.

Always fold the flour and liquid in gently by hand. If you beat or stir vigorously at this stage, the cake will not rise properly and will be tough.

185 g (6 oz) butter
185 g (6 oz) caster sugar
3 large eggs, beaten
185 g (6 oz) self-raising flour
pinch of salt
1–2 tablespoons milk

TO FINISH:
3 tablespoons warmed jam
extra caster sugar for dredging

To prepare and bake, see step-by-step pictures at left.

Victoria Sandwich; Dundee Cake

Angel Cake

This is the great American contribution to fine dessert cakes: a fluffy confection baked in a special deep ring tin, usually with a removable base, which is 'hung' upside down after baking to set the fragile structure.

1 cup flour	*1½ teaspoons cream of tartar*
1½ cups caster sugar	*1½ teaspoons vanilla essence*
1½ cups egg whites (10–12 medium eggs)	*¼ teaspoon almond essence*
¼ teaspoon salt	

Mix the flour with ½ cup sugar and sift three times. Place a shelf just below the centre of the oven and set the oven at moderate (180°C/350°F).

Beat the whites until foamy, add salt and cream of tartar and beat until soft peaks form. Add the remaining sugar gradually, beating until stiff and glossy. Fold in the essences, sift the flour mixture over in four lots and fold in.

Turn the mixture into a 23 cm (9 inch) angel cake tin, which must have no trace of grease, and cut through the mixture to break up any large bubbles. Bake for 45 minutes or until a light touch leaves no imprint.

Turn the tin upside down and hang on a bottle or inverted funnel. Leave for at least 1 hour, then remove the cake from the tin. To serve, pull apart with two forks. A knife would squash this delicate cake.

Dundee Cake

To many a Scot, a well-run household should always have some Dundee cake on hand for family or visitors.

250 g (8 oz) butter	*1 cup sultanas*
grated rind of 2 oranges	*1 cup currants*
1 cup caster sugar	*½ cup chopped candied peel*
5 eggs, beaten	*1 tablespoon strained orange*
2½ cups flour	*juice*
pinch of salt	TO FINISH:
1 teaspoon baking powder	*extra blanched almonds*
½ cup blanched almonds, chopped	*milk*
	glacé cherries (optional)

Grease a deep 20 cm (8 inch) round cake tin and line with greased brown paper, then greased greaseproof paper. Set the oven to slow (150°C/300°F).

Cream the butter with the orange rind and add the sugar gradually, beating until fluffy. Add the eggs a little at a time, beating well between additions. If the mixture begins to curdle, stir in a spoonful of flour with each addition of egg.

Sift the flour, salt and baking powder together and mix in the almonds, fruits and peel. Fold into the butter mixture with the orange juice.

Put the mixture into the prepared tin, smooth the top and make a large shallow depression in the centre with a spoon. This will level out during baking, giving a flat top rather than a dome. Split the extra almonds, toss in a little milk and arrange on top of the cake with a few glacé cherries if desired.

Bake in the centre of the oven 2 to 2½ hours, or until a skewer inserted in the middle of the cake comes out clean.

Allow the cake to cool in the tin. If the top has cracked, turn upside down on a cooling tray and the weight will close the crack. Remove the tin and paper when cool. When quite cold, store in an airtight tin or plastic bag and allow the cake to mature – for 4 weeks if possible – before cutting.

Make a depression in the top to give a flat top when baked

Simnel Cake

This rich fruit cake, layered and topped with marzipan, was originally made for Mothering Sunday halfway through Lent, but is now the traditional centrepiece for Easter Sunday. It is surrounded by fascinating associations. 'Simnel' probably came from the name of a fine wheat flour used by the Romans, while the traditional decoration of 11 marzipan balls represents all the apostles, except Judas.

750 g (1½ lb) marzipan	2 teaspoons grated lemon rind
2 cups flour	1 cup caster sugar
¼ cup rice flour	4 eggs, separated
large pinch of salt	sieved, warmed jam
¼ teaspoon baking powder	beaten egg, to finish
1½ cups raisins	ICING (OPTIONAL):
½ cup currants	1 cup sifted icing sugar
2 tablespoons chopped	vanilla essence
candied peel	hot water
250 g (8 oz) butter	

Grease and line a deep 20 cm (8 inch) round cake tin (page 263). Set the oven at moderate (180°C/350°F).

Set aside about one-quarter of the marzipan. Divide the rest in half; roll each piece out and cut to a round to fit the inside of the cake tin. Add the trimmings to the reserved marzipan.

Sift the flours, salt and baking powder together and mix in the fruits and peel.

Cream the butter with the lemon rind until soft and add the sugar gradually, beating until light and fluffy. Beat in the egg yolks.

Whip the egg whites until stiff, then fold the flour mixture and egg whites alternately into the butter mixture.

Put half the cake mixture into the prepared tin, level it out and cover with a circle of marzipan, then put in the rest of the cake mixture. Bake in the centre of the oven for 2 hours, then reduce the heat to slow (150°C/300°F); cover the tin with a double thickness of greased foil or greaseproof paper and cook for about 30 minutes more, or until a skewer inserted in the centre comes out clean. Allow the cake to cool a little in the tin, then turn out, slide it onto a baking sheet and cool completely.

When quite cold, brush the top of the cake with a little warmed jam and place the second circle of marzipan on top, pressing it down well. Roll the reserved marzipan into 11 balls and arrange round the edge, securing each with a dab of beaten egg. Brush the balls lightly with beaten egg and tie a band of greaseproof paper round the sides of the cake to hold them in position. Place the cake in a hot oven (200°C/400°F), or under the grill for a few minutes, to brown the tops of the balls. Remove and cool.

To ice: mix icing sugar with a few drops of vanilla and just enough hot water to give a smooth paste, and stir over simmering water until glossy. Pour the icing over the centre of the cake and decorate, if you wish, with Easter decorations such as chicks or tiny marzipan eggs, tinted with food colouring.
NOTE: Without the marzipan and special decorations, the mixture for Simnel Cake makes an excellent, well-flavoured fruit cake for any time of the year. The egg whites, stiffly beaten and added separately, give it a crusty outside. The top may be iced or decorated with almonds or walnuts, and ½ cup nuts may be added to the mixture. Like all rich fruit cakes, it improves in both flavour and texture with keeping, so long as it is stored in an airtight tin.

Basic Génoise

Génoise is a light butter sponge. It is ideal for cutting into fancy shapes because it is close-textured and cuts without crumbling. It can be used for Petits Fours, the pretty little mouthfuls served with coffee, or for making Lamingtons, one of the great traditions of Australian home cooking and so delectable that they're due for a revival.

Génoise may also be baked in a round tin, and filled and decorated to make an elegant afternoon tea or dessert cake.

1 cup flour	½ cup sugar
60 g (2 oz) butter, melted	¼ teaspoon vanilla essence
4 eggs	

Grease a shallow lamington tin, 28 × 18 cm (11 × 7 inches) and line the base. Set the oven to hot (200°C/400°F).

Sift the flour. Have the melted butter just warm, not hot. Place the eggs, sugar and vanilla in a bowl and set over a gentle heat (a saucepan in which a little water has been brought to the boil and which has been removed from the heat). Beat until the egg mixture is thick and pale, and leaves a ribbon visible on the surface for a few seconds when allowed to drop from the beater. Remove the bowl from the saucepan and continue beating for 3 minutes more.

Sift about two-thirds of the flour over the egg mixture and fold in lightly with a large metal spoon. Sift the remaining flour over, pour the butter on top and fold in very quickly and lightly, then pour into the prepared tin. Don't worry if you don't fold the butter and flour in completely, turning the mixture into the tin will combine it a little more and you can 'tickle' in any unmixed pockets with the edge of the spoon as you pour. The great thing is to handle a Génoise mixture as little as possible after adding the butter.

Bake in the centre of the oven for about 30 minutes, or until risen and golden, with a centre that is springy to the touch. Cool in the tin for 5 minutes before turning out.

Petits Fours

1 Basic Génoise	ICING:
APRICOT GLAZE:	double quantity Glacé Icing
1 cup sugar	(page 215)
½ cup water	
1 cup sieved apricot jam	

When the cake is cool, trim off the crusty edges and cut into little squares or rectangles, or stamp into fancy shapes with a small cutter.

Place the sugar and water in a small heavy saucepan and heat, stirring, until the sugar is dissolved. Stir in the jam and boil steadily without stirring until the glaze will coat a wooden spoon – this takes about 5 to 8 minutes. Brush each piece of cake, tops and sides, with the hot apricot glaze and place on a rack to set. The glaze holds down any loose crumbs which might spoil the surface.

Place the rack over a tray and pour the warm glacé icing, coloured and flavoured as desired, over each cake. The icing should be thin – add a little more boiling water if necessary, and keep the bowl over hot water while working. Any surplus icing that drips off may be warmed and used again.

Decorate with nuts, chocolate caraque or curls (page 215), stars or sprinkles, silver cachous or shapes cut from jelly beans, angelica or cherries.
NOTE: Any surplus glaze can be cooled and stored in a screw-top jar, and can be reheated when required.

Lamingtons, plain and filled with jam

Lamingtons

Make the Basic Génoise the day before required to make it easier to cut into neat squares. If you have frozen the cake, allow it to thaw for a full 24 hours before using for Lamingtons.

1 Basic Génoise	⅓ cup cocoa
desiccated coconut	½ cup boiling water
3 cups icing sugar	few drops of vanilla essence

Cut the cake into three strips lengthwise, then cut each strip into eight even pieces. Scatter a thick bed of coconut on a large sheet of paper.

Sift the icing sugar and cocoa into a bowl, add water and vanilla and stir over hot water until smooth and shiny. The icing should be thin – add a little more boiling water if necessary, and keep the bowl over hot water while working.

Spear each piece of cake on a fork and dip into the icing, hold a moment to allow it to set slightly, then roll in coconut, using the paper to help. Place on a wire rack to dry.

Variation

Jam Lamingtons Each piece of cake may be cut in half and sandwiched together with a little jam before dipping into icing and rolling in coconut. Be careful to use only a small amount of jam so that it does not run out while the cake is being coated.

Parkin

This is an old Yorkshire recipe. It is good buttered and eaten with cheese and improves if kept for a few days, well wrapped to keep it moist.

2 cups flour	1 cup brown sugar, firmly
¼ teaspoon salt	packed
2 teaspoons bicarbonate of	125 g (4 oz) butter
soda	⅓ cup golden syrup (see note)
1 teaspoon ground ginger	½ cup milk
1 cup medium oatmeal	¼ cup slivered almonds

Grease a small roasting tin, approximatley 25 × 23 × 5 cm (10 × 9 × 2 inches) and line with greaseproof paper. Set the oven at moderate (180°C/350°F).

Sift the flour with the salt, bicarbonate of soda and ginger and mix together with the oatmeal and sugar. Warm the butter and syrup together and add the milk. Stir into the dry ingredients. Turn the mixture into the prepared tin, level the top, and bake for 15 minutes; then pull forward and scatter the slivered almonds over the top. Return to the oven and bake for a further 35 minutes, or until a skewer inserted in the centre comes out clean.

Cool on a wire rack, wrap in foil, and keep for a few days before cutting. To serve, cut into squares and spread with butter. NOTE: To measure a sticky ingredient such as golden syrup, first rinse the measuring cup or spoon in hot water. The syrup will run off more cleanly. A spray with cooking spray also helps. Pour the syrup into the measure rather than dipping the measure in, to avoid getting extra syrup on the back.

Saffron Buns

Saffron and other spices have been prominent in the cooking of Cornwall for hundreds of years, since the days when Spanish and other traders brought exotic goods to that coast.

large pinch of saffron	20 g (¾ oz) fresh yeast
2½ cups hot milk	½ cup caster sugar
4 cups flour	¾ cup cream
pinch of salt	2 eggs, beaten
½ teaspoon cinnamon	¾ cup currants
125 g (4 oz) butter	beaten egg, to glaze

Stir the saffron into hot milk and leave to infuse for 30 minutes.

Sift the flour, salt and cinnamon together into a bowl and rub in the butter with the fingertips until resembling breadcrumbs.

Mix the yeast with about half the sugar and stir gently until liquid. Strain on the saffron-flavoured milk (which must be no hotter than lukewarm) and add the cream and the beaten eggs.

Make a well in the centre of the flour mixture, pour the yeast mixture into it, then add the currants and stir all together. Beat vigorously by hand, then cover and leave in the refrigerator overnight.

Next day, set the oven at moderately hot (190°C/375°F). Turn the dough out onto a floured board, knead and divide into 20 even-size pieces and shape these into buns. Place on a greased oven slide and leave to prove in a warm place for 15 minutes. Brush the tops with a little beaten egg, sprinkle with the remaining sugar and bake for 15 to 20 minutes.
NOTE: Compressed yeast is usually available at health food and cake shops. Active dried yeast, stocked by most supermarkets, may be substituted for the compressed variety but should be added by a different method. Stir 2 teaspoons active dried yeast into the warm, strained saffron-infused milk, leave about 10 minutes until frothy, then add half the sugar, the cream and beaten eggs. Pour the yeast mixture into the flour as directed and proceed with the recipe.

Guinness Cake

This is today's version of an old Irish recipe for Porter Cake (porter was a weak form of stout). Guinness gives an intriguing flavour and makes the cake moist and rich.

250 g (8 oz) butter	1 cup blanched almonds, chopped
4 cups flour	1 cup chopped mixed peel
3 cups brown sugar	
large pinch of mixed spice	4 eggs
1 cup raisins	1¼ cups warm Guinness
½ cup currants	1 teaspoon bicarbonate of soda
½ cup sultanas	
1 cup glacé cherries, halved	

Line a deep 23 cm (9 inch) round cake tin (page 263). Set the oven to very slow (120°C/250°F).

Rub the butter into the flour until resembling breadcrumbs. Add the sugar, spice, fruits, nuts and peel, and mix well. Beat the eggs with the Guinness and stir in the bicarbonate of soda. Mix this very well with the flour mixture and turn into the prepared tin. Lay a sheet of greaseproof paper over the top.

Bake in the centre of the oven for 3 to 3½ hours, or until a skewer inserted in the centre comes out clean. Remove the paper for the last 30 minutes. Cool on a wire rack and store in an airtight tin for a week before cutting. Guinness cake may be iced or decorated with almonds and used as a Christmas cake.

Christmas Cake

Make the cake 3 or 4 weeks ahead so that it can mature, but do not ice more than a week ahead. Decorate with almonds or with snowy icing.

375 g (12 oz) raisins, chopped	1 tablespoon golden syrup
250 g (8 oz) sultanas	2 tablespoons marmalade
125 g (4 oz) currants	5 eggs
125 g (4 oz) glacé cherries, halved	2½ cups flour
	1 teaspoon mixed spice
3 tablespoons brandy	1 teaspoon cinnamon
3 tablespoons sherry	¼ teaspoon salt
125 g (4 oz) dried apricots, chopped	125 g (4 oz) blanched almonds, chopped
2 tablespoons hot water	extra almonds, to decorate (optional)
250 g (8 oz) butter	1 tablespoon brandy
1¼ cups brown sugar	
grated rind of 1 lemon	

The day before baking, mix the raisins, sultanas, currants, cherries, brandy and sherry in a bowl. Soak the apricots separately for 1 hour with the hot water, then add to the other fruit. The next day, line a deep 23 cm (9 inch) round or 20 cm (8 inch) square cake tin with 2 layers each of brown and greased greaseproof paper (page 263). Set the oven to slow (150°C/300°F).

Beat the butter and sugar with the lemon rind until fluffy. Beat in the golden syrup and marmalade. Then add the eggs, one at a time, beating well after each; if there are signs of curdling, stir in a spoonful of flour with each additional egg. Sift the flour, spices and salt and fold into the butter mixture alternately with the fruit and almonds. Turn into the prepared tin and decorate with almonds if you wish.

Bake in the centre of the oven for about 4 hours, or until a skewer inserted in the centre comes out clean. Remove from the oven and sprinkle with brandy. Remove from the tin, leaving the paper on, wrap in a tea-towel and cool. Store in an airtight container.

To Ice the Cake
Allow 3 days to cover the cake with almond paste and complete the icing.

GLAZE:	90 g (3 oz) icing sugar
2 tablespoons sieved apricot jam	1 teaspoon lemon juice
	1 egg yolk
1½ tablespoons water	few drops of almond essence
¼ teaspoon lemon juice	ROYAL ICING:
ALMOND PASTE:	2 egg whites
185 g (6 oz) ground almonds	500 g (1 lb) pure icing sugar
90 g (3 oz) caster sugar	1 teaspoon lemon juice

To make the glaze: Boil the jam and water together for 4 minutes, add the lemon juice and continue boiling until the glaze coats a wooden spoon. Brush hot glaze evenly over the top of the cake.

To make the almond paste: Sift the ground almonds and sugars together. Add the remaining ingredients, mix well and knead lightly on a board. Roll out to fit the top of the cake, place on and press gently with a rolling pin. Leave for at least 48 hours.

To make the royal icing: Whisk the egg whites to a light froth and beat in the sifted icing sugar, 1 tablespoon at a time. Add the lemon juice and beat until soft peaks form. Spread all over the cake, roughening the surface to look like snow. Add decorations and leave for at least one day to set.

Simnel Cake (page 206); Dundee Cake (page 205)

A Cheer for Chocolate

Ask anyone to name their favourite cake and 'chocolate cake' will be the popular answer. Whether you use cocoa or chocolate you get that rich, dark, irresistible flavour. As well as cakes, here are other kinds of chocolate delights for you to try.

Honey-Rum Chocolate Cake

Honey, rum and sherry are added to cocoa to give this light-textured cake a luscious blend of flavours. It's a good family cake.

185 g (6 oz) butter	2 tablespoons cocoa
1 cup brown sugar, lightly packed	1¾ cups self-raising flour
⅓ cup honey	pinch of salt
2 eggs	½ cup sweet sherry
1 tablespoon rum	TO FINISH:
½ teaspoon vanilla essence	1 cup cream, whipped
	icing sugar

Grease a 23 cm (9 inch) round cake tin and line it with greased greaseproof paper. Set the oven temperature at moderate (180°C/350°F).

Have the butter at room temperature, and cream well with brown sugar. Add the honey, and continue beating until the mixture is light and fluffy. Beat in the eggs one at a time, then stir in the rum and vanilla. Sift the cocoa, flour and salt together three times (this helps to give a light texture to the finished cake).

Chocolate Pots de Crème

Fold into the creamed mixture alternately with the sherry, beginning and ending with flour. Turn into the prepared tin and bake in a moderate oven for 45 minutes, or until cooked when tested with a fine skewer. Allow to cool in the tin for a few minutes, then turn out onto a wire rack to finish cooling. Split the cake in two, fill with whipped cream and dust the top with icing sugar.
NOTE: If desired, the top may be iced. See page 215 for Chocolate Butter Icing.

Chocolate Pots de Crème

Use the prettiest individual moulds you can find for this smooth-as-silk, French chocolate custard.

1 cup milk	1 tablespoon finely grated orange rind
1 cup cream	
250 g (8 oz) dark chocolate, grated	Sugared Violets, to decorate (see below – optional)
6 egg yolks, lightly beaten	

Heat the milk, cream and chocolate in a bowl set over a pan of simmering water. Stir until the chocolate is melted but do not allow to boil. Cool, and combine with the beaten egg yolks and orange rind. Pour into 6 individual pots or moulds, and arrange them in a baking dish. Pour enough hot water into the dish to come halfway up the sides of the custards, and bake in a preheated moderately slow oven (160°C/325°F) for 25 minutes, or until set. (Test with a sharp knife – it should come out clean, with no custard clinging to it.) Remove moulds from the water, cool, then chill before serving. If you like, decorate with sugared violets. *Serves 6*
Sugared Violets Choose fresh, perfect violets and cut the stems very short. Froth a little egg white with a fork, brush gently onto violets with a soft brush and sprinkle with caster sugar. Dry on a wire rack.

Chocolate-Rum Dessert Cake

This superb cake contains no flour, and has a texture as meltingly rich as chocolate mousse.

185 g (6 oz) dark cooking chocolate	185 g (6 oz) ground almonds
185 g (6 oz) unsalted butter	pinch of salt
¾ cup sugar	TO DECORATE:
6 eggs, separated	whipped cream
2 tablespoons dark rum	chocolate caraque (page 215)

Grease a 23 cm (9 inch) springform pan and line the bottom with greased greaseproof paper. Set the oven at moderately hot (190°C/375°F).

Chop the chocolate and melt in a basin set over simmering water. Allow to cool a little. Cream the butter and sugar until light and fluffy, then add the egg yolks one at a time, beating after each addition. Fold in the chocolate, rum and almonds. Whisk the egg whites with salt until they form stiff peaks. Fold a large spoonful of the egg whites into the chocolate mixture, then fold in the remaining whites in two or three batches. Be gentle – you don't want to beat the air out of the mixture.

Pour into the prepared tin and level the top. Place on a rack set about one-third of the way up from the bottom of the oven, and bake at moderately hot for 20 minutes. Reduce the temperature to moderate (180°C/350°F) and bake for a further 45 minutes. The cake will still be soft and moist in the centre.

Allow the cake to stand in the tin until cold. Carefully remove the sides of the springform pan and peel away the paper. Pile whipped cream in the centre (which may have fallen a little). Decorate with chocolate caraque. *Serves 8 to 10*

Sour Cream Chocolate Cake

This is a truly superb cake, which I like to serve as a dessert with whipped cream, or in thin slices with afternoon coffee. It has a deep chocolate flavour, melting texture, and a cooked-on coating of buttery almonds.

TO COAT TIN:	250 g (8 oz) butter
15 g (½ oz) butter	1½ cups caster sugar
4 tablespoons flaked almonds	3 eggs, separated
CAKE:	1 teaspoon vanilla essence
1 cup boiling water	2½ cups flour
125 g (4 oz) dark chocolate, chopped	pinch of salt
	1 teaspoon baking powder
1 teaspoon bicarbonate of soda	⅔ cup light sour cream

Generously butter a 12-cup bundt tin or two 20 cm (8 inch) fluted ring tins. Sprinkle with flaked almonds, pressing them well into the butter to coat the bottom and sides of the tin.

Put the boiling water, chocolate and bicarbonate of soda in a bowl and stir until smooth. Cream the butter and sugar until light, and add the egg yolks one at a time, beating after each addition. Stir in the vanilla, then add the chocolate mixture a little at a time. Sift the flour, salt and baking powder and fold in alternately with the sour cream, mixing lightly until just combined. Beat the egg whites until stiff and fold into the creamed mixture with a large metal spoon.

Turn gently into the prepared tin and bake in a preheated moderate oven (180°C/350°F) for 1 to 1¼ hours for the large cake or 45 minutes for the small cakes, or until cooked when tested with a skewer. Leave in the tin for a minute, then turn out and cool on a wire rack.

Chocolate Chiffon Pie

This pretty party dessert can be made well beforehand ready for its last-minute decoration of bananas and cream.

1 × 23 cm (9 inch) baked pie shell (page 224)	4 eggs, separated
	1 cup sugar
FILLING:	1 teaspoon vanilla essence
1 tablespoon gelatine	TO DECORATE:
¼ cup cold strong coffee	2 ripe bananas
6 tablespoons cocoa	1½ cups cream, whipped
½ cup boiling water	

Soak the gelatine in cold coffee until it expands and softens (this is called 'sponging'). Mix the cocoa to a paste with the boiling water, then stir in the gelatine and blend well. Lightly beat the egg yolks, stir in half the sugar, and combine with the gelatine mixture. Chill until almost set, then add the vanilla and beat well with a whisk until light and fluffy. In another bowl, beat the egg whites until they stand in soft peaks, and fold them into the chocolate mixture with the remaining sugar. Spoon into the pie shell and chill until serving time. Just before serving, slice the bananas thinly and arrange over the top of the pie, then spread with whipped cream. *Serves 6 to 8*

Variation

If you wish, the filling can be poured into a chocolate crumb crust instead of a pastry crust. To make it, mix together 1½ cups finely crushed chocolate wafer biscuits (about 36 wafers) and 90 g (3 oz) melted butter. Press firmly into a 23 cm (9 inch) pie plate and chill before adding the filling.

Double Chocolate Cake

The method of making this cake is intriguing. The luscious chocolate frosting is mixed first, and goes into the cake batter as well as on the finished cake.

FROSTING:	CAKE:
185 g (6 oz) Philadelphia cream cheese	60 g (2 oz) butter
	2 cups chocolate frosting
125 g (4 oz) butter	3 eggs
1 teaspoon vanilla essence	2¼ cups flour
6 cups icing sugar, sifted	1½ teaspoons bicarbonate of soda
½ cup hot water	
125 g (4 oz) dark chocolate, melted	1 teaspoon salt
	¾ cup milk
	2 tablespoons raspberry jam

First make the frosting. Allow the cream cheese and butter to soften at room temperature, add the vanilla and beat well. Add half the icing sugar and blend in, then add the rest of the icing sugar alternately with hot water. Stir in the melted chocolate, and mix until smooth.

Grease and lightly flour two 23 cm (9 inch) round sandwich cake tins, and set the oven at moderate (180°C/350°F).

For the cake: Cream the butter with 2 cups of frosting. Mix in the eggs one at a time, beating well after each addition. Sift together the flour, bicarbonate of soda and salt, and stir into the creamed mixture alternately with milk (beginning and ending with flour). Turn the mixture into the prepared tins and bake in a moderate oven for 30 to 40 minutes, or until cooked when tested with a fine skewer. Cool in the tins for a few minutes, then turn the cakes out onto a wire rack to cool completely. Join together with raspberry jam and top with the remaining frosting, spreading it over the top and sides of the cake.

Perfect Sponges

A sponge cake is one of the lightest and most delicate cakes of all. It is the amount of air beaten into the eggs and sugar and held in the mixture that makes the cake rise and, fortunately for those who enjoy it, a sponge cake is relatively quick and easy to make.

There are two ways of making a sponge cake and many different ways of presenting it. A whisked sponge is made by beating the whole eggs and sugar together until the mixture is thick and light, and then folding in the flour. For a sponge sandwich, the eggs are separated and the whites beaten until thick, with the sugar added gradually; then the yolks are added and the flour folded in. Included in the next few pages are recipes using both methods.

Generally speaking, the Australian sponge has a raising agent (self-raising flour or plain flour and baking powder) which helps make the sponge rise spectacularly. This type of sponge tends to become dry very quickly and is best eaten soon after it is made. However, this high and fluffy sponge sandwich is superlative when topped and filled with tart-sweet passionfruit or strawberries and lashings of whipped cream. The English sponge, or whisked sponge, does not rise as high as its Australian counterpart, but what it lacks in height it makes up for in flavour and keeping ability. It is served split in half and filled with jam.

The French have the Génoise (see page 206), to which a little melted butter is added, and Italy has the Pan di Spagna flavoured with lemon rind.

Swiss rolls belong to the sponge family; they are baked in a shallow pan, spread with jam and rolled while warm.

Once you master the few basic rules, you will be able to whip up a tender sponge roll for afternoon tea or dessert without a moment's thought. Remember:
● Eggs for a sponge should be at least three days old and should be at room temperature to give the greatest volume.
● Have the oven ready, tins prepared and all ingredients assembled and measured before you begin to mix. Once you begin, don't leave the mixture standing or the air that you have beaten in will begin to escape. Your sponge won't rise to its expected heights!
● Close the oven door gently when you put the cake in, and don't open it until two-thirds of the way through the cooking time.

Whisked Sponge

This basic sponge is quick to make, especially with an electric beater. Fill with a butter icing or jam and a little whipped cream.

Use a large metal spoon for folding. Cut down and through the batter, lifting some of the mixture from the bottom up and over the top each time.

3 eggs	FILLING AND TOPPING:
$\frac{1}{4}$ teaspoon vanilla essence	1 quantity Chocolate Butter
$\frac{3}{4}$ cup caster sugar	Icing (page 215)
1 cup self-raising flour	2 tablespoons finely chopped
1 teaspoon butter, melted	walnuts
2 tablespoons hot water	9 walnut halves
	angelica leaves, to decorate

Grease two 18 cm (7 inch) sandwich tins and dust with a mixture of 1 teaspoon each of sugar and flour. Set the shelf just above the centre of the oven. Preheat the oven to moderately hot (190°C/375°F).

Whisk the eggs, vanilla and sugar together until thick and pale; the mixture should fall off the whisk in ribbons which hold their shape on top of the mixture in the bowl for several seconds before sinking.

Sift half the flour and fold it into the egg mixture quickly and lightly. Sift and fold in the remaining flour. Fold in the melted butter and hot water quickly and lightly. Pour the mixture into the sandwich tins and tilt them to spread it out evenly. Bake the cakes on the same oven shelf for 20 minutes until they are well risen and golden, and the tops are springy to the touch. Remove the cakes from the oven and allow to shrink slightly before turning out onto a wire tray to cool, tops up.

Take one-third of the chocolate butter icing and mix in the chopped nuts. Sandwich the two sponges together with this filling. Spread the rest of the butter icing neatly over the top of the cake. Make a swirling pattern with a knife, or mark it into squares with the tines of a fork. Arrange the walnut halves on top and finish with small angelica leaves.

Swiss Roll; Whisked Sponge

Swiss Roll

This impressive cake is cooked at a higher temperature than an ordinary sponge cake. Be sure to have the jam warming and the tea-towel and greaseproof paper at the ready (see Step 2) before the cake comes out of the oven.

¾ cup self-raising flour	1 teaspoon butter
pinch of salt	1 tablespoon hot water
3 eggs	caster sugar for dredging
¾ cup caster sugar	3–4 tablespoons warm jam

Prepare a 23 × 30 cm (9 × 12 inch) Swiss roll tin (see Step 1). Preheat the oven to hot (220°C/425°F).

Sift the flour with the salt three times. Beat the eggs and sugar until very thick and lemon coloured; an electric beater makes easy work of this. Fold in the flour as lightly as possible using a metal spoon. Add the butter to the hot water and fold in quickly and lightly.

Follow Steps 2, 3 and 4 at right, to bake and roll the sponge.

Lemon Curd

A refreshing tangy filling for sponge cakes and rolls.

3 medium lemons	60 g (2 oz) butter
2 eggs	2 teaspoons cornflour
¾ cup sugar	

Grate the rind from the lemons, then squeeze out the juice. Beat the eggs with the sugar until light and creamy, then add the lemon rind and strained juice and butter. Place in the top of a double boiler. Blend the cornflour with a little water and add to the mixture. Place over simmering water and stir until thick enough to coat a spoon. This takes about 15 minutes. Cool. NOTE: This also makes a delicious spread for your breakfast toast or muffins, and keeps well in a covered jar in the refrigerator.

Swiss Roll

1 First line a 23 × 30 cm (9 × 12 inch) Swiss roll tin with greaseproof paper, cut to a rectangle 5 cm (2 inches) larger on all sides than the tin. Grease the bottom of the tin to prevent the paper slipping about. Lay the paper in the tin and, using the handle of a metal spoon, press the paper into the angle all round the base of the tin, making a firm crease. Using scissors, snip the paper from each corner down to the corner of the tin. Brush with oil. (This is not necessary with non-stick parchment.)

2 Preheat the oven to hot (220°C/425°F). Make up the sponge mixture (recipe at left). Pour into the tin and spread it evenly into the corners with a spatula. Bake near the top of the oven for 8 to 10 minutes, until golden and springy to the touch. Meanwhile, wring out a clean tea-towel in hot water. Spread it on the table, place a sheet of greaseproof paper on top and dredge lightly with sugar. This will make it easier to roll the sponge.

3 When the sponge is ready (do not overcook it or it will be brittle to roll up), turn upside down on the sugared paper. Carefully ease up the edges of the lining paper and peel it off. With a long knife, trim off the crisp side edges of the sponge. Cut a shallow slit, parallel with the bottom edge and 1 cm (½ inch) above it.

4 Spread the warmed jam over the sponge. Turn the bottom edge up and tuck it in so the first roll is fairly tight. Then, using the paper, continue rolling more lightly and evenly into a neat roll with the join underneath. Place the Swiss roll on a serving plate and dredge with a little more caster sugar. NOTE: You could also roll the sponge with lemon curd (this page) or whipped cream.

Sponge Sandwich

This high tender sponge cake is the one that takes pride of place at many afternoon teas and country shows. It is at its best when freshly baked and takes well to a simple jam filling or luscious cream with passionfruit or strawberries (see below).

3 eggs, separated	1 teaspoon butter
pinch of salt	TO FINISH:
¾ cup caster sugar	3 tablespoons raspberry jam
1 cup self-raising flour	icing sugar
3 tablespoons warm milk	

Grease two 18 cm (7 inch) sandwich tins and dredge lightly with a little flour. Set the oven at moderate (180°C/350°F). Set the shelf just above the centre of the oven.

Place the egg whites in a clean, dry bowl with a pinch of salt. Beat the whites until stiff peaks form. Add the sugar gradually, beating until thick and glossy. Add the egg yolks all at once and beat lightly until combined. Sift the flour into the egg mixture and with a large metal spoon fold in lightly and evenly. Combine the warm milk and butter, and fold in quickly.

Pour the mixture into prepared sandwich tins and tilt them to spread it out evenly. Place on the same oven shelf to ensure that the cakes will have constant heat and bake evenly. Make sure that the tins do not touch each other; it may be necessary to place one towards the back and one towards the front if the oven is a small one. Bake for 20 minutes. Turn out and cool on a wire rack, top side up (page 263). When cold, fill with raspberry jam and top with a dusting of icing sugar.

Variation

For a 20 cm (8 inch) sponge sandwich, follow the method for the basic sponge described above, with the following quantity adjustments:

4 eggs, separated	1½ cups self-raising flour
pinch of salt	4 tablespoons warm milk
1 cup caster sugar	1 teaspoon butter

Strawberry Cream Sponge

3 tablespoons strawberry jam	1 tablespoon caster sugar
1 Sponge Sandwich	1 punnet strawberries
1 × 300 ml carton cream	
(1¼ cups)	

Spread the strawberry jam on one sponge cake. Whip the cream with the sugar until it holds its shape, and use some to sandwich the cakes together. Decorate the top with rosettes of the remaining whipped cream or simply spread cream on top and decorate with whole strawberries.

Passionfruit Cream Sponge

1 × 300 ml carton cream	⅓ cup passionfruit pulp
(1¼ cups)	1 Sponge Sandwich
1 tablespoon caster sugar	

Whip the cream with the sugar until it holds its shape. Fold half the passionfruit pulp through the whipped cream and use to fill and top the sponge sandwich. Cover the top with the remaining passionfruit.

Ginger Sponge Sandwich

4 eggs, separated	FILLING AND TOPPING:
1 cup caster sugar	6 tablespoons sugar
1¼ cups self-raising flour	6 tablespoons water
1 tablespoon cornflour	185 g (6 oz) butter
2 teaspoons ground ginger	½ teaspoon vanilla essence
1 tablespoon butter	2 tablespoons sliced glacé or
4 tablespoons water	preserved ginger

Grease two 20 cm (8 inch) sandwich tins. Set the oven temperature at moderate (180°C/350°F).

Beat the egg whites until stiff and gradually beat in the sugar, keeping the mixture stiff. Beat well, then add the egg yolks and beat again. Add the flour, cornflour and ginger to the mixture. Heat the butter and water together and fold in gently. Pour into the prepared tins and bake for 20 minutes.

Filling: Heat sugar and water together until sugar dissolves. Allow the syrup to cool. Cream the butter until light, then gradually add the cooled syrup and continue to beat until the mixture is light and fluffy. Divide the cream in half, then flavour one half with the vanilla and use as a filling. Add half the ginger to the remaining cream and use to top the sponge. Decorate the top with the remaining sliced ginger.

Walnut Roll

Ground walnuts add interesting texture to a roll filled with coffee-flavoured butter cream. It freezes well, so you can make it in advance for a party.

about 3 tablespoons fine cake	¼ cup self-raising flour
or breadcrumbs	whipped cream or Coffee
3 large eggs, separated	Butter Cream (see below)
½ cup caster sugar	for filling
½ cup ground walnuts	

Prepare a Swiss roll tin as described in Step 1, page 213. Sprinkle with the crumbs, coating the surface evenly, then tip out any excess crumbs. Set the oven temperature at moderate (180°C/350°F).

Beat the egg whites until stiff. Beat the yolks with the caster sugar until the mixture is light and creamy. Gently fold in the walnuts and sifted flour alternately with the stiffly beaten egg whites. Spread in the prepared tin and bake for about 15 minutes, or until the cake springs back when the centre is lightly touched.

Turn out on a tea-towel sprinkled with caster sugar. Peel off the paper and roll up the cake. Allow to cool. Unroll the cake, spread with whipped cream or coffee butter cream and re-roll, using the tea-towel as an aid.

Coffee Butter Cream

1 egg yolk	125 g (4 oz) unsalted butter
2–3 tablespoons caster sugar	2 teaspoons coffee essence or
¼ cup milk	dissolved instant coffee

Cream the egg yolk with half the sugar. Dissolve the remaining sugar in the milk, bring slowly to the boil and pour onto the yolk mixture. Return to the pan and stir over a gentle heat until it coats the back of the spoon. Do not allow to boil. Strain and cool.

Cream the butter and, when soft, add the custard mixture by degrees. Flavour with the coffee essence, beating well.

Sponge Sandwich

Butter Icing

90 g (3 oz) butter   1–2 *teaspoons warm water*
1 *cup icing sugar*
¼ *teaspoon vanilla essence or*
   other flavouring

Cream the butter until soft and gradually beat in the icing sugar. Add the flavouring essence and a little warm water, if necessary, to give a smooth pliable texture. *Sufficient to cover the top and sides of an 18 cm (7 inch) sponge sandwich or for a filling and topping.*

Variations

Chocolate Butter Icing Replace 2 tablespoons icing sugar with 2 tablespoons cocoa or chocolate powder. Flavour to taste with vanilla.
Orange and Lemon Butter Icing Cream the butter and sugar with the finely grated rind of 1 lemon or 1 small orange. Add the strained juice a little at a time or the butter cream will curdle.
Coffee Butter Icing Add 2 teaspoons instant coffee powder to the icing sugar. Cream with the butter, adding a little water if necessary.
Mocha Butter Icing Add 1 teaspoon instant coffee powder and 1 tablespoon cocoa or chocolate powder to the icing sugar. Cream with the butter, adding a little water if necessary.
Walnut Butter Icing Add 2 tablespoons finely chopped walnuts to the finished vanilla, chocolate, coffee or mocha butter icing.
Peanut Butter Icing Cream 60 g (2 oz) of butter and 1 tablespoon smooth peanut butter with the icing sugar. Add water only if needed to give a spreading consistency. Sprinkle chopped peanuts on the iced cake if you wish.
Passionfruit Butter Icing Omit the water and stir the pulp of 1 passionfruit into the creamed butter and icing sugar.

Glacé Icing

¾ *cup icing sugar, sifted*   ½ *teaspoon vanilla essence*
1 *tablespoon boiling water*

Mix the icing sugar, water and vanilla in a bowl. Stir over boiling water until smooth, then quickly pour over the top of the sponge and smooth with a knife dipped in hot water. *Sufficient to coat the top of an 18 cm (7 inch) cake.*

Variations

Lemon or Orange Glacé Icing Use strained lemon or orange juice instead of water to mix, and add a few drops of yellow or orange colouring if desired.
Coffee Glacé Icing Sift 1½ teaspoons instant coffee powder with the icing sugar.
Passionfruit Glacé Icing Use 1 tablespoon of passionfruit pulp instead of water.

Chocolate Caraque

This is the classic finish for many desserts and cakes.
   Grate about 90 g (3 oz) plain dark chocolate and melt on a plate over a pan of hot water, working with a palette knife until smooth. Spread this thinly on a marble slab or laminated surface and leave until nearly set. Then, using a long sharp knife, shave it off the slab slantwise, using a slight sawing movement and holding the knife upright. The chocolate will form long scrolls and flakes. Store in an airtight tin.

Chocolate Curls

An easy but pretty chocolate decoration.
   Have a thick block of milk chocolate at room temperature. Then, using a swivel-bladed vegetable peeler, shave thin curls of chocolate from the side of the block.

Little Cakes are Charming

There is all the charm of childhood in little cakes – memories of birthday parties and licking the icing bowl! On the practical side, small plain cakes and ones with simple icing are very convenient to wrap and freeze, ready to go into lunch boxes. At home, they thaw out to their original freshness almost as quickly as it takes to boil the kettle for tea.

Honey Buns

125 g (4 oz) butter, softened	2 tablespoons honey
½ cup brown sugar, firmly packed	1¾ cups self-raising flour
	pinch of salt
1 egg, beaten	creamed honey for spreading

Grease two scone trays and set the oven at moderate (180°C/350°F). Cream the butter with the brown sugar, then beat in the egg and honey. Sift the flour with the salt and work into the mixture until it forms a soft dough. Chill until firm.

Shape the dough into small balls the size of a walnut and place well apart on scone trays. Bake for 12 minutes, or until risen and golden. Cool, then sandwich together in pairs with honey.
Makes 10 to 12

Almond Cream Fancies

A light slab cake is cut into fancy shapes, then decorated with butter icing. The look of a French pâtisserie for a fraction of the price – and fun to do as well.

185 g (6 oz) butter	Butter Icing (page 215)
¾ cup caster sugar	green food colouring
2 eggs	2 teaspoons cocoa
1½ cups self-raising flour	½ teaspoon instant coffee
½ teaspoon almond essence	dissolved in 2 teaspoons
GLAZE:	water
⅔ cup apricot jam	blanched almonds
about 1 tablespoon water	glacé cherries, angelica, silver
TO DECORATE:	cachous, etc.
1½ cups crushed toasted almonds (or use plain crushed nuts)	

Grease a deep, oblong tin about 33 × 23 cm (13 × 9 inches) and line the bottom with greased greaseproof paper. Set the oven at moderate (180°C/350°F).

Cream the butter and sugar together until light and fluffy, then beat in one egg. Fold in a tablespoon of flour, then beat in the remaining egg and add another tablespoon of flour (this stops the mixture from curdling). Sift the remaining flour over the top, and fold in lightly with the almond essence. Turn into the prepared tin and bake for 30 minutes, or until well risen,

Almond Cream Fancies; Honey Buns

golden brown and firm to the touch. Cool in the tin for a minute, then turn out onto a cake rack to finish cooling.

Cut the cake into different shapes as illustrated, using a 5 cm (2 inch) round scone cutter, and making some into squares and triangles.

Heat the jam with the water and push through a sieve. Brush the sides of the shapes with jam, then roll in crushed nuts.

Divide the butter icing among three small bowls. Tint the first a pale green with food colouring, add the cocoa to the second and the coffee to the third. Spread or pipe the butter icing over the tops of the cakes and decorate with rosettes of contrasting cream. Add blanched almonds, a cherry, or other decorations to your own design. *Makes about 20*
NOTE: If desired, the green icing may be flavoured with a drop or two of peppermint essence, but use a light touch – peppermint can easily become overpowering.

Peanut Butter Cupcakes

90 g (3 oz) butter	*1 teaspoon vanilla essence*
½ cup crunchy peanut butter	*2 eggs*
1½ cups brown sugar, lightly packed	*2 cups self-raising flour*
	½ teaspoon salt
	1 cup milk

Grease muffin tins and set the oven at moderately hot (190°C/375°F). Beat the butter and peanut butter together, then gradually add the sugar and beat until light. Stir in the vanilla, then the eggs one at a time. Sift the flour with the salt and add alternately with the milk. Spoon into the tins, filling half full, and bake for 20 minutes, or until cooked when tested with a skewer. Cool in the tins for a minute, then turn out onto a rack. *Makes about 24*

Butterfly Cakes

125 g (4 oz) butter	*⅔ cup milk*
¾ cup sugar	FILLING:
1 teaspoon vanilla essence	*strawberry jam*
2 eggs, beaten	*1 cup cream, whipped*
2 cups self-raising flour	*icing sugar for dusting*
pinch of salt	

Place paper cases in 24 patty tins, and set the oven temperature at hot (200°C/400°F).

Have the butter at room temperature and cream well, then gradually beat in the sugar until the sugar is dissolved. Stir in the vanilla and add the eggs, a little at a time, beating well after each addition. Sift the flour and salt together three times and add to the mixture alternately with milk, beginning and ending with flour. (You should add about half a cup of flour at a time, folding into the butter and egg mixture lightly with a metal spoon. Be careful not to over mix.) Fill each patty case half full with the mixture and bake on the centre shelf for 15 minutes, or until well risen in the middle and cooked when tested with a skewer. Allow to cool for a minute in the tins, then turn the cakes onto a wire rack.

To make 'butterflies', cut a circle from the top of each cake and cut the circles in half. Put a small dab of strawberry jam on each cake, then a generous spoonful of whipped cream and top with two half-circles of cake to form 'wings'. Dust with icing sugar. Serve freshly made. *Makes 24*

Variations

Plain Cupcakes Bake in a moderate oven (180°C/350°F) instead of a hot oven. Dust with icing sugar when cool, or ice if desired. (See icings, page 215.)
Sultana Cupcakes   Add ½ cup sultanas to the creamed mixture before folding in the flour and milk. Bake in a moderate oven.

Speedy One-Bowl Cakes

For most traditional cakes, the butter and sugar are creamed together first, then the eggs are beaten in and the flour and liquid added last.

However, with the pace of life today, a delicious cake is often wanted in a hurry – and new methods have been developed to hasten the mixing process. Now we have 'one-bowl cakes', where the ingredients all go in together and are blended in one easy operation.

It's as convenient and quick as opening a packet of cake mix, but of course you have the advantage of using your own fresh ingredients and adding your favourite flavourings.

The evergreen favourite, boiled fruit cake, was the forerunner of this new style of cake. Here, the butter is heated with the sugar, fruit and liquid to make blending easy. Another shortcut is to use oil instead of butter or margarine, so mixing is super-quick.

If you have to cook, but time is of the essence, you will appreciate these recipes for speedy, one-bowl cakes.

Carrot-Pineapple Health Cake

This is a moist cake made with oil, wholemeal flour, a fruit and a vegetable. If you add the Cream Cheese Frosting, it makes it even more nourishing and an excellent choice for children's school lunches and afternoon snacks.

1½ cups wholemeal self-raising flour
1 cup brown sugar, loosely packed
1 teaspoon bicarbonate of soda
1 teaspoon cinnamon
½ teaspoon salt
⅔ cup polyunsaturated oil
2 eggs
1 cup finely grated carrot
½ cup crushed pineapple (with syrup)
1 teaspoon vanilla essence
Cream Cheese Frosting (see below – optional)

Grease a 23 cm (9 inch) square cake tin and line the base with greased greaseproof paper. Set the oven temperature at moderate (180°C/350°F).

Place the flour, sugar, bicarbonate of soda, cinnamon and salt in a large bowl and stir well to mix. Add the remaining ingredients and blend well together with a wooden spoon. Pour into the prepared tin and bake until a skewer inserted in the centre comes out clean, about 35 to 40 minutes. Cool for 10 minutes in the tin, then turn out and finish cooling on a cake rack. Ice with Cream Cheese Frosting if desired.

Cream Cheese Frosting

60 g (2 oz) Philadelphia cream cheese, about ½ small packet
30 g (1 oz) butter, softened
1 teaspoon vanilla essence
1½ cups sifted icing sugar
a little milk (optional)

Combine the cheese, butter and vanilla in a small bowl and beat with an electric mixer, or by hand, until light and creamy. Beat in the sugar, little by little, until the frosting is fluffy. If necessary, beat in a little milk to give a good spreading consistency.

Boiled Whisky Fruit Cake

750 g (1½ lb) mixed dried fruit
185 g (6 oz) butter
¾ cup water
1¼ cups brown sugar, firmly packed
¼ cup whisky
3 large eggs
1 cup plain flour
1½ cups self-raising flour
1½ teaspoons mixed spice
¼ teaspoon salt
½ teaspoon bicarbonate of soda

Grease a deep 20 cm (8 inch) cake tin and line with greased brown paper or two layers of greased greaseproof paper. Set the oven at moderate (180°C/350°F).

Place the dried fruit in a large saucepan with the butter, water and brown sugar. Bring slowly to the boil, then simmer for 5 minutes. Remove from the heat and cool until lukewarm. Stir in the whisky and add the eggs to the mixture one at a time, beating well each time with a wooden spoon. Sift the flours with the spice, salt and bicarbonate and stir into the mixture, combining thoroughly.

Spoon into the prepared tin and bake for 45 minutes. Reduce the heat to moderately slow (160°C/325°F) and cook for a further 45 minutes, or until a skewer inserted in the centre of the cake comes out clean. Leave the cake for a minute or two in the tin, then turn out onto a wire cake rack and allow to cool before removing the paper.

Lunch Box Vanilla Cake

This cake keeps well and cuts well. Enjoy it plain or lightly buttered, or serve with Marshmallow Topping as a dessert.

90 g (3 oz) butter, softened
1¾ cups self-raising flour, sifted
¾ cup sugar
½ teaspoon salt
1 egg
¾ cup milk
2 teaspoons grated lemon rind
1½ teaspoons vanilla essence

Grease a loaf tin about 23 × 10 cm (9 × 4 inches) and line base with greased greaseproof paper. Set the oven at moderately hot (190°C/375°F).

Place the butter, flour, sugar, salt, egg and half the milk in a large mixing bowl. Beat for 2 minutes at medium speed on an electric mixer, or blend well by hand with a wooden spoon. Add the remaining milk, lemon rind and vanilla and beat for 2 minutes longer. Turn into the prepared loaf tin and bake for 30 minutes, or until cooked when tested with a skewer. Leave in the tin for 2 minutes, then turn out onto a wire cake rack to cool.

Marshmallow Topping

A lovely pineapple-flavoured topping to dress up any kind of plain cake, or to spoon over ice-cream or sliced bananas.

2 egg yolks
3 tablespoons sugar
½ cup pineapple juice
1 cup marshmallows, snipped into small dice (measure after snipping)
½ cup cream, whipped
½ teaspoon vanilla essence

Beat the egg yolks and sugar until thick and lemon coloured. Beat in the pineapple juice, then place in a saucepan and cook, stirring, over a gentle heat until very thick, about 5 minutes. Remove from the heat and stir in the marshmallows. Chill, and fold in the cream and vanilla. *Makes 1⅔ cups*

Banana Cake

Date and Nut Cake

1 cup boiling water	*1½ cups self-raising flour*
250 g (8 oz) pitted dates,	*1 teaspoon bicarbonate of*
coarsely chopped	*soda*
90 g (3 oz) butter, softened	*¼ teaspoon salt*
1 cup sugar	*1 teaspoon cinnamon*
1 teaspoon vanilla essence	*½ cup chopped walnuts*
1 egg	

Grease a 33 × 23 cm (13 × 9 inch) cake tin and line with greased greaseproof paper. Set the oven at moderate (180°C/350°F).

Pour the water over the dates in a large bowl and leave for 2 to 3 minutes until they soften. Add the butter and sugar and beat with a wooden spoon until combined with the dates, then add the vanilla and egg and blend in. Fold in the flour sifted with bicarbonate, salt and cinnamon, and stir in the nuts. Turn into the prepared cake tin and bake for 25 to 30 minutes, or until cooked when tested with a skewer. Leave in the tin for a minute, then turn onto a cake rack to cool.

NOTE: This cake is also delicious served warm as a dessert, with a dollop of whipped cream. It keeps well wrapped in foil and stored in an airtight container, or may be cut into slices, wrapped in foil and frozen, ready for lunch boxes.

Banana Cake

This makes two round sandwich cakes. Eat one fresh and freeze one for later, or sandwich the two together and decorate the top with whipped cream and sliced bananas.

2 teaspoons lemon juice plus	*185 g (6 oz) butter, softened*
enough milk to make ⅔ cup	*⅔ cup mashed, very ripe*
2⅓ cups self-raising flour	*bananas (about 2 large*
1⅔ cups sugar	*bananas)*
1 teaspoon bicarbonate of	*2 eggs*
soda	*⅔ cup chopped walnuts*
1 teaspoon salt	

Grease two 23 cm (9 inch) sandwich tins. Set the oven at moderate (180°C/350°F).

Leave the lemon juice and milk for 5 minutes until the milk thickens a little. Sift the flour into a large bowl and add the sugar, bicarbonate and salt. Add the softened butter, bananas and milk. Mix well with an electric mixer on low speed, or by hand with a wooden spoon. Add the eggs and beat for 2 minutes longer. Stir in the walnuts. Turn into the sandwich tins and bake until cooked when tested with a skewer, about 35 minutes. Cool for 5 minutes in the tins, then turn out.

Cakes that Keep . . . and Keep

Some cakes need to be eaten fresh, others taste just as delicious (or more so) after keeping for a week or more. Here is a cross-section of cakes that keep well.

Orange Semolina Cake

Serve this cake with tea or coffee, or as a dessert with whipped cream. It stays moist and light for a week or more, wrapped in foil and kept in the refrigerator. Allow to stand at room temperature for 20 minutes or so before serving.

125 g (4 oz) butter	1 teaspoon baking powder
½ cup caster sugar	125 g (4 oz) ground almonds
1 tablespoon grated orange	SYRUP:
rind	1¼ cups orange juice
2 eggs	½ cup sugar
2 tablespoons brandy	3 tablespoons Grand Marnier,
1 cup semolina	Cointreau or brandy

Grease a 20 cm (8 inch) round or square cake tin with butter, then line with buttered greaseproof paper – a circle or square for the base and a strip for the sides. Set the oven temperature at hot (200°C/400°F).

Cream the butter, sugar and orange rind together until light and fluffy. Beat in the eggs one at a time, beating thoroughly after each addition, then stir in the brandy.

Stir the semolina, baking powder and almonds together and fold lightly into the mixture. Turn into the prepared tin and place on the centre shelf of the oven, lowering the temperature to moderate (180°C/350°F) as you do so. Bake for 30 minutes or until golden on top and risen. (A skewer inserted in the middle should come out clean.)

While the cake is cooking, make the orange syrup. Place the juice and sugar in a saucepan, bring to the boil and boil briskly for 5 minutes. Cool slightly and add the spirits.

Take the cake from the oven, pour the syrup over, then return to the oven and cook for a further 15 minutes. Allow to cool in the tin, and turn out carefully onto a plate to serve.

Cherry Rum Balls

These are more of a confection than a cake and are excellent served with coffee. Store in the refrigerator, covered with plastic wrap.

2 cups cake crumbs (butter or	1 tablespoon rum
sponge cake)	2 tablespoons hot apricot jam
2 tablespoons cocoa	18 glacé cherries
½ cup caster sugar	chocolate sprinkles
½ cup desiccated coconut	
1 teaspoon instant coffee	

Mix all the ingredients together except the jam, cherries and sprinkles. Add enough hot apricot jam to bind the mixture together, and mould small pieces around the cherries. Dip in sprinkles, then arrange in paper cases and chill before serving. *Makes 18*

Old-Fashioned Gingerbread with apple sauce and cream

Pumpkin Spice Cake

Mashed pumpkin in the mixture keeps this cake moist for a week or more if stored in an airtight container. The flavour's as delicious as pumpkin pie!

125 g (4 oz) butter, softened	*¾ cup milk*
1¼ cups sugar	*1 cup cooked, drained and mashed pumpkin*
2 eggs	
2¼ cups self-raising flour	*½ teaspoon bicarbonate of soda*
½ teaspoon salt	*½ cup chopped walnuts*
1 teaspoon cinnamon	*Caramel Frosting (see below – optional)*
1 teaspoon ground ginger	
1 teaspoon nutmeg	
¼ teaspoon ground cloves	

Grease a rectangular cake tin about 33 × 23 cm (13 × 9 inches) and line the base with greased greaseproof paper. Set the oven at moderate (180°C/350°F).

Cream the butter and sugar together until light and fluffy, then beat in the eggs one at a time. Sift together the flour, salt and spices. In another bowl, combine the milk with the pumpkin and bicarbonate of soda.

Add the flour and pumpkin mixtures alternately to the creamed mixture, beginning and ending with flour. Stir in the nuts. Turn into the prepared tin and bake in a moderate oven for 50 to 55 minutes, or until cooked when tested with a skewer. Cool in the tin for a few minutes, then turn out onto a rack to finish cooling. Ice with caramel frosting or serve plain.

Caramel Frosting

125 g (4 oz) butter	*¼ cup hot milk*
1 cup brown sugar, firmly packed	*about 3 cups icing sugar, sifted*

Melt the butter in a saucepan, add the brown sugar and stir until boiling. Turn the heat down and continue cooking and stirring for 1 minute, or until slightly thickened. Cool for 15 minutes, then add the hot milk and beat until smooth. Stir in enough icing sugar to give a spreading consistency, and use to frost cold cake.

Honey Cake

This is the traditional Middle Eastern honey cake, which contains only a tiny amount of butter and no eggs. It should be baked at least 2 weeks before serving and stored in an airtight tin, wrapped in foil. This gives the flavour and texture time to mellow.

½ cup honey	*½ cup chopped candied peel*
1 cup sugar	*½ cup raisins*
½ cup raspberry syrup	*4 teaspoons cinnamon*
1 cup warm black coffee	*½ teaspoon pepper*
1 cup flour	*2 teaspoons bicarbonate of soda*
15 g (½ oz) butter	
2 cups finely chopped nuts	

Grease a 30 cm (12 inch) square cake tin and line with greased brown paper. Set the oven at moderate (180°C/350°F).

Bring the honey to boiling point in a large saucepan and remove from the heat. Stir in the remaining ingredients in the order given. Turn the mixture into the prepared tin and bake until brown on top and cooked when tested with a skewer, about 45 minutes. Allow the cake to cool in the tin, then turn out and carefully remove the paper. Wrap in foil and store in an airtight container for 2 weeks before cutting.

Old-Fashioned Gingerbread

It's spicy, dark and rich – and even nicer after maturing for a few days, tightly wrapped in foil.

125 g (4 oz) butter	*2 cups flour*
¼ cup treacle	*2 teaspoons mixed spice*
2 tablespoons golden syrup	*2 teaspoons ground ginger*
⅓ cup brown sugar, firmly packed	*1 teaspoon bicarbonate of soda*
½ cup plus 1 tablespoon milk	*½ cup flaked almonds, to decorate*
2 eggs, beaten	

Grease a 23 cm (9 inch) square cake tin and line the bottom with greased greaseproof paper. Set the oven at slow (150°C/300°F).

Put the butter, treacle, golden syrup and brown sugar in a saucepan and heat very gently, stirring until melted. Remove from the heat, add the milk and allow to cool a little, then stir in the eggs.

Sift the flour, spice, ginger and bicarbonate into a bowl. Make a well in the middle and pour in the butter mixture. Stir from the middle, gradually incorporating the dry ingredients, then beat until the surface is covered with small bubbles.

Pour the gingerbread mixture into the prepared tin and scatter almonds over the top. Bake on the middle shelf for 1½ to 2 hours, or until a fine skewer inserted in the middle comes out clean. Allow to cool in the tin, then turn out, remove the paper and wrap in foil.

NOTE: For a delicious dessert, serve squares of warm gingerbread topped with stewed apples and whipped cream – a favourite idea from the United States.

Old-Fashioned Gingerbread
1 For gingerbread, butter is first melted with treacle, golden syrup and sugar, then milk and eggs are added. (Treacle and golden syrup won't stick to the spoon or cup if you first rinse utensils in boiling water or spray with a little cooking spray.)

2 Dry ingredients are mixed together in a bowl and the liquid mixture is poured into the centre. Start stirring from the centre out, blending in a little more of the dry ingredients each time. When all the flour is dampened, beat well with a wooden spoon until smooth.

3 Grease the pan and line with greased greaseproof paper, and have oven set at slow before pouring mixture into the pan. Gingerbread needs long, slow cooking, about 1½ to 2 hours. It is cooked when it shrinks away slightly from the sides of the pan and is firm to the touch. Cool in the pan before turning out.

Those Luscious Continental Cakes

There's a certain magic about Continental cakes; they include rich and buttery, almond-crusted German Bundt Cake, tender light Chocolate Roll and fabulous rum-soaked Coffee Cake from Austria. No cook's repertoire is complete without one of these famous cakes.

German Bundt Cake

A rich cake with a golden crust of butter-fried almonds.

200 g (7 oz) butter	¼ teaspoon almond essence
⅓ cup whole blanched almonds	2¼ cups flour
¾ cup icing sugar, sifted	1½ teaspoons baking powder
¾ cup caster sugar	pinch of salt
3 eggs, separated	¾ cup milk
¾ teaspoon vanilla essence	extra icing sugar, to finish

Set the oven at moderate (180°C/350°F). Grease a 6–7 cup fluted ring cake mould with 30 g (1 oz) butter, putting large dabs in the creases of the mould and embedding an almond in each dab. Put in the refrigerator to set while preparing the mixture.

Cream the remaining butter well. Gradually beat in the sugars, beating well between each addition. Add the egg yolks one at a time, and beat until smooth. Stir in the vanilla and almond essences. Sift the flour, baking powder and salt three times and fold into the creamed mixture alternately with the milk.

Whisk the egg whites until stiff, stir a spoonful into the cake mixture and, when incorporated, fold in the remaining whites carefully and lightly using a large metal spoon.

Pour into the prepared tin and bake for about 1½ hours, or until the cake is cooked when tested with a skewer. Allow to stand for about 15 minutes before turning out. Allow the cake to cool completely before dusting with sifted icing sugar. Cut this rich cake into thin slices to serve.

Chocolate Bundt Cake

This is a variation of the great basic cake. It has a coating of flaked almonds and a rich chocolate ribbon running through it.

30 g (1 oz) butter	3 tablespoons grated chocolate
⅓ cup flaked almonds	icing sugar, to finish
1 quantity German Bundt Cake mixture	

Set the oven at moderate (180°C/350°F). Butter a 6–7 cup fluted ring cake mould or deep 18 cm (7 inch) cake tin and sprinkle with the flaked almonds. Put in the refrigerator to set while preparing the cake mixture.

Carefully spoon half the cake mixture into the mould. Sprinkle the grated chocolate over the mixture in the tin. (The chocolate mustn't go near the edges.) Spoon in the remaining cake mixture and bake for 1½ hours or until cooked when tested with a fine skewer. Allow to stand for about 15 minutes before turning out. Cool completely, then dust with sifted icing sugar.

Austrian Coffee Cake

fine, dry breadcrumbs	1–2 tablespoons milk
185 g (6 oz) butter	Coffee Syrup (see below)
¾ cup caster sugar	TO DECORATE:
3 eggs, lightly beaten	¾ cup cream, whipped
1½ cups self-raising flour	marrons glacé
pinch of salt	

Grease an 18 cm (7 inch) round cake tin. Sprinkle with fine, dry breadcrumbs. Set the oven at moderate (180°C/350°F).

Beat the butter until soft and gradually add the sugar, beating until the mixture is light and fluffy. Gradually add the eggs, beating well after each addition. Fold in the sifted flour and salt alternately with enough milk to make a dropping consistency. Pour into the tin and bake for 40 to 45 minutes or until a skewer inserted comes out clean. Leave to cool in the tin for 5 to 10 minutes and turn onto a rack to cool. When cold, replace in the tin and slowly pour the coffee syrup over the cake. Refrigerate and remove from the tin just before serving.

Spread whipped cream over the top and around the sides of the cake and decorate with marrons glacé.

Coffee Syrup Put 1¼ cups strong black coffee into a jug. Boil ⅓ cup sugar and ⅔ cup water together for 2 minutes, then add to the coffee. Allow to cool and then add 2 tablespoons rum.

Chocolate Roll

This is a special European approach to sponge roll, using less flour and extra egg for a meltingly light texture.

½ cup flour	¼ teaspoon bicarbonate of soda
¼ teaspoon salt	2 tablespoons cold water
½ teaspoon baking powder	sifted icing sugar
60 g (2 oz) cooking chocolate, roughly chopped	TO FINISH:
4 eggs	1 × 300 ml carton cream (1¼ cups), whipped
¾ cup caster sugar, sifted	1 tablespoon caster sugar
1 teaspoon vanilla essence	chocolate caraque (page 215)

Grease and line a 38 × 25 × 2.5 cm (15 × 10 × 1 inch) Swiss roll tin (see page 213). Set the oven temperature at hot 200°C/400°F.

Sift together the flour, salt and baking powder onto a piece of paper. Melt the chocolate gently in a bowl over hot water. Break the eggs into a large bowl and beat with the sifted sugar until very light and thick. Fold the flour mixture and vanilla all at once into the egg mixture. Add the bicarbonate of soda and cold water to the chocolate, stirring until smooth. Fold quickly and lightly into the egg and flour mixture.

Turn into the prepared tin and bake for about 15 minutes, or until the centre springs back when touched. Loosen the edges and turn onto a tea-towel generously sprinkled with icing sugar. Peel off the paper and trim the edges of the cake with a sharp knife. Roll immediately in the towel, folding the hem of the towel over the edge of the cake and rolling the towel in the cake to prevent sticking. Cool on a wire rack for at least 1 hour.

Before serving, carefully unroll the cake and quickly spread with whipped cream sweetened with sugar. Re-roll the cake, using the tea-towel to help. Decorate with rosettes of whipped cream and chocolate caraque.

From front to back: Chocolate Roll;
Chocolate Bundt Cake;
German Bundt Cake;
Austrian Coffee Cake

Perfect Pastry

Making perfect pastry may be an art, but it is one art within everybody's reach. The step-by-step pictures on this page have been carefully designed to help you achieve the best possible results and the following special hints will also prove a useful guide.

● Start with cool ingredients and equipment. In hot weather, chill your mixing bowl and rolling pin before you begin. Rinse your hands in cold water and dry them, so your fingers will be cool. Have the butter ice cold, and use iced water for mixing.

● You will notice that only approximate amounts of water are given in shortcrust pastry recipes. Add just enough to work the dough into a soft ball, without getting sticky. If you have to add more flour, this changes the proportion of fat to flour and the pastry may be tough.

● Chilling the dough after mixing it helps to keep it tender, makes it easier to handle and reduces shrinkage during baking. Wrap in plastic film and refrigerate for 30 minutes, or until required.

● Handle the dough lightly, for two reasons: to keep as much air as possible in the dough and to slow down the development of gluten. Your pastry will be flakier and more tender if you have a light touch.

● Never stretch pastry when covering a pie or lining a tin, as this causes it to shrink back during baking and spoils the shape of your pie or flan.

● To make two pie or tart shells, divide the dough into two even pieces before rolling it. For a double-crust pie (like a meat or apple pie) make one piece slightly larger than the other, keeping the small one for the top.

● Keep your pastry board and rolling pin floured to prevent sticking. Roll the dough from the centre out, lifting the rolling pin and giving the dough a half-turn each time. Don't roll backwards and forwards, as this can stretch the dough. If the dough tears, dampen the edges around the tear and patch it carefully with another piece of pastry. Don't try to re-roll.

● Pastry is mixed with a cool hand, but needs a hot oven. Always preheat the oven to the stipulated temperature before baking the pie. The contrast between the coolness of the pastry and the heat of the oven causes rapid air expansion and helps to give a crisp, light texture.

● Baking times can vary according to the type of pan used. Tins that have lost their shine or have a special brown base help produce a nicely browned crust.

● For double-crust pies, always cut a few slits in the top to allow steam to escape. For an attractive, shiny finish, glaze with a little beaten egg or cream. A sprinkle of sugar can be added to fruit pies, and a little paprika or grated cheese adds interest to savoury pies.

● Allow 4 cups of sweet or savoury filling for a 23 cm (9 inch) pie and 3 cups for an 18 cm (7 inch) pie. To seal the edges, moisten the bottom rim and press the top crust firmly onto it (being careful not to stretch it). The rim can be fluted or simply marked with the tines of a fork. Another method of sealing is to cut the bottom crust large enough to give a 1 cm (½ inch) overhang, and to turn it up over the top crust like a hem.

Unfilled Pie Shells

If a pie shell is to be baked unfilled, prick it all over with a fork after you have placed it in the tin to prevent it rising during cooking. Or place a sheet of greaseproof paper over the pastry and weight it with dried beans or rice, or, as they do in France, with small, clean round pebbles. This keeps it from baking unevenly. (See Steps for Baking Blind opposite.)

If you wish to heat a filling in a baked pie crust, place it still in its pan inside a larger pan to protect it from too much heat. Otherwise it may over brown while the filling is heating.

Plain Shortcrust
1 Sift the flour and salt into a cool mixing bowl. Cut fat into chunks, and rub into the flour with the fingertips. You will incorporate more air into the mixture if you keep your hands well above the bowl. (Air helps to keep your pastry light and crisp.)

2 When the mixture is the texture of coarse breadcrumbs, shake the bowl and any lumps will rise to the surface. Rub them in but don't overdo it or the dough may become sticky before the water is added.

Lining a Flan Ring
1 Place a flan ring on a greased baking tray but do not grease the ring itself. Roll the pastry out into a circle about 3 mm (⅛ inch) thick and large enough to extend about 3.5 cm (1½ inches) beyond the rim of a 23 cm (9 inch) flan ring.

2 Lift the pastry up in the hands, or on the rolling pin, and place it over the flan ring. Ease it into the ring carefully, then press well into the angle all round the base of the tin. (It is easy to do this with the forefinger.) Hold the ring steady with one hand while you press the pastry firmly into the flutes with the

Plain Shortcrust

2 cups flour
pinch of salt
125 g (4 oz) lard or firm
  cooking margarine, or a
  mixture of half and half

3–4 tablespoons iced water

To prepare and bake, see step-by-step pictures below.

Curried Seafood Filling

You can vary the seafood for this filling as you like, using any combination of canned or fresh cooked fish or shellfish. You will need about 250 g (8 oz) after draining or removing skin, bones or shells. Flake or cut into small pieces before adding to the sauce with the cheese and lemon juice.

30 g (1 oz) butter
½ green pepper, seeded and
  finely chopped
2 spring onions, chopped
2 teaspoons curry powder
1 tablespoon flour
½ cup milk
½ cup cream
salt

1 × 185 g can tuna in oil,
  drained
125 g (4 oz) peeled prawns
1 tablespoon grated Parmesan
  cheese
1 tablespoon lemon juice
paprika, to garnish

Melt the butter in a heavy saucepan and gently fry the pepper and onions until soft. Stir in the curry powder, and cook for 1 minute, then stir in the flour off the heat. Add milk and cream to the mixture and blend well, then return to the heat and simmer for 3 minutes. Add salt to taste, tuna, prawns, cheese and lemon juice. Heat through, taste for seasoning, and spoon into a hot baked flan case (see below). Sprinkle with paprika to serve.
Serves 4 to 6

3 Add cold water a little at a time, using a knife with a round-ended blade. When the dough starts to cling together, use the fingers of one hand to gather it into a ball. Add a little more water if it seems too dry and crumbly.

4 Continue gathering the dough into a soft ball until it leaves the sides of the bowl clean and dry. Wrap in plastic film and chill for 30 minutes in the refrigerator before rolling out. (Or it may be left as long as required.)

5 Lightly flour a pastry board or clean work surface and a rolling pin (a marble slab is an excellent investment if you make a lot of pastry). Knead the dough lightly, then shape it into a round for a round tin, or into an oval if you are making an oval-shaped pie.

6 Roll the dough away from you with short, quick strokes. A heavy 'steamroller' action will roll out the air and make the dough heavy, so keep movements light. Turn the pastry on the board to keep it even and prevent sticking, but never turn it over.

other hand. A little flour on your fingers will prevent sticking.

3 Roll across the top of the flan ring with your rolling pin. This will automatically trim off the surplus pastry. (Don't throw the trimmings away, they can be used to make small tartlets.)

Baking Blind
1 Flan cases are often baked 'blind' (without filling), and care must be taken to see they don't rise or cook unevenly. Either prick the pastry all over with a fork, or line it with greaseproof paper and weigh down with a layer of rice or dried beans.

2 To cook the flan, have the oven preheated to hot (200°C/400°F). Bake for 15 to 20 minutes until the sides of the flan are crisp and set, then remove from the oven and carefully remove the paper and beans. Using oven gloves or a cloth, lift off the flan ring.

3 Leave the pastry case on the baking tray, and return to the oven for 5 minutes to crisp and brown the base. The pastry may now be filled with a hot savoury filling or it can be cooled and filled with custard, cream and fruit, etc., or frozen for later use.

Savoury Pastries

When you can make good pastry (and it's not difficult) a whole world of good cooking is at your fingertips. The shortcrust pastry shown step-by-step on the preceding pages is excellent for most pies, pastries, and other savoury double-crust pies. The rich shortcrust on the opposite page is used for flans and quiches, where a small amount of crisp pastry provides the perfect texture contrast for a large amount of creamy filling.

Cheese shortcrust, on this page, is a versatile pastry. You can shape it into straws or tiny biscuits, make it into boat shapes (barquettes) to hold a savoury filling, or use it for small tart shells.

Pastry freezes well, so it's sensible to make a double batch and freeze half for later use. Wrap it in plastic film, then in foil or a freezer bag; when required, leave at room temperature to thaw.

Cheese Shortcrust

A rich, well-flavoured pastry for making cheese straws and biscuits or small pastry cases.

¾ cup flour	pinch of dry mustard
60 g (2 oz) butter	pinch of cayenne
¾ cup grated mature Cheddar	1 egg yolk
cheese	½ teaspoon lemon juice
½ teaspoon salt	

Sift the flour into a mixing bowl. Cut the butter into small pieces and rub through the flour with the fingertips until the mixture resembles coarse breadcrumbs. Mix in the cheese, salt, mustard and cayenne. Beat the egg yolk with lemon juice, add to the flour mixture, and mix to form a dough. (If necessary, add a little iced water; but the dough should be soft, not sticky.) Wrap the dough in plastic film and chill for 30 minutes or until required. Use in any of the following ways.

Cheese Biscuits

Roll the dough out thinly and cut into small rounds with a floured glass or scone cutter. Bake in a preheated hot oven (200°C/400°F) for 5 to 7 minutes, or until crisp and golden. If desired, sandwich the biscuits together with a little anchovy paste when cooled. *Makes about 36 single biscuits*

Cheese Straws

Roll the dough out to a strip about 10 cm (4 inches) wide and trim the edges. With a 6 cm (2½ inch) scone cutter, cut three rounds from the pastry and stamp out the middles, or cut with a sharp knife, to make hollow circles. Cut the remaining pastry into straws (see illustration left, below) and arrange the pastry shapes on a greased baking tray. Bake in a preheated hot oven (200°C/400°F) for 5 to 7 minutes, or until crisp and golden. Cool on a wire tray, and arrange the straws in bundles pushed through the pastry circles. (You will also have the little rounds cut from the centre.) *Makes about 30*

Anchovy Plaits or Twists

Cut strips of cheese shortcrust and place two strips side by side. Place an anchovy fillet in the middle and plait the anchovy with the pastry strips. Or twist a single strip with an anchovy fillet. Bake plaits and twists in a preheated hot oven (200°C/400°F) for 5 to 7 minutes, and serve hot or cold. *Makes 15 to 20*

Asparagus Barquettes

Small boat-shaped moulds are available from specialty kitchen shops and large department stores. They look especially attractive on the savoury tray. How to line them with pastry is described in the method.

1 quantity Cheese Shortcrust	2 tablespoons grated
15 g (½ oz) butter	Parmesan cheese
2 rashers streaky bacon, diced	2 eggs, beaten
2 spring onions, chopped	salt
1 cup cream or evaporated	freshly ground pepper
milk	1 × 340 g can asparagus tips

Roll the pastry thinly on a lightly floured board. Grease 8 moulds with butter or spray with a non-stick cooking spray. Arrange close together. Lift the sheet of pastry on a rolling pin

and place loosely over the tins. (There may be only enough to cover 6 tins.) Roll a small piece of pastry into a ball and dip into flour. Use to press the pastry into the moulds, then roll a well-floured rolling pin over the top (first one way, then the other) to remove surplus paste. Roll the trimmings out again and use to line the remaining moulds, if there is enough.

Heat the butter and fry the bacon and spring onions until the bacon is beginning to crisp. Add the cream or evaporated milk and heat just until bubbles form, but do not bring to the boil. Remove from the heat, stir in the cheese, then the eggs, and season with salt and freshly ground pepper.

Drain the asparagus and place a few tips in each pastry case. Arrange the moulds on a baking tray and carefully pour the filling in to come almost to the top of the moulds. Bake in a preheated moderate oven (180°C/350°F) for 15 to 20 minutes, or until the filling is puffed and golden and a knife inserted in the centre comes out clean. Serve warm or cold on the hors d'oeuvre tray, or as a snack. *Makes 6 to 8*

Rich Shortcrust

1 cup flour	*1 egg yolk*
pinch of salt	*1–2 tablespoons iced water*
pinch of baking powder	*good squeeze lemon juice*
60 g (2 oz) butter	

Sift the flour, salt and baking powder into a bowl. Rub in the butter lightly and evenly until the mixture resembles breadcrumbs. Beat the egg yolk with 1 tablespoon of water and lemon juice and sprinkle evenly over the flour, stirring with a knife to form a dough. Add a little extra water if necessary. Knead lightly on a floured board, wrap in plastic film and chill for 30 minutes or until required. *Makes one 23 cm (9 inch) flan case*

Cheese Straws; Anchovy Plaits and Twists; Cheese Biscuits; Asparagus Barquettes; Asparagus Quiche; Quiche Lorraine

Quiche Lorraine

The addition of cheese to the classic quiche filling is one I think you will enjoy.

1 quantity Rich Shortcrust	*½ teaspoon salt*
FILLING:	*pinch of cayenne*
4 rashers streaky bacon	*½ cup cream*
90 g (3 oz) sliced Swiss or	*½ cup milk*
Gruyère cheese	*30 g (1 oz) butter, melted*
2 eggs	*watercress or bacon rolls,*
1 teaspoon flour	*to garnish*
pinch of nutmeg	

Roll the dough out on a lightly floured board to fit a 23 cm (9 inch) flan tin, following the step-by-step method on the previous pages. Chill while preparing the filling.

Remove the rind from the bacon and grill until crisp. Cut into 1 cm (½ inch) squares, and cut the cheese the same size. Place in layers in the pastry case. Beat the eggs with the flour, nutmeg, salt, cayenne, cream and milk until just combined (over beating causes bubbles on top). Stir in the melted butter. Strain over the bacon and cheese and bake in a preheated hot oven (200°C/400°F) for 10 minutes. Reduce the heat to moderate (180°C/350°F) and bake for a further 20 minutes, or until a knife inserted in the centre comes out clean. Serve the quiche warm, garnished with watercress or grilled bacon rolls. *Serves 4 to 6*

Variation
Asparagus Quiche Follow the recipe for Quiche Lorraine. Arrange cooked asparagus tips over the base of the flan case, and pour over the filling. Bake as for Quiche Lorraine.

Sweet Pies

Begin with the beautiful pastry (it really does melt in the mouth) and add a luscious filling.

Rich Sweet Shortcrust (Pâte Sucrée)

1½ cups flour	½ cup caster sugar
pinch of salt	2 egg yolks
60 g (2 oz) butter	few drops vanilla essence

Sift the flour and salt onto a pastry board or marble slab. Make a well in the centre, so the flour forms a ring. Place the remaining ingredients in the centre and work together into a smooth paste, using the fingertips of one hand. With a metal spatula, gradually draw the flour into the butter and egg mixture, and knead lightly to form a dough. Wrap in plastic film and chill for at least 1 hour before rolling out. *Makes one 23 cm (9 inch) flan case*

French Strawberry Flan

1 cooked and cooled 23 cm (9 inch) sweet shortcrust flan case, baked blind (page 225)	1 tablespoon cream
	1 punnet strawberries
FILLING:	GLAZE:
1 × 125 g packet Philadelphia cream cheese	½ cup redcurrant jelly
	1 tablespoon water
⅓ cup sugar	2 teaspoons Grand Marnier or orange juice
2 teaspoons grated orange rind	
1 tablespoon orange juice	

For the filling, cream the cheese well with sugar, then blend in the orange rind, juice and cream. Spoon into the pastry case. Hull and wash the strawberries, pat dry and arrange over the top.

Stir all the ingredients for the glaze together over a gentle heat until smooth. Cool a little, stirring occasionally, and spoon over the strawberries. Chill until serving time. *Serves 6*

French-Canadian Sugar Tart

Superb caramel flavour, creamy texture and plump sultanas!

1 uncooked, chilled 23 cm (9 inch) sweet shortcrust flan case (reserve pastry trimmings)	1 cup cream
	30 g (1 oz) butter
	½ teaspoon vanilla essence
	pinch of salt
FILLING:	2 eggs, beaten
2 cups brown sugar	1 cup sultanas

Combine the brown sugar and cream in a saucepan and bring to the boil, stirring all the while. Simmer gently for 15 minutes, stirring now and again. Remove from the heat and add the butter, vanilla and salt. Cool until lukewarm, then add the beaten eggs and mix well.

Sprinkle the sultanas over the base of the flan case and carefully pour in the filling. Knead the pastry trimmings together and roll out, then cut into strips. Arrange the strips lattice-fashion over the tart, moistening the ends and pressing them firmly to pastry sides, so they won't shrink away during cooking. Bake in a preheated hot oven (200°C/400°F) for 45 minutes, or until the filling is just set and the pastry crisp and golden. Cool the pie a little, then remove the metal ring. Finish cooling on a wire rack.

Cherry Almond Tart

1 uncooked, chilled 23 cm (9 inch) sweet shortcrust flan case	2 eggs, beaten
	500 g (1 lb) cooked and drained fresh black cherries, or 1 × 425 g can black cherries, drained
FILLING:	
125 g (4 oz) ground almonds	
½ cup caster sugar	¼ cup slivered almonds

Line the pastry case with greaseproof paper, half fill with dried beans and bake in a moderately hot oven (190°C/375°F) for 10 minutes. Remove the paper and beans and cook for a further 3 minutes. Remove from the oven, but leave the oven on. (Pastry will be only half cooked.)

Mix the ground almonds and sugar and stir in enough beaten egg to give a soft paste. Pit the cherries and arrange over the base of the flan case, then spread the almond paste over the top. Spike with slivered almonds and bake for 30 minutes, or until the filling is set and golden. Cool a little, remove the flan ring and serve at room temperature (not chilled).

Flow the glaze carefully over the strawberries from the side of a large metal spoon. For a pretty finish to the pastry, save a little glaze and brush the top edge of the crust. Serve with whipped cream if desired.

French Strawberry Flan; Lemon Meringue Pie

Fresh Banana-Prune Pie

No-one will believe you created the luscious filling in 5 minutes!

1 cooked and cooled 23 cm (9 inch) sweet shortcrust flan case, baked blind (page 225)	*teaspoon cinnamon*
FILLING:	*2 cups soft, pitted dessert prunes*
⅔ cup honey	*2 cups sliced medium-ripe bananas*
60 g (2 oz) butter, softened	*1½ cups cream, whipped*
1 tablespoon lemon juice	*2 tablespoons crushed nuts*
pinch of salt	

Combine the honey and butter in a bowl and beat well. Stir in the lemon juice, salt, cinnamon and fruit. Spoon into the flan case, cover with whipped cream and sprinkle with nuts.

Marbled Rum Cream Pie

You'll love the look of this pie when it's cut – swirls of vanilla cream and rum-flavoured chocolate. A real party pie!

1 cooked and cooled 23 cm (9 inch) sweet shortcrust flan case, baked blind (page 225)	*pinch of salt*
FILLING:	*2 eggs, separated*
1 envelope (3 teaspoons) gelatine	*¾ cup milk*
¼ cup water	*¼ cup dark rum*
1 cup sugar	*375 g (12 oz) dark chocolate, chopped into small pieces*
	1 cup cream
	1 teaspoon vanilla essence

Sprinkle the gelatine over the cold water and allow to sponge. Place in the top part of a double boiler (or in a bowl placed over simmering water) with ¼ cup of the sugar and the salt. Stir well until the gelatine dissolves, then remove from the heat and beat in the egg yolks, milk and rum. Return to the heat and continue stirring until the mixture is slightly thickened, about 4 minutes. Remove from the heat and stir in the chocolate until thoroughly blended. Chill until thickened but not set.

Beat the egg whites until foamy, then gradually beat in ½ cup of the remaining sugar and continue beating until stiff. Fold into the chilled chocolate. Whip the cream with the remaining ¼ cup sugar and vanilla.

Pile alternate spoonfuls of chocolate and cream into the cold flan case. Cut through with a knife several times for a pretty marbled effect, then chill until firm.

Lemon Meringue Pie

1 cooked and cooled 23 cm (9 inch) sweet shortcrust flan case, baked blind (page 225)	*grated rind of 1 medium lemon*
FILLING:	*60 g (2 oz) butter*
¾ cup sugar	*3 eggs, separated*
pinch of salt	*½ cup lemon juice*
3 tablespoons cornflour	*extra 4 tablespoons sugar*
1 cup water	*TO DECORATE:*
	glacé cherries
	angelica leaves

Place the sugar, salt and cornflour in a saucepan. Mix to a paste with the water, add the lemon rind, and bring slowly to the boil, stirring. Simmer for 5 minutes and stir in the butter. Remove from the heat. Beat the egg yolks with lemon juice and gradually add to the hot cornflour mixture, stirring well to combine. Cook over a gentle heat for 1 to 2 minutes, but do not allow to boil. Cool the filling and spoon into the flan case.

Beat the egg whites until they stand in peaks, then gradually beat in the 4 tablespoons of sugar. Continue beating until stiff and shiny. Spread the meringue over the pie, taking it right to the edge, and bake on the centre shelf of a preheated slow oven (160°C/325°F) until set and golden, about 20 minutes. Cool and decorate. Chill until ready to serve.

Lemon Meringue Pie
1 To make meringue for the pie, beat whites into soft peaks, gradually beat in sugar, and beat until stiff and shiny.

2 Cover the filling completely with meringue, taking it right to the edges. Swirl the top with a spatula for a pretty effect.

Rough Puff Pastry

This is the simplest of the rich pastries that rise in layers to give a proud professional finish to your baking. Rough puff pastry is excellent for sweet or savoury hot pies or turnovers, sausage rolls and those delightful confections from Lancashire, Eccles Cakes.

This light, crisp pastry is surprisingly easy to make as long as you remember a few points:

Don't make it in a tearing hurry; it is vital that the pastry is allowed to rest in the refrigerator or other very cool place between rollings and before baking, so that it won't shrink in the oven. Fortunately, this type of pastry freezes and reheats perfectly, either cooked or uncooked, so you can make it when it suits you best.

At all stages, handle the pastry quickly and lightly (at London's Cordon Bleu Cookery School, students are told to 'handle pastry as if it were red hot'), and use the fingers only – the palm of the hand is too warm and may melt some fat into the flour, making the finished pastry greasy and heavy.

There is a special way of rolling rough puff or other flaky pastries: bring the rolling pin down firmly on the pastry, give a short, sharp back-and-forth roll, lift the pin and repeat the process. The idea is to roll the pastry thinner without pushing the fat about so that it bursts through the surface. Work your way from front to back with these short, quick rolls but stop just before you get to the back edge so that the pastry is not pushed out of shape. To keep straight edges, pull the corners out gently rather than pushing the sides in.

When the pastry is shaped for baking, all edges must be cut cleanly with a sharp knife so that the layers can separate as they rise, giving the airy look and texture characteristic of this lovely pastry.

Rough Puff Pastry

Butter gives its special flavour to the pastry, but firm margarine and lard are easier to work with and still give good flavour. Have the fat cool and firm but not hard.

2 cups flour	*1 teaspoon lemon juice*
pinch of salt	*about ½ cup cold water*
185 g (6 oz) butter, or 90 g	
(3 oz) each firm margarine	
and lard	

To prepare, see step-by-step pictures at right.

This quantity is called '250 g (2 cups) pastry', by the amount of flour used. *Sufficient to make a 20 cm (8 inch) diameter crust or 16 to 20 sausage rolls.*

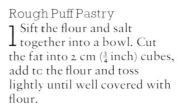

Rough Puff Pastry
1 Sift the flour and salt together into a bowl. Cut the fat into 2 cm (¾ inch) cubes, add to the flour and toss lightly until well covered with flour.

2 Mix the lemon juice and water and stir into the flour with a round-ended knife, without breaking up the pieces of fat. Don't add all the liquid unless it is necessary – use just enough to make the dough cling together.

Sausage Rolls

1 quantity Rough Puff Pastry
500 g (1 lb) sausage mince

1 beaten egg

To prepare and cook, see step-by-step pictures below. *Makes 16 to 20*

Sausage Rolls
1 Place a shelf just above centre of the oven and set oven to hot (220°C/425°F). Roll out the pastry about 5 mm (¼ inch) thick into a rectangle about 15 cm (6 inches) wide, and cut in half lengthwise. With floured hands, divide the meat in half and roll it on a floured board into 2 long thin sausage shapes. Lay one piece just off-centre on each pastry strip. Brush one edge of the pastry with beaten egg and fold the other side over to meet it.

2 Press the edges of pastry firmly together. With the back of a knife held horizontally, lightly tap the cut edges to help it to rise in flaky layers (this is called 'knocking up' the pastry). Cut the long rolls into 5 cm (2 inch) lengths, or larger if you like. Place on a dampened baking tray and chill for 20 minutes. Brush with beaten egg, cut 2 or 3 slits across the top of each roll for the steam to escape and bake for 25 to 30 minutes until golden brown. Serve hot with mustard or tomato sauce.

3 Flour your fingers and gently gather the mixture together, then turn it out onto a floured board. Use your fingers and a rolling pin to shape it into a rectangular block.

4 With a floured rolling pin, roll the pastry out to a rectangle about 1 cm (½ inch) thick. Use the rolling technique, and keep the edges and corners neat, as explained in the introduction on the opposite page. Lightly mark the pastry across into 3 equal parts.

5 Fold up the bottom third, keeping fingers inside and the thumb on top of the pastry so that you trap a little air between the layers, and press the ends with the rolling pin to seal. Fold the top third of the pastry down over this layer in the same manner and seal the ends and the long open edge. Give the pastry a quarter-turn.

6 Repeat Step 5, wrap pastry in greaseproof paper and put it into the refrigerator for 15 minutes. Repeat the rolling, folding and turning 3 or more times, resting the pastry in the refrigerator for 15 minutes after every second rolling. Then rest the finished pastry for at least 20 minutes. Rest again after shaping and cutting ready for baking.

232

Fruit Pie

$3\frac{1}{2}$–$4\frac{1}{2}$ cups prepared fresh, canned or bottled fruit	1 quantity Rough Puff Pastry (page 230)
$\frac{1}{3}$–$\frac{1}{2}$ cup caster sugar and 2–3 tablespoons water, or 2–3 tablespoons fruit syrup	GLAZE: 1 egg white, slightly beaten caster sugar
lemon juice (optional)	

Use any fresh fruit in season such as apples, pears, peaches, apricots or plums, or canned or bottled fruit. Prepare and slice fruit, if necessary, and put it into a 3–4 cup pie dish with a rim. The fruit should fill the dish and mound up a little in the centre. Spoon over the sugar and water for fresh fruit, or syrup in which canned or bottled fruit was packed. Add lemon juice to point up the flavour, if you wish.

Set the oven to hot (220°C/425°F). On a floured board, roll out the pastry about 4 cm (1½ inches) larger than the top of the dish. It should be about 5 mm (¼ inch) thick. Cut off a 2.5 cm (1 inch) strip all round, dampen the rim of the dish and lay the strip round it, cutting and joining the ends if necessary. Press down onto the rim and dampen this strip. Lay the pastry lid over and press together to seal. Trim off any surplus with a sharp knife. Press the lid out towards the edge with a finger and at the same time 'knock up' the pastry by lightly tapping the cut edge all round with a knife. Chill for 20 minutes, then brush with egg white and sprinkle with caster sugar. Cut two or three small slits in the lid for steam to escape.

Place the pie dish on a baking tray and bake for 20 minutes. Then, if using fresh fruit, lower the heat to moderately hot (190°C/375°F), and bake for a further 40 minutes or until the fruit is cooked (test with a skewer). If the pastry is becoming too brown, cover loosely with greaseproof paper. If using canned or bottled fruit, bake without lowering heat until the top is well risen and golden brown. Serve with cream or custard. *Serves 4*
NOTE: To use leftover pieces of pastry, arrange them in a rectangle, cutting as necessary. Paint an edge of each piece with cold water, overlap it slightly on the next piece and press the join together with your fingers. Roll out lightly on a floured board to make the surface even. Spread two-thirds of the pastry with butter and fold in three as in Step 5 of the recipe for Rough Puff Pastry, then chill, roll and fold once or twice more as in Step 6. Chill this re-rolled pastry overnight before using.

Eccles Cakes

30 g (1 oz) butter, melted	1 quantity Rough Puff Pastry (page 230)
2 tablespoons brown sugar	GLAZE:
2 tablespoons chopped mixed peel	milk
$\frac{3}{4}$ cup currants	caster sugar
$\frac{1}{4}$ teaspoon mixed spice	

Stir the butter, sugar, fruit and spice together. Cool.

Place an oven shelf in the second top position and set the oven to hot (220°C/425°F). Roll out the pastry about 3 mm (⅛ inch) thick and cut 9–10 cm (3½–4 inch) rounds, using a floured cutter.

Place a scant tablespoon of filling in the centre of each round. Dampen the edges of the pastry with water, then draw them up to meet in the centre and seal by pressing together. Turn them over, and roll gently to make circles 8–9 cm (3–3½ inches) across.

Place the cakes on a dampened baking tray and chill for 15 minutes. Brush the tops with milk and sprinkle with caster sugar. Cut 3 slits across the top of each cake and bake for 15 to 20 minutes until golden brown. *Makes 16*

Sweet or Savoury Turnovers

These are treats for a main course or dessert, for picnics, packed lunches, snacks or (made half-size) as nibbles with drinks.

| 1 quantity Rough Puff Pastry (page 230) | beaten egg or egg white caster sugar (for sweet turnovers) |
| 1 cup cold filling (see below) | |

Place a shelf just above the centre of the oven and set the oven at hot (220°C/425°F).

Roll out the pastry about 5 mm (¼ inch) thick and cut into 8 squares or circles. Place 1½ tablespoons of cold filling on one half of each piece of pastry (a triangular half for squares), brush the edges with beaten egg or egg white, fold the other half over and press to seal. 'Knock up' the cut edges (see Sausage Rolls, Step 2, page 231), place on a dampened baking tray and chill for 20 minutes. Brush savoury turnovers with beaten egg, sweet ones with beaten egg white with sugar sprinkled over. Cut two or three slits in the tops to allow steam to escape and bake for 25 to 30 minutes until golden brown. Serve warm or hot. *Makes 8*

Savoury Fillings

Cheese and Tomato Skin, seed and chop 2 large tomatoes and mix with 1 tablespoon soft breadcrumbs, 4 tablespoons grated cheese, 1 tablespoon grated onion, 1 egg and salt and pepper.
Savoury Mince Chop 1 small onion and fry, without extra fat, with 250 g (8 oz) hamburger mince, breaking the meat down with a fork. When the meat has changed colour, sprinkle with 2 teaspoons flour and stir until brown. Add ¼ cup water or stock, ¼ teaspoon Worcestershire sauce, 1 teaspoon tomato sauce and salt and pepper to taste. Stir until thickened. Two teaspoons of chopped parsley or other herbs, a pinch of dried herbs or ½ small carrot, grated, may be added. Cover and simmer for 10 minutes, then cool.
Cooked or Canned Fish, Meat or Chicken Flake or chop finely and mix with your choice of chopped tomato, celery, herbs, green pepper, grated onion, mustard or grated lemon rind. Add just enough chutney, cream, yogurt, mayonnaise, gravy or any suitable sauce you may have to moisten slightly. Season well with salt and pepper. Half a thick slice of the softer type of Continental sausage, spread with Dijon mustard, is excellent too.
Vegetable Sliced mushrooms or chopped cooked vegetables are good mixed with chopped herbs or grated cheese and seasoned well with salt and pepper. Moisten slightly, if needed.

Sweet Fillings

Fruit Use apples or pears, stewed or thinly sliced, and sprinkled with sugar and lemon juice. Or use berries or other fresh or canned fruits. Drain canned fruits well.
Dried Fruit Use fruit mincemeat or raisins, sultanas or mixed fruit, sprinkled with brown sugar and lemon juice. Jam or lemon curd also makes a good filling.
Cream Cheese or Ricotta Use cream cheese, or Ricotta cheese mixed with a little cream; sweeten to taste with brown or white sugar, then add your choice of flavourings: ground cinnamon, cardamom or mixed spice, brandy or rum, chopped dried or glacé fruits, grated orange or lemon peel.

From the back: Large Savoury Turnovers; Eccles Cakes; Sweet Turnovers; Small Savoury Turnovers; Cocktail Turnovers

Choux Pastry

Choux pastry is wonderfully useful. It is best known as the basis of sweet éclairs and cream puffs, but it also makes sensational hot or cold savouries, first course and luncheon dishes, or Lilliputian puffs for a soup garnish.

Like many other preparations that are surrounded by some mystique, choux pastry is quite easy to make if you know the rules. It is really just a panada (a sauce so thick as to be solid) with eggs beaten into it. When it is cooked, it swells into a crisp golden shell that is hollow inside.

The panada is made by adding flour to butter and water at boiling point and cooking for a few moments until the mixture forms a solid mass.

The eggs should be added gradually, beating hard after each addition. An electric beater is a great help.

Choux pastry is sometimes considered temperamental because shells that look beautiful when they come from the oven sometimes collapse as they cool, but the solution is simple. The secret of making shells that do not collapse is to be sure that the pastry is cooked and dry right through. It is placed first in a very hot oven so that it puffs quickly, then the heat is reduced so that the pastry will dry without over-browning. A well-cooked shell is golden brown and firm to the touch and feels very light in the hand. To be fail-safe, leave the cooked shells in the turned-off oven with the door half open, or put them into a warming drawer for 20 minutes or so to ensure that they are thoroughly dried out. Slit éclairs along the side and make a slit or a hole with the point of a knife in round puffs as soon as they are cooked, to allow any steam to escape and make an opening for filling.

Coffee Éclairs; Raspberry Éclairs

Choux Pastry

1 Put the water, butter, salt and sugar (if using) into a small heavy saucepan and heat slowly. The butter must be melted before boiling point is reached. Meanwhile, sift the flour onto a piece of greaseproof paper. The moment the butter mixture boils, remove from the heat and tip in all the flour at once.

2 Stir vigorously with a wooden spatula until well blended; return to a low heat and beat briskly with the spatula until the mixture leaves the sides of the saucepan, forms a mass and begins to film the bottom of the saucepan. Remove from the heat immediately and cool a little.

3 Turn the mixture into the bowl of an electric mixer, or leave it in the saucepan. Add the eggs gradually, beating after each addition until thoroughly incorporated. Do not add all the egg unless it is needed; the pastry is right when it is as shiny as satin and holds its shape on a spoon. Use warm.

Choux Pastry

1 cup water
125 g (4 oz) butter
½ teaspoon salt
2 teaspoons sugar (for sweet
shells)

1 cup flour
4 eggs, beaten

To prepare, see step-by-step pictures on opposite page. *Makes 12 éclairs*

Choux pastry will keep in the refrigerator for a day or two. Store in a covered container, with plastic food wrap pressed down onto the surface of the pastry itself to prevent a skin from forming. Bring to lukewarm by standing the container in warm water when you are ready to shape and bake it.

Baked shells freeze well. When required, place straight from the freezer in a moderately slow oven (160°C/325°F) for 5 to 15 minutes, depending on size, to thaw and crisp.
NOTE: A wooden spatula, mentioned in Step 2 (opposite), is like a spoon without a bowl. It is best for stirring flour mixtures because the mixture cannot collect into a lump.

Chocolate Éclairs

1 quantity Choux Pastry
1 cup cream
1 teaspoon caster sugar
GLOSSY CHOCOLATE ICING:
2 tablespoons cocoa

1½ tablespoons sugar
3 tablespoons water
1 cup icing sugar, sifted
few drops vanilla essence

To prepare, fill and ice, see step-by-step pictures below. *Makes 12*
Variations
Coffee Éclairs Make as for Chocolate Éclairs, but ice with Coffee Glacé Icing (page 215).
Strawberry or Raspberry Éclairs Make as for Chocolate Éclairs, but fill with sliced strawberries or whole raspberries and cream and ice with Lemon Glacé Icing (page 215), tinted pink.

Cream Puffs

Fill a forcing bag with choux pastry as for Éclairs, Step 1, below. Grease and flour a baking sheet and press out the pastry into well-spaced, high 4 cm (1½ inch) mounds. Hold and guide the bag as for Éclairs, Step 2, but work from directly above. Pipe each mound with one steady pressure. To stop, release the pressure before lifting the bag away, to avoid a long tail. Alternatively, take spoonfuls of the pastry and push off onto the baking sheet in one movement. Don't try to change the shape of choux pastry when putting it out, or it will rise in cottage loaf shapes instead of round puffs. Brush the puffs with beaten egg, pushing down the tails.

Bake and dry as for Éclairs, making a slit or a hole with the point of a knife in each puff where there is a crack in the shell. Cool and fill as for Éclairs and dust the tops with icing sugar.

Savoury Puffs and Éclairs

Unsweetened choux pastry, shaped as éclairs or puffs, may be filled with any hot savoury filling and served as a first course or luncheon dish; or you may make cheese-flavoured shells by beating 2 tablespoons of grated cheese into the finished pastry. Cut off the tops of the shells with a serrated knife, spoon in the hot filling and replace the lids. Reheat for 10 minutes in a moderate oven (180°C/350°F). Miniature puffs with hot or cold savoury fillings are excellent with drinks.

Choux pastry doubles in size when baked, so judge the amount to put out accordingly.

Tiny Puffs for Soup

Make dots of pastry mixture by squeezing it from a forcing bag fitted with a plain 5 mm (¼ inch) nozzle and cutting off in 5 mm (¼ inch) lengths. Set out on a greased baking sheet and bake in a moderate oven (180°C/350°F) for about 10 minutes or until crisp and brown. Pass separately as a garnish for clear soup.

Chocolate Éclairs
1 Place a shelf just above the centre of the oven and set the oven to very hot (230°C/450°F). Stand a forcing bag in a jug. Turn back the top third of the bag and spoon in the pastry. Turn the top up, hold the bag up in one hand and slide the other hand down it, pressing between thumb and fingers to pack the mixture down and eliminate air bubbles.

2 Grease and flour a baking sheet. Mark evenly spaced lines 8 cm (3 inches) long with the handle of a wooden spoon. Pleat the top of the bag together, twist it and pull it up between your thumb and forefinger until your fingers are against the mixture. Using the other hand to guide the nozzle, press out the pastry onto the lines, cutting it off at the ends with a knife.

3 Bake for 12 minutes, then turn heat down to moderate (180°C/350°F) and bake for 15 to 20 minutes more, or until golden brown, firm and light in the hand. Slit each éclair along the side and leave in the turned-off oven with the door half open for 20 minutes, then cool on a rack. When cold, whip the cream with the sugar and fill the éclairs, using a forcing bag and nozzle as before.

4 Stir the cocoa, sugar and water over a low heat until the sugar is dissolved, then bring to the boil without stirring. Remove from the heat and stir in the icing sugar and vanilla, adding a little boiling water if necessary to make a coating consistency. Spread the tops of the éclairs with icing, using a knife dipped in hot water, or dip éclairs, top down, in the icing. Leave to set.

Drop Biscuits

They're easy to make, quick to bake and keep for ages (if you hide them!). Here are a few general points to keep in mind when you're making biscuits:
- Shiny baking trays help biscuits brown evenly. The best size to look for is one about 5 cm (2 inches) shorter and narrower than your oven shelf.
- Cool biscuits on wire racks to help prevent sogginess. If baking more than one batch, use a cool tray each time.
- To stop biscuits spreading too much, chill the dough a little before baking. Also be sure to cook at the correct temperature.
- Store biscuits in an airtight container; if they become soft, crisp them for a few minutes in a moderately slow oven (160°C/325°F).

Lemon Crispies

A not-too-sweet biscuit that's perfect with tea or coffee.

1½ teaspoons vinegar	1¾ cups self-raising flour, sifted
½ cup milk	¼ teaspoon bicarbonate of soda
125 g (4 oz) butter, softened	¼ teaspoon salt
¾ cup sugar	LEMON GLAZE:
1 egg	¾ cup sugar
2 teaspoons finely grated lemon rind	¼ cup lemon juice

Combine the vinegar and milk. Cream the butter and sugar until light and fluffy, then beat in the egg and lemon rind. Sift the dry ingredients together and add to the creamed mixture alternately with the milk, beating after each addition. Drop from a teaspoon, about 5 cm (2 inches) apart, onto ungreased baking trays. Cook in a preheated moderate oven (180°C/350°F) for 12 to 14 minutes until crisp and golden.

Combine the sugar and lemon juice. As soon as the biscuits are cooked, remove them from the oven and brush with the glaze. Cool on wire racks. *Makes about 4 dozen*

Peanut Oaties

1¾ cups self-raising flour	2 eggs
½ teaspoon salt	¼ cup milk
125 g (4 oz) butter, softened	1 teaspoon vanilla essence
½ cup chunky peanut butter	2½ cups rolled oats (plain or quick-cooking)
1 cup white sugar	½ cup raisins
1 cup brown sugar, firmly packed	½ cup chopped raw peanuts

Sift the flour and salt. In a large bowl, beat the butter, peanut butter and both sugars together until creamy. Add the eggs, milk and vanilla and mix well. Stir in the flour, then the oats, raisins and peanuts. Drop by rounded tablespoonfuls onto ungreased baking trays, about 7 cm (3 inches) apart. Bake in a preheated moderate oven (180°C/350°F) for 15 minutes, or until golden brown. Cool on wire racks. *Makes about 42*

Vanilla Snaps

A thin, crisp biscuit that's so useful to serve with ice-cream, stewed fruit and creamy desserts. Makes dozens!

250 g (8 oz) butter, softened	½ teaspoon salt
1 cup sugar	2 eggs
2 teaspoons vanilla essence	2½ cups self-raising flour

Cream the butter and sugar until light and fluffy. Blend in the vanilla and salt. Add the eggs one at a time, beating well, then stir in the flour. Drop from a teaspoon, 5 cm (2 inches) apart, onto cool ungreased baking trays. Flatten with the bottom of a glass dipped in flour. Bake in a moderate oven (180°C/350°F) for 8 to 10 minutes, or until a pale straw colour. Remove at once and cool on wire racks. *Makes 7 to 8 dozen*

Apple Dapples

These interesting biscuits are like tiny tarts with an apple filling and little 'lids' of biscuit mixture.

1 cup finely chopped unpeeled apple	2 eggs
¼ cup raisins	2 cups flour, sifted
¼ cup chopped walnuts	2 teaspoons baking powder
½ cup sugar	½ teaspoon salt
2 tablespoons water	1 teaspoon cinnamon
250 g (8 oz) butter, softened	½ teaspoon ground cloves
1 cup brown sugar, firmly packed	½ cup milk
	2 cups rolled oats (quick-cooking)

Place the apple, raisins, walnuts, sugar and water in a small saucepan and cook and stir until the apple is tender, about 5 minutes. Cream the butter and sugar together, and beat in the eggs one at a time. Sift the flour with the baking powder, salt and spices. Add to the creamed mixture alternately with milk. Stir in the oats.

Put ¾ cup of the dough aside. Drop the remainder from a teaspoon onto greased baking trays. Make a hollow in the centre of each biscuit with the back of a spoon, add a little apple filling, and top with a dab of reserved dough. Bake in a preheated moderately hot oven (190°C/375°F) for 10 to 12 minutes, until crisp and golden. Cool on wire racks. *Makes about 3 dozen*

Butternut Wafers

These are very thin, crisp lacy biscuits. It is just as well the recipe makes such a lot, because most people find them hard to resist.

125 g (4 oz) butter, softened	1 teaspoon baking powder
1 cup brown sugar, firmly packed	½ teaspoon salt
1 teaspoon vanilla essence	½ cup very finely chopped nuts (e.g., almonds, walnuts, Brazils, pecans)
1 egg	
¾ cup flour, sifted	

Cream the butter and sugar, then add the vanilla and egg and beat until light. Sift the flour with the baking powder and salt and add to the creamed mixture with the nuts. Drop by scant teaspoonfuls, 5 cm (2 inches) apart, onto ungreased baking trays. Bake in a preheated hot oven (200°C/400°F) for 5 minutes, until crisp and golden. (Watch carefully, they mustn't colour too much.) Cool for 30 seconds on the trays, then remove to wire racks to finish cooling. *Makes about 6 dozen*

Muesli-Sesame Biscuits

Sesame seeds provide flavouring and extra crunch in these economical, nutritious biscuits.

¼ cup sesame seeds	125 g (4 oz) butter
¾ cup muesli (untoasted kind)	1 tablespoon golden syrup
1 cup sugar	1½ teaspoons bicarbonate of
1 cup flour, sifted	soda
pinch of salt	2 tablespoons boiling water

Spread the sesame seeds on a flat ovenproof dish, place in a medium oven and toast until golden. You can toast them under the grill, if preferred, but watch carefully in case they burn. Cool.

Combine the sesame seeds, muesli, sugar, flour and salt in a large bowl. Melt the butter in a small saucepan over a very low heat, add the golden syrup and mix well. Remove from the stove and stir in bicarbonate of soda and boiling water. Add this mixture to the dry ingredients and stir until blended. Drop by teaspoonfuls onto greased baking trays, 5 cm (2 inches) apart, and bake in a slow oven (150°C/300°F) for 20 minutes, or until golden brown. Leave on trays for 1 to 2 minutes to set, then carefully remove with a spatula to wire racks. *Makes 3 dozen*

Variations

Butterscotch Muesli Biscuits Use 1 cup firmly packed brown sugar instead of white sugar.

Spice Biscuits Add 1 teaspoon ground cardamom, ½ teaspoon ginger and ½ teaspoon ground cloves.

Jam Sandwiches

These drop cookies have a firmer texture than most, and will need to be pushed off the spoon. To get biscuits of the same size, use a standard measuring teaspoon, and chill the dough for 20 minutes in very hot weather. Fill only when required.

½ cup self-raising flour	FILLING:
½ cup cornflour	30 g (1 oz) butter, softened
pinch of salt	3 tablespoons icing sugar
125 g (4 oz) butter	few drops vanilla essence
2 tablespoons icing sugar	raspberry jam for spreading
½ teaspoon vanilla essence	

Sift the flour, cornflour and salt together. Cream the butter with the icing sugar and vanilla and beat until light. Add half the flour to the butter mixture and combine, then add the remaining flour and mix to a smooth dough. Place teaspoons of the mixture on greased baking trays and flatten a little with a fork. Bake in a preheated moderate oven (180°C/350°F) for 15 to 20 minutes, or until pale golden. Leave to cool.

For the filling beat the butter, sugar and vanilla together until light and creamy. When required, sandwich the biscuits together in pairs with jam and cream filling. *Makes about 30*

Variation

Chocolate Mint Sandwiches Sandwich biscuits with the above filling, adding 2 teaspoons cocoa with the icing sugar. Place a thin chocolate mint (after-dinner mint) in between. Rich, but delicious with coffee.

At the back: Peanut Oaties; In front: Butternut Wafers and Jam Sandwiches

Refrigerator Biscuits

Welcome to one of the most useful and versatile of modern cookery ideas – refrigerator biscuits. Dough is moulded into a roll, chilled to make it firm for easy slicing, then simply cut into biscuits as required. (Uncooked dough keeps for up to 2 weeks in the refrigerator and months in the freezer.)

They are not only quick to make, but have a delicate texture because chilling permits a reduction in flour content. And as they're so easy to slice thinly, refrigerator biscuits are economical – one roll of dough makes dozens!

Experiment with different ideas once you have mastered this interesting biscuit technique. For example, you can roll two sheets of different coloured dough together, to give a pretty pinwheel effect when the roll is sliced. Nuts can be combined with the dough, or the entire roll can be rolled in crushed nuts before chilling for a crunchy border to each biscuit.

I am also including recipes for another type of refrigerator biscuit. The dough is not moulded, but simply chilled before cooking to help the biscuits stay a good shape during baking. Once again, it is a delicate mixture with a minimum of flour, giving a light, lacy texture.

Herb and Coconut Slices

These little savoury biscuits have the interesting flavour of fresh herbs and a coconut topping.

1 cup self-raising flour	125 g (4 oz) butter, softened
1 teaspoon salt	¾ cup grated Parmesan cheese
½ teaspoon cayenne	¾ cup desiccated coconut
2 teaspoons finely chopped fresh rosemary, thyme or oregano	

Sift the flour, salt and cayenne into a bowl. Mix in the herbs, then rub in the butter and cheese. The mixture will form a soft dough. Shape into a roll about 3.5 cm (1½ inches) in diameter, wrap in foil and chill for several hours or overnight.

Cut into thin slices and sprinkle with coconut (pressing lightly into tops of biscuits). Bake on greased trays in a preheated moderately hot oven (190°C/375°F) until lightly browned, about 15 minutes. *Makes about 24*

Butternuts

These crisp little slices contain no flour. The nuts can be ground in an electric blender or food processor fitted with the steel blade, but be careful to process only until finely chopped – you don't want a paste.

1½ cups almonds or pecans, ground	1 egg white, lightly beaten
1 cup brown sugar	1½ teaspoons butter

Combine all the ingredients in a saucepan, and stir over a low heat until well blended. Cool the mixture, then form into a roll about 2.5 cm (1 inch) in diameter. Wrap in foil, chill for several hours and cut in thin slices.

Bake on well-greased trays in a preheated slow oven (160°C/325°F) for 30 to 40 minutes, or until delicately browned. Leave on the trays to cool. *Makes about 3½ dozen*

Sesame Cheese Bites

Keep a roll of this dough in the refrigerator or freezer over the holidays, or whenever you might have guests calling in. In 15 minutes, you'll have hot, crisp biscuits to serve with drinks.

2 tablespoons sesame seeds	1½ cups flour
185 g (6 oz) butter, softened	1 teaspoon curry powder
1½ cups finely grated mature Cheddar cheese	1 teaspoon salt
¼ cup grated Parmesan cheese	pinch of cayenne
	4 tablespoons poppy seeds

Toast the sesame seeds in an ungreased frying pan over medium heat, stirring until they turn golden. Set aside to cool. Cream the butter and cheeses together until soft. Sift the flour with the curry powder, salt and cayenne and work into the butter mixture with the toasted sesame seeds. Form into a roll about 3.5 cm (1½ inches) in diameter and roll in the poppy seeds, coating all over. Wrap in foil and chill for several hours or overnight (or refrigerate or freeze until required).

Cut in slices about 5 mm (¼ inch) thick and bake on greased trays in a preheated moderately hot oven (190°C/375°F) until golden, about 15 minutes. Cool a little on the trays, then remove to wire racks to finish cooling. *Makes about 3 dozen*

Variations

Instead of rolling the dough in poppy seeds, it can be rolled in crushed nuts or a light dusting of paprika.

Pinwheel Cookies

125 g (4 oz) butter, softened	¼ teaspoon salt
1 cup sugar	1½ teaspoons baking powder
1 egg, beaten	½ cup crushed nuts
½ teaspoon grated lemon rind	30 g (1 oz) dark chocolate, melted over hot water
1½ cups flour	

Cream the butter and sugar until light and fluffy, and mix in the egg and lemon rind. Sift the flour with salt and baking powder and stir into the creamed mixture (if it seems too soft, add a little more flour, but no more than ¼ cup). Stir in the nuts, then divide the dough in half. Blend the melted chocolate into one half, then wrap both balls of dough in foil, and chill in the refrigerator for half an hour. Roll dough out on a lightly floured board into oblongs about 3 mm (⅛ inch) thick. Place the chocolate dough on top of the white dough, trim the edges to make an even rectangle, and roll up. Wrap in foil, chill for several hours or overnight, then cut into thin slices.

Bake on greased baking trays in a preheated moderately hot oven (190°C/375°F) for about 10 minutes, or until the white part is lightly browned. Cool for a minute on trays before removing to wire racks. *Makes about 40*

Variation

The dark dough may be flavoured with 1½ teaspoons of instant coffee instead of chocolate.

Jelly Bean Gems

The sliced biscuits are decorated with jelly beans, making them a special treat for the younger set. Discard (or eat) the black ones, which may stain the biscuits during baking.

250 g (8 oz) butter, softened	1 teaspoon cream of tartar
1½ cups icing sugar, sifted	¼ teaspoon salt
1 teaspoon vanilla essence	1 cup jelly beans, cut into
1 egg	pieces or slices
2½ cups flour	
1 teaspoon bicarbonate of soda	

Cream the butter with the icing sugar and vanilla, and beat in the egg. Sift the flour with the bicarbonate, cream of tartar and salt. Gradually stir into the creamed mixture and blend well. Shape the dough into a roll about 5 cm (2 inches) in diameter and 30 cm (12 inches) long. Wrap in greaseproof paper or foil and chill for several hours or overnight.

Cut into 5 mm (¼ inch) slices and place on ungreased baking trays. Decorate the tops with jelly beans, pressing lightly into dough. Bake in a preheated moderately hot oven (190°C/375°F) until lightly browned, about 12 minutes. Cool for a minute on trays before removing to wire racks. *Makes about 4 dozen*

Lemon Lace Cookies

Very delicate biscuits with oatmeal for texture and lemon for extra flavour.

125 g (4 oz) butter, softened	½ teaspoon lemon essence
½ cup white sugar	about ¾ cup flour
½ cup brown sugar, firmly packed	½ teaspoon bicarbonate of soda
1 egg	½ teaspoon salt
1 tablespoon milk	1 cup rolled oats (plain or quick-cooking)
1½ teaspoons grated lemon rind	

Either side: Lemon Lace Cookies; In the middle: Whisky Wafers

Cream the butter with the white and brown sugars. Beat in the egg, milk, lemon rind and essence. Sift the flour with the bicarbonate and salt and blend into the creamed mixture, adding a little more flour if the dough seems too soft (but no more than ¼ cup). Work in the rolled oats with the hands. Chill for several hours.

Using two teaspoons dipped in hot water, spoon the mixture onto greased trays and flatten slightly. Bake in a preheated moderately hot oven (190°C/375°F) for 10 minutes, or until lightly browned on top. Allow to cool for a minute on the trays before removing to wire racks. *Makes about 5 dozen*

Whisky Wafers

These are lovely biscuits to pass with coffee for a party, or to serve with ice-cream.

⅔ cup honey	½ teaspoon ground cloves
1 cup sugar	½ teaspoon ground cardamom
60 g (2 oz) butter	½ cup whisky
2½ cups flour	1 cup blanched slivered almonds
1 teaspoon baking powder	
½ teaspoon bicarbonate of soda	1 cup chopped mixed peel
2 teaspoons cinnamon	

Place the honey, sugar and butter in a saucepan and heat gently until the butter melts, stirring constantly. Remove from the heat and cool to lukewarm. Sift the flour with the baking powder, bicarbonate and spices, and stir into the butter mixture. Add the whisky, almonds and peel and blend well. Chill for several hours.

Using two teaspoons dipped in hot water, spoon the mixture onto greased trays and flatten slightly. Bake in a preheated moderately hot oven (190°C/375°F) for 10 minutes, or until lightly browned on top. Allow to cool for a minute on the trays before removing. *Makes about 70*

Bars and Slices

Biscuits made by this method are baked in the tin, cooled a little, then cut into the desired shapes. Be sure to follow the tin sizes recommended, because this will affect the texture of the finished biscuit.

Grandma's Best Chocolate Bars

2½ cups brown sugar, firmly
   packed
6 eggs
125 g (4 oz) dark chocolate,
   grated
3 cups flour
1 tablespoon cinnamon
1½ teaspoons ground cloves

1 teaspoon allspice
1 teaspoon bicarbonate of soda
1 teaspoon salt
½ cup honey
2 cups chopped candied peel
½ cup chopped blanched
   almonds
Chocolate Icing (see below)

Preheat the oven to moderate (180°C/350°F) and grease two 23 × 33 cm (9 × 13 inch) tins.

Sift the sugar to remove any lumps. Beat the eggs until light, then gradually beat in the sugar and stir in the chocolate. Sift together the flour, cinnamon, cloves, allspice, bicarbonate and salt. Add to the egg mixture alternately with the honey, beginning and ending with flour. Stir in the candied peel and almonds. Spread the dough evenly in the two tins, and bake for 25 minutes, or until a skewer inserted in the mixture comes out clean. Cool in the tins, then ice with chocolate icing and cut into bars. *Makes about 9 dozen 2.5 × 5 cm (1 × 2 inch) bars*

Chocolate Icing

90 g (3 oz) dark chocolate
30 g (1 oz) butter
¼ cup hot black coffee
1 egg, lightly beaten

pinch of salt
1 teaspoon vanilla essence
about 2½ cups icing sugar,
   sifted

Place the chocolate and butter in a saucepan over simmering water, and stir until melted. Remove from the heat and blend in the coffee, egg, salt and vanilla. When cool, stir in the icing sugar until the mixture is a good spreading consistency.

Orange Date Slices

60 g (2 oz) butter, softened
½ cup brown sugar, firmly
   packed
1 egg
2 teaspoons grated orange rind
1 cup flour

½ teaspoon baking powder
½ teaspoon bicarbonate of soda
¼ cup orange juice
½ cup chopped walnuts
½ cup chopped dates
icing sugar

Cream the butter and sugar, then stir in the egg and orange rind. Sift the flour with the baking powder and bicarbonate and add to the creamed mixture alternately with the orange juice. Stir in the nuts and dates, and spread in a greased 28 × 18 cm (11 × 7 inch) shallow tin. Bake in a preheated moderate oven (180°C/350°F) for 25 minutes. When cold, sprinkle with icing sugar and cut into bars. *Makes 24*

Peanut Slices and Chocolate Toffee Bars

Rich Fruit Bars

250 g (8 oz) butter, softened	4 tablespoons sugar
⅔ cup sugar	4 tablespoons water
1 egg	1 teaspoon grated lemon rind
1 teaspoon vanilla essence	pinch of salt
2½ cups flour, sifted	½ teaspoon cinnamon
½ teaspoon salt	30 g (1 oz) butter
FILLING:	1 tablespoon dark rum
1 cup mixed fruit	

Cream the butter and sugar; beat in the egg and vanilla and stir in the flour and salt. Wrap the dough and chill for several hours.

To make the filling, place all the ingredients in a saucepan, except the rum, and simmer until thick, stirring often. Stir in the rum. Cool completely before using.

Divide the dough into two pieces, one a little larger than the other. Roll the larger to a rectangle 23 × 33 cm (9 × 13 inches). Place on a greased baking tray and spread with the filling almost to the edges. Roll out the second piece of dough and cover the filling completely, pinching edges to seal. Bake in a preheated moderate oven (180°C/350°F) for 25 minutes. Cut into bars when cold. *Makes 32*

Peanut Slices

125 g (4 oz) butter, softened	TOPPING:
¼ cup sugar	2¼ cups finely chopped
1 egg	unsalted peanuts
½ teaspoon vanilla essence	1 cup sugar
1¼ cups flour, sifted	1 teaspoon cinnamon
pinch of salt	2 teaspoons grated lemon rind
¾ cup raspberry jam (optional)	4 egg whites, lightly beaten

Cream together the butter and sugar, then beat in the egg and vanilla. Sift the flour with the salt and add in three parts to the butter mixture, blending well each time. Pat the dough into a greased 23 × 33 cm (9 × 13 inch) shallow tin. Bake in a preheated moderate oven (180°C/350°F) for 15 minutes, until set but not cooked.

Meanwhile make the topping. Place all the ingredients in a large saucepan and combine well. Cook over gentle heat, stirring all the time, until the sugar has dissolved. Increase the heat slightly and continue cooking and stirring until the mixture leaves the sides of the pan.

Spread the pastry with jam, if using, and then with nut topping. Bake for a further 15 minutes, until the pastry is crisp and the topping firm. Cut into slices when cold. *Makes about 4 dozen 2.5 × 5 cm (1 × 2 inch) slices*

Chocolate Toffee Bars

250 g (8 oz) butter, softened	1 teaspoon vanilla essence
1 cup brown sugar, firmly packed	2 cups flour, sifted
	1 cup chocolate bits
1 egg yolk	1 cup chopped walnuts

Cream the butter and sugar; beat in the egg yolk and vanilla, then stir in the remaining ingredients. Pat into an ungreased tin about 31 × 21 × 2.5 cm (12½ × 8 × 1 inch). Bake in a preheated moderate oven (180°C/350°F) for 20 minutes. Cut into bars while warm, then cool in the tin. *Makes about 4 dozen 2.5 × 5 cm (1 × 2 inch) bars*

Biscuits for Keeping

Homemade biscuits are so delicious it's hard to keep the cookie jar full. You rarely need to worry whether they'll keep or not! However, if you're in the mood for baking a double batch, or want to send biscuits to someone as a delicious 'message from home', here are recipes for biscuits that are easy to store and stay fresh for days or more.

A hint on packing biscuits for posting:

Bars and slices should be individually wrapped in foil. Wrap other biscuits individually in plastic film, then place inside a plastic bag and tie firmly. Make a bed of popcorn in a cardboard box and place the biscuits on top. Fill all nooks and crannies with popcorn right to the lid. Secure the lid with tape, and then wrap the box in brown paper. Your biscuits should arrive crisp, fresh and unbroken.

Marmalade Chews

90 g (3 oz) butter, softened	½ cup thick marmalade
⅔ cup sugar	1½ cups flour
1 egg	1½ teaspoons baking powder

Cream the butter and sugar until light. Beat in the egg and marmalade. Sift the flour with the baking powder and stir into the creamed mixture. If it seems too soft, add a little more flour; if too dry, add a touch more marmalade. Drop the batter from a teaspoon onto greased baking trays, spacing the biscuits well apart.

Bake in a preheated moderately hot oven (190°C/375°F) for about 8 minutes, or until golden brown on top and firm underneath. Cool for a minute on the trays, then finish cooling on a wire rack. *Makes about 4 dozen*

Light Peppernuts

125 g (4 oz) butter	1 teaspoon cinnamon
½ cup sugar	⅛ teaspoon crushed anise seeds
2 eggs, well beaten	⅛ teaspoon ground cardamom
1 cup flour	¼ cup ground almonds
¼ teaspoon salt	1¾ cups chopped mixed peel
¼ teaspoon bicarbonate of soda	
½ teaspoon each black pepper, nutmeg, ground cloves and allspice	

Cream the butter and sugar well together, then gradually beat in the eggs. Sift the flour with salt, bicarbonate and spices and stir into the creamed mixture. Add the almonds and peel and mix well. Drop the dough by teaspoonfuls onto well-greased baking trays, leaving about 5 cm (2 inches) between the biscuits to allow for spreading. Bake in a preheated moderate oven (180°C/350°F) for 10 to 12 minutes, until brown on top and crisp on the edges. Cool a little on the trays, then remove to wire racks. *Makes about 3 dozen*

Little Rocks

125 g (4 oz) butter, softened	1 teaspoon nutmeg
¾ cup brown sugar, firmly packed	pinch of salt
2 eggs	¼ cup sherry or orange juice
1½ cups wholemeal flour	½ cup raisins
½ teaspoon bicarbonate of soda	1 cup coarsely chopped blanched almonds
1 teaspoon cinnamon	½ cup chopped dried apricots

Cream the butter and sugar until soft, then beat in the eggs one at a time. Sift the flour with the bicarbonate, cinnamon, nutmeg and salt and add to the creamed mixture alternately with the sherry or orange juice. Stir in the raisins, nuts and apricots. Drop the mixture from a teaspoon onto well-greased baking trays, and bake in a preheated moderately hot oven (190°C/375°F) for 12 minutes, or until golden on top. *Makes about 30*

Chocolate Kisses

No-one will guess how you made these delicious biscuits!

¼ cup sugar	⅔ cup sugar
30 g (1 oz) dark chocolate	3 tablespoons crushed, salted, crisp crackers (type used as a base for cheese or savouries)
2 egg whites	
½ teaspoon vanilla essence	
¼ teaspoon cream of tartar	

Place the ¼ cup of sugar and chocolate in a small bowl over simmering water and stir until melted. Put aside to cool. Beat the egg whites until stiff; add the vanilla and cream of tartar, then beat in the ⅔ cup of sugar, little by little. Gently fold in the melted chocolate and crushed cracker biscuits.

Drop from a teaspoon onto well-greased baking trays, and bake in a preheated moderate oven (180°C/350°F) for 10 to 12 minutes. (They are cooked when a glazed puff has formed on top of a biscuit base.) Allow to cool a little on the trays, then transfer with a spatula to racks to finish cooling. *Makes about 5 dozen*

Currant Cakes

These large round biscuits are often called Easter cakes. At Easter time they are offered as gifts, tied in bundles with ribbon.

4 cups flour	1 cup currants
½ teaspoon bicarbonate of soda	2 eggs, beaten
¼ teaspoon salt	1 teaspoon vanilla essence
125 g (4 oz) butter	1 egg white, lightly beaten
125 g (4 oz) lard	sugar for sprinkling
½ cup caster sugar	

Sift the flour, bicarbonate and salt into a mixing bowl. Cut the butter and lard into small pieces and rub into the flour until the mixture resembles coarse breadcrumbs. Stir in the sugar, currants, eggs and vanilla, mixing to a dough.

Knead lightly on a floured board and roll out thinly. Brush with egg white and sprinkle with sugar. Cut into rounds about 7.5 cm (3 inches) across, and arrange on greased baking trays. Bake in a preheated moderate oven (180°C/350°F) for 15 minutes, until golden. Cool for a minute on the trays, then transfer to wire racks. *Makes about 5 dozen*

Gingerbread Ladies and Gentlemen

Gingerbread Men

These children's favourites keep well if wrapped individually in plastic film and then stored in an airtight container. (They also freeze beautifully, so can be made well ahead for parties.) You can make fat gingerbread men by moulding the dough into shapes; for trimmer gentlemen, the dough is rolled out and stamped with a cutter. Either way, they have that marvellous, old-fashioned gingerbread flavour.

60 g (2 oz) butter, softened	1 teaspoon ground ginger
½ cup brown sugar, firmly packed	¼ teaspoon ground cloves
½ cup golden syrup	½ teaspoon salt
3½ cups flour	about ⅓ cup water
1 teaspoon bicarbonate of soda	currants, cherries, silver cachous, icing, etc., to decorate
1 teaspoon cinnamon	¼ cup icing sugar

Cream the butter and sugar well, then mix in the golden syrup. Sift the flour with the bicarbonate, spices and salt and add to the creamed mixture in three parts, alternately with the water. (Use just enough water to give a firm but pliable dough.)

For fat gingerbread men, use the modelling method: roll a small ball for the head, a larger one for the body, and cylinders for arms and legs. Stick them together on a greased tray, overlapping the pieces and pressing firmly so they won't come apart during baking.

If you have a gingerbread cutter, roll the dough out thinly and stamp out the figures. Or you can make a pattern out of stiff cardboard and cut around it with a sharp knife.

Decorate before baking with currants for eyes, a piece of cherry for a mouth, silver cachous for buttons, etc. (Other decorations may be added later with icing.) Bake on greased trays in a preheated moderate oven (180°C/350°F) for 8 minutes or longer, depending on thickness. Test to see if they are cooked by pressing with a finger – the dough should spring back. Remove and cool on a wire rack.

Mix the icing sugar to a thick paste with a few drops of water. Then use a toothpick dipped in the thick icing to add details to faces and bodies: hair, caps, moustaches, belts, shoes, etc. *Makes about eight 12.5 cm (5 inch) fat men, or 16 thin ones.*

Magic Batters

If you want a sure-fire success, bake a sweet or savoury batter. These are the great dishes of the people, developed not by chefs but in farm and village kitchens. Many of the names – Toad-in-the-Hole, Popovers, Yorkshire Pudding – suggest their homely origins. There's something about the crisp golden crust and the promise of delight within, that makes them not only top favourites with children but irresistible to even the most sophisticated grown-ups.

Basic Batter

1 cup flour	*1 egg*
pinch of salt	*1¼ cups milk*

For instructions on making the batter by hand, see the step-by-step pictures below. It may also be made by putting all the ingredients into a blender, egg and milk first, then flour and salt, and blending until smooth; or by putting the dry ingredients into a food processor fitted with the steel blade, then adding egg and milk through the feed tube with the motor running and processing until smooth.

Basic Batter

1 Sift the flour and salt into a mixing bowl and make a well in the centre so that you see the bottom of the bowl. Put in the egg and about one-third of the milk and stir them together with a wooden spatula or spoon.

2 Use a rapid circular motion, gradually extending it to allow the flour to wash into the liquid, little by little. It should fall in a thin film onto the surface. Add more liquid as more flour is drawn in.

3 When all the flour is incorporated, stir in the remaining milk and beat the batter with a whisk or a rotary beater until very smooth with bubbles on top. Cover and leave to stand for at least 30 minutes to allow the flour grains to swell. The batter may stand for several hours if you wish.

Yorkshire Pudding

Make Basic Batter and stand for at least 30 minutes. It may thicken as it stands. Check the consistency and stir in a little water, if needed, to make it like that of very thick cream, just dropping from the spoon. Pour into a jug.

Brush muffin tins generously with melted butter or dripping and place them on the top shelf of a preheated hot oven (220°C/425°F) for a few minutes until the fat begins to smoke. Remove from the oven, stir the batter and pour in quickly to fill each tin about two-thirds full.

Replace in the top of the oven and bake for 15 to 20 minutes or until well risen, crisp and golden brown. Serve immediately as an accompaniment to roast beef. *Makes 12*
NOTE: If you prefer, make one large pudding and cut it into squares. In this case, heat 2 or 3 tablespoons of dripping in a baking tin 25 × 23 × 5 cm (10 × 9 × 2 inches) and bake as above.

Toad-in-the-Hole

Make Basic Batter and stand for 30 minutes. Check the consistency and correct it, if necessary, as for Yorkshire Pudding.

Put 8 large sausages into a small roasting tin or baking dish about 25 × 23 × 5 cm (10 × 9 × 2 inches) and bake just above centre in a preheated hot oven (220°C/425°F) for 7 to 8 minutes, turning two or three times until browned all over. Arrange the sausages evenly spaced in the dish, stir the batter and pour it over. Replace in the oven and bake for 20 to 30 minutes or until well risen, crisp and golden brown. Serve immediately, with Onion Gravy if you wish. *Serves 4*
Onion Gravy Peel and chop a medium onion. Fry in 2 tablespoons butter or dripping until soft, then stir in 1½ tablespoons of flour and cook gently, stirring, for 1 minute. Remove from the heat, cool a little and blend in 1½ cups of warm stock, stirring until smoothly mixed. Return to the heat and stir until boiling. Season with salt and pepper.

Variations

This hearty dish seems always to be made with sausages nowadays, but there are recipes going back a century or more which use other meats. Try ham steaks spread with mustard, or boned lamb chops browned quickly on both sides and spread with chutney. Arrange in the baking dish, pour batter over and bake as above. You could also substitute well-seasoned cooked vegetables for meat.

*Toad-in-the-Hole; Clafoutis Limousin;
Apple Batter Pudding*

Clafoutis Limousin

Clafoutis is made when the cherries are ripe in the Limousin region of France. It may also be made with plums, apricots, apples or pears, either fresh or canned.

500 g (1 lb) ripe cherries	2 eggs
¼ cup flour	1¼ cups milk
pinch of salt	1 tablespoon Kirsch or rum
3 tablespoons caster sugar	45 g (1½ oz) butter

Stem the cherries and stone them if you wish (use a cherry pitter or cut in half). Sift the flour and salt into a mixing bowl and stir in 2 tablespoons of sugar. Blend in the eggs, milk and Kirsch or rum as described in the method for Basic Batter. Cover and stand for 30 minutes.

Melt the butter and use some to brush a shallow 4–5 cup baking dish. Whisk the remaining butter into the batter. Put the cherries into the dish and pour the batter over. Place on the centre shelf of a preheated hot oven (220°C/425°F) and bake for 30 to 35 minutes, or until golden brown and set. Sprinkle with the remaining sugar and serve warm. *Serves 4 to 6*

Apple Batter Pudding

Make Basic Batter and allow to stand for 30 minutes. Check the consistency and correct it, if necessary, as for Yorkshire Pudding.

Peel, core and thickly slice 500 g (1 lb) cooking apples. Generously butter a shallow 6-cup ovenproof dish and place it just above the centre in a preheated hot oven (220°C/425°F) for 5 minutes to heat. Put in the apples and sprinkle generously with brown sugar. Return the dish to the oven for 10 minutes. Stir the batter and pour it over the apples.

Bake for 30 minutes or until well risen and golden brown. Dredge with caster sugar and serve immediately with ice-cream, custard or cream. *Serves 4 to 6*

Popovers

An American specialty – crisp little batters that puff up like magic!

2 eggs	¼ teaspoon salt
1 cup milk	1 tablespoon vegetable oil
1 cup flour, sifted	

Place the eggs in a mixing bowl. Add the milk, flour and salt and beat all together with a rotary beater, just until smooth. Add the oil and beat for 30 seconds more. Do not over beat. Cover and stand for 30 minutes.

Generously grease 8 deep muffin tins. Fill two-thirds full and bake in a preheated very hot oven (250°C/475°F) for 15 minutes; then, without opening the door, reduce the heat to moderate (180°C/350°F) and bake for a further 20 to 25 minutes until browned and firm. A few minutes before removing from the oven, prick each popover gently with a skewer or sharp pointed knife to allow steam to escape. Serve immediately, with butter and jam or honey for morning tea, or for breakfast with grilled sausages and bacon. *Makes 8*

Triumphant Soufflés

Do make up your mind to become adept at soufflés. As always, success is simply a matter of knowing the rules and following them. Soufflés acquired a reputation for temperament in the days when the heat of the oven was a matter for expert judgement; but today, when the turn of a knob gives precisely the right temperature, any cook can experience the pleasure of producing this most triumphant of dishes.

A soufflé does have to be eaten as soon as it's ready, and it's sensible to give everyone due warning. However, it's my experience that family and guests alike are so charmed at the prospect of a soufflé that they cooperate beautifully.

Traditional soufflés are based on a thick, flavoured sauce, into which stiffly beaten egg whites are folded. When the mixture is baked, the air trapped in the whites expands and the soufflé puffs up.

Another style which is especially light and delicate is made with egg whites folded directly into a fruit or vegetable purée.

Checkpoints

The main point to watch when making a soufflé is that the egg whites are beaten correctly. The whites should be at room temperature and must have no trace of yolk, and the bowl and beaters must be dry and free of grease.

Beat the whites until foamy, add cream of tartar and beat to a velvety snow. Test by gathering a little mixture on the beater and holding it upright: at the right consistency, the beaten whites will stand on the beater in a firm peak with a slightly drooping top. If they sag, beat a little longer and test again. Don't beat past the stage described or the whites will begin to break down, becoming brittle and dry and losing their ability to trap air.

Have the sauce or purée base warm. (If you have made it ahead, stand the bowl in warm water.) Stir a big spoonful of the whites into the base mixture to lighten it, then scoop the rest of the whites onto the surface and fold in by cutting down through the mixture with a large metal spoon or rubber spatula. Lift some of the mixture up and over onto the top each time, but don't try to be too thorough. Folding in the whites should only take a minute or so. The mixture will blend a little more as you turn it into the soufflé dish.

Cheese Soufflé

Serve as a first course or light luncheon dish.

45 g (1½ oz) butter	freshly ground pepper
3 tablespoons flour	pinch of cayenne
1 cup warm milk	pinch of nutmeg
45 g (1½ oz) freshly grated	4 egg yolks
Parmesan cheese	5 egg whites
½ teaspoon salt	½ teaspoon cream of tartar

Have the eggs at room temperature. To prepare and bake, see step-by-step pictures below. *Serves 4*

Cheese Soufflé

1 Butter an 18 cm (7 inch) soufflé dish. Cut a doubled sheet of greaseproof paper long enough to wrap around the dish and overlap by 5 cm (2 inches). It should be deep enough to extend 5 cm (2 inches) above the rim. Butter the paper and tie firmly with string just under the rim of the dish. (Tie with a bow for quick removal.) Place a baking tray on a shelf in the centre of the oven and set the oven to hot (200°C/400°F).

2 Melt the butter, stir in the flour and cook over low heat for 1 minute. Remove from heat, cool a little, and blend in milk, stirring until smooth. Return to heat and stir until boiling, then take from heat and stir in the cheese and seasonings. Beat in the egg yolks, one at a time. Whisk the egg whites with cream of tartar until firm but not brittle (see introduction) and fold into the cheese mixture.

3 Pour the mixture into the prepared dish, tap the bottom of the dish lightly on the work surface to expel any large air pockets, and smooth the top of the soufflé. Quickly run a spoon around the top of the mixture about 2.5 cm (1 inch) from the edge to make the soufflé rise evenly in a 'crown'. Immediately place the soufflé dish on the baking tray in the centre of the oven, close the door gently, and turn the oven down to moderately hot (190°C/375°F). Do not open the oven door for the next 20 minutes.

4 Bake the soufflé until it is well puffed up, golden brown on top and just firm, about 24 minutes. Have a heated serving platter ready and a warmed serving spoon and fork. Place the soufflé dish on the platter, remove the paper and take immediately to the table. To serve, pierce the top lightly with the spoon and fork held vertically, and spread the soufflé apart. Include some of the outside crust and some of the creamy centre with each serving.

Chocolate Soufflé

Chocolate Soufflé

This is one of the classic sweet soufflés – an impressive dessert.

125 g (4 oz) plain dark chocolate	*2–3 tablespoons dark rum or coffee-flavoured liqueur*
4 tablespoons black coffee	*½ teaspoon vanilla essence*
45 g (1½ oz) butter	*3 egg yolks*
4½ tablespoons flour	*4 egg whites*
1 cup warm milk	*pinch of cream of tartar*
¼ cup caster sugar	*sifted icing sugar for dredging*

Prepare a 15 cm (6 inch) soufflé dish and set the oven as in Step 1, opposite page. Chop the chocolate and melt with the coffee in a small bowl over a pan of hot, not boiling, water.

Melt the butter, stir in the flour and cook over a low heat for 1 minute. Remove from the heat, cool a little, then blend in the milk and sugar, stirring until smooth. Return to the heat and stir until boiling, then remove from the heat and stir in the melted chocolate, rum or liqueur and vanilla. Beat in the egg yolks one at a time. Whisk the egg whites with cream of tartar until firm but not brittle, and fold into the chocolate mixture. (For instructions on folding mixture, see Checkpoints on opposite page.)

Turn the mixture into the prepared dish and bake as directed in Steps 3 and 4. When the soufflé is cooked, dredge the top with icing sugar before removing the paper. Serve with cream or custard flavoured with vanilla, coffee, sherry or coffee liqueur. *Serves 4*

Delicate Banana Soufflé

This soufflé is easier to make than the conventional one because it uses only egg whites. However, it is more fragile than soufflés based on a sauce, and tends to fall rapidly when taken from the oven. The lovely flavour won't be affected, and the texture is light and delicious, but be warned that the 'high-rise' look may be fleeting!

This is one of my favourite ways of dealing with small amounts of fruit or vegetable purées. Instead of the bananas you may use 1½ cups of well-drained, puréed peaches, apricots, prunes, plums or apples for another version of a dessert soufflé. Or you can use puréed spinach, broccoli or green peas for a savoury soufflé to serve as a first course or light luncheon dish. In this case, you will of course omit the sugar and add salt, freshly ground pepper and grated nutmeg to taste.

5–6 ripe bananas (1½ cups when mashed)	*2 tablespoons slivered almonds or chopped walnuts*
grated rind and juice of 1 medium orange	*4 egg whites*
1 tablespoon lemon juice	*pinch of salt*
½ cup caster sugar	*pinch of cream of tartar*

Peel the bananas and mash with a fork. Add the orange rind and juice, lemon juice, sugar and nuts. Whip the egg whites to a firm snow with the salt and cream of tartar, then gently fold into the banana mixture. Turn at once into a prepared soufflé dish (see Step 1 on opposite page) and bake in a preheated moderate oven (180°C/350°F) for 25 to 30 minutes, or until well risen, golden brown and firm on top. Remove the paper collar and serve immediately with whipped cream or ice-cream. *Serves 4*

The Cheesecake Theme

Each country seems to have its own favourite cheesecake, from the light Curd Cake of Austria to the chocolate and rum confections of the United States. They can be filled with cottage cheese or cream cheese and baked in a pastry shell or with a biscuit crust. The unifying theme is the subtle cheese flavour, which has made cheesecake one of the most popular desserts in the world. The following recipes illustrate just a few of the deliciously endless variations on 'the cheesecake theme'.

Manhattan Cheesecake

A superb blend of cream cheese, Ricotta and sour cream.

2 × 250 g packets Philadelphia cream cheese	3 tablespoons cornflour
500 g (1 lb) Ricotta cheese	2 teaspoons vanilla essence
1½ cups sugar	2 teaspoons grated lemon rind
4 large eggs	2 cups light sour cream
60 g (2 oz) butter, melted	TOPPING (OPTIONAL):
3 tablespoons flour	2 cups cream, whipped
	freshly grated nutmeg

Have the cream cheese at room temperature, and beat in a large bowl until soft and creamy. Beat in the Ricotta and sugar, then add the eggs one at a time, beating well after each addition. Add the butter, flour, cornflour, vanilla and lemon rind, and combine well. Fold in the sour cream and pour the mixture into an ungreased 23 cm (9 inch) springform pan.

Bake on the middle shelf of a preheated moderately slow oven (160°C/325°F) for 1 hour. (The cake will still be soft in the centre at this stage.) Turn off the heat, but do not open the oven door, and leave the cake in the closed oven for 2 hours. Remove the cake to a rack and allow it to cool in the pan, then chill for at least 2 hours. Remove the sides of the pan and transfer the cake to a serving dish. If you like, top with whipped cream and grate fresh nutmeg over.

Mexican Cheesecake

A chocolate crust enfolds a cheesecake flavoured with coffee liqueur.

BAKED CRUMB CRUST:	1 teaspoon cinnamon
1½ cups plain chocolate biscuit crumbs	pinch of salt
⅓ cup sugar	2 × 250 g packets of Philadelphia cream cheese, softened
125 g (4 oz) butter, melted	
FILLING:	3 large egg whites
½ cup coffee-flavoured liqueur	pinch each cream of tartar and salt
½ cup cold water	
2 tablespoons gelatine	1 cup cream
3 large egg yolks	grated chocolate, to decorate
¼ cup sugar	
2 teaspoons instant coffee dissolved in 1 tablespoon hot water	

Combine all the ingredients for the crumb crust and press the mixture into the base of a 23 cm (9 inch) springform pan and halfway up the sides. Bake in a preheated moderate oven (180°C/350°F) for 8 minutes. Remove and place the pan on a rack to cool.

Choose a bowl that will fit into the top of a saucepan. Combine the liqueur and cold water in the bowl, sprinkle with gelatine, and leave for 10 minutes to soften. Beat in the egg yolks one at a time. Add the sugar, coffee, cinnamon and salt and mix well. Set the bowl over boiling water (the bottom mustn't touch the water) and beat the mixture until it begins to thicken, about 5 minutes. Remove from the heat and cool a little.

Place the softened cream cheese in a large bowl and beat until light and fluffy. Add the gelatine mixture, combine well, and chill for 30 minutes.

Have the egg whites at room temperature and beat with a pinch of salt and cream of tartar until they form stiff peaks. In another bowl, whip the cream until stiff. Fold the egg whites and cream into the chilled cheese mixture, then turn into the prepared crust and chill for at least 3 hours to set the filling. Remove the sides of the springform pan, transfer the cake to a serving dish, and decorate with grated chocolate.

Double Chocolate Cheesecake

Luscious chocolate filling baked in a chocolate crust. The topping is rum-flavoured whipped cream.

1 baked crumb crust (see Mexican Cheesecake)	2 tablespoons cornflour
FILLING:	1 teaspoon cinnamon
1 cup cream	1 teaspoon vanilla essence
250 g (8 oz) dark chocolate, chopped	4 egg whites (at room temperature)
4 large egg yolks (at room temperature)	pinch each cream of tartar and salt
½ cup sugar	TOPPING:
3 × 250 g packets Philadelphia cream cheese, softened	1½ cups cream
	1 tablespoon icing sugar
1 cup light sour cream	1 tablespoon dark rum
	chocolate buttons or curls

Bring the cream just to the boil in a saucepan, remove from the heat and cool for 2 minutes. Add the chocolate and stir until the chocolate is melted.

Beat the egg yolks in another bowl until light and foamy, then beat in the sugar until the mixture is thick. Add the chocolate mixture and stir until well blended.

Place the cream cheese, sour cream, cornflour, cinnamon and vanilla in a food processor fitted with the steel blade, and blend until creamy. Alternatively, beat together by hand.

Combine the cheese mixture with the chocolate mixture. Beat the egg whites with the cream of tartar and salt until they stand in stiff peaks, then gently fold into the chocolate-cheese mixture. Pour into the crust. Bake in a preheated slow oven (150°C/300°F) for 1½ hours. Turn off the heat, but do not open the oven door, and leave the cake to cool completely. When cooled, chill for at least 2 hours. Remove the sides of the pan and spread the top of the cake with the cream whipped with icing sugar and rum. Decorate with chocolate buttons or curls and transfer to a plate for serving.

Manhattan Cheesecake

Almond Cheesecake with Sour Cream Topping

An unforgettable cheesecake for a special celebration.

CRUMB CRUST:
$\frac{3}{4}$ cup plain biscuit crumbs
$\frac{1}{2}$ cup ground almonds
125 g (4 oz) butter, melted
3 tablespoons sugar
FILLING:
2 × 250 g packets Philadelphia cream cheese
$\frac{2}{3}$ cup sugar
3 large eggs
$\frac{1}{2}$ cup ground almonds
1 teaspoon almond essence
pinch of salt
TOPPING:
1 cup sour cream
3 tablespoons sugar
$\frac{1}{2}$ teaspoon almond essence
$\frac{1}{2}$ teaspoon vanilla essence
TO DECORATE:
$1\frac{1}{2}$ cups cream, whipped
toasted whole almonds

Combine all the ingredients for the crumb crust and press on the bottom and halfway up the sides of a 23 cm (9 inch) springform pan. Chill.

Beat the cheese until light. Beat in the sugar and eggs, one at a time. Add the almonds, almond essence and salt. Pour into the crust and bake on the middle shelf of a preheated moderate oven (180°C/350°F) for 45 minutes. Cool in the tin on a wire rack for 20 minutes.

Combine the topping ingredients and spread evenly over the cake. Return to a moderate oven and bake for 10 minutes. Cool on a wire rack, then chill for at least 2 hours. Remove from the pan and decorate with cream and almonds.

Austrian Curd Cake

This mixture is not quite as rich as the usual cheesecake. It is made with cottage cheese, ground almonds and semolina.

$1\frac{1}{2}$ cups cottage cheese
75 g ($2\frac{1}{2}$ oz) butter
$\frac{2}{3}$ cup caster sugar
2 eggs, separated
$\frac{1}{2}$ cup raisins
30 g (1 oz) ground almonds
2 tablespoons semolina
grated rind and juice of 1 medium lemon
sifted icing sugar

Set the oven at moderately hot (190°C/375°F). Grease the base of an 18 cm (7 inch) sandwich tin and line with greased greaseproof paper.

Rub the cheese through a fine sieve. Cream the butter and gradually add the sugar, beating well after each addition. Add the sieved cheese bit by bit, beating until light and fluffy. Beat the egg yolks lightly, add to the mixture and beat well again. Blend in the raisins, almonds, semolina, lemon rind and juice. Beat the egg whites until stiff peaks form, then lightly fold them into the creamed mixture. Spoon into the prepared tin and bake for 50 to 60 minutes, or until a rich golden brown. Allow to cool in the tin on a wire rack, then carefully transfer to a serving plate and dust with sifted icing sugar.

Pavlovas, Meringues and Heavenly Pies

In this day of the electric mixer, show-off meringue cakes and desserts have become effortless to make. They are all based on egg whites, sugar and lots of air, and they're easy so long as you understand the basic rules. What's more, in spite of their delicacy they freeze beautifully, or can be stored unfrozen for a few days in an airtight tin (but count on only one day in damp weather).

Use whites from eggs at least a few days old; very fresh whites will not achieve good volume. Egg whites which have been stored in the refrigerator or freezer tend to be thin, but they still beat up very well if you bring them to room temperature beforehand.

Do make sure that beaters and bowl are clean, dry and free from grease, and that there is no trace of yolk in the whites. Yolks contain fat and even a little yolk will prevent the whites from whisking stiffly.

Don't beat egg whites and leave them standing. Have everything ready before you start so that you can shape and bake the meringue immediately, before the air bubbles begin to break down.

Meringues Chantilly

2 large egg whites	1 teaspoon caster sugar
¼ cup caster sugar	few drops vanilla essence
FILLING:	chopped walnuts, to finish
½ cup cream	(optional)

To prepare and bake, see step-by-step pictures at right.

Meringues Chantilly

Meringues Chantilly

1 Place a shelf in the coolest part of the oven and set oven to cool (120°C/250°F). Line a baking tray with non-stick cooking parchment. Alternatively, grease and flour the pan: brush with melted lard or unsalted butter or oil, or spray with cooking spray; dredge with flour, rap to distribute flour evenly, then reverse and rap once to dislodge excess flour. Using a rotary beater or an electric mixer, beat the egg whites until they form soft peaks. Sift 2 tablespoons caster sugar over the whites and beat again until the mixture is stiff and shiny.

3 Take 2 dessertspoons or tablespoons (depending on the size you want the meringues) and, with one, scoop up a heaped spoonful of the mixture. With the other spoon, scoop the meringue out onto the baking tray to form a half-egg shape. Neaten with a knife dipped in cold water. If preferred, the meringue can be formed by piping, using a large plain or rose nozzle. Dredge with caster sugar and bake for about 1 hour in a very cool oven (120°C/250°F) until a delicate beige colour. Peel the parchment off the meringues, if used, or lift carefully off the tray with a thin knife.

2 Sift half the remaining sugar over the whites and, using a large metal spoon, fold it in. To do this, cut gently down through the mixture and lift some mixture up and over onto the top, repeating until the whites and sugar are lightly mixed. Don't worry about mixing thoroughly; it is important not to over work the meringue or the air bubbles will break down. Shaping the meringues will mix the whites and sugar a little more.

4 Gently press the base of each meringue, while still warm, to make a hollow. Replace upside down on the tray and return to the oven for a further 30 minutes to complete cooking. Cool on a wire rack. An hour or two before required, whip the cream with sugar and vanilla until stiff, and use to sandwich the meringues together in pairs. The cream may be piped or spread on. Place in the refrigerator until serving time. If you wish, sprinkle chopped walnuts on the cream just before serving.

Peach Meringue Pie

Make this when you want to impress. It would be lovely, too, with fresh raspberries, strawberries or other fresh or canned fruit such as plums or apricots. Be sure that canned fruits are very well drained. The finished masterpiece can wait in the refrigerator for an hour or two before serving.

4 egg whites
1 cup caster sugar
½ cup cream
1 cup sliced fresh or canned peaches

chopped pistachio nuts, to decorate

To prepare and cook, see step-by-step pictures below.

mixture into the other circle and spread it evenly into a flat disc.

Peach Meringue Pie

Hazelnut Pavlova

4 egg whites
pinch of salt
1½ cups caster sugar
1½ teaspoons vinegar
1½ teaspoons vanilla essence
1 cup ground hazelnuts (see note)

Chocolate Sauce, to serve (see below)
TO DECORATE:
whipped cream
chopped hazelnuts

Oil and flour a 23 cm (9 inch) springform pan and set the oven at slow (150°C/300°F).

Beat the egg whites and salt using an electric mixer at full speed, until they stand in peaks. Sift the sugar and sprinkle in 1 tablespoon at a time, beating each time. Stop when all the sugar has been added. Lastly, fold in the vinegar, vanilla and ground hazelnuts. Put into the prepared tin. If using an electric oven, bake for 1 hour, then turn the heat off and leave the Pavlova in the oven until cold. If using a gas oven, bake for 1 hour, turn the heat to 120°C/250°F for a further 30 minutes and then turn the heat off and leave the Pavlova in the oven until cold.

When the Pavlova is cold, remove from the tin. The Pavlova will collapse slightly. Before serving, decorate with whipped cream, spoon some of the chocolate sauce over and sprinkle with chopped hazelnuts. Serve the remaining sauce separately.
NOTE: For best flavour, grind the hazelnuts freshly yourself. Use a small rotary hand grinder, the kind that also grates cheese; or put them through the grating blade of a food processor. Alternatively, grind them in several batches in a blender, by dropping them through the hole in the lid onto the blades going at high speed, then switching off quickly before the nuts are blended to a paste.

Chocolate Sauce

90 g (3 oz) dark cooking chocolate
¼ cup sugar
1 teaspoon cocoa

¾ cup water
piece of vanilla pod or vanilla essence

Chop the chocolate into small pieces and put into a large saucepan with the sugar, cocoa and half the water. Stir over a moderate heat until boiling and the chocolate is dissolved. Simmer for 2 to 3 minutes, then add the rest of the water and vanilla to taste. Simmer for a further 15 to 20 minutes or until the sauce is syrupy. Serve cold.

Peach Meringue Pie
1 Place a shelf in the coolest part of the oven and set the oven to 140°C/275°F. Line a baking tray with non-stick cooking parchment or greaseproof paper. Draw on it in pencil two circles 18 cm (7 inches) in diameter. Lightly grease with melted lard or unsalted butter or oil, or spray with cooking spray. Make meringue mixture as for Meringues Chantilly.

2 Fit a large plain or rose nozzle into a forcing bag and fill it with meringue (see page 235 for detailed instructions). Pipe a ring of meringue round one circle just inside the pencilled line. Pipe onto the paper 8 to 12 baby rosettes with bases the same width as the meringue ring. Pipe the remaining meringue

3 Bake the meringue for 1 hour or until crisp when tapped. Remove from the oven, lift off the rosettes with a thin knife and place on a rack. Turn the paper upside down and carefully peel it off the meringue ring and disc. (If you try to prise these pieces off the paper, they are likely to splinter.) Lift very carefully and place on a rack to cool.

4 Shortly before serving, whip the cream until stiff and fill into a forcing bag fitted with a 1 cm (½ inch) rose nozzle. Place the meringue disc on the serving plate and pipe a ring of cream round the edge. Set the meringue ring on top and press down very gently. Arrange the peach slices inside the ring in concentric circles. Pipe a little cream on the base of each rosette and arrange the rosettes evenly spaced on the ring, pressing each down gently to secure. Pipe the remaining cream in rosettes round the ring to decorate, and top with chopped pistachios. Chill until serving time.

Meringue Crust

This basic crisp crust can be used with a variety of luscious fillings.

2 egg whites	½ cup finely chopped walnuts
pinch of salt	or pecans
pinch of cream of tartar	½ teaspoon vanilla essence
½ cup sugar	

Beat the egg whites with the salt and cream of tartar until light and foamy. Add the sugar 2 tablespoons at a time, beating well after each addition. Continue to beat until the mixture stands in soft peaks, then fold in the nuts and vanilla.

Grease a 20 cm (8 inch) pie plate lightly and spoon in the meringue. Make a depression in the middle and mould the edges up slightly so they come about 1 cm (½inch) up the sides of the pie plate, but not over the rim. Bake the meringue in a preheated slow oven (150°C/300°F) for 50 to 55 minutes, or until crisp and a light straw colour. Cool in the plate before filling.

German Sweet Chocolate Pie

Meringue Crust (see above)	1 cup cream
FILLING:	chocolate curls, buttons or
125 g (4 oz) cooking chocolate	squares, to decorate (see
3 tablespoons water	below)
1 teaspoon vanilla essence	

Roughly chop the chocolate and place with the water in a small bowl. Set over hot water on a low heat and stir until the chocolate has softened. Leave to cool, then add the vanilla essence. Whip the cream and fold the chocolate mixture into it. Pile into the cooled meringue crust and chill in the refrigerator for 2 hours before serving.

Decorate with chocolate curls, buttons or squares.

Variations

Add 1 teaspoon instant coffee to the melted chocolate and continue as above. Or add 1 tablespoon cognac with the vanilla and continue as above.

Chocolate Decorations

Chocolate buttons or thin squares are available from good delicatessens. To make chocolate curls, see page 215.

Apricot Cream Pie

Meringue Crust (see above)	1¼ cups cream
FILLING:	8–10 ripe apricots or 1 × 425 g
3 egg yolks	can apricots, drained
⅓ cup caster sugar	
finely grated rind and juice of	
1 lemon	

Cream the egg yolks and sugar in a small basin and blend in the lemon rind and juice. Place over a saucepan of very hot, but not boiling, water. Cook, whisking constantly, until the mixture forms a thick, smooth cream. Cool completely.

Whip the cream until it holds its shape; don't over beat. Fold all except a few spoonfuls of cream into the cold lemon mixture.

Remove the stones from the apricots and cut into thin slices. Fold through the lemon cream, saving a few slices for decoration. Fill into the cooled meringue crust and decorate with the reserved whipped cream and apricot slices.

Basic Pavlova

This is the traditional recipe for Australia's favourite Pavlova – crisp on the outside, and with a delicate marshmallow texture inside.

6 egg whites	1½ teaspoons vinegar
pinch of salt	1½ teaspoons vanilla essence
2 cups caster sugar, sifted	fruit filling (see below)

If you have a gas oven, set the temperature to very hot (220°C/450°F) before starting to mix the Pavlova. Just before you put the Pavlova in the oven, reduce the temperature to slow (150°C/300°F). If you have an electric oven, preheat the oven to slow from the beginning.

Beat the egg whites with salt, using a rotary beater or an electric mixer set at the highest speed. When soft peaks form, add the sugar, a tablespoon at a time, beating well between each addition. Stop beating when the last tablespoon of sugar has been added, and lightly fold in the vinegar and vanilla.

Draw a circle 18 cm (7 inches) in diameter on greaseproof paper or aluminium foil and place on a baking tray. Brush the paper with oil. Heap the Pavlova mixture into the circle and use the back of a spoon to make a slight depression in the centre, moulding up the sides a little so there will be room for the topping.

Place the Pavlova in the oven (remembering to turn the heat down if using a gas oven) and bake for 40 to 50 minutes, until crisp on top and a pale straw colour. Turn off the heat and leave in the oven until cold.

Suggested Fillings

Top the Pavlova generously with whipped cream and then with your choice of fruit. Passionfruit and strawberries, kiwi fruit, fresh or canned peaches, plums or apricots, or sliced banana dipped in lemon juice and sprinkled with toasted coconut are all delicious. Drain canned fruits well.

NOTE: For a party, you might like to sprinkle the Pavlova with blanched slivered almonds before baking. They will toast to a golden brown, adding crunch as well as flavour.

Apricot Pavlova

10 dried apricots	APRICOT SAUCE:
4 egg whites	125 g (4 oz) dried apricots
pinch of salt	1½ cups water
1 cup sugar	½ cup sugar
	icing sugar, to sweeten

Make an apricot purée by simmering the dried apricots in a saucepan with water to cover for about 30 minutes, or until very tender. Drain, and push through a sieve. (You should have ¼ cup purée.)

Beat the egg whites and salt until they stand in peaks, then gradually whisk in the sugar, a little at a time. Fold a little of the meringue into the cooled apricot purée and, when it is incorporated, fold into the remaining meringue. Do this gently and evenly. Spread onto a prepared tray and bake in a preheated slow oven (150°C/300°F) for 1½ hours, until crisp on the outside.

Meanwhile, prepare the sauce. Cook the dried apricots in the water for 15 minutes. Add the sugar and simmer for about 3 minutes. Strain the syrup off and reserve. Push the apricots through a nylon sieve with a metal spoon. Measure the reserved syrup and, if necessary, add water to make up to 1 cup liquid. Stir in the apricot purée and sweeten to taste with icing sugar, then leave to cool. Serve the Pavlova with the apricot sauce and, if you like, whipped cream.

Gâteau Rolla

A magnificent meringue cake layered with a rich butter cream.

4 egg whites
⅛ teaspoon cream of tartar
1½ cups caster sugar
½ cup ground almonds
icing sugar for dusting

MOCHA BUTTER CREAM:
2 egg yolks
½ cup sugar
½ cup warm milk
2 tablespoons cocoa
125 g (4 oz) chocolate
250 g (8 oz) butter

Beat the egg whites and cream of tartar with an electric beater until they stand in stiff peaks. Add 2 tablespoons sugar and continue to beat for a few minutes. Fold in the remaining sugar and ground almonds with a metal spoon.

Cut out 4 rounds of baking paper (you can get Bakewell paper at good kitchen shops) 20 cm (8 inches) in diameter. Spray with a cooking spray or oil lightly. Spread each round with meringue and cook on a baking tray in a slow oven (150°C/300°F) for 15 minutes, or until the meringue is dry on top. Turn the layers over and continue baking for 5 minutes until the tops are dry. Cool before sandwiching with mocha butter cream.

Pavlova

Place the egg yolks and sugar in a bowl over hot, but not boiling, water and beat until thick and lemon-coloured. Gradually add the milk and cocoa. Add the roughly chopped chocolate and blend in to soften, beating well. Allow to cool. Cream the butter until it resembles whipped cream, and gradually beat in the cooled custard.

Spread the filling on three of the meringue layers and sandwich together with the fourth layer on top. Make a lattice of 2.5 cm (1 inch) wide strips of paper on top of the cake and dust over the icing sugar. Carefully remove the paper and you will have a pretty pattern. Refrigerate for 24 hours before serving.

Extra Ideas for Fillings

Meringue crusts are delicious with Lemon Cream (equal parts of lemon cheese and whipped cream folded together). Or you can fold 2–3 sliced bananas through your favourite thick custard for a Banana Cream Pie (top with whipped cream and a sprinkle of nutmeg).

For a quick and easy filling, soften a small carton of vanilla ice-cream and fold in crushed peanut brittle, grated chocolate, or a few spoonfuls of strawberry jam.

The Joys of Home-Baked Bread

Home-baked bread gives pleasure all year round. It fills the house with an aroma that is both reviving and soothing. Kneading and baking the dough is a uniquely satisfying and creative experience for the cook, and the crusty loaves are as good to eat as they are to look at.

There is time involved in baking bread, but most of it is 'waiting' time, so you can be doing other things, or just relaxing, while the dough is rising and proving.

Don't be put off by the apparent length of the recipes. Once you have made a few loaves you will discover the basic procedures are generally the same, and only the ingredients vary. The whole process soon becomes automatic, and then you can discover endless pleasure in creating new flavours, shapes and textures for your delicious home-baked bread.

Here are a few simple hints to help you achieve perfection:

Yeast: Fresh compressed yeast is available from most cake shops and health food shops. Well wrapped, it will keep for several days in the refrigerator. Dried yeast, sold in granular form in packets, is obtainable in supermarkets and delicatessens and will keep up to 6 months in a cool dry place. It is concentrated, so you need only approximately $2\frac{1}{2}$ teaspoons granular yeast for every 30 g (1 oz) of fresh yeast, but it must first be reconstituted in some of the water used in the recipe and it will take longer to raise the dough.

Flour: The right type of flour is important for successful bread-making. For white bread, try to get the special bread flour sold at health food shops. This is a 'strong' flour, which means it contains more gluten than plain white flour, and gives a better texture to your bread. For brown bread, you can use all wholemeal or a mixture of wholemeal and white flour. (All wholemeal produces a denser, more solid loaf.)

Kneading: This is an important step; it strengthens the dough and is essential if you want a light, fine texture and a well-risen loaf. The step-by-step pictures show the basic technique.

Rising: In most recipes, rising occurs twice, the first time when the dough is still in a ball and the second time after the bread is shaped into a loaf. When the dough rises the second time it is said to 'prove'.

Baking: Try to get the regulation bread tins. They give a good shape for slicing, and the quantities in recipes are worked out to suit them. You can use one 1 kg (2 lb) tin, or two 500 g (1 lb) tins. Health food shops stock them, as well as kitchen shops and department stores.

A Few Problems Explained

Whatever happens, your bread is going to taste delicious but it may not be quite as perfect as you'd hoped. Here are the reasons behind some common problems:

Crust too thick: A thick, tough crust means some water has been trapped underneath, which hardens the crust as it cools. This can be caused by insufficient sugar in the dough, or insufficient baking, or too low a baking temperature. Always check to see if the bread is cooked by turning it out of the pan and tapping the underside. It should sound hollow. If it is still soft, return it to the oven for further baking.

Loaf too crumbly: If the loaf is crumbly and difficult to slice you may have used too much liquid. Other causes are insufficient kneading, too low a baking temperature, or proving the dough for too long.

Texture too open (with holes) or too 'chewy': An open texture is usually caused by excess yeast, insufficient salt or not enough mixing. A too-dense texture means the loaf has been proven too rapidly (in too warm a place), the baking time was too short, or the oven temperature was too low.

Basic White Bread

6 cups white bread flour (strong white flour)	15 g ($\frac{1}{2}$ oz) fresh yeast, or $1\frac{1}{2}$ teaspoons dried yeast and 1
2 teaspoons salt	teaspoon caster sugar
15 g ($\frac{1}{2}$ oz) lard or butter	2 cups lukewarm water

To prepare and cook, see step-by-step pictures.

Basic White Bread

1 Sift the flour and salt into a warmed bowl and rub in the lard or butter. Cream the fresh yeast in a small bowl, and gradually blend in the lukewarm water. If using dried yeast, dissolve the caster sugar in the water, sprinkle the yeast on top and leave until frothy. Make a well in the centre of the flour and pour in the yeast liquid all at once. Stir from the centre with a wooden spoon, gradually stirring in a little extra flour each time, until all the flour is incorporated. Continue stirring until the dough leaves the sides of the bowl.

2 Gather the dough into a ball, then turn it out on a floured board and flatten slightly. Hold the front of the dough firmly with one hand, and with the other hand pull up the piece of dough on the other side, stretching it out and folding it over towards you.

Bread dough, finished White Bread and Dinner Rolls

3 Press the folded dough together, then push it away from you with a punching movement, using the heel of your hand. Give the dough a quarter turn and repeat the stretching, folding and punching, developing a rocking movement. This is called 'kneading' the dough, and should be continued until the dough feels firm and elastic and doesn't stick to the fingers – it will take at least 10 minutes.

4 Shape the dough into a round, and place it in a lightly oiled plastic bag big

enough to allow room for expansion. The dough is now left to rise, that is, to double in bulk as the yeast works. Rising will be more rapid if the dough is placed in a warm spot, on a sunny bench in the kitchen, near a warm oven or a sink full of hot water. Times are only approximate, but you can expect dough to double in bulk in an hour in a warm place, or 2 hours at room temperature.

5 Grease two 500 g (1 lb) bread tins or one 1 kg (2 lb) tin. For 2 small loaves, divide the risen dough into two pieces. Punch each one firmly, using the knuckles to knock out any air bubbles. (The technical name for this is – as you might expect – 'punching down'.) Knead each piece of dough for 3 minutes as before, then stretch into a rectangle with a width equal to the length of the tin. Fold

each piece of dough in three, or roll them up like a Swiss roll, and place in the tins with the join underneath. Pat them into shape to fit the corners. If you are making just the one loaf, treat the one quantity of dough in the same way.

6 Brush the tops of the loaves with lightly salted water. Place each loaf in a lightly oiled plastic bag, and again leave in a warm place to prove. (A loaf should be left until the dough reaches the top of the tin, and is springy to the touch.) Remove the tins from the bags, place on a baking tray, and again brush the tops with lightly salted water for a nice crisp crust. Bake in the centre of a preheated very hot oven (230°C/450°F) for 35 to 40 minutes, until loaves are well risen, golden brown, and have shrunk away slightly from the sides of the tins. As an extra check, tap the bottom

of the loaves – they should sound hollow. If they're not quite cooked, return to the oven for a further 5 minutes or so. Turn loaves out and cool on a wire tray.

Variations

Rich White Bread Instead of 2 cups water, use 1 cup milk and 1 cup water. Add a lightly beaten egg to the yeast mixture before incorporating with the flour, and sprinkle the top of the loaf with poppy seeds or sesame seeds before baking.

Dinner Rolls After the risen dough has been divided in half and 'punched down' (Step 5), shape each half into a round and divide into 6 or 8 equal portions. Roll each portion into a ball between floured hands, then press down on a floured board and flatten slightly. Arrange the rounds on a greased baking tray, allowing room between them for expansion, and cover with lightly oiled plastic. Leave until doubled in size, then bake in a preheated very hot oven (230°C/450°F) for 15 to 20 minutes, until crisp and golden, and hollow when tapped. *Makes 12 to 16*

Farmhouse Bread

Wholemeal bread flour (from health food stores) is best because of its high gluten content, but you will still get good results with ordinary wholemeal flour.

6 cups wholemeal bread flour	1¾ cups lukewarm water
2 teaspoons salt	1 tablespoon oil
1 tablespoon sugar	beaten egg, to glaze
30 g (1 oz) fresh yeast or 2½ teaspoons dried yeast	

Place the flour, salt and sugar in a warmed bowl and stir well to mix. Blend the yeast with a little of the water, then stir into the remaining water and add to the flour mixture with the oil. Mix to a soft dough.

Turn out onto a lightly floured surface and knead for 10 minutes, until the dough is smooth and doesn't stick to the fingers. Place the dough in a lightly oiled plastic bag that allows room for expansion, cover, and leave in a warm place for 1 hour, or until doubled in size.

Punch down firmly with the knuckles to remove air bubbles, then turn out onto a floured surface and knead again for 5 minutes. Divide the dough into two pieces. Pat each one out to a rectangle, then fold into three and place in greased 500 g (1 lb) bread tins. Cover with a damp cloth or lightly oiled plastic and leave in a warm place for 30 to 40 minutes, until the dough has risen to the tops of the tins. Brush the tops with beaten egg and bake in a preheated very hot oven (230°C/450°F) for 40 minutes, or until well risen, brown, and hollow when tapped on the bottom. Turn out onto a wire rack to cool. *Makes 2 × 500 g (1 lb) loaves*

High Fibre Loaf

5 cups wholemeal bread flour	2 cups lukewarm water
2 cups unprocessed bran (from health food shops)	1 tablespoon oil
1½ teaspoons salt	TOPPING:
1¼ teaspoons sugar	2 tablespoons cold water
30 g (1 oz) fresh yeast or 2½ teaspoons dried yeast	pinch of salt
	2 tablespoons rolled oats

Place the flour, bran, salt and sugar in a warm bowl and mix well. Blend the yeast with a little of the water, then stir into remaining water. Make a well in the centre of the dry ingredients and pour in the yeast liquid and oil. Stir from the centre outwards with a wooden spoon until all the flour is incorporated. Stir until the dough is firm and leaves the bowl cleanly.

Turn out onto a lightly floured surface and knead for 10 minutes until smooth and elastic. Shape the dough into a ball and place in a lightly oiled plastic bag, allowing room for expansion. Leave in a warm place for 1 hour, or until doubled in size.

Remove the dough and knead again on a floured surface for 5 minutes, then divide in half. Pat each piece of dough out into a rectangle, then fold into three or roll up like a Swiss roll. Place in greased 500 g (1 lb) bread tins, shaping to fit into the corners, and cover with greased plastic. Leave in a warm place for 30 minutes, until the dough has risen to the tops of the tins.

Mix the cold water and salt together and brush over the tops of the loaves, then sprinkle with rolled oats. Bake in a preheated very hot oven (230°C/450°F) for 35 to 40 minutes, until well risen, crisp on top and hollow when tapped. Turn out onto a wire rack to cool. *Makes 2 × 500 g (1 lb) loaves*

Wholemeal Buns

6 cups wholemeal bread flour	2 cups lukewarm water
1 teaspoon salt	1 tablespoon oil
1½ tablespoons sugar	a little extra flour
30 g (1 oz) fresh yeast or 2½ teaspoons dried yeast	

Place the flour, salt and sugar in a warmed bowl and mix well. Blend the yeast with a little of the water, then stir into the remaining water and add to the dry ingredients with the oil. Mix to a soft dough.

Turn out onto a lightly floured surface and knead for 10 minutes, until the dough is smooth and elastic and doesn't cling to the bowl. Place the dough in a warm greased bowl, turning it over to grease all surfaces, cover loosely with greased plastic wrap and leave for 1 hour or until doubled in bulk.

Punch the dough firmly to remove air bubbles, then turn out onto a floured surface and knead again for 5 minutes. Divide into 12 pieces and shape into round flat buns (like English muffins). Place them on warm, greased baking trays, sprinkle with a little wholemeal flour and cover with greased plastic wrap. Leave to rise in a warm place until doubled in size. Bake the buns in a preheated hot oven (220°C/425°F) for 15 minutes. Serve split and buttered, with cheese, honey or other fillings. *Makes 12*

Fruit Malt Loaf

This beautifully flavoured loaf keeps fresh for days wrapped in plastic and stored in a bread tin. Store in the refrigerator in hot, humid weather.

2 cups wholemeal bread flour	30 g (1 oz) fresh yeast or 2½ teaspoons dried yeast
½ teaspoon salt	
¾ cup sultanas	⅓ cup lukewarm water
60 g (2 oz) butter	1 tablespoon honey, to glaze
3 tablespoons malt extract	
1½ tablespoons molasses (both from health food shops)	

Place the flour, salt and sultanas in a warmed bowl and mix together. Place the butter, malt and molasses in a small saucepan and heat gently until the butter melts. Allow to cool for 5 minutes.

Blend the yeast with a little of the water, stir into the remaining water, then add to the dry ingredients with the butter-malt mixture. Stir with a wooden spoon until the dry ingredients are moistened and the mixture forms a soft dough.

Turn out onto a lightly floured surface and knead for 10 minutes until smooth and elastic. Place the dough in a warmed greased bowl, turning it to grease all surfaces, and cover with greased plastic wrap. Leave in a warm place for 1 hour or until doubled in size.

Punch down to knock out air bubbles, turn out onto a floured surface and knead again for 5 minutes. Pat the dough into a rectangle, fold into three, and fit into a warm, greased 500 g (1 lb) bread tin, shaping it into the corners. Cover with plastic or a clean cloth and leave in a warm place for 30 minutes, until the dough has risen to the top of the tin. Bake in a preheated hot oven (200°C/400°F) for 45 minutes. Turn out onto a wire rack, brush the top with honey and allow to cool. *Makes 1 × 500 g (1 lb) loaf*

Fruit Malt Loaf; High Fibre Loaf; Wholemeal Buns; Farmhouse Bread

Festive Breads

Colourful eggs nestling in buns and topped with the symbolic cross, little doves in flight, an almond-browned Swedish coffee ring; these are just a few of the yeast breads that play a special role in the celebrations of many lands. From a basic rich bread dough you can make many breads to serve at Christmas and Easter. Included in these triumphs are spicy and fruity Hot Cross Buns.

Hot Cross Buns

4 cups flour	*1 egg, lightly beaten*
1½ teaspoons mixed spice	PASTE:
1 teaspoon salt	*4 tablespoons flour*
60 g (2 oz) butter	*2 tablespoons cold water*
¾ cup currants or sultanas	GLAZE:
¼ cup chopped mixed peel	*¼ teaspoon gelatine*
30 g (1 oz) fresh yeast	*2 tablespoons water*
½ cup caster sugar	*1 tablespoon sugar*
1 cup lukewarm milk	

Sift the flour with the spice and salt into a bowl. Rub in the softened butter, then stir in the fruit and peel. Make a well in the centre. Cream the yeast with the sugar and add a little warm milk to dissolve the yeast completely. Add the remaining milk and pour, with the beaten egg, into the well in the flour. Mix to form a soft dough. Turn onto a lightly floured board and knead until smooth and elastic. Shape into a ball, then place in a greased bowl, and turn over so that the top of the dough is greased. Cover with a damp cloth and leave to rise in a warm place until doubled in bulk, 1 to 1½ hours.

Turn the risen dough onto a lightly floured surface and gently press out to 1 cm (½ inch) thickness. Divide into 12 to 14 even-size pieces and shape each into a ball. Place the buns in greased round cake tins. Cover and leave to rise in a warm place for a further 20 to 30 minutes.

Combine the flour and water and beat to a smooth paste. Fill into a greaseproof paper funnel or small piping bag and, just before baking, pipe the paste into a cross on the buns. Bake in a hot oven (200°C/400°F) for about 15 minutes.

Meanwhile, sprinkle the gelatine over the water in a small pan. When soft, dissolve over a low heat. Add the sugar and stir until dissolved.

Remove the buns from the oven and brush with the warm glaze while still hot. Stand near the turned-off open oven so that the glaze will dry on the buns. *Makes 12 to 14.*

Variation

If you prefer, omit the paste and decorate the buns with icing crosses; mix 1 cup of sifted icing sugar with about 2 teaspoons of hot milk to make a firm icing. Fill an icing bag fitted with a small plain nozzle and pipe crosses onto the warm glazed buns.

Sweet Bread Dough

From this basic dough you can make a lovely variety of sweet festive breads – add fruits, spices and icings as you wish.

4 cups flour	*30 g (1 oz) fresh yeast*
large pinch of salt	*½ cup caster sugar*
¾–1 cup milk	*2 eggs, beaten*
125 g (4 oz) butter	

Sift the flour with the salt into a large bowl. Heat ¾ cup milk to lukewarm, then add the butter and allow to melt. Add the milk and butter mixture to the yeast, stirring until dissolved. Mix in the sugar and eggs.

Make a well in the flour, pour in the milk and yeast mixture and mix until smooth and elastic, adding more milk if necessary to make a soft dough. Place the dough in a greased bowl, turning it over in the bowl so that it is lightly greased all over. Cover with a damp cloth and leave to rise in a warm place for 45 to 50 minutes or until doubled in bulk. Knock down the dough, pull sides to centre, turn it over, then cover and allow to rise again for 30 minutes before shaping and proving. *Makes 1 loaf, 6 to 8 large or 12 medium buns.*

Italian Festive Bread

Eggs are dyed with natural food colouring or Easter dye (from many Greek delicatessens) to decorate this rich Easter bread.

½ quantity Sweet Bread Dough	*½ teaspoon aniseed (optional)*
¼ cup finely chopped mixed peel	*3 raw eggs in shell (coloured or plain)*
¼ cup chopped blanched almonds	*Glacé Icing (see Folares) chopped nuts, to decorate*

Prepare the sweet bread dough and leave in a warm place to rise. After the second rising, turn out onto a floured board. Combine the peel, almonds and aniseed, if using, and knead into the dough.

Divide the dough in half and roll each half into a rope about 60 cm (24 inches) long. Twist the ropes loosely together and shape in a ring on a large greased baking tray. Arrange the eggs in the hollows of the loaf. Cover with a cloth and leave in a warm place to rise, about 30 to 40 minutes. Set the oven at moderately hot (190°C/375°F). Bake the bread for 30 to 35 minutes. Remove to a wire rack to cool, coating with the icing while still warm and sprinkling with chopped nuts.

Easter Dove Bread

Visit Rome at Easter time and you will be entranced by the symbolically shaped breads, a favourite being a dove.

½ quantity Sweet Bread Dough	*1 egg, lightly beaten*
8 cloves	

Prepare the dough and allow to rise. After the second rising, punch it down and roll out on a lightly floured board to 1 cm (½ inch) thickness. Cut the dough into strips 2.5 cm (1 inch) wide and roll each into a rope 23 cm (9 inches) long. Tie each rope into a loose knot with one end short. Pinch the short end to shape a head and beak, and press a clove in the head for an eye. Flatten the other end for the tail and snip the end 2 or 3 times for the feathers.

Brush with lightly beaten egg and allow to rise. Bake in a preheated hot oven (200°C/400°F) for 15 minutes. *Makes 8*

Folares

At Easter time these little bread baskets, each one with its own coloured egg, are part of the breakfast scene in Portugal.

½ quantity Sweet Bread Dough	*Soft Glacé Icing (see below)*
6 coloured eggs (see below)	

Prepare the dough and allow it to rise. After the second rising, turn it onto a floured board and punch down lightly, then divide it into 6 even pieces. Cut off about a quarter of each piece and reserve. Form the large pieces into balls and flatten down into rounds about 1 cm (½ inch) thick. Put an egg in the centre of each round. Divide each of the remaining small pieces of dough in half and roll each half into a rope about 15 cm (6 inches) long. Cross two of the dough ropes over each egg and seal the ends by pressing onto the base of the bun.

Put the rounds on a buttered baking tray, cover them, and leave to rise in a warm place for about 30 minutes, or until doubled in bulk. Bake the Folares in a preheated moderate oven (180°C/350°F) for 25 to 30 minutes, or until golden brown. Brush icing over the bread while still warm. Serve warm. *Makes 6*
Coloured Eggs Dye the raw eggs with either natural food colouring or Easter egg dye, a powder obtainable from many Greek delicatessens. Use small bowls and allow 2 eggs to each, cover with water and add the dye. Stand until you get the required colour. Lift the eggs and allow to dry off before using.
Soft Glacé Icing Mix ½ cup sifted icing sugar with 1 tablespoon boiling water to make a smooth paste of a running consistency. Tint a pale pink, if you wish, and add a squeeze of lemon juice. NOTE: To have Folares freshly baked for your Easter breakfast, make the dough and give it its first rising the day before. Then knock down, cover, and place it in the refrigerator for a slow second rising overnight. Shape and bake in the morning.

Swedish Coffee Bread Ring

Almonds flavour and decorate this beautiful Easter bread. It can be prepared ahead of time, frozen and reheated.

½ quantity Sweet Bread Dough	TOPPING:
MARZIPAN FILLING:	*1 egg white, lightly beaten*
250 g (8 oz) marzipan	*3 tablespoons flaked almonds*
30 g (1 oz) butter	*1 tablespoon caster sugar*
2 egg yolks	
½ cup crushed almond macaroons	

Prepare the dough and allow it to rise. After the second rising, turn it onto a floured board, punch down lightly to release any bubbles and roll it out into a 20 × 45 cm (8 × 18 inch) rectangle.

To make the marzipan filling, soften the marzipan with the butter and egg yolks, and add the macaroons, mixing well.

Spread the filling over the dough, roll it up lengthwise and place on a buttered baking tray, seam side down, pinching the ends together to form a ring. With a pair of scissors, snip the dough almost to the centre of the ring at 2 cm (¾ inch) intervals. Pull and twist each slice, laying it flat on the baking tray, to form a wreath.

Cover the dough and leave to rise in a warm place for about 30 minutes, or until it is doubled in bulk. Brush with the egg white, and sprinkle with flaked almonds and sugar. Bake in a preheated moderately hot oven (190°C/375°F) for about 30 minutes or until golden brown. Transfer the wreath to a rack and serve it warm.

Quick Breads

The marvellous thing about quick breads is that they really are so quick! Scones, coffee cakes, savoury loaves and muffins are mixed with a light touch for melt-in-the-mouth texture. They're at their best fresh from the oven, so, if possible, enjoy them while they're still warm.

Old-Fashioned Scones

3 cups self-raising flour	60 g (2 oz) butter
1 teaspoon salt	1 cup milk
2 teaspoons sugar	

Set the oven at very hot (230°C/450°F) and arrange a shelf in the top third of the oven.

Sift the flour and salt into a bowl, then stir in the sugar and rub in the butter. Make a well in the centre and add the milk in a steady stream, stirring in the flour to make a soft dough. Knead lightly on a floured surface, then pat into a rectangle about 2 cm (¾ inch) thick. Cut into squares, or into rounds with a 4 cm (1½ inch) floured cutter. Arrange on a lightly greased scone tray, and brush the tops with a little milk to glaze. Bake for 12 to 15 minutes, until well risen and golden brown. *Makes 12*
NOTE: If you like scones with crisp tops, serve straight from the oven. For softer scones, wrap in a clean tea-towel for 5 minutes before serving.

Apple Cider Muffins

2 cups flour	185 g (6 oz) butter, melted
1 tablespoon baking powder	1 egg, lightly beaten
¼ teaspoon salt	TOPPING:
½ cup raisins	¼ cup sugar
1 cup apple cider (plain or alcoholic)	1½ teaspoons cinnamon

Sift the flour, baking powder and salt into a bowl and stir in the raisins. Combine the cider, butter and beaten egg and pour over the flour mixture. Stir lightly just until the flour is moistened – the batter will still be lumpy. Spoon into greased muffin tins, filling them two-thirds full. Combine the sugar and cinnamon and sprinkle over the batter. Bake in a preheated hot oven (200°C/400°F) for 20 to 25 minutes, or until well risen and golden brown. *Makes 12*

Savoury Olive Bread

Serve sliced with a salad, or make into sandwiches with slices of cheese in between.

2 eggs	2 cups flour
1 cup stuffed green olives, coarsely chopped	1 tablespoon sugar
2 tablespoons olive oil	2 teaspoons baking powder
½ cup milk	¼ teaspoon salt

Brush a 20 × 10 cm (8 × 4 inch) loaf pan with olive oil and line with greased greaseproof paper.

Beat the eggs until frothy and stir in the chopped olives, oil and milk. Sift the flour, sugar, baking powder and salt together and add the egg mixture, stirring lightly just until the flour is moistened – be careful not to over mix. Spoon into the prepared tin and bake in a preheated moderate oven (180°C/350°F) for 1 hour, or until hollow when tapped. Leave in the tin for a minute, then turn onto a wire rack to cool.

Superb Banana Bread

This is the best banana bread recipe I know. It has a rich, moist texture and deep banana flavour.

125 g (4 oz) butter	¼ cup thick sour cream
1⅓ cups brown sugar, firmly packed	¾ cup wholemeal flour
	¾ cup plain flour
2 eggs, lightly beaten	¼ teaspoon salt
1 teaspoon vanilla essence	1 cup mashed, ripe bananas (about 3–4)
1 teaspoon bicarbonate of soda	

Grease a 25 × 10 cm (10 × 4 inch) loaf pan, and line the base and long sides with greased greaseproof paper.

Cream the butter and sugar until light and fluffy, then add the eggs and vanilla and combine well. Dissolve the bicarbonate in the sour cream and stir into the butter mixture. Sift the flours with salt and add to the mixture with the mashed bananas, stirring until well blended. Bake in a preheated moderate oven (180°C/350°F) for 1 hour, or until a skewer inserted in the centre comes out clean. Cool in the tin for a minute then turn onto a wire rack.

Jasmine Tea Bread

You'll find jasmine tea at Chinese groceries and health food shops. Use 1 teaspoon to ½ cup boiling water.

60 g (2 oz) butter	1 teaspoon baking powder
¾ cup sugar	1 teaspoon bicarbonate of soda
1 egg, beaten	
1 tablespoon grated orange rind	pinch of salt
	½ teaspoon cinnamon
1 teaspoon each grated lemon and lime rind, or 2 teaspoons lemon rind	½ cup orange juice
	½ cup cooled jasmine tea
	½ cup chopped pecans or walnuts
3 cups flour	

Grease a 25 × 10 cm (10 × 4 inch) loaf pan and line with greased greaseproof paper.

Cream the butter and sugar until light and fluffy, then stir in the egg and grated rinds. Sift together the flour, baking powder, bicarbonate, salt and cinnamon. Add to the butter mixture with the juice and tea, stirring until combined, then fold in the chopped nuts. Spoon into the prepared tin and bake in a preheated moderate oven (180°C/350°F) for 45 minutes, or until a skewer comes out clean. Cool in the tin for a minute, then turn onto a wire rack. Serve cold, sliced and buttered.

From front to back:
Savoury Olive Bread; Apple Cider
Muffins; Jasmine Tea Bread

Better Baking

A pot-pourri of hints, explanations and techniques to help you enjoy your baking even more.

Ingredients Used in this Book

Eggs: Unless otherwise stated, all the eggs used in the recipes are medium-size – that is, 55 g.

Fats: Butter is the fat nominated in most recipes, but you may substitute cooking margarine if desired (the firm type of margarine), or use half butter and half margarine.

In pastry recipes, a mixture of half lard and half butter may also be used; many cooks find this gives a flakier, more tender result than all butter.

Flour: Unless otherwise stated, the term 'flour' in the recipes refers to plain flour.

Sugar: Where brown sugar or caster sugar is called for, the recipe will say so. In all other cases 'sugar' is ordinary white crystal sugar.

Creaming Butter and Sugar: Many cakes and biscuits are made by the 'creamed' method where butter and sugar are beaten together until light and fluffy. This is easier to do if the butter is allowed to soften at room temperature first, and creamed with a wooden spoon (or in an electric mixer) before adding the sugar.

When using an electric mixer, a tablespoon of the liquid used in the recipe can be added to the butter and sugar to help dissolve the sugar.

If mixing by hand, it is easier to add the sugar in three or four additions, beating in between, instead of all at once. If you are a perfectionist, the ideal to aim for is to have the sugar dissolved completely. However, this is a long process, and as long as the mixture is light and smooth you have done a good job!

Steps in Baking

Read the recipe through carefully and assemble the ingredients. Prepare the cake tins or baking trays and set the oven temperature before starting to mix.

Choose tins and baking trays that fit the oven shelves, leaving room for heat to circulate in the oven.

Avoid opening the oven door until the minimum time given in the recipe is reached, otherwise you run the risk of the cake falling.

The cooking time given in recipes is a guide, but make the following tests before taking the cake from the oven:

Sponge cakes are cooked when they are well risen and golden brown, and have shrunk slightly from the sides of the tin.

Creamed cake mixtures should be risen and brown, and spring back if pressed lightly with the fingertips. (This test also applies to 'one bowl' cakes where all the ingredients are mixed together.)

Fruit cake should be tested with a fine skewer. If it comes out clean, with no unbaked mixture clinging to it, the cake is cooked.

Preparing Cake Tins

A carefully prepared tin is your insurance against trouble when turning cakes out.

Shallow tins up to 5 cm (2 inches) in depth: Brush the inside of the tin with melted butter, lard or oil, or spray with a cooking spray. Cut a piece of greaseproof paper to fit the base of the tin, grease it and fit it in carefully, smoothing out any creases.

Sponge cake tins: Brush the inside of the tin with melted butter, lard or oil, or spray with a cooking spray. Cut a circle of greaseproof paper to fit the bottom of the tin, and grease the paper. Sprinkle a little flour and caster sugar into the tin, rotate the tin to distribute them evenly and shake out any excess.

Deep round cake tins: Cake tins that are deeper than 5 cm (2 inches) should have the sides lined with paper as well as the base. Grease the tin first, then cut a strip of paper long enough to wrap around the inside of the tin with an overlap to keep it in place. Clip the paper at intervals so it curves easily. Cut a circle to fit the bottom and brush with a little melted butter or oil.

Square cake tins: Take a square of greaseproof paper big enough to fit the bottom of the tin and come about 4 cm (1½ inches) up the sides. (For a 20 cm/8 inch tin you will need paper 27.5 cm/11 inches square.) Fold the paper to give a centre square the size of the base of the tin, and make a diagonal cut in each corner. Grease the tin and fit the paper into the tin, overlapping the corner pieces. Brush with a little oil or melted butter.

Adding Flour and Liquid

You will notice that many recipes advise you to add flour and milk (or other liquid) alternately with the creamed mixture. Use a large metal spoon to cut and fold the flour into the mixture, in two or three batches with the milk, beginning and ending with flour. Mix lightly but thoroughly between each addition for a smooth texture.

Turning out of the Tin

Unless otherwise stated, allow the cake to **cool for** 3 or 4 minutes in the tin before turning it out onto a wire cake rack. Place the rack over the tin, hold the rack and tin together with both hands, reverse and rap on the table, then gently lift the tin off the cake. Immediately place another rack on the bottom of the cake and reverse again so that the top of the cake is the **right way up**. This prevents the wire mesh pattern of the rack from marking the top of the cake.

The Right Conditions for Baking

The temperature of the kitchen has an important role to play in successful baking. For bread baking, choose a warm day or a warm part of the kitchen – the temperature should be 22°C/72°F or more.

Yeast is a living organism which does its work best at just the right warm temperature; if it is too cold the yeast action is sluggish.

Mixing bowls should be warmed by soaking in hot water and drying thoroughly. Also, make sure the liquid is lukewarm before adding to the flour.

For pastry making, it is best to work in a cool, airy kitchen. A humid, hot atmosphere doesn't suit pastry, so plan to make your pies and tarts before the kitchen becomes warm from other cooking. Keep bowls and fingers cool as well – the rule for perfect pastry is 'cool hands, hot oven'.

Beverages for all Occasions

Here are ideas for good things to drink . . . for reviving, soothing, warming and refreshing. A selection of recipes to lift your spirits!

Summer-Time Refreshers
Tropical Frost

2 cups unsweetened pineapple juice	*6 scoops fruit-flavoured ice-cream or gelato (strawberry, passionfruit, etc.)*
2 cups orange juice	*sprigs of mint*
¼ cup lemon juice	

Mix the juices together. Put a scoop of ice-cream or gelato in 6 tall glasses, pour the juice over and stir lightly. Garnish with a sprig of mint. *Serves 6*

Fruity Yogurt Cooler

1 cup sliced ripe strawberries, peaches, apricots or plums	*1 cup milk (skim or whole)*
1 small carton fruit-flavoured yogurt	*sugar*

Have the fruit, yogurt and milk icy cold. Purée the fruit in a blender (or push through a sieve) and mix well with the yogurt, milk and sugar to taste. *Serves 3*

Egg and Fruit Flip

This is not only refreshing, but very nutritious. Served with crisp bread rolls and preserves it would make a lovely summer breakfast.

4 cups ice-cold milk	*½ cup orange juice*
4 eggs	*freshly grated nutmeg*
4 tablespoons honey	
1 teaspoon grated orange rind	

Blend all the ingredients, except the nutmeg, in an electric blender, or whip until frothy with a rotary beater. Sprinkle with grated nutmeg to serve. *Serves 4*

Lemon Buttermilk Delight

No-one will guess buttermilk is the main ingredient in this deliciously tart-sweet, frosty drink.

1 cup cream	*4 tablespoons lemon juice*
1 litre buttermilk (2 cartons)	*½ cup sugar*
2 teaspoons finely grated lemon rind	*ground cinnamon*

Whip the cream until soft peaks form. Using the same beater, whip the buttermilk with the lemon rind, juice and sugar until frothy. Fold the cream and buttermilk together, and serve in tall chilled glasses with a sprinkle of cinnamon on top. *Serves 6 to 8* NOTE: The drink may be made beforehand and refrigerated. Whip again just before serving.

Fresh Tomato Juice

Nothing matches the flavour of homemade juice. When tomatoes are cheap, make this in double or triple quantities and keep tightly covered in the refrigerator.

12 medium-size ripe tomatoes	TO SEASON:
½ cup water	*1–2 teaspoons salt*
1 medium onion, sliced	*freshly ground pepper*
2 sticks celery (with leaves), sliced	*1 teaspoon Worcestershire sauce*
1 bay leaf	*1 teaspoon sugar*
3 sprigs parsley	

Chop the tomatoes coarsely and simmer with the water, onion, celery, bay leaf and parsley for 15 minutes. Strain and add the seasoning ingredients. Chill before serving. *Serves 4 to 6*

Blender Temptations

If you have an electric blender you can transform many fruits and vegetables into delectable liquids. They are the perfect, between-meal pick-me-ups – satisfying and nourishing, yet comfortingly low in kilojoules. Here are some combinations I think you'll enjoy.

Apricot Cream

This is a thick drink, almost like a sherbet. It would also make a refreshing dessert after a rich meal.

6 ripe apricots, pitted and coarsely chopped	*1 tablespoon lemon juice*
½ cup milk	*2 tablespoons sugar*
½ cup cream	*½ cup finely crushed ice*

Whirl all the ingredients in a blender until smooth and creamy. *Serves 3 to 4*

Variation

This is also delicious made with ripe peaches. Use 3 medium-size for 3 servings.

In the tall glasses: Orange-Melon Frost; Apricot Cream
In front: Lemon Buttermilk Delight; Fruity Yogurt Cooler; Tropical Frost

Orange-Melon Frost

2 medium oranges, peeled, seeded and coarsely chopped	*2 tablespoons lemon juice*
	pinch of salt
1 cup chopped peeled melon (honeydew, rockmelon or watermelon)	*½ cup finely crushed ice*

Whirl all the ingredients in a blender until frothy. *Serves 3 to 4*

Pineapple-Cucumber Cooler

1 cup unsweetened pineapple juice	*2 tablespoons lemon juice*
	6 sprigs parsley
1 medium cucumber, peeled, seeded and coarsely chopped	*½ cup finely crushed ice*

Whirl all the ingredients in a blender until frothy. *Serves 3 to 4*

Mango Delight

2 ripe mangoes	*2 tablespoons honey*
3 tablespoons lemon or lime juice	*2 cups orange juice*

Peel the mangoes, cut the flesh away from the seed and chop coarsely. Whirl with the remaining ingredients in a blender. *Serves 3 to 4*

Tropical Fizz

2 cups chopped peeled pawpaw	*2 cups unsweetened pineapple juice*
4 passionfruit	*1 ripe banana, sliced*

Whirl all the ingredients in a blender until frothy. *Serves 3 to 4*

Non-Alcoholic Punches

The emphasis these days is on light, cooling drinks for a party, especially if it's a day-time affair. These punches are just right for children and teenagers, too.

Fruit Tea Punch

1¼ cups sugar	*6 oranges*
1¼ cups water	*6 lemons*
4 cups strong hot tea	*1 punnet strawberries, hulled and sliced*
1 × 440 g can crushed pineapple	*4 large bottles soda water*
1 × 425 ml can apricot nectar	*ice, to serve*

Boil the sugar and water for 10 minutes, add the tea and allow to cool. Stir in the crushed pineapple with juice, the apricot nectar, and the juice from the oranges and lemons. Chill until serving time. Add the sliced strawberries and soda water. Pour over large pieces of ice in a punch bowl to serve. *Serves 20 to 30*

Mocha Punch

This rich, chocolate-coffee punch would be lovely to serve with homemade shortbread or fruit cake when friends drop in at Christmas time.

8 cups strong freshly made black coffee	1 teaspoon rum or almond essence
2½ cups cream	¼ teaspoon salt
1 litre carton chocolate ice-cream	freshly grated nutmeg or grated chocolate, to decorate

Chill the coffee, and whip the cream until stiff. Put 1 cup of cream aside to decorate the punch for serving. Pour the chilled coffee into a large bowl and add half the ice-cream. Beat until the ice-cream is almost melted, then stir in the rum or almond essence and salt. Fold in the remaining ice-cream and the whipped cream.

Pour into tall glasses and decorate with reserved cream and grated nutmeg or chocolate. *Serves about 15*

Quick Golden Punch

So easily made, but sparkly and delicious.

1 litre fresh orange juice	½ cup finely chopped mint
1 litre fresh grapefruit juice	2 large bottles ginger ale
½ cup lemon juice	mint sprigs, to garnish

Combine the juices and chopped mint and chill. At serving time, pour over ice in a punch bowl, add the ginger ale and garnish with mint sprigs. *Serves 15 to 20*

Punches with Alcohol

These punches are easier on the budget than strong drinks, and can be put out in pretty punch bowls or containers for guests to help themselves. Nice for weddings, anniversaries and birthdays, and for outdoor entertaining if you set the containers in a bed of cracked ice.

Champagne Wedding Punch

This is a superb punch and not too expensive when locally produced champagne is available at very reasonable prices. If you wish to extend the quantity of punch, you can add extra pineapple juice.

3 large ripe pineapples	2 cups brandy
500 g (1 lb) caster sugar	2 cups light rum
2 cups fresh lemon juice	6 bottles chilled champagne
1 cup cherry brandy	

Peel, core and slice the pineapples and whirl the fruit in an electric blender until crushed, or process in a food processor fitted with the steel blade. (Failing this, chop very finely by hand.)

Place in a bowl, sprinkle with sugar and allow to stand for 1 hour or more. Stir in the remaining ingredients, except the champagne, then cover and chill for 4 hours.

Pour over a block of ice in a punch bowl and just before serving add the chilled champagne. *Serves 35 to 40*

Strawberry Punch

A pretty pale-pink punch with a delicate flavour. Keep it in mind if you grow your own strawberries or there's a strawberry farm nearby.

6 punnets ripe strawberries	3 bottles dry white wine
1½ cups caster sugar	3 bottles rosé (or use your favourite flagon wine)
2 cups brandy or Madeira	
½ cup lemon juice	

Hull and wash the strawberries and slice most of them, keeping a few whole ones for decoration. Place in a bowl, add the sugar, brandy and lemon juice and allow to stand for several hours or overnight. At serving time, stir well and pour over a block of ice in a punch bowl. Add the wine and reserved whole strawberries and serve. *Serves 25 to 30*

Hot Spiced Wine Punch

Serve it around the fire on a winter's night.

2 bottles burgundy or claret	½ whole nutmeg, crushed
thinly peeled zest of 1 small orange and lemon	6 whole cloves
piece cinnamon stick about 7 cm (3 inches) long	2 tablespoons sugar or more to taste

Combine all the ingredients in a large saucepan, bring to just under boiling point, turn off heat and stand for 10 minutes, then pour into mugs and drink hot. *Serves 8 to 10*
NOTE: Some like this hot punch quite sweet. Taste before serving and stir in more sugar to suit your own palate, if necessary.

Glögg

This is another hot punch, which is made the day before so the flavours can mellow overnight, then reheated for serving. Serve in mugs or glasses, with spoons to fish out the fruits and nuts.

¾ cup water	½ cup raisins
6 cardamom seeds	1 cup pitted prunes
8 whole cloves	1 large bottle red wine
2 tablespoons grated orange rind	1 bottle port
½ cup blanched almonds	1½ cups vodka
	sugar (optional)

Bring the water to the boil in a saucepan. Tie the cardamom, cloves and orange rind in a muslin bag, add to the water and simmer with the lid on for 10 minutes. Add the almonds, raisins, prunes and enough water to cover the fruit. Replace the lid and simmer for 20 minutes. Stir in the red wine, port and vodka, bring to the boil and immediately remove from the heat.

Cool, then chill overnight in a covered container in the refrigerator. When ready to serve, remove the spice bag and gently reheat the punch. If desired, add sugar to taste. Divide the fruit and nuts among the glasses and top up with punch. *Serves 15 to 20*

Champagne Wedding Punch; Strawberry Punch

Index

Acknowledgments

Special photography:
Melvin Grey: endpapers, 2–3, 8–9, 10–11, 72–3, 74–5, 136–7, 138–9,
200–1, 202–3; Robert Golden: 185, 220–1, 249, 250–1, 264, 267; Norman
Nicholls: 5, 15, 19, 20, 21, 33, 36, 39, 41, 49, 52, 53, 57, 58, 60, 65, 69, 70,
87, 91, 92, 95, 101, 107, 120, 125, 132, 133, 135, 154, 159, 161, 164, 165,
166, 167, 168, 169, 170, 173, 175, 189, 190, 195, 196, 207, 237, 239.

All other photography by Bryce Attwell, Melvin Grey and Paul Kemp.